# THE
# DOPE

# THE DOPE

## THE REAL HISTORY OF THE MEXICAN DRUG TRADE

BENJAMIN T. SMITH

EBURY
PRESS

1

Ebury Press an imprint of Ebury Publishing,
20 Vauxhall Bridge Road,
London SW1V 2SA

Ebury Press is part of the Penguin Random House group of companies
whose addresses can be found at global.penguinrandomhouse.com

First published in the United Kingdom by Ebury Press in 2021
First published in the United States by W. W. Norton & Company in 2021

www.penguin.co.uk

A CIP catalogue record for this book is available from the British Library

Hardback ISBN 9781529105674
Trade Paperback ISBN 9781529105681

Typeset in 12/16 pt Fairfield LT Std
by Integra Software Services Pvt. Ltd, Pondicherry

Printed and bound in Great Britain by Clays Ltd, Elcograf S.p.A.

The authorised representative in the EEA is Penguin Random House Ireland,
Morrison Chambers, 32 Nassau Street, Dublin D02 YH68

*To my mum and dad, thank you. And to Ernest who always*

*knew how to tell a good story.*

*People see what they want to see and what people want to see never has anything to do with the truth.*

—Roberto Bolaño, 2666

# CONTENTS

# ACRONYMS

BNDD—Bureau of Narcotics and Dangerous Drugs
DEA—Drug Enforcement Administration
DFS—Ministry of Federal Security (Mexico)
FBN—Federal Bureau of Narcotics
ICE—Immigration and Customs Enforcement
PAN—National Action Party
PGR—Attorney General's Office (Mexico)
PJF—Federal Judicial Police (Mexico)
PRI—Institutional Revolutionary Party

# A NOTE ON NAMES

Spanish names comprise first names (e.g., Joaquín) and then two surnames (e.g., Guzmán Loera). The first surname is the patronymic of the father (Guzmán) and the second surname is the patronymic of the mother (Loera). Normally, to reduce repetition, writers use simply the patronymic to refer to the person in question. However, occasionally with certain common first surnames, both the first and second surnames are used (President Ávila Camacho, the trafficker Caro Quintero). Just to confuse matters, because traffickers usually live in the shadows, sometimes we have confirmation of their first but not their second surnames.

Finally, the world of Mexican drug trafficking is rich in evocative nicknames. However, unless they are short for proper names or infamous on their own, such as "El Chapo," I have translated them into English.

# Prologue

## *The Lookout*

Cruz never wanted to be in the narcotics business. But he had little choice. The youngest of eleven children, he was born in Carácuaro in 1989. Once the base for Mexico's nineteenth-century Independence army, now the small, nondescript village in the Michoacán hot lands boasted few opportunities. Most villagers produced agricultural goods for the local market or—if they could afford to pay for passage—migrated north to find work. It was one of the poorest townships in one of Mexico's poorest states. Four in every five families lived in poverty. Cruz's family was one of them. "We didn't have a TV or a car or anything. We just had a house with a dirt floor and that was only because my father left to be with his other woman."

Cruz's hometown, however, did have one advantage. It lay on a beautiful, winding road that ran up from Mexico's west coast to the center of the country and from there to the United States. By the mid-1990s the road was a major drug highway.

Cruz learned the business young. Five of his brothers drove narcotics from the coast to the state capital of Morelia. So did three of his brothers-in-law and all his cousins. "They were all involved. I didn't know anyone who wasn't. But no one said anything. It was just a job." Even his mother was drawn in. She stored guns and narcotics in a wooden hut overlooking the small ranch on which they all lived. And when Cruz was seven years old he also started to work as a *halcón*, or lookout, for the stash.

In his decade in the drug business, Cruz demonstrated a singular lack of ambition. As his brothers moved up the hierarchy from transporters to gunmen to local chiefs, they often mocked their shy, diminutive sibling. But Cruz didn't mind. He liked being a lookout. The job allowed him to wander the stunning, rolling landscape above his ranch. It allowed him to look after his ageing mother. He also showed a complete lack of interest in experimenting with any of the drugs. He never opened the packages, never looked inside, and certainly never used them. "They were for the gringos."

He did, however, notice that the *mercancia*—the merchandise—changed. At first, in the mid-1990s, it was cocaine. "When I first started, my brothers used to bring in loads of *perico* ["parakeet," but also the slang term for cocaine]. It was wrapped tightly in cellophane packets with names and numbers on the side. No one ever told me what they meant and I never asked." Then by the end of the decade, his brothers also brought in weed. Marijuana was Cruz's least favorite narcotic. "I had to carry it up to the hill to the hut in these massive sacks. It was so heavy … and it stank." Then, at the turn of the century there was another change. "It was all *hielo* ["ice," or methamphetamine] and *chiva* ["goat," or heroin]. They said it all came from down the mountains around Zihuatanejo and Petatlán."

He also observed the changes in the trade's local protection rackets. At first, it was the state cops who were in charge. When Cruz was just a child, they would come up to the ranch, sling a few packages of cocaine into a squad car, and then drive back to the state capital. "A local politician even came once. He wanted to thank my brothers for their work." But by the turn of the century it was traffickers themselves. "When the Zetas came, they demanded that we work for them now. If you didn't, they just killed you. Just like that."

Violence accompanied these changes in the protection rackets. In just three years two of Cruz's brothers and four of his cousins were killed; another brother disappeared together with one of his brothers-in-law. The genealogy he sketched looked like a family tree from the plague years.

At this point, Cruz's mother decided that she needed to protect at least one of her children. So in October 2007, she put Cruz on a bus to Morelia. From there he took another bus to Tijuana where he had the address of more family. Eventually, in early 2008, he managed to cross to the United States and lived with extended family in the Northwest. He got married, had three children, and started to work picking fruit. He was safe for a time.

In 2018, Immigration and Customs Enforcement (ICE) agents raided Cruz's place of work in Middleton, Idaho. They bused him four hours to the nearest detention facilities in Weber County, Utah. It was here, as he awaited deportation, that I first spoke to him. His lawyer had asked me to work pro bono as an expert witness in his case.

Talking to Cruz on the crackly detention center phone line, he seemed quiet and thoughtful. He was devoted to his wife and kids, and scared about the future. He feared that if he was returned, the government officials and cartel hitmen that had wiped out half his family would come after him.

In the end he was right to be afraid. After a decade of watching America's changing narcotics needs, he now witnessed its grinding mechanisms of narcotics prevention. ICE lawyers used Cruz's testimony to portray the slight, nervous farmhand as a hardened narco—a violent psychopath bent on feeding drugs to America's vulnerable youths. They knocked his claims of forced recruitment, questioned his tale of family tragedy, and intimated that he had actually come north to sell drugs. They were playing on a set of common assumptions and stereotypes. It was enough to persuade the judge. Two months after the hearing, Cruz was put on a plane back to Mexico.

Over the past decade, Cruz's story has become depressingly common. Myths about the Mexican drug trade have become one of the twenty-first century's most persistent narratives. Beyond the narrow world of cops and traffickers, such myths provide the scripts for TV series, the stock characters for action flicks, and the prejudices underlying a thousand law-yers' arguments and judges' decisions.

Such myths started over a century ago. In the same breath that American moralizers lauded the prohibition of narcotics, they started to accuse the Mexicans of providing them. And as these myths took hold, they started to shape popular culture. They provided the backdrop for Dashiell Hammett's detective fiction and 1950s teen exploitation flicks. Mexican traffickers supplied the cocaine for Billy and Wyatt in *Easy Rider* and played the bad guys in Evel Knievel's first excursion on the silver screen—*Viva Knievel!*

Though the drugs have changed and the slang modified, these myths have remained disconcertingly constant. ("Mexican Cartel Threatens to Drown El Paso in Dope," reads a strangely timeless 1932 headline.)

They tell simple stories of a war between north and south, between white and brown, between noble and well-intentioned cops and a threaten-ing cabal of vicious kingpins, simpering gangsters' molls, corrupt Mexican politicians, and shadowy, powerful cartels.

Such myths serve a purpose. They demonize the drug traffickers and cement the narrative of the drug war as a struggle between good and evil. They legitimize official violence. Drug cops carry guns because they must fight well-armed traffickers; they shoot but only when shot at; they torture but only because pulling some farmer's fingernails prevents some conven-iently vague future death.

Now drug war myths provide the essential background for the upsurge in U.S. nativism, the expansion of a massive deportation industry, and the popularity of Trump's demands for a wall.

Unpacking these myths and discovering the real story of Mexico's drug trade has not been easy. These stereotypes are firmly entrenched; they configure the way documents are written; they structure the way we read them; and they shape the way we have told these stories in the past.

Together with a handful of colleagues, I have spent nearly a decade tracking down narcos, narcotics, and the police that pursued them. I have visited over thirty archives, ranging from grand, air-conditioned national collections to the dusty, scorpion-infested cells that pass for municipal depositories. I have applied for a plethora of classified documents in the United States and Mexico. Some, I have received. Others have been refused or redacted to the point of incomprehensibility.

Private collections, in particular, have proved a boon. Friends and contacts have lent me classified documents, grand jury transcripts, the Drug Enforcement Administration's (DEA) in-house review of the famous international smuggling ring known as the French Connection, the photo album of a Sinaloa kingpin, and the sole known snapshot of the legendary trafficker Pedro Avilés Pérez. He lies on a mortuary slab with half his head missing.

Over the past decade, I have also talked to dozens of DEA officers who worked in Mexico during the 1970s and 1980s. They introduced me to the murky world of overseas U.S. drug policy—the characters, the clashes, and the cavalier attitude to lives and laws. I have also talked to those involved in the other side of the business, from 1960s weed smugglers to the poor, mostly rural drug workers like Cruz who populate the very lowest rungs of the trade.

Some of these sources are disconcertingly blunt. DEA agents, in particular, are often upfront about the amount of violence they and the Mexicans deployed against the traffickers. The unapologetic use of force is testament to how powerful drug myths have become. It is also a measure of how these myths have insulated federal agents (and, perhaps most important, their pensions) against legal challenge.

But most sources only tell a fraction of the truth. They inflate the numbers, exaggerate the threat, and weave what happened into recognizable tales of good cops and bad traffickers. To draw out the history of the trade has taken constant fact-checking, triangulation with other documents, and a persistent cynicism about the motives underlying what appear to be factual statements.

The stories these sources reveal cover a century of Mexican drug production. They recount the shifting organizations that have specialized in growing, processing, and transporting narcotics from the small, mountain clans of the early twentieth century to the so-called cartels of today. They offer snapshots of many of the characters involved, from Mexico's first heroin chemist to Ciudad Juárez's legendary queen pin to right-wing hitmen turned cartel mafiosi. And they pull back the curtain on the U.S. and Mexico's counterproductive attempts to limit a flourishing market.

This history presents, I believe, four distinct findings.

Least surprising is that the driving force of the drug trade is and always has been economic. America has an enduring and enormous appetite for narcotics. In the late nineteenth century, according to some estimates, between 2 and 4 percent of the U.S. population was addicted to morphine. A century later, America was consuming up to 70 percent of all the world's cocaine.

The American hunger for intoxication has always dwarfed that of Mexicans. In the 1970s, for example, the CIA conservatively estimated that there were around 450,000 heroin addicts in the United States. (Other reports claimed over 600,000.) In comparison, there was "almost no evidence of heroin use" in Mexico. At the time, Mexico's largest survey of recreational drug use struggled to find any individuals who had even tried opiates.

Marijuana did have a Mexican market. (The name itself is probably Mexican in origin.) But after a brief surge in popularity during the Mexican Revolution, the herb rarely penetrated beyond a small, bohemian subculture. During the 1970s, when 40 percent of U.S. high schoolers were using marijuana on a regular basis, barely 4 percent of Mexico City's kids had smoked the herb even once. Outside the capital's student hipsters, rates of usage barely climbed above 1 percent.

This ceaseless U.S. demand has merged with the persistent poverty of the average Mexican. Even during the middle decades of the twentieth century—when Mexico was riding an unparalleled wave of economic growth—average wages rarely reached 10 percent of those to the north. Now, after two decades of economic turmoil and a further two decades of stagnation, they barely reach 6 percent of those in the United States. You can earn the average annual Mexican wage by working for fifteen days in the United States.

This combination of high demand and low wages has generated enormous incentives to produce and traffic drugs. There is no established way to assess these incentives. (One suspects that the World Bank's economists are rarely asked to measure the intersection of salaries and drug prices.) So, I have come up with my own: an estimate of the quantities of various narcotics a Mexican would have to sell wholesale in the United States to earn the average annual Mexican wage.

This calculation is not meant to mirror real life. Few individual Mexicans have had the wherewithal to sell the drugs that they grew on their own land directly to American users. (Though some have. As journalist Sam Quinones discovered, in the early 2000s a handful of enterprising Mexican poppy farmers started to sell their homemade black tar heroin directly to U.S. OxyContin addicts.) The figure does not take into account the (comparatively minimal) costs of drug production and processing or the (less minimal) costs of networking and bribery. Instead, what it does is suggest why the drug trade has been so attractive to so many Mexicans.

The results are telling. Over the past fifty years, to earn the median wage, a Mexican has had to sell an average of 700 grams of marijuana, 18 grams of heroin, or 66 grams of cocaine on the U.S. streets. It amounts to weed weighing two cans of soup, coke weighing a tennis ball, or smack weighing just three U.S. quarters. And this is only the average. During the economic collapse of the mid-1980s, it took only 280 grams of marijuana and 4.8 grams of heroin to make the annual wage. You could earn as much growing a single marijuana plant or a window box of poppies as driving a cab for a year.

The second—perhaps more surprising—finding concerns the relationship between the drug trade and the authorities. Since governments prohibited drug trafficking in the 1910s, many Mexican politicians have sought to harness the income from the illegal trade. As long as the drugs went north, the trade caused limited social or political fallout, and no one blamed the politicians—who cared? In general, these politicians have taken a cut by instituting what we might call drug "protection rackets." They have charged certain favored wholesalers or traffickers a fee or a percentage of profits to protect their enterprises and not to apply the law. Those that have refused to pay, they have arrested or—at times—murdered. To put it another way, state agents were Mexico's mafia, trading protection for a cut of narcotics proceeds.

For over a century, observers deemed this system corruption. ("Corrupt officials are in league with the traffickers," reported the same 1932 El Paso newspaper.) Yet corruption is an imprecise and unhelpful term. Such a blanket expression obscures what has always been a subtle and shifting set of arrangements. Up until the 1970s, these protection rackets were controlled by state governments and manned by the state police. (Mexico, like the United States, has a federal system.) Though many of these officials got very rich, there were limits. Authorities sought to distribute at least some of these funds either through official state programs (like school- or road-building) or individual philanthropy. And they sought to check violent disputes associated with the trade. To do otherwise was to risk U.S. or Mexican federal intervention.

During the 1970s, national institutions—in particular the Federal Judicial Police (PJF)—took over these local protection rackets. And they referred to their regional protection rackets as their plazas. Corruption changed from a mechanism that greased the wheels and oiled the machine to what political scientists now term "grand corruption." These new racketeers no longer hailed from the region they controlled; they had no links with the communities they extorted. So they stole more, they distributed less, and they became increasingly casual about the use of violence. They, after all, were the highest authorities in the land. This scaled-up corruption started to undermine the functioning of the state.

Since 1990, corruption has shifted once more. Increased drug profits and declining state power have upended the old protection rackets. In many regions of Mexico, the traffickers still pay the authorities. But now the traffickers are in charge; they control the protection rackets and decide the rules of the game. Political scientists have come up with a term for the new arrangement. They call it "state capture." (Though it should be said that they have only captured a small part of the state—the part that used to run the protection rackets.)

Mexican corruption has attracted headlines and oversimplified cultural explanations. "It is as eternal as the Aztec sun," declared one Mexico foreign correspondent. And it has become firmly entrenched in the myths surrounding the drug trade. Yet, as I also discovered, corruption never stopped at the border. Stories of hard-nosed sheriffs and principled drug agents mask similarly entrenched corruption on the U.S. side. Just as in Mexico, the enormous profits from the drug trade have been tough to resist. And they have persuaded many agents from local law enforcement,

Customs, the DEA, and the CIA to either look the other way or overtly protect the trade. However, unlike in Mexico, American observers have been resistant to investigate these claims or declare any systemic fault.

The third finding relates to counternarcotics policies. Drug myths suggest that punitive policies are logical and necessary responses to genuine threats. Policy hawks target kingpins or peddlers or cultivators because they believe this is the most efficient way to stop Americans injecting or smoking or snorting drugs. But studying a century of south-of-the-border counternarcotics efforts reveals that such policies are rarely implemented for their effectiveness. They are driven instead by invented panics, the need for bureaucratic fundraising, and managerial scapegoating. They target whatever group is deemed easiest to cow, capture, and sell to the public as a victory. And they are supported by the relentless manipulation of facts and figures through administrative sleight of hand, the deliberate distortion of evidence, or straight out lying.

Furthermore, these policies never actually fulfill their aims. Cutting supply never raises prices and lowers U.S. addiction rates for more than a few months. American drug demand is simply too large; the incentives are too great. And patterns of drug-taking are broadly independent of supply. In fact, the two "successful" campaigns against Mexican drug production—which did genuinely bring down narcotics production in the late 1940s and late 1970s—were followed by a massive rise in U.S. heroin addiction and a huge escalation in U.S. cocaine addiction respectively.

What unforgiving counternarcotics policies do cause, however, is increased violence. This brings me to my fourth finding, which concerns the connection between the drug trade and the use of force. Many commentators argue that the narcotics business inevitably generates violence; it is "in the DNA of the trade." They give many reasons for the inevitability of violence. The stakes are high; the trade attracts criminals and sociopaths; and without official regulation, disputes are decided by force. Over the past fifteen years, at least in Mexico, this has not been a difficult claim to make. Yet it is important not to let contemporary horror obscure both the history of the trade and the origins of the violence.

Up to the 1970s, violence was rarely employed to sort out disputes between drug traffickers. The trade was relatively peaceful. Cooperation was the rule. Deep ties of blood, marriage, friendship, and neighborhood, which linked many of the traffickers, prevented the frequent use of force. In general, so did the local protection rackets. Both state governors and state cops were keen to avoid conflicts that risked exposing their own ties to the traffickers.

Instead, the causes of violence were twofold. These causes originated not from inside the drug trade, but from inside the state.

Occasionally, new state authorities attempted to overturn the old protection rackets and institute their own. To do so, they frequently tracked down powerful traffickers and arrested or killed them. They then placed their own compliant traffickers in their place. New state authorities could claim to the U.S. and Mexican federal authorities that they were taking serious action on counternarcotics while also capturing the protection racket for themselves. Yet the strategy was high-risk. If the new authorities failed to control or eliminate the powerful traffickers, the attempted takeover could develop into a bloody conflict.

Such conflicts over drug protection rackets dot the early years of the trade. There were outbreaks of violence in Ciudad Juárez in the early 1930s, in Sinaloa in the 1940s, and again in Sinaloa in the late 1960s. Yet such conflicts have become more frequent. Over the past forty years, increasing numbers of groups have vied for control of the drug protection rackets. They no longer comprise just warring local politicians, but also federal cops, secret service agents, and the drug traffickers themselves. What is described as a conflict over the drug trade is often a conflict over the control of the protection racket.

Furthermore, over the past fifteen years, many gangs have attempted to extend these protection rackets from narcotics to other commercial enterprises. It is these attempts that have spread violence beyond the areas where drugs are traditionally grown and smuggled. Criminals now demand protection money from everyone, from car thieves and human traffickers to local businessmen, truck drivers, and avocado farmers. These new victims might be different. But the rules are the same. Pay up or get killed.

The other principal cause of the violence has been the war on drugs itself. In Mexico, aggressive counternarcotics policing was slow to take off. U.S. diplomatic bullying forced law changes in the late 1940s. And by the early 1950s there was a relatively forceful militarized eradication campaign. Conflicts increased. But for the most powerful traffickers, punishments were rare. And there were multiple ways to avoid capture or long imprisonment.

In the early 1970s, Nixon's drug war transformed counternarcotics policing south of the border. U.S. drug agents, Mexican cops, and Mexican soldiers descended on areas of drug production and trafficking like an invading army. They arrested tens of thousands; they tortured thousands; and they killed hundreds. They racked up their own body count. There were similar rapid U.S.-backed escalations of drug policing after the murder of DEA agent Enrique "Kiki" Camarena in 1985 and again with the election of President Felipe Calderón in 2006.

Yet, beyond the direct victims, such uncompromising policing also had a crucial secondary effect. As the risks increased, drug traffickers turned on one another to avoid the threat of capture or worse. The cooperation that had marked the first half-century of the trade decreased and then evaporated almost completely. Traffickers gave evidence on each other to escape long sentences, avoid torture, or save their families; and traffickers killed anyone they suspected of being a police informer.

Nowadays there are plenty of other underlying causes for Mexico's spiraling murder rate—the explosion of other forms of crime, the expansion of Mexico's own retail drug market, the ongoing smuggling of guns from the United States, and the almost complete collapse of the country's judicial system.

Yet these two causes, which have marked the history of the Mexican drug trade, remain important today. Struggles over the control of drug protection rackets still generate conflicts among diverse state institutions and their allied traffickers. Aggressive antidrug policing still produces state-backed murders and divides drug-trafficking networks against one another.

Violence, then, is not so much in the DNA of trading in narcotics as in the DNA of prohibiting the trade.

It was something that Cruz, the teenage lookout, grasped effortlessly. Looking back on his decade in the Michoacán drug trade, he recalled two moments when violence spiked. The first was when a new cartel—the Zetas—arrived and attempted to take over the protection racket from local officials. They murdered a handful of local traffickers (including Cruz's relatives), kidnapped the others, and then forced them to pay a fee for moving the narcotics through Carácuaro. The second was in 2007 when the army arrived in response. "They just made things worse. They didn't care who they killed."

This book, then, is the story of how America's unending demand for narcotics first shaped, then transformed the economy, social makeup, and politics of modern Mexico. It is a story that starts in a minor key with the small-scale networks of pharmacists, criminals, farmers, and merchants that teamed up to sate U.S. needs in the wake of the first drug prohibition decrees. These networks were limited in scope and based on cooperation, not conflict; they were protected by local politicians; and at least some of their profits were distributed to broader society.

Yet from the 1970s onward, these networks started to expand and these arrangements between traffickers and the state started to break down. First there was the spiraling demand for marijuana, then heroin, then cocaine, then meth, and then heroin again. Next there were the attempts to curtail supply through harsher laws, more aggressive policing, and military force. Together such changes beefed up the power of the drug-trafficking networks, allowed them to take over chunks of the state, and set these networks against one another. The Mexican drug trade had become the Mexican drug war.

It is a reality that Mexico still lives with today.

# Part I

## First Puffs
## 1900–1940

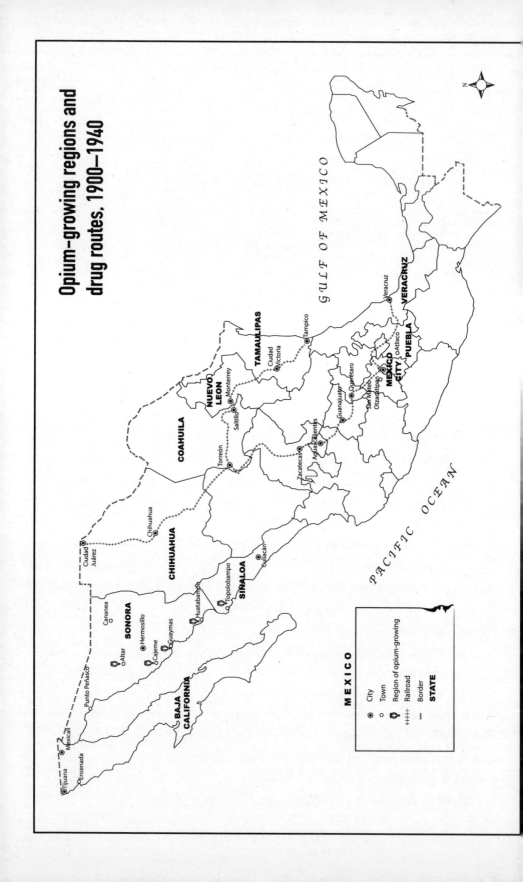

## Opium-growing regions and drug routes, 1900–1940

**GULF OF MEXICO**

**PACIFIC OCEAN**

BAJA CALIFORNIA

SONORA

CHIHUAHUA

SINALOA

COAHUILA

NUEVO LEON

TAMAULIPAS

VERACRUZ

PUEBLA

MEXICO CITY

Tijuana
Ensenada
Mexicali
Punto Peñasco
Cananea
Altar
Hermosillo
Cajeme
Guaymas
Huatabampo
Topolobampo
Culiacán
Ciudad Juárez
Chihuahua
Torreón
Zacatecas
Aguascalientes
Saltillo
Monterrey
Ciudad Victoria
Tampico
Veracruz
Guanajuato
Querétaro
San Mateo
Otzacatipa
Atlixco
Veracruz

### MEXICO

- ◉ City
- ○ Town
- ◐ Region of opium-growing
- ╬╬╬ Railroad
- --- Border
- **STATE**

## Chapter 1

─────────────

## The King of the *Grifos*

MEET MEXICO'S FIRST NARCO. FOR PUBLIC ENEMY NUMBER ONE, JOSÉ del Moral, was a bit of a disappointment. As the police dragged him out of his house on Calle San Jeronimo in the center of Mexico City on July 20, 1908, he cut a disheveled figure. Grimacing from his toothless mouth, he was in his late fifties, grey-haired, and dressed in a tattered waistcoat and trousers. Of course, the tabloid press of the time didn't call him a narco. They had yet to come up with such convenient short-hand. Instead, he was "the capital's poisoner in chief" and "the king of the grifos [stoners]."

Del Moral was not royalty, but he was the capital's biggest marijuana wholesaler. Three days earlier the police had raided his warehouse south of the city. Here they had discovered thousands of marijuana cigarettes. The newspapers had reacted with full-blown hysteria. "Marijuana factory" with enough marijuana "to poison the whole capital" ran *El Imparcial*. "The ter-rible cannabis indica of the healers is the opium of our lower classes," opined the slightly more cerebral *El País*.

Mexico's first narco—meet Mexico's first drug panic.

Tabloid censure brought swift justice. Within a month, Del Moral was tried and sentenced to five months in jail. His crime was a new one—selling marijuana without a proper license.

Del Moral might have been Mexico's first bulk dope slinger but he was not illiterate. "The king of the grifos" was something of an autodidact. And his appeal letter—written from inside Mexico City's notorious Belén prison—outlined rather neatly the tension between this first drug panic and his and many others' more reasoned appreciations of the drug.

Doctors, he claimed, had denounced marijuana while knowing nothing about it. They quoted no studies and ignored the everyday application of the drug. Instead, they simply adopted the popular prejudices of women and children, he said, "who run when they hear its very name and believe the herb has come from hell." The tabloids were even worse. They parroted the doctors' lies and added to them, making up tales of marijuana-induced madness and weed-fueled murders. "How," Del Moral asked, "can marijuana be considered dangerous for health ... when it is used as a medicine for infinite ailments?" Surely Mexicans should trial the drug rather than rashly condemn it?

Lost for over a century beneath a stack of case files, Del Moral's appeal letter now seems oddly prescient. Two years after his imprisonment, the outbreak of the Mexican Revolution would drive thousands of his countrymen to start using marijuana both as a medicine and as a relaxant. It was a trial—albeit a wild and impromptu one. Marijuana would go from a rarely used herbal remedy to the drug of choice for the Revolution's soldiers. After the Revolution, it would gain an audience among urban bohemians and the city's poor.

Yet, the marijuana craze was never more than a subculture. It was localized, short-lived, and by the 1930s had started to fizzle out.

In contrast, the panic that Del Moral described did not go away. It proved much more enduring. It was one of the world's first drug panics. It was an important moment, a turning point in Mexico's attitudes to narcotics. It would provide the template and many of the stories for subsequent panics, including America's own terror over marijuana use during the 1930s. And it would inspire a set of laws and prejudices against marijuana that would shape a century of Mexican drug policing. To this day, Mexicans hold some of the least progressive attitudes in the world to marijuana. Sadly, the first marijuana panic had little to do with the drug's actual effects. It had much more to do with prejudices about the people involved in the trade.

As Del Moral was keen to point out, he was not the instigator of marijuana use. Mexicans had been using the drug's healing properties for well over a hundred years. The Spanish had originally brought cannabis to the country in the sixteenth century. Their idea was to make hemp. But it soon escaped. A hardy plant, it sprang up on the edge of cornfields and dotted the hills of Mexico's dry Sierras. Around the end of the eighteenth century, Mexicans discovered its calming properties. And within a few decades it was a medicinal staple. In the countryside, many people just self-medicated, using recipes passed down from parents or grandparents.

But in the towns and cities, wholesalers like Del Moral usually sold the narcotic to *herbolarias* or traditional healers. These herbolarias were a common sight in nineteenth-century Mexico. Most were indigenous women. They sold their advice and their bewildering array of herbs, barks, and potions from mats strewn on the floor of the country's hundreds of markets. Snooty health inspectors were not impressed.

> Their ignorance is enormous, they don't know how to read or write, the Spanish they talk is very poor and the sicknesses and the herbs they know by their indigenous or vulgar names. Their business is mostly done on the outskirts of the markets on the edges of the pavement, setting up their wares on shabby blankets and separating them in vague overlapping piles. Their measures are handfuls and branches and their prices always extremely low.

What they lacked in formal training, they made up for in price and choice. Their "shabby blankets" were piled with an A to Z of powders and leaves from achiote (seeds from the *Bixa orellana* shrub for measles) to zoapatle (*Montanoa tomentosa* for abortions).

Marijuana was one of their most versatile remedies. It was rolled up and smoked to cure asthma, bronchitis, and laryngitis; it was pounded into a powder, dissolved in alcohol, and rubbed on rheumatic joints, hernias, or the stomachs of women struggling to give birth; and its seeds were dissolved in water and used for urinary infections and bladder pains. Popular prescriptions included marijuana dissolved in water combined with jimson weed and butter to make "a calming pomade" and boiled in water to produce a rough form of hash and then mixed with cinnamon syrup. Tasty and relaxing.

If marijuana was most often employed as an herbal remedy, two groups also occasionally smoked it as a narcotic—soldiers and prisoners.

Most of the early references to marijuana concern soldiers. As early as 1846 as the Americans threatened to bombard the port of Veracruz, one

*Herbolarias or traditional healers were held to be ill-educated indigenous women prone to poisoning their clients. Their use of marijuana simply confirmed this prejudice.*

worried newspaper reported that Mexican troops had been struck down "by a strange sickness." "They are without strength, languid, confused and often end in a profound stupor." The cause of this strange illness—"marijuana, which the soldiers smoke as if it was tobacco." By the 1870s, the weed-addled soldier—stuck in his barracks or on the prowl looking for trouble—had been a stock character in the Mexican imagination. In fact, one of the most persuasive theories for the origins of the very word marijuana reflects this use. Juan was the name given to the average Mexican soldier. His camp wife was often termed María. María-Juan became Marijuana.

The second group that smoked marijuana was prisoners. They shared many of the soldiers' experiences. They were locked indoors for long periods of time; they were bored; and they were looking for some form of escape. Again marijuana provided the answer. It was smuggled inside food, beneath women's plaits and underclothes, or grown openly on the roof of prisons. In 1895, a journalist of the demimonde, Heriberto Frías, was jailed for exposing a vicious military campaign against peasant rebels. He described the poor men he met inside. They included a luckless thief who was busted every few months and returned to jail, where he would survive by selling marijuana cigarettes. And they included a wife beater who had been arrested for hitting his errant lover and who calmed his pain (if not hers) with the herb. "With marijuana he felt happy, the smoke of the cigarette bathed his brain, killed his memories, and submerged him in shadowy oriental ecstasy."

At the end of the nineteenth century, then, marijuana consumption was minimal. It was relegated to a corner of the healers' stalls. And it was contained in barracks and prisons. Places you might expect to find mentions, like criminology books, anthropology texts, and folk literature, barely mentioned the drug. The 600-page *Diccionario de Mejicanismos* (Dictionary of Mexican Slang) included only two words connected to weed—*marihuano*, or marijuana smoker; and *grifo*, or stoned. (In comparison, there were thirty-five colloquialisms for "drunk.")

So the roots of the panic lay not in the level of marijuana's use. Del Moral's warehouse—with its thousands of cigarettes and piles of weed—probably accounted for most of the capital's sales. Rather, like the roots of most drug panics, they lay in the type of people that used it.

By the 1890s the ruling dictator Porfirio Díaz (in office most of the years 1876–1911) was trying to modernize Mexico. Foreign capital was flowing in. Railways and roads were being built. Entrepeneurs were reopening mines, extending sugar, cotton, and wheat plantations over peasant lands, and sending their goods north. Mexico was going places. And there was no room for an embarrassing lumpen proletariat of Indian healers, drunken soldiers, and stoned criminals. Marijuana—the medicine of the poor and the stimulant of the downtrodden—started to represent everything that was wrong with Mexico.

Doctors began the campaign. They argued that marijuana smoking produced hallucinations, temporary insanity, and, if smoked for long enough, full-blown dementia. They argued that mixed with booze or tobacco it could also cause outbursts of stunning violence. They also attacked the principal vendors of the drug—the herbolarias. "How many lives has your ignorance cost? How many pounds of marijuana have you sold? How many times have you given a poison rather than a cure?"

Because it was the late nineteenth century, they overlaid this intolerance with the vacuous veneer of race science. For Mexico's elites, anyone indigenous (like most healers and soldiers) was at the bottom of the racial pyramid. Their habits and customs risked polluting the country's population. So soldiers shouldn't smoke it and healers shouldn't sell it, not because it harmed them (who cared?), but because its cumulative use risked "degenerating the Mexican race." Who better to blame for Mexico's lack of progress than the dope-smoking, baby-bearing poor themselves?

If doctors started the myths, Mexico's new tabloid press popularized them. From the 1890s onward, stories of prisoners, soldiers, and criminals attacking their fellow citizens under the influence of marijuana became widespread.

February 1894, Alberto Guttman robs a man and slices him with a machete. The cause—"the excitation that this powerful narcotic produces." December 1899, former soldier Eulalio Andagua comes back to the barracks to visit friends, "turns into a madman after smoking marijuana," attacks a guard, is placed in a holding cell and then tries to kill himself by beating his head against the wall. January 1901, Margarito Trujano punches a passerby, tears off his clothes, and gnaws at his arm before he is finally placed in a straitjacket. As the paper explained, "Trujano was not crazy … he was crazy under the influence of the marijuana which he smoked in large quantities."

Though strict prohibitions against marijuana would come later, this first panic also caused a crackdown. Suppression started in the barracks, where sergeants threatened soldiers with court-martials. It moved into the prisons, where weed-smuggling visitors were caught and thrown inside with their relatives. Finally, by the turn of the century, it extended to the markets, where health inspectors now demanded a license for the sale of weed. And if you were poor, a woman, and without any letters after your name, your chances of getting one were basically nil. Inspectors scoured the stalls of the capital's markets for the drug. If they found it, they busted the offending healer for dealing in harmful medicines. Then they moved on to the wholesalers like Del Moral.

No doubt the first marijuana panic was influential; it put hundreds behind bars; and it established the template for thinking about the drug for decades. Yet, initially at least, it was unable to hold up weed's use. In the short term, tabloid alarm was little match for the forces of Revolution.

In 1910, after two decades of declining democracy, sliding wages, and aggressive land takeovers, Mexico's masses rose up against the dictator. Within less than a year they drove him from power. On departing, Porfirio Díaz allegedly whispered that the revolutionaries "had unleashed a tiger. Let's see if they can control it." On this, at least, he was right. They couldn't. And the conflict rolled on for another decade. Different armed groups stressed different aims. Some, like the followers of Emiliano Zapata, wanted the return of stolen lands. Others, like the more middle-class followers of Venustiano Carranza, demanded political power. Others still, like the supporters of the charismatic former bandit Francisco "Pancho" Villa, coupled both calls with demands for higher wages.

In peak years—like 1914, when a right-wing general attempted to install a military regime—army numbers soared to around 250,000. Add to this the thousands of irregular rebel militias, local defense units, and robber bands and there were around double that number under arms at any one time. Some of these revolutionaries were rather puritanical. (Pancho Villa—whose face now adorns dozens of brands of tequila—was actually a teetotaler.) Yet many were not. The Revolution proved a boon for the booze business. Domestic beers and cactus-based liquors like pulque, tequila, and mezcal soaked the nights, numbed the pain, and fueled the fireside songs of the Revolution's soldiers.

But also, as soldiers left the barracks, so did marijuana. What had been a drug for the few became a solace for the many. Writings on the Revolution, from autobiographies to thinly veiled fictional accounts, point to the drug's everyday use. Cannabis became campfire consolation. Perhaps the most famous account was in former soldier Francisco Urquizo's tale of army life, *Tropa Vieja*. Urquizo described the military authorities desperately searching camp visitors for liquor and drugs. In a passage that would echo with any contemporary prison officer, their searches were in vain. Visitors hid firewater in the chorizo sausages, mezcal in their bras, their underskirts, and the nappies of newborns. They put black dye in the tequila to make it look like coffee and hid marijuana inside sandwiches and tortillas. Trumpeters hid the drug in their instruments. Soldiers secreted it in the linings of their jackets and in the barrels of their guns.

Inside camp the drug functioned as both medicine and narcotic. Camp wife Chata gives marijuana to one injured soldier to stop the pain. "Here's a marijuana cigarette to suck on, let's see if it can stop your agony and you can cope with the journey ... he took a few puffs and was calmed."

But it was also a drug for the downtimes. For the wannabe poet Jacobo Otamendi, it was blessed relief; alcohol was nothing in comparison.

Liberating herb! Consolation of the overwhelmed, the sad and the afflicted. You ... can make us forget the miseries of life, the pain of the body, and the malaise in our heart. You shake up the weight of time, you make us take flight and dream in what could be the supreme being. You are the consolation of the imprisoned, the music of the heart that sings a song for the free man, free of other men, free of the body, absolutely free.

The poet's paean was not a solitary one. The revolutionary *corridos*, or songs, that passed news from town to town also testified to marijuana's extensive consumption. Most famously, revolutionary troops changed the lyrics of the popular ditty "La Cucaracha" (The Cockroach) to infer that the cockroach in question—the famously immoderate dictator Victoriano Huerta—"didn't want to walk, because he lacks, because he lacks, marijuana to smoke." But beyond the greatest hits, there were other mentions. In "Imprisoned they take me north," the prisoner claimed that he was being dragged away "for my love of Juanita." It wasn't a girl; it was a slang term for marijuana.

But perhaps the most telling testament to the army's drug use was the flood of stories about military marijuana smoking after the Revolution. Doctor's accounts, medical theses, and judicial trials all pointed to the popularity of the narcotic. As late as 1938, a doctor asked battalion medics to fill in a questionnaire on camp marijuana use. No doubt harsh penalties had decreased smoking. But in some barracks—especially in weed-growing areas—the practice was still endemic.

In fact, this later study highlighted one of the key aspects of military marijuana. It was a balm and a way to relax. But it also had a practical use for battalion brass band players. The reason, one doctor explained, was simple. Weed dried the palate. So brass players smoked it to "lessen their secretion of saliva and hence play well." Perhaps "the cockroach" of the corrido had no marijuana because the band playing the tune had smoked it all?

The Revolution was a truly transformative event. Over a million were dead; Mexico was changed forever. Revolutionaries now took control of the country. Change was often conflictive and painstakingly slow. But improvements were made. Farmlands were handed out to the peasants. The oil and rail industries were brought under public ownership. And the new Constitution of 1917 introduced a bill of workers' rights so radical it would only be surpassed by the Russian Bolsheviks.

The Revolution also brought cultural change. Deference diminished; standards of behavior altered. Women chopped their hair short and wandered the streets alone at night. Men—some from the lowest social ranks—now walked with the confidence of soldiers that had fought a dictatorship in the front lines. Among some of the popular classes, attitudes to marijuana also changed. Weed gradually became a drug for literary bohemians and the urban poor.

A subculture was born.

In 1920, the year the Revolution ended, we catch a glimpse of this new subculture from a rather strange source. Eugenio Gómez Maillefert was not a journalist or an anthropologist or a poet of the Mexican underground. He was a bureaucrat and a posh one. But he had a keen eye for a good story. And his article—"Marijuana in Mexico"—was revelatory.

In it he claimed that marijuana smoking now spanned the capital's society. There were former prisoners and soldiers (of course), thieves and sex workers (expected), but also workers, artisans, youths, and even professionals from the middle classes. Though it was officially illegal, "you can basically say it is tolerated because of the ease in acquiring it."

A new market brought new vendors. Market healers now competed with street dealers, newspaper vendors, and sandwich sellers. They bought the weed wholesale, then rolled cigarettes for sale at around 10–20 centavos each. It was an easy and relatively risk-free income. Perhaps the capital's most famous marijuana sellers were a husband and wife team called Cockerel Face and the Little Cockerel. Officially, they were candle makers, but the business was just a front. At the back of the shop they produced the best-quality weed in Mexico City—"pure sheep's tail," or marijuana exclusively drawn from the bushy top of the plant.

Market growth also opened up new spaces for smoking. There were high-class joints like the old convent where poets read out their reefer-inspired poems surrounded by papier-mâché skulls and other macabre decorations. And there were down-at-the-heels cafés off Plaza Garibaldi where thieves, ruffians, and youths added a few shots of firewater to their coffee and puffed on marijuana cigarettes.

This subculture also started to generate its owns rituals and language. Joints were wetted before smoking; they were passed around in a circle; and smokers often chewed sweets after taking three drags on the herb. There was even a song that the stoners sang: one wit termed it the Marijuana Marseillaise.

> I'm a marihuano and I can't
> Even lift up my head
> With my bloodshot eyes

*And my mouth dry, oh so dry*
*Here comes the devil*
*With his twenty-five brothers*
*He says that he's going to take away*
*All the marihuanos*

If the rituals were rather formulaic, the language surrounding marijuana was ostentatiously jokey and imaginative. There were multiple words for weed—*grifa*, *mota*, and *shora*, which could be combined into a real post-smoking tongue twister, *Motishorigrif*. There were words for being under the effects of marijuana—*vacilar* (to dither or stumble) and *ahuitarse* (to be disturbed). There was even a word for the roach, the *tecolote* (owl, or a colloquial term for policeman). And there was a whole series of games of verbal jousting, punning, and wordplay that went along with the experience.

It was this wordplay—what we might term this *"gramática grifa"*—that moved marijuana culture into another arena: music hall theater. It was this connection that cemented the changing meaning of marijuana in the popular imagination. For the music hall audiences of workers, youths, and partygoers, it was an antidote to all the deference and daintiness of the dictatorship. It was a mirror—albeit a distorted one—of a new, revolutionary Mexico.

Music hall, and particularly satirical music hall, was as much part of the Revolution as campfire songs or Diego Rivera murals. Big theaters like the Apolo and the Lírico shared the center of Mexico City with hundreds of cabarets and bars. Outside the center, dozens of tents put on satirical romps that mixed dances and stock characters with political lampoons. The plays were strong stuff. U.S. ambassador Josephus Daniels was shocked to witness satirists holding up "public officials to devastating ridicule" and compared Mexico's comedic candidness favorably with that of the United States.

These music hall productions reflected the new openness of revolutionary Mexico. The big battles were over. Now it was time to remake national culture and, perhaps more important, enjoy it. Music hall, together with drinking at a cantina and taking in a late-night cabaret, became a weekend for all but the most uptight.

Marijuana was central to this. During the Revolution, playwrights had started to frame the chaos of the civil war as some kind of hallucinatory marijuana dream. And by the end of the conflict, the idea had taken hold. The weed smoker was a stock character—revolutionary Mexico's version of the medieval jester—whose comedic wordplay, staggering gait and intoxicated condition not only made people laugh but also allowed the actor to speak truth to power. Half a century before Cheech and Chong, the stoner comedy was born.

Perhaps the first actor to really nail the role was Lupe Rivas Cacho, who regularly played the role of "La Grifa" or "The Stoner." She started in the cheap cabarets but soon made it to the high-profile theaters. In 1919 journalists applauded her talent for playing "a neighborhood woman." She drank pulque, smoked "that pestilent herb," and declared—in a garbled way—what all the audience was thinking.

The shift in marijuana's meaning was perhaps best expressed not by the jumbled argot of the comedy stoner, but rather by the brilliant Jewish intellectual Anita Brenner. With an ear for street talk that bypassed most foreign observers, Brenner explained that what best summed up the mood of postrevolutionary Mexico were not the self-important speeches of the politicians or the art of the muralists, but the predominance of the *vacilada* or the semidemented laughing state caused by smoking marijuana. For Brenner, for the playwrights, and for their audience, it acted as "a simile for a strain, a tone, an attitude that runs through Mexican life."

It meant laughing at the solemn, mocking the pompous, and ridiculing the pious. It reflected contemporary Mexico. After the Revolution, the country was a world turned upside down. Or for a moment in the 1920s it seemed so. The rich of the dictatorship were cowed or had fled. The crowd and its populist representatives now ruled. It was carnival. The jesters were in charge. What better way to indulge in this, describe it, and maybe even memorialize it than the laughter produced by the revolutionary soldiers' drug of choice?

As the meaning of marijuana changed, new adherents emerged from among the Revolution's more bohemian artists. They did not include La Grifa's sometime boyfriend, Diego Rivera, at least not for long. Sometime around 1923 he declared that he and his fellow painters should attempt to channel the energies of their forebears and "officially smoke cannabis ind-ica." This was no idle trial and they even invited in a "professional" weed smoker, Chema, to guide them. Chema clearly recognized his audience, and his sales pitch was pure pretention. Opening his briefcase, he claimed that inside was "the only transcendental value that Mexico, our country, has given the world. . . . Marijuana." Here, he claimed, pointing at the con-tents, "is science, love, politics, everything that you need to construct the monumental art that you dream of." After taking a few puffs, Rivera declared that the drug had little or no effect. Mexico's muralists were nat-ural marihuanos. They didn't need the drug.

Others, however, did. Perhaps the most prominent was the poet and journalist Porfirio Barba Jacob. Barba was an exile from Colombia who wandered Mexico from the 1910s on as a pen for hire. He claimed that he first tried the drug in Monterrey during a torrential storm. It was love at first puff. And that night, as he put it, he "celebrated his nuptials with the Lady with the Burning Hair." He even celebrated her in a poem of the same name. According to one of his friends, he used to hang around shabby cafés with "counterfeiters, marijuana sellers, criminals and killers." By the 1930s, he was smoking more than ever. The soirées at his apartment at the Hotel Sevilla were legendary. They included journalists, poets, artists, and even (allegedly) the future president Adolfo López Mateos. His rooms were always thick with marijuana smoke. And at one particularly wild reading of "The Lady with the Burning Hair" one guest took it rather too literally and set fire to his wife's locks.

Marijuana now had a market; it had sellers; it had rituals; it had a lingo; and it had a distinct set of acceptable venues from hole-in-the-wall bars to the Hotel Sevilla. It was still very much a subculture. But it demanded more intensive production than picking random hillside plants or investing in a few patio flower pots. Now it needed agricultural land outside the city. And soon a few villages started to specialize in growing the weed.

In San Mateo Otzacatipan, a predominantly indigenous village some 50 miles west of the capital, it was the crop of choice for the revolutionary peasants that had taken over the big landlord's farm. In September 1928 a sanitary agent tried to enter the village and collect what he described as "enormous quantities of cannabis indica." He was met by its armed and "aggressive" new owners. The local army commander was no fool and refused to intervene. As a result, the agent got only a sample of 10 kilos to send back to his superiors. It was a gift from the local teacher who felt sorry for his powerless federal colleague.

Another key growing zone surrounded the beautiful colonial town of Atlixco, in the foothills of the volcano Popocatépetl. Its reputation for fine marijuana would last decades. Rarest of accolades, it even got a hippie nickname—Popo Oro or Popo Gold. Informants estimated that the village produced around 500 kilos, which they delivered to a female wholesaler from the western fringes of Mexico City.

Mexico's marijuana subculture made for entertaining anecdotes and financed a small circle of suburban villages. And a dampened version of it would go on to inspire American Beat poets and protohippies during the 1950s. But it failed to penetrate much beyond the capital's partygoers. And as the initial enthusiasm for the Revolution diminished, use waned. By the end of the 1930s, users were limited to a few army regiments and the capital's lower classes. Mexico would have to wait another century for the return of widespread recreational drug use.

What did stick, however, was the panic over the drug.

The Revolution's leaders were—in general—more middle class than the armies they led and the crowds they addressed. And among many of the leaders, the panic that linked marijuana to violence died hard. In fact, to make matters worse, it now combined with a U.S.-influenced temperance movement in vogue at the time. (Pancho Villa was not the only dry revolutionary at the party.) It would take another twenty years for revolutionary thinking to reform the drug laws.

So while the capital's theatergoers smoked and partied, doctors continued to produce hysterical articles listing the drug's dangerous effects. And the tabloids continued to print imaginary stories of marijuana-induced murders.

Now to cap it off, the Mexican authorities introduced a series of punitive laws against marijuana. In 1920, the government prohibited the "cultivation and commerce of all products that degenerate the race." It included marijuana. With a stroke, the herb—in all its forms—medicinal or narcotic—was banned. Mexico had prohibited marijuana seventeen years before the United States. And further laws backed this up. The penal codes of 1929 and 1931 stipulated sentences of up to ten years for growing or trafficking the drug.

Soon the new laws brought seizures and arrests. In Mexico City the authorities created a new sanitary police. It was their job to prowl the markets and backstreets looking for illegal dealers. The Del Moral bust now looked trifling in comparison. In 1925 they seized over 4 tons of marijuana in the capital alone. Two years later they confiscated 27 tons. In the early 1930s they trawled the city's nightspots, arresting hundreds of small-time peddlers and giving them fines and six-month sentences.

Up on the border, local cops were also clamping down on everyday use. In just eighteen months in the early 1920s they indicted 559 people for drugs in the cities of Mexicali and Tijuana alone. A lot were Chinese opium addicts and U.S. visitors, but there were also many Mexican marijuana smokers.

Though it was stuttering, underpowered, and rested uneasily on a prerevolutionary racial panic, the war on drugs had begun.

## Chapter 2

# White Lady, Black Market

IT WAS SEPTEMBER 1924 AND JOSÉ MASCORRO WAS AT A LOW EBB. HE WAS a secret service agent. He should have been infiltrating counterrevolutionary sects or hunting down bandits. Instead, he was stuck in the bowels of the capital. Two months ago he had been charged with investigating the Mexico City heroin trade; it was not a glamour job. His days were full of backstreet meetings with desperate addicts, slippery dealers, and bent cops. He was bored and frustrated.

On the upside, he had recently made a useful informant—a chauffeur and heroin addict called Juan Hernández. Mascorro liked Hernández. Hernández wanted to get clean. And Mascorro had promised him a free stint in a government hospital if he coughed up what he knew. Hernández was more than forthcoming. Driving Mascorro around in the back of his cab, he started to point out the network of criminals, doctors, and pharmacists who channeled Mexico City's dealers large quantities of morphine, heroin, and cocaine originally registered for medical use.

But the double act didn't last long. Hernández had continued to buy and shoot heroin. And soon he fell ill from blood poisoning. His arm went purple, then black. Mascorro called a doctor, but the prognosis wasn't good. Ten days later Hernández was dead. In a letter to his superiors Mascorro raged against the trade that had claimed his contact. He raged against the dealers who "were killing people with their drugs, not just this victim, but many others." And he raged against the officials that were protecting them.

Anger bred action. And over the next six months Mascorro would start a one-man crusade to unmask Mexico's first drug-trafficking ring. It was an investigation that would take him into the worlds of organized crime, professional medicine, and corrupt cops. It would lead him from the capital's notorious Lecumberri jail, to squalid morphine stash houses, upscale pharmacists' labs, and the Caribbean port city of Veracruz. It was an inquiry that demonstrated the sources of Mexico's early trade in hard drugs and the strange alliances that these produced. It was also one that was meticulously recorded in Mascorro's increasingly outraged letters to his secret service bosses.

Without Hernández's help, Mascorro struggled to reenter the world of Mexico's drug addicts. It was, as he knew, a fairly narrow world. Morphine, heroin, and cocaine were European and American vices. They were expensive medicines; they were prescribed by doctors; and morphine—in particular—was used to combat World War I field injuries. By contrast, Mexico's soldiers either relied on booze and marijuana or died in pain. As a result, even in the wake of the Revolution, addiction to morphine, heroin, and cocaine was extremely low. And it would continue to be so for the next century. Experts observed that even on the border very few Mexicans aped their U.S. neighbors. "The poverty of the patients and the disinclination of Mexican physicians to prescribe narcotics makes for a very low ... per capita use."

In Mexico City, abuse was also limited. The most comprehensive medical study of heroin and morphine addiction counted only 458 cases in private hospitals, the general state asylum, or the city jail between 1920 and 1924. Though it was the epicenter of Mexican addiction, there was an average of less than one case every thousand inhabitants. By comparison, in some U.S. cities, addiction could be as much as ten times as prevalent.

So Mascorro started his inquiry in the one place where he knew there were addicts—Mexico's City's imposing new jail—the Lecumberri prison.

Hard drugs had started to blight the prison in the late 1910s. Morphine and heroin, in particular, had started to contend with marijuana as the prisoner's preferred release.

Prison doctor Dr. Juan Peón del Valle was there at the beginning and described the drug's gradual incursion into everyday life.

At first the traffickers didn't have an important market in this penitentiary. But little by little it grew to become one of the biggest subjects of commerce.... Soon we realized that around Cell Block F there were drug traffickers. First it was hidden in a milk bottle with a false bottom, then a few morphine capsules lodged in the nasal passages of a woman wearing a veil, then in the hollow of a wooden leg, then behind the photo of a girlfriend, then stuck behind the stamp of a letter, until at last there were innumerable ways that it was entering. Later we realized that inside that cell block there was an entire market established as the family members of the addicts brought in clothes, money, food, and even the drug itself and that there was not enough money in the world to establish an incorruptible vigilance on the trade.

Prison changed hard drugs almost overnight. As use grew, the profile of the average addict changed. Middle-class addicts—who had got hooked on prescription morphine or heroin—started to decline. They were replaced by what the prison doctor—with a rare eye for the subtleties of Mexico's class distinctions—described as a crew of "tramps, beggars, lottery ticket sellers, drivers, and newspaper vendors."

Hard drugs also gained a popular argot. Heroin became *la dama blanca* (the white lady) or more inexplicably *chiva* (goat). As it moved from the medicine cabinet to the street, it also got cut—with sodium bicarbonate, milk powder, and ammonium carbonate. Nicknames snowballed; heroin mixtures were called *gaviotas* (seagulls) and were snorted by the new addicts before they took to injecting.

As morphine and heroin moved down the social hierarchy, legislation against abuse of the drugs hardened. External pressure played a role. In 1914, the United States passed the Harrison Act, which started to regulate the medicinal use of morphine, heroin, and cocaine. Over the next decade pressure on U.S. doctors to stop prescribing the narcotics increased until finally in 1924 the production of heroin was banned altogether. In some ways Mexico simply followed the northern neighbor's lead. U.S. authorities on the border in particular were concerned that Mexico might become an avenue for the illegal drug trade. So the Mexican government signed on to international accords with limited, if any, cajoling.

But like the marijuana ban, this was also prohibition *a la mexicana*. It was tied up with old ideas of race science—the fear of cumulative use poisoning the nation's bloodstock. In 1917 the new constitution gave the government control over any substance that might "degenerate the race." And in 1920 the government decreed that opium and morphine could only be imported with the state's permission. Decrees in 1923 and 1925 tightened up imports even further. And the new penal laws of 1929 and 1931 established new prison sentences for trafficking in the substances illegally.

As the state gradually clamped down on domestic use, the white lady gained a black market.

Inquiries in the prison led Mascorro to the first tier of Mexico's new drug trade—the organized criminals. According to his sources, they stored large quantities of drugs in what we might now term stash houses. Here they doled them out to small-time peddlers, who would either smuggle them into the jail or sell them to ex-cons on the streets.

The organized criminals involved in the business were not just any old thugs. They were some of Mexico's most well-known felons. "Pugnose" Bernabé Hernández and Luis Lara had been members of the infamous Grey Automobile Gang, described by one scholar as Mexico's first "modern criminals." In 1915, in the midst of the Revolution, they had posed as policemen or soldiers and preyed on the city's elites, robbing their houses of money, jewelry, and valuable possessions.

The gang was legendary. There were corridos, news stories, exposés, and carefully staged photo shoots. In the tabloids they gained a reputation as revolutionary Robin Hoods, stealing from the rich if not exactly giving to the poor. Instead, they disbursed their gains on the arms of beautiful women, in fancy restaurants and upscale bars. Such spending patterns

were not the only things that made them very much of the moment. They
were a metropolitan crew that included Spanish, Mexican, and even
Japanese members. Their getaway vehicle, the eponymous grey automobile,
was the same limo that had driven the first revolutionary president,
Francisco Madero, to his execution in 1913.

There was even a movie, and not just any movie but Mexico's first real
narrative film. Enrique Rosas's 1919 work *El Automóvil Gris* followed the
story of the police investigation into the gang, The film was part action
flick, which entertained audiences with car chases, daring rooftop escapes,
and heated confrontations. And it was part documentary. The film ends
with actual footage of the execution of the gang filmed by Rosas three years
earlier. The scene is quite shocking. We not only witness the soldiers shooting a volley at the prisoners, we also see the soldiers approaching the quiv-
ering bodies to give them the *coup de grâce*. The film was a massive
commercial success and it seemed to offer Mexicans a simple lesson—
crime doesn't pay.

Yet, as Mascorro discovered, for at least two members of the gang, it
still did.

Hernández and Lara somehow managed to dodge the firing squad (or
at least the *coup de grâce*). Instead, they did a few years in Lecumberri
prison, where they built on their fame, posed for pictures with reporters,
and picked up on the new market for morphine and heroin use. When they
got out in 1923, they established two bases of operations. One run by Lara
was in the center of the poor barrio of Tepito. The other, managed by
Hernández, was to the east of the city, next to the Veracruz–Mexico City
train line and the Lecumberri prison. Hernández's pad appeared to be the
main storage space for the city's drugs. Dealers and addicts came from all
over the city to buy produce. Trade was brisk. When Mascorro staked out
the address for just fifteen minutes, he saw over twenty people entering and
leaving. According to an informant, Hernández was raking in over 500
pesos a day from the trade.

Many of the sellers were related to the two gangsters. The narcotics
trade was and still is a business predominantly run along family lines.
Hernández's mother-in-law was a prominent dealer in the center of the city,
just six blocks from the National Palace; so was his sister-in-law "La Cholita"

Soledad and her husband "Tiny" Pepe. (The trade has always also been big on nicknames.)

The question now arose, where were the organized criminals acquiring the drugs? The answer, Mascorro found, was quite simple—where the rich had got theirs—from the medical world. During the early years of the drug trade, doctors and pharmacists were absolutely crucial to the development of the black market in narcotics in both the United States and Mexico.

Before World War II, morphine, heroin, and cocaine were predominantly made in Europe by massive pharmaceutical companies like Bayer and Merck. During the first decades of drug prohibition, specialists were allowed to import set amounts of these drugs for medical use with a government license. But there were multiple ways around the rules. You could import legal amounts, cut it, fake a series of prescriptions, and then sell it for a greater price on the black market. Or, if you really wanted to make a serious profit, you could make contacts in Europe and import it in secret.

During the 1920s, both tricks were extremely common. The newly created health police kept a close eye on suspect doctors and pharmacists. In the last two months of 1927, there was a big crackdown on these rule-breakers throughout the republic. Over a hundred fines were given out for importing morphine, heroin, or cocaine without a license or in illegal amounts, or adulterating it and selling it without prescription. There was barely a state without at least one case. What seven years ago had been healthcare had now been declared "the selling of poisons."

Such cases demonstrated the arbitrary lines between formal medicine and drug dealing. Medicine was just filling out the right forms, going through the right channels, and prescribing relief to the rich. Drug dealing was giving out a slightly weaker version of the product but to a poorer clientele and while cutting a couple of bureaucratic corners. Though the crackdown on narcotics was—even in its earliest days—portrayed as a struggle between good and evil, the difference between medicine and dealing was not really one of ethics or morality, but rather of attitudes to class and the state.

In Mexico City, Mascorro discovered that the most important corner-cutters were the pharmacist Félix Sánchez and his brother Othon. Félix had the technical know-how. He was a chemist. He was described as "thin faced, with a curly moustache, and three gold teeth." At least part of the morphine and heroin the brothers sold was ordered legally through the government health department. It was delivered to his pharmacy, the Apothecary San Pedro, in the center of the city. Félix then took the product to his laboratory in a quiet middle-class neighborhood, mixed it with various other chemicals, lowered its purity to around 30 percent, and handed it over to his brother Othon for sale.

Othon was the link between the fastidious chemist and the wider world. Mascorro described him as "clever and pretentious," always going on about how he was "friends of this person or close to that person." This was not all bluster. He knew the Grey Automobile Gang, through a *comadre* (co-godparent) who was Lara's lover. This clearly gave him a link to the prison market. He also had friends in almost every layer of Mexican authorities. An able political player, his job was to ensure protection and distribution.

On November 8, 1924, Mascorro sat nursing a beer in a cantina around the corner from the apothecary and observed how the two brothers worked. At 7 P.M. both brothers arrived in matching two-door Fords. They chatted to friends, handed over a few bags of narcotics to the cantina owner (who also dealt on the sly), and then exchanged car keys. Félix drove off in Othon's car; Othon drove off in Félix's complete with a boot full of adulterated narcotics fresh from the lab. Othon then spent the night distributing the drugs to dealers throughout the city.

What made the Sánchez brothers the main Mexico City wholesalers was not simply their connections to the underworld and but also their ability to bring in narcotics above and beyond what they were licensed to import. This took two further links—contacts in the ports and contacts in the police.

The port contacts were in the sweltering Caribbean city of Veracruz, around 300 miles east of the capital. Veracruz was—and still is—Mexico's principal trading port with Europe. In the 1920s, Italian, German, French, and Spanish freighters carried clothes, ceramics, and luxury goods in and then left for the return journey weighed down with agricultural and mining products. These same freighters also delivered the majority of Mexico's medicines. These were still imported from Europe's big pharmaceutical factories.

One of Mascorro's contacts, the repentant former owner of an opium den, explained how the system worked. Traffickers paid stevedores to skim off licensed packages of morphine, heroin, or cocaine or pick up unlicensed ones from visiting ships. They would then pass these packages to dock laborers who would smuggle the drugs out of the port and drop them off at nearby wholesalers. Just like in Mexico City, these were respectable pharmacists. They had simply neglected to get licenses for the import or sale of the drugs. These pharmacists would rebadge the narcotics as patent medicines and send them by train to Mexico City. They would arrive at the railway station, only a few blocks from Bernabé Hernández's stash house and the Lecumberri prison. It was door-to-door service.

The foreign drugs provided for the Mexico City market and increasingly fed a lot of the cross-border traffic. But they also created a small chemical mecca in Veracruz itself. The pharmacies were at the center of this. One local writer remembered that during the 1920s you could buy

> [c]ocaine chloride and German morphine from the Merck company or French stuff ... as no one bothered with the register of narcotics. In many pharmacies drugs were sold without fear and there were silversmiths who sold little silver boxes perfect to carry them in.... It was common to give 3 pesos to any street urchin, send him to a pharmacy, and get a gram of magnificent Merck cocaine. No one got scared, people knew about the traffic and everyone knew who liked snow and who injected themselves with morphine and heroin.

Veracruz's surprisingly lively drug scene also inspired Mexico's first drug flick. *El Puño de Hierro* (The Iron Fist) of 1927 was no *El Automóvil Gris*. The acting was wooden and the narrative confusing; it was watched by virtually no one. But what it lacked in technical brio and commercial success, it made up for with a strange mixture of journalistic truth-telling and sheer, unhinged weirdness.

The film was the story of a young, well-to-do man gradually pulled into morphine addiction. Depravity ensues. He leaves his girlfriend, strokes and kisses a donkey, and hangs out in an increasingly odd shooting gallery where young men caress an older man wearing what appears to be a diaper. The film then changes pace. We leave the den and move to the center of the city where a respectable doctor is giving a speech on the dangers of opiates. His preaching is interspersed with disturbing footage of genuine operations, addicts trussed in straitjackets, and their children hobbling on deformed limbs. Over the next hour, there are robberies, fights, a pipe-smoking child detective, and strange goings-on in the den. But the punch comes at the end. The shady owner of the morphine den is revealed as none other than the sanctimonious doctor.

Strange it may have been, but it was also close to the truth. In revolutionary Mexico surrealism and social realism, morphine and medicine, dealers and doctors, intermingled and overlapped.

By the end of 1924, Mascorro had tracked down the heavies, discovered the wholesalers, found the source of the drugs, and traced their route to the capital. Yet the really explosive breakthrough was still to come. Over the next two months he also managed to piece together the officials who protected the trade. Like the criminals and the pharmacists, they were from the top tier.

The traffickers' principal ally was the chief detective of the capital's police, Valente Quintana. Quintana was to Mexican policing what the Grey Automobile Gang was to Mexican crime. He was the first modern detective and the first tabloid gumshoe. He, like the gang, would even go on to star in his own films. (Though he had a better survival rate.)

Quintana was born in the border state of Tamaulipas in 1890. A thin, handsome man, he was a natural raconteur. His early career was shrouded in myth, most of it of his own making. He claimed that he first came to detective work when falsely accused of stealing by a U.S. shop owner. To prove his innocence he tracked down the real thief. Such skills brought him to the attention of a Brownsville police training college called the "Detective School of America." Here gringo teachers honed his natural abilities. It was the perfect origin story for revolutionary Mexico—detective work as part natural intuition and part nationalist counterpunch. It was also probably untrue.

But certificate in hand and with a thirst for justice, he arrived in Mexico City in 1917 and joined the police. Four years later he made his name tracking down a gang of famously violent train robbers. From then on, he barely left the headlines. He drifted through the Mexican underworld, often in disguise, picking up gossip, breaking cases, and taking down high-profile felons. After arresting a U.S. armed robber on the lam, he was even nicknamed "the Mexican Sherlock Holmes." The moniker stuck. It was meant to refer to Quintana's investigative skills but was perhaps as much a knowing wink to their shared penchant for hard drugs. Holmes injected them; Quintana peddled them.

Mascorro first started to suspect Quintana's involvement when he interviewed a sex worker and high-class heroin dealer in early August 1924. She claimed that it was Quintana that protected the Sánchez brothers. It was also Quintana who helped move the drugs over the border in Matamoros, where his brother was a Mexican customs officer. A few days later his suspicions grew. Mascorro ordered a raid on the chemist Félix Sánchez's house. Within minutes Quintana had arrived and demanded to take over the operation. In case Mascorro was in any doubt, the police commander then generously placed his own lawyer in charge of the chemist's defense.

For months Quintana managed to brazen out the steady drip-drip of accusations. He had most of the city's major newspapers paid off. They said nothing. But around the close of the year, rumors started that he was involved in the kidnapping and ransom of several members of the city elite. Quintana was starting to cross the line. Beating up street dealers for pesos was one thing; ransoming the rich for hundreds of thousands of pesos something else entirely.

At the same time, Mascorro made a breakthrough. On January 4, 1925, he finally managed to turn one of Quintana's agents. The insider confirmed that Quintana had pocketed most of the money from his famous train robbery bust. He said that the police chief had invested it in a fizzy drink factory, an entertainment firm, and a bullfighting ring. And he combined these interests with a slice of the capital's drug and robbery businesses.

Mascorro's investigation probably broke Quintana. On January 25, Quintana was reported to have called in his squad of cops and demanded that they no longer take bribes. It was too late. Less than a week later, he was sacked. His replacement—José Mascorro. The secret agent had not only won; he had taken over the Mexican police department.

Yet Mascorro's victory was little more than an illusion. None of the wholesalers or dealers went to prison. And nor did Quintana. His friends in the media kept silent. His removal was rebranded retirement and he started his own private detective agency. His record was clean.

Most ironically, by the end of the year Mascorro, the man who had railed against the heroin wholesalers, was being accused of exactly the same forms of revenue collection as Quintana. In return for bribes, he was allowing certain brothel owners and drug dealers to remain open.

No doubt it looked bad. Yet at the time it was the way policing worked—both in Mexico and in the United States. Policing was about catching criminals. But it was also about effectively regulating and taxing criminal enterprise; it was a protection racket. Some of the money went to the police; but often it also went into the state coffers.

Moreover, it was something that the government might have been unwilling to publicly flaunt, but it still understood. So, despite the accusations, Mascorro survived, job intact. In fact, he was only forced to resign in May 1928 when he drunkenly insulted the presidential candidate, Álvaro Obregón. It seems that taking drug bribes was a job requirement; laughing at the president was a sackable offense.

## Chapter 3

## Pipes and Prejudice

CHEN TA FAN WAS FURIOUS. IT WAS 1906 AND HE HAD SPENT NEARLY TEN years in Mexico. He had settled in the capital with hundreds of other Chinese immigrants. They had worked hard in cafés, restaurants, laundries, and shops. He himself ran a flourishing import-export business, which catered to both Chinese and Mexican buyers. Yet during this decade, most Mexicans had learned nothing about his culture. Their sole guide to his homeland was a popular, racist theater show called *Chin Chun Chan*.

In a letter to Mexico's biggest selling tabloid, *El Imparcial*, Fan claimed that such ignorance bred disdain. Mexicans, he wrote, thought that all the Chinese "spoke with a funny accent, wore pigtails ... and ate rats." How would Mexicans feel, he asked, if they were solely defined as "never washing ... and living off a diet of cockroach eggs, iguanas and cactus worms"?

What was worse, the Mexican tabloids had now started to rail against what their journalists called "the Chinese mafia." It was a shady and ill-defined group, "an octopus with claws," which—they claimed—had started to import tons of opium and open smoking dens wherever there were Chinese addicts. Why, he inquired, had they given a Chinese group a Sicilian name? Why did the octopus have claws? (Was this as dangerous, he asked, as a lion with tentacles?) And most important, why did they tar the entire Chinese community with the actions of a small group of opium smokers? Would Mexicans want to be dismissed as a nation of marihuanos?

Chen Ta Fan was a talented satirist—and he had a point. By the early 1900s, Mexicans had started to deploy a variety of ugly racial stereotypes against the Chinese. They were dirty, diseased, lazy, and sexually promiscuous. And their food was strange. Even *El Imparcial*'s editors agreed with the criticism. Though—in classic tabloid style—even their apology was cast as a racial stereotype. The letter, they admitted, "contained a little truth like those Chinese sandalwood boxes inside which there is a grain of rice wrapped in silk."

Chen Ta Fan was also prescient. Over the next two decades, the Mexican authorities would use regulations against smoking opium to demonize and persecute the country's Chinese minority. Punishments started with arrests and fines, grew to jail sentences, and culminated in forced exile. Just like the panic over marijuana penalized the poor, the panic over smoking opium demonized the Chinese.

Where the Chinese writer did perhaps err was in underestimating the importance of the Chinese opium trade. It was never run by a mafia; it never risked "poisoning" Mexico; and it never reached the popular usage of marijuana, let alone alcohol. Yet, as more and more Chinese moved to Mexico, the prevalence of smoking opium did increase. And it did change the Mexican drug trade. It was the Chinese who first planted opium poppy in Mexico on an appreciable scale. And it was Chinese merchants who first showed how to use the enormous capital generated by the trade to finance legal businesses.

Chinese migrants first arrived in Mexico during the seventeenth century. Some were merchants based in the Philippines who sold the Spanish colonists luxury porcelains and silks. Others were servants who worked for the galleons that plied the Manila–Acapulco route. But most Chinese immigrants—like Chen Ta Fan—arrived at the turn of the twentieth century. They fled a Chinese mainland where population growth had long outstripped agricultural supply, and hunger, banditry, and rebellion were now rife. Some fled to the United States. But with the Chinese Exclusion Act of 1882, Mexico's northern neighbor barred further immigration. So eventually many started to arrive in Mexico. It was trying to attract cheap labor and in 1899 had signed a treaty that allowed for free movement between the two countries.

No doubt some of the migrants simply passed through Mexico on their way to being smuggled over the border into the United States. But others stayed. The country's Chinese community grew. By 1926 there were 24,218 Chinese immigrants. They were the second-largest foreign community in Mexico, second only to the Spanish.

The new arrivals spanned the social spectrum. Some came voluntarily. They were relatively well off and used family networks to set up transnational trading companies, general stores, and farms. But others were closer to indentured servants, forced to pay back heavy transportation costs. Life was tough. They worked in mines, in cotton plantations, in sugar refineries, or building railways. Some of the earliest arrivals were sent to the baking desert of Sonora, where they built the coastal railway line in the midst of a brutal race war. Here, Chinese workers not only sought shelter from 40°C heat; they also ducked for cover while the Mexican army attempted to annihilate the Yaqui Indians in a bloody conflict over land.

By the 1920s, Chinese immigrants spanned Mexico. Every state had a small Chinese population, usually in the capital city, a port, or around a major railway terminal. But the largest communities flourished where the opportunities were—in the big metropolitan areas of Mexico City and Guadalajara, around the northern mines of Cananea, and the cotton-growing regions of La Laguna and Mexicali. The majority of these settlers were men; they were in Mexico to work for wages in the expanding economy.

But they also brought some of China with them. By the early 1900s, concentrations of immigrants started to build their own "Chinatowns." These were collections of inns, cafés, shops, and restaurants that offered not only a taste of home, but also support networks and working opportunities. In the dusty border city of Mexicali they not only built one Chinatown above ground, but also one underneath. La Chinesca was a subterranean labyrinth of rooms and passageways, which Chinese migrants used to escape the sweltering heat and, with time, the immigration authorities.

No doubt some also brought a taste for opium. During the nineteenth century many mainland Chinese used opium. Most smoked the treated poppy gum in a pipe. It started as an elite habit, an exotic commodity, which was taken socially in heavily ritualized ceremonies. Gradually, opium smoking spread down the social spectrum. But it never lost its convivial appeal. It was smoked openly at weddings, parties, and religious observances. "The welcome smoke" for the arriving guest was an indispensable part of everyday etiquette.

Addiction was not unknown. But it was not frequent. Many used the same amount every day for decades, smoking a few pipes with friends, or at work in the fields, or while pulling a rickshaw. It seemed to have little damaging effect. Others went on and off the gum depending on medical circumstances. Opium was—before the invention of aspirin in the 1890s—the world's most effective painkiller. Smoked, swallowed, or dissolved in liquid, it was a popular remedy for digestive problems, respiratory difficulties, fevers, and diseases affecting the nervous system. In a refrain that would echo with any Mexican marijuana smoker, one contemporary Chinese soldier said, "Opium was our medicine, it was all we had."

Sometimes users smoked their pipes in what became known as opium dens. Yet these were far from the dank spaces of degradation, suffering, and criminality that most U.S. and British commentators portrayed. They were often light, clean, tidy areas where smokers talked, ate, conducted business transactions, and played board games. They were much less rough than the average U.S. bar, British pub, or Mexican cantina. Reports of violent confrontations between patrons were rare.

Reading the Mexican press of the time, it is often difficult to separate the reality from the racist hysteria. Nevertheless, it seems that in Mexico some Chinese smoked opium as they had done in China. Some smoked for leisure at home. Others smoked at work, to break up the tedium of the day. Others still continued to use the medicine as a painkiller.

But many still smoked socially in dens. As in China, class divided these more official smoking spots. There were the high-class joints. In 1918 an inquisitive journalist infiltrated a place called Cabaret X in Mexico

City. When he arrived there, he found the place "shone with light, happiness and love." It was a place not only for the Chinese, but also for "high ranking military officials, rich playboys, incorrigible Bohemians, and well-dressed women." It was "the most elegant and comfortable opium den in Mexico." It had multiple rooms for talking, drinking, and gambling. Finally, after "an hour of chit chat and several cocktails," the journalist was invited into a room reserved for smoking. The walls were painted with pictures of scantily clad women, which, the journalist delicately admitted, "while not obscene, awakened certain passionate energies." He was given a pipe, inhaled the opium, and saw "the classical goddesses on the wall come alive."

But there were also rougher places that catered to a working-class crowd. The U.S. consul in Mexicali fancied himself a part-time detective. In February 1927 he looked into the city's drug scene. His contact brought him to a small alleyway just off the main drag behind the Chinese casino. Here they approached a rickety wooden house and rapped on the window ledge. A Chinese man poked his head out of the window and asked what they wanted. The consul's accomplice replied with the code word "Q." The door creaked open and the Americans entered. They found that the den was actually split in two. There was an orthodox opium smoking room populated by local Chinese workers. But there was also another, grubbier area where a multinational group of heroin addicts bought the product and injected it. Even on the border, where opium dens catered to a clientele of varying tastes, the smoking space itself was kept separate from areas where non-Chinese addicts took other narcotics.

Whatever the reality of opium smoking, as our satirist, Chen Ta Fan, predicted, it was soon used as a way to demonize Mexico's Chinese minority. Some of the assumptions were foreign imports. During the 1890s, Mexico's newspapers were full of horror stories—often directly reprinted from U.S. or European publications—of Chinese opium addiction and the depravities it caused.

As more immigrants arrived, the myths coalesced with Mexico's own brand of antidrug rhetoric. Just as with marijuana, the panic focused not on the actual effects of the drug, but rather on the smokers. And the poor Chinese laborers—like the poor indigenous healers or the stoned prisoners—didn't mesh with Mexico's modernizing self-image. Just like marijuana, smoking opium was held to "degenerate the race." According to this thinking, as more and more Chinese married Mexican women, their opium-addled children risked polluting the nation's bloodstock.

Just like the panic over marijuana, such thinking started in the era of dictator Porfirio Díaz, but it continued well into the Revolution. In fact, ideas about smoking opium mixed with increasingly violent prejudices against the Chinese population in general. Like so much xenophobia, these prejudices were rooted in the group's perceived economic success. In the north of the country, a handful of Chinese businessmen had used migrant networks to secure favorable loans and cross-border trading deals. In many towns they ran prosperous wholesale businesses or local shops.

The perceived success bred resentment. Roaming bands of revolutionary soldiers vented their anger on the country's Chinese minority. There were riots, shop burnings, lynchings, and murders. This peaked in early May 1911, when revolutionary forces invaded the city of Torreón, destroyed Chinese businesses, and killed over 300 immigrants.

There was no visible remorse. (Still to this day, the Torreón massacre has no lasting memorial.) In fact, during the 1920s such feelings hardened. In states with large Chinese populations, like Sonora, Sinaloa, and Baja California, politicians harnessed anti-immigrant sentiments to official economic nationalism. Progressive calls for lands, jobs, and the distribution of wealth became entangled with old-school racism. Such politics eventually led to the forced exile of tens of thousands of Chinese migrants during the following decade.

Such ideas also cemented the laws against smoking opium. Mexico was the second Latin American country to sign on to the Hague International Opium Convention, which sought to stamp out the trade in smoking opium. And after three Chinese men requested permission to monopolize the import of the paste in 1912, the government's health authorities made a definite pronouncement. They decided that smoking opium "was universally recognized as having noxious results." The request was denied. Four years later the president generalized the decision and prohibited the import of smoking opium. Heroin—a much more addictive substance but one originally taken by the rich—would only be banned a decade later. During the 1920s, subsequent antinarcotics laws were always careful to lump smoking opium together with other drugs.

As Chen Ta Fan realized, these laws provided useful shorthand—the Chinese were a threat because they were all drug addicts. In 1923, Torreón's broadsheet preached that the surviving Chinese population—which had congregated for self-protection in the nearby town of San Pedro de las Colonias—embraced "congenital vices, a peculiar filthiness, repulsive sicknesses, and a habit of taking money from our country back to theirs." Among the vices were preying on Mexican women and, of course, "enjoying the artificial paradises dreamed up by the smoke of an opium pipe."

The laws also provided a means to start arresting the country's Chinese population. During the 1920s, raids on Chinese lodging houses, tearooms, and market gardens were frequent. Often the police weren't fussy. Being Chinese and in a house with a pipe (or really any thin, hollow object) was often treated as sufficient evidence of addiction. In 1927 police raided a Chinese grocery store in the port city of Mazatlán for the second time in two years. This time they claimed to find two opium pipes, a lamp for burning opium, a large tray with opium residue, and two small trays. As the prosecuting attorney later found out, these were actually two bamboo sticks, a standard lamp, a tray, two pieces of foil, and some clay.

Beyond persecuting the Chinese, the new laws also shaped the trade itself. As importing opium was now banned, some Chinese entrepreneurs started to grow opium poppies in the Mexican countryside. Though not even our seer Chen Ta Fan would have guessed it at the time, this short-term solution to the ban changed the geography of the Mexican drug trade and the social profile of its traffickers forever. The focus shifted from the ports, where medicines were imported, and the cities, where they were sold, to the countryside, where the narcotics were grown.

Though chemists, pharmacists, and customs officers would still play major roles, peasants and farmers now entered the trade as the major producers of narcotics.

No doubt some Chinese farmers had grown small crops of opium poppies since they arrived in Mexico. Poppies were attractive garden flowers. And it was relatively easy to extract the gum necessary for the most elementary opium medicines. As early as 1906, the geographical society of the eastern state of Yucatán claimed that local Chinese farmers grew "coconut trees, white sapotes [often called Mexican apples] and a plant that looks a bit like mint that they called opium."

But the most credible claims emerged in the early 1920s. At first, most Mexicans simply didn't know what they had stumbled upon. In 1923, Rafael Muñoz, a health inspector from the steamy Pacific port of Topolobampo, explained to journalists that his first encounter with the plants was entirely by chance. He was riding a train between Topolobampo and the next port of San Blas when the train came off the rails. Some of the passengers got off the vehicle to wait for the repair. Wandering to some nearby fields, they started to pick the bright red flowers that were growing all around them. Returning to the train, they showed the flowers to the inspector. He identified them as opium poppies. When he eventually got into San Blas, he asked the local authorities about the fields. They claimed that a group of Chinese men had rented them for the purposes of farming an unspecified crop.

Without any real contacts in the Chinese underworld, accidental encounters seem to have been one of the Mexicans' most popular investigative techniques. Two years later another health inspector, this time from the northwest city of Culiacán, was out hunting with "an esteemed local family." They were tracking down deer and rabbit in the foothills just to the east of the city when suddenly they came across "an enormous valley sowed with poppies, a Chinese industry in the middle of the mountains of Sinaloa." At first, the hunters doubted their find. They had never seen such a quantity of the red flowers. But after inspecting the fields, they had no doubt that they were "poppies, the primary material for opium."

If Mexican laws pushed Chinese farmers to start growing the crop, they also made some Chinese businessmen extremely rich. Prohibition generated a black market in both Mexico and the United States. By providing for it, a handful of wholesalers became the country's first drug millionaires. Consciously or not, they established a way of doing business that set a pattern for many Mexican drug capitalists in the subsequent years.

In particular, these early traffickers of smoking opium carefully trod the line between what was legal and what was illegal. Difficult to catch and risk-averse, they were neither entirely legitimate businessmen nor entirely devoted to the drug trade. They moved between licit and illicit enterprises depending on an estimate of relative risk and return. When returns were high—perhaps the quality of the crop was good or demand was high—they invested in drugs. When returns were low or the risks were particularly severe (maybe the health inspectors were in town), they avoided the trade and survived on their legitimate businesses.

Many of these savvy entrepreneurs served the Chinese cotton farmers based around Mexicali. It was a favorable location. It was the capital of Baja California and had the largest Chinese population in Mexico.

But perhaps the most impressive was Antonio Wong Yin. Making money from a blend of business and opium selling in Mexico's Chinese capital was one thing. Doing the same in the heartland of anti-Chinese racism was quite another. But this is what Wong did. For two decades he surfed the limits of licit and illicit enterprises in the northern city of Torreón, the site of the 1911 massacre.

Wong was born in Canton in 1895. He and his brothers came over as adolescents and settled in the small market town of San Pedro de las Colonias just east of Torreón. San Pedro was the agricultural center of the area's cotton and farming business. Wong and his brothers started out during the 1920s buying up produce from local Chinese farmers and then selling it in the downtown market of Torreón. Over the next two decades, the Wong family would continue in the produce business, but they would also buy up cantinas, restaurants, and other general stores around the market. Antonio Wong also became the main shareholder in the Casino Unión, a club for Chinese workers. The Casino, he stressed, was a respectable place. It was definitely not geared toward gambling and opium smoking. Rather it was "a space where the Chinese come to rest from their daily labors, and dedicate themselves to talk, business and other distractions."

Wong's wealth gave him access to high society. Here he had a good start. He married the daughter of Mexican landowners also from San Pedro. She opened doors to the social world of the provincial city. They had their children baptized in Torreón's central Guadalupe church; they acquired Mexican godparents; they gave money to worthy charities; and they were invited to the area's most upscale parties. In 1936, they attended the wedding of the governor's sister. All the state's bigwigs were there, including generals, statesmen, and large cotton farmers. But Wong's gift of "delicate Japanese silks" was at the top of the gift list. Invites were reciprocated. When his own daughter was married six years later, he invited the same crowd to a Catholic service and a champagne lunch.

Here was a man so rich and so well connected that the combination seemed to overcome (or at least subdue) ingrained prejudice. Even in a place with such a bleak history of anti-Chinese sentiment, Wong built a network of powerful political backers. According to one 1932 police report, he was so close to the mayor of Torreón, the state governor, and the local military commander, he was untouchable.

For Wong, maintaining an aura of respectability was obviously of great concern. He realized the delicate line he walked between approval and condemnation. He understood the power of the press and fancied himself a bit of a wordsmith. Whenever he was arrested for drug offenses, he immediately wrote a formal letter to the local newspaper that laid out his case. In 1924, for example, he explained that he had been picked up in a random raid of commercial establishments outside the market. His cantina simply happened to be next to the intended target. He was kept inside because certain unnamed "enemies" had framed him for opium possession. They were jealous of the cheap rates at which he sold his goods. "The jealousy of these persons," he claimed, "has reached the level of intrigue."

Despite Wong's remonstrations, the accusations were so frequent that either the jealousy was exceptionally bitter and long-lasting or (much more likely) he was heavily involved in the opium trade.

At first, Torreón might seem a strange place to become a kingpin. It was no tourist hotspot, but a rather nondescript agricultural center in the midst of flat, featureless cotton fields. There was a native population of Chinese smokers, but never more than a few dozen. Most were killed during the massacre. It wasn't near opium-growing regions; they were much further to the west. But for a brief moment, it served—rather like Veracruz—as a kind of narcotic sorting center. The reason was simple—the train.

For the first decades of the twentieth century, getting around the interior of Mexico was extremely hard. One could try the roads, but most were muddy, potholed, and impassable during the rainy season. One could ride a horse, but the journey would take weeks and one would be vulnerable to bandits and thieves. The most reliable form of transport was the train. And here Torreón was important. It was at the intersection of four railways. Each of these routes was crucial to the development of the drug trade. One reached south to Mexico City, the source of much of the country's drugs. Another reached east to the port of Tampico, which like Veracruz also shipped in medicines and narcotics. Another reached north to the border town and vice capital of Ciudad Juárez. And another still reached west to the mountain city of Durango. This would go on to become an important marketplace for opium plants grown further west.

Wong's trade relied on this strategic position. Two investigations—one in 1925 and one in 1930—showed the unchanging simplicity of his plan. Wong would buy smoking opium (and increasingly heroin) from drug wholesalers in Mexico City or Tampico. These contacts would then post the goods by train to Torreón. In case of capture, the packages were all sent to fake names from fake addresses. (As one detective noted, all the Mexico City addresses were actually written with the same hand.) Wong's wife or other accomplices would then go to the post office and pick up the packages using fake IDs. Some drugs were skimmed off for local smokers. But most were sorted at a stash house, divided up into individual packages, and then sent by post to the border. Here they sold for double the price.

Even when things went wrong, Wong had sufficient social capital and political muscle to ride out any trouble, as even agent Mascorro, the Mexico City antidrug crusader, soon discovered. On April 4, 1925, two months into his new job as head of the Mexico City police, Mascorro ordered four of his men to track a package on the northern railway line out of the capital. The package contained 8 kilos of smoking opium and was addressed to a Mr. Bueno of Torreón. On April 6, 1925, a woman arrived at the Torreón post office and demanded the package. The postal employee refused and the woman fled. Apparently, she was Wong's wife using a fake ID.

But Wong didn't give up; the opium was worth over 60,000 pesos. So two days later an official from the mayor's office arrived and demanded the package once more. Again, the postal employee refused. This time he called Mascorro's men. In reply, the official rang the local police. The two groups of cops arrived, aimed their pistols at each other, and demanded the narcotics.

By the end of the 1970s such confrontations—between police units over the ownership of drugs—would become remarkably common. But in 1925 it was a first. In this case, the Mexico City cops backed down; they were outside their jurisdiction. The local police took the drugs. These promptly disappeared, presumably on the next train up to Ciudad Juárez. Fittingly, we shall follow the drugs; it is to this border town that we now turn.

## Chapter 4

## Vice and Violence

ENRIQUE FERNÁNDEZ PUERTAS WASN'T A FREQUENT CROSS-DRESSER. YET AS he hobbled down the station platform in Ciudad Juárez in early January 1934, he was decked in a blouse and a long dress; a modest shawl covered his face. There was a reason for his attire. He was on the run. His enemies were trying to kill him, and he was trying to reach Mexico City to firm up his political support. As he stepped onto the train, perhaps for a moment he dared to hope that he would make it.

Nevertheless, he remained on his guard. He changed out of the disguise and put on another. As he collapsed on the wooden seat of the second-class carriage, he wore an old cap, dark glasses, and a fake moustache. He was posing as a poor Mexican worker recently ejected from the United States. According to one of his associates, he was "unrecognizable."

Fernández was right to be cautious. Nearly 300 miles of desert south of Ciudad Juárez was the state capital, Chihuahua City. This was the stronghold of his most powerful opponent, the state governor Rodrigo M. Quevedo. And when the train pulled up there, three of the governor's gunmen got on board. They scoured the train looking for Fernández. But the disguise held. No one identified the poor, dusty tramp slumped in the second-class carriage as the millionaire Ciudad Juárez businessman. Finally, as the train approached the Torreón station, he could breathe a sigh of relief. He was in friendly territory. His business partner, the Torreón opium trafficker Antonio Wong Yin, would protect him.

Fernández lay low in Torreón for nearly a week, hoping that the chasing gunmen would give up. When he eventually got on the train to continue his journey, he thought that they had returned north. Yet this time he was wrong. In fact, they had gone south together with two of the governor's brothers. They had arrived in Mexico City before Fernández and managed to locate his safe houses. They were now staking them out.

When Fernández finally arrived at one of these houses in the upscale Roma neighborhood, the Quevedo brothers started to make their plan. They didn't employ a gunman who could be traced back to them. Instead, they found a convenient patsy, a former police officer. Poor and down on his luck, he agreed to assassinate the businessman in return for cash and the promise of legal support. He was true to his word. On January 13 he shot Fernández in the head as walked out into the street. The killer immediately gave himself up. In his statement the Quevedos were not mentioned.

Fernández's story should have ended there, in a pool of blood, in a posh Mexico City street. But in Ciudad Juárez at least, Fernández's legend lived on. His body was returned to the city where he was born and where he had built his fortune. His funeral attracted thousands. Workers and waiters, bureaucrats and schoolchildren all lined the muddy road that led to the city graveyard. In the evening, the balladeers sang a new song.

> *His death was deeply felt*
> *We are always grateful.*
> *He gave money with open hands*
> *And ordered schools to be built*
> *For the good of all the young people.*

It was a touching memorial to a man the city's newspaper remembered as a "businessman, a merchant, a bar owner, and a mining entrepreneur." It was also a rather unexpected memorial for the man who up to January 1934 had been Ciudad Juárez's leading drug trafficker. One of the world's first *narcocorridos* was actually a paean to education spending.

Fernández was a different order of Mexican drug trafficker. He wasn't a small-time weed slinger or a prison heroin peddler. He didn't service Mexico's own small markets in marijuana, morphine, heroin, and smoking opium. He was one of the first border smugglers. He fed the enormous drug market to the north in the United States. And he encountered the two interlinking products of the business, which made it both so attractive and so dangerous. They were its enormous capacity for making money but also, indirectly, for generating violence.

During the first decades of the twentieth century, the U.S. black market in narcotics grew, especially on the border. It made a lot of traffickers—including Fernández—very rich. Yet it also generated the first big drug protection rackets. These were run not by the traffickers but by the state. Along the border the local authorities charged drug traffickers fees to not implement antidrug laws. And they used these fees to pay for government buildings, soldiers, police forces, pen pushers, and schools. Fernández wasn't the first drug trafficker to prop up a local administration. In fact, to the west of Ciudad Juárez on the California–Mexico border, the state governor established the first lucrative state-run drug protection racket as early as 1915.

But these protection rackets also had a crucial side effect. They introduced violence to the trade. New local governments asserted their authority over the protection rackets by arresting or murdering the old traffickers and putting their own smugglers in their place. For the new governments, such an approach had multiple advantages. It gave the illusion to the Americans and the Mexican federal authorities that the new governments were serious about drug crime. It took out established, powerful traffickers that might balk at paying what was demanded. And it demonstrated immediately the harsh penalties for not paying the required fee.

But, for the traffickers and for Mexico over the long term, it was a disaster. Such practices often developed into spiraling conflicts between the new governments and the old traffickers. This is exactly what happened in Ciudad Juárez. Government hitmen not only killed Fernández, but also dozens of his associates. It was the first real massacre of the Mexican drug business.

For most of the nineteenth century two groups had dominated the use of what would become illegal narcotics in the United States. Chinese men smoked opium and well-to-do women were prescribed morphine to combat pain. (The figure of Mary the ailing morphine addict in Eugene O'Neill's *Long Day's Journey into Night* was based on his own mother.) But as the century came to an end, a new group of addicts started to join these traditional users. They were young, male pleasure seekers. Contemporaries referred to them as "the sporting classes." They visited bars, gambled, frequented brothels, and took drugs.

Getting any sort of meaningful figures for what some have termed "the great binge" is extremely difficult. (Though the scale of drug taking may have resembled the 1960s, the ability to measure and quantify it did not.) But one can get some idea of the use at least in comparison to other countries. In 1896, a total population of 70 million Americans imported around 76,000 pounds of opiates. In comparison Germany (population 60 million)—no stranger to the use of narcotics—imported a mere 17,000.

Doctors and politicians gradually attempted to curb use. Prejudices shaped laws and their enforcement. The old distrust of Chinese opium smokers was joined by new panics over immigrant heroin users, "negro cocaine fiends," and predatory pimps turning white sex workers into morphine addicts. In 1906 the Pure Food and Drug Act banned the excessive use of heroin and cocaine in patent medicines. Finally, in 1914 the U.S. Congress passed the Harrison Act. The law imposed a new sales tax, required that all narcotics transactions be registered with the federal government, and outlawed selling narcotics without a prescription. Over the next few years, a series of landmark cases cracked down on doctors or pharmacists who sought to bend the law or sell narcotics on the sly. And in 1924 all manufacture of heroin was banned.

Initial results were not terribly impressive. World War I undermined the effort. Some young men used drugs to dodge the draft. Others who were not so fortunate came back from the front addicted to the pain relief provided by morphine. By 1919, one survey claimed—no doubt exaggeratedly—that there were as many as a million drug users in the United States.

If prohibition failed to substantially curb drug use, it did change the system of buying and selling drugs. What had been visible disappeared underground. Users became criminalized as addicts; sellers became dealers; and importers became traffickers. The trade in medicine gradually transformed into a black market in drugs. Organized criminals and smugglers now controlled the smoking opium, morphine, and heroin that arrived in the United States. A lot was shipped through New York. But it was also increasingly smuggled over the U.S.–Mexico border.

Moving narcotics over the country's southern frontier had some obvious advantages. Crossing was easy; the area was underpopulated and mostly unguarded. Mexico's revolutionary conflicts made strict vigilance even more difficult. And a new clientele for narcotics had started to emerge in the growing cities of the Southwest and the military bases that dotted the border. (One scholar estimated that as many as 10,000 soldiers stationed on the border used hard drugs. If true, there were more addicts in frontier military forces than in all of Mexico.)

The first trafficker to take advantage of this market wasn't a career criminal, a dodgy pharmacist, or a morally pliable entrepreneur. He was Baja California's most celebrated governor. His name was Esteban Cantú. He was a revolutionary, a peacemaker, a modernizer, a builder of roads, and a firm believer in the education of the masses. He was also the architect of the first large-scale border narcotics business.

Cantú wasn't from Baja California; in the nineteenth century few people were. He was born in the small, dusty town of Linares in northeastern Mexico in 1880. His family wasn't poor, but it was by no means rich. And Cantú followed his father into one of the few careers that offered social advancement—the army. He went to the capital's Military College in 1897. After attaining rather underwhelming grades, he joined a cavalry battalion. For the next decade he traipsed through various late dictatorship warzones. He killed Yaquis in the Sonoran Desert (while the Chinese finished the railway line), and he hunted bandits in the mountains of Durango. His reports remained distinctly subpar. He was described as "apathetic," "constantly in debt," and a drunkard.

But—like a handful of other soldiers—the Revolution made him. Perhaps the movement better suited his lower-middle-class upbringing. Perhaps he needed a rather more constructive challenge than hunting down those poorer or browner than him. Whatever the reason, when the revolutionary president Francisco Madero took over the army in 1911, Cantú agreed to stay on. His first mission was to defeat a group of radicals that had taken control of the border state of Baja California. After he had completed this, he bided his time, outlasting his senior officers. Finally, in 1914, he was made military commander of the state. The following year he was appointed governor.

The state he inherited was not a normal Mexican state. Baja California is a huge desert peninsula jutting out of California, joined to the Mexican mainland by only a thin strip of land. During the nineteenth century the parched landscape made it one of the least inhabited regions of the Americas. Population centers were sparse. The Pacific port of Ensenada was home to a boisterous, multinational mix of smugglers, ex-convicts, and deserters. And the two border crossing points of Mexicali and Tijuana were tiny villages. In general, the place was poor. There were no mines, no factories, and no large agricultural enterprises. Most important for Cantú, there was nothing for the state to tax. When he took over the governorship, the treasury stood bare.

What Baja California did have was potential. And it was this potential for farming, for trade, and, crucially, for vice that allowed Cantú to fill the treasury's coffers. As such, the drug trade formed one part—admittedly a rather financially lucrative one—of a broader relationship between the creation of the state and the expansion of the border vice industry.

Like the drug trade, the vice industry arrived from the north. During the first decades of the twentieth century, U.S. politicians not only clamped down on narcotics, but also other "unhealthy" leisure activities. Many of these measures were state-level laws. In 1915, for example, the California government banned horse racing and prostitution. And four years later it signed on to the national Volstead Act, which prohibited the manufacture and sale of alcohol. From now on, California was a dry state.

Luckily for its thrill seekers, Mexico was not. The U.S.'s puritanical laws only succeeded in pushing the vice industry a few miles south. In what would become a familiar tale, America outsourced what it desired but didn't want to see. Overnight its problem became Mexico's. But so did at least part of its cash. And Cantú's state now provided the booze, the betting, and the brothels that the United States did not.

Nowhere was this more apparent than the two tiny border crossings of Tijuana and Mexicali. In just a few years, Tijuana grew from a few wooden shacks and a muddy main road to the go-to venue for California's smart set. Festivities began in 1915 when U.S. and Mexican businessmen held the Tijuana Fair. The giant jamboree offered visitors bars, restaurants, nightclubs, casinos, boxing, and bullfighting. The next year the same entrepreneurs built a massive horse-racing circuit. The establishment dwarfed the town's buildings and attracted high rollers from Los Angeles and San Francisco.

In 1919 as alcohol prohibition started to bite in America, Tijuana's reputation for pleasure seeking rose still higher. On July 4, 1919, 22,000 Americans—around twenty times the town's actual population—spent their national holiday in the border city. A contemporary tourist guide, transparently titled *Gambling, Liquor, Ponies, Girls, the High Life 'n' Everything*, described the place as a "Mecca for all those who wish to cast off restraint and kick up their heels." There was the Monte Carlo casino—"a great barn of a place with a dozen roulette tables, blackjack, craps, chuck luck, and wheel of fortune." Beside it were numerous bars with English-language names like the Blue Fox, El Foreign Club, and the Turf Bar. The writer approvingly noted that there were no grocery shops or any other "useless places." (Who had space for food?)

In contrast to Tijuana's reputation for "the high life 'n' everything," Mexicali catered to a less starry crowd. During the 1910s, Mexicali's landowners were attracting Chinese workers to farm the newly irrigated lands just outside the town. But it was developments on the other side of the border that really shaped the place. Imperial Valley had become one of the United States' richest agricultural areas. Thousands of laborers ploughed, picked, and weeded the fields every day. But on the weekends they had money to spend. And they spent it in Mexicali, where bars, dancehalls, brothels and gambling dens quickly sprang up to service their needs. The most famous was the Owl, a giant hangar with three cantinas, two casinos, a restaurant, and over a hundred bedrooms. It had room for 1,500 gamblers and at least 300 sex workers. For moralizing Americans, Mexicali—even more than Tijuana—was a modern Gomorrah. As early as 1913, a U.S. priest gothically declared that "gambling was unrestrained, vice was rampant and unspeakable specters stalked the town unregarded." He advised that if anyone cared for the health of the valley workers "this hellhole must be relegated to the past."

It seems no one did.

Instead, Cantú built a wealthy, stable, and (at the time perhaps most important) well-armed government by nurturing and taxing just those industries the priest deplored. They included the brothels that had to pay 100 pesos a month, the bars 300, the bullfights 100, and the gambling joints up to 1,000. The proto-Vegas entertainment complex, the Owl, paid 15,000 pesos a year and the Tijuana hippodrome alone brought in 400 pesos a day.

Cantú also started to tax the narcotics business. In 1915 the new governor introduced three laws to regulate the trade. The first taxed the importation of opium at 3.50 pesos a kilo. The second charged the Chinese-run establishments, which refined the raw opium into smoking opium. The third demanded opium sellers pay 400 pesos a month and opium dens an extra 250 pesos. The laws were not overtly prodrugs. But they were resigned to the fact that "extirpating this vice" was "impossible." What is more, the money was needed to "cover the most urgent necessities of the public services."

Over the border, such hard-nosed realism was not popular; Cantú's attitude to the drug trade was widely condemned. Newspapers railed against the effects of the narcotics business on American tourists. They claimed Tijuana's "midnight hophead specials" were making "San Diego boys and girls slaves to demoralizing drugs." They even started an unsubstantiated rumor that Cantú himself was a drug addict. Allegedly, he "had made such use of the hypodermic needle that one leg and one arm were partially black and covered with perforations." Pressure also came from the Mexican capital. In 1916, President Venustiano Carranza banned the sale of smoking opium altogether.

Cantú's response was the first example of a political maneuver that would cement the association between local governments and the drug trade. Rather than publicly tax the narcotics business, he imposed Mexico's first off-the-books drug protection racket. Now the state would receive money for protecting the drug business and not implementing antidrug laws. It was a turning point—the first use of a trick that would be repeated by border governors for decades to come.

Imposing this protection racket involved a law change and a propaganda campaign. But it also involved an unpleasant errand. To prove his antinarcotics credentials and to persuade traffickers to pay up, Cantú killed a group of the established traffickers.

On the surface, then, Cantú prohibited the manufacture and sale of narcotics. The three edicts that taxed the opium trade were canceled; and in June 1916 the federal laws prohibiting smoking opium were finally passed in the state. Cantú also ordered all opium to be handed in to the authorities and all opium dens to be closed.

Cantú made sure that the measures were well publicized. He invited U.S. policemen and journalists to attend the official reading of the new law. Newspapers quoted approving U.S. officials who ditched the accusations of addiction and now claimed that "whole squads of drug users were sitting about on the Mexicali lumber piles looking woebegone and already plainly showing their crying need for their opium, morphine, or cocaine."

He also combined this press campaign with the violent suppression of a few traffickers. Such tactics played well with the U.S. authorities and the opinion-forming crime reporters. In January 1917, Mexican police raided the Sam Sing opium den in Mexicali. Ma Toon and Lee Wee Get, two Chinese immigrants wanted for drug offenses in the United States, were the owners. According to the official version, they opened fire on the cops as soon as they entered. The cops then called in the army and after a "fierce shoot out" the Chinese businessmen were dead. Lee Wee Get was "riddled with bullets as he sought to escape." He fell "with a smoking revolver in one hand and a hatchet in the other." Police raid had become crowd-pleasing crime caper. The dead—they were wanted by the gringos anyway.

These public performances worked. By 1917, Americans were applauding Cantú's crackdown. San Diego's grandees even invited Cantú to their celebration of cross-border cooperation—the Fiesta de Amistad—as the guest of honor.

The reality, however, was rather different. The returns from the drug business were simply too big to ignore; the state treasury needed them. So, despite his claims, Cantú let it continue. Merchants still imported opium through the port of Ensenada; Chinese opium makers continued to produce smoking opium in the artisan refineries of Mexicali; street peddlers continued to sell the drugs; and opium dens remained open. They now secretly paid the state not to impose the laws.

One U.S. agent, who visited Ensenada in September 1916, described how this new system worked. A select group of Chinese importers, led by a Patricio Hong, imported the opium into the port of Ensenada. They were connected to a group of local businessmen. They included Cantú's in-laws—the Dato family, Ignacio del Corte (a former United Sugar employee and perfume maker), and David Goldbaum (a U.S. immigrant and merchant, the head of the Ensenada chamber of commerce, and a keen amateur historian). The local businessmen had a deal with the port customs official who allowed the opium to be brought on land disguised as paint tins and cans of preserves, or inside crates of cigarettes.

The merchandise was then taken by cart to a ranch just outside the town to be divided up. Some of it was sent north to the border towns, where it was sold by a network of protected opium dens and dealers. The rest of it was sent by fishing boat to the United States. It was delivered to Los Angeles, where a member of San Francisco's Chinese community bought it and then transported it further north.

Cantú protected this system and his services didn't come cheap. The gang was rumored to pay around $11,000 per month for the concession. But there were additional benefits. If the police caught independent opium dealers, they were fined and their opium sold to the gang. It was win-win. Cantú looked like a serious prohibitionist and the money kept coming in.

Increasingly, many Americans and many Mexicans would term such protection rackets corruption. Strictly, they were. Yet in the early years of the twentieth century, many Mexicans, and, one suspects, some of the more pragmatic Americans, saw the system as an intelligent and productive solution to a problem that had been imposed on the region from the outside. Drug users were going to get drugs no matter what the government did. At least under this scheme, the government could channel some of the money from the trade into beneficial services.

This is exactly what Cantú did. The money from the vice trade made the government of the underpopulated, underdeveloped state one of the richest in Mexico. Official tax earnings increased fourfold in the five years Cantú was in charge; unofficial earnings probably pushed the amount collected even higher. Yet individual citizens paid some of the lowest property taxes in the country. The money came from the big vice concessions.

Furthermore, unlike some of his successors, Cantú spent the money wisely. A U.S. journalist who investigated the area after the governor's fall had to admit that though "his methods of getting money were not approved of … every cent of it was spent within the limits of the district." His achievements were impressive. He used policemen and soldiers to hunt down bandits and make the place safe. He brought in expert engineers who helped construct the roads that by the end of his tenure crisscrossed the peninsula, climbed over the imposing Sierra Juárez, and connected all the major population centers. He built the governor's palace, a prison, a barracks, a fire station, and a public park. He introduced drainage, drinkable water, garbage collection, and a functioning postal service. And he did so while paying his workers U.S.-level wages.

But perhaps Cantú's most notable success lay in the field of education. As governor, he made education compulsory for all children between the ages of seven and fourteen. He built schools in the growing rural communities east of Mexicali. He even persuaded the architect of the Mexico City opera house to design a state-of-the-art school in Mexicali itself. There were secondary schools, adult evening classes, and even scholarships for smart kids. One inspector who visited the district in the same year was amazed to discover that "it was very rare to come across anyone that doesn't know how to read and write."

Cantú was a remarkable character. He seems to have been scrupulously honest. And though his in-laws clearly made serious money out of the trade, there is no evidence that he secreted away millions. He lived out the rest of his life in Mexicali in a relatively humble house. And he still had to make ends meet by working surprisingly ordinary administrative jobs in the state government for the next two decades. Few of his successors were so trustworthy. Many employed similar schemes to line their own pockets.

But if he was remarkable, he was not entirely exceptional. During the early years of the drug trade, other local governments also set up similar drug protection rackets. The exchange of drug money for schools was no one-off. To the east of Baja California on the Texas border, local politicians established a similar deal.

There were two variations, which perhaps indicated the direction in which the Mexican drug trade was going. First, whereas Cantú had channeled drug money directly to the state treasury, in Ciudad Juárez the principal drug trafficker played the role of independent philanthropist. Second, these protection rackets often struggled to outlast changes of local government. New leaders wanted their own men (and, as we shall see, women) in charge. The violence used to impose new rackets often spiraled out of control. So in Ciudad Juárez the new authorities not only killed the cross-dressing fugitive, Fernández, but also orchestrated the first massacre connected to the drug trade.

For the first few years of the twentieth century, Ciudad Juárez's northern neighbor, El Paso, had been the original American vice city. Farm laborers, railway workers, and soldiers from nearby Fort Bliss all swarmed to the city's bars and bordellos. But by the 1910s, reformers had started to close down the entertainment districts on the U.S. side of the Río Bravo. El Paso got bourgeois. Men now "shaved daily ... changed their clothes by the clock and began to play golf." When Texas introduced its own alcohol prohibition law in 1918, sin moved south.

Ciudad Juárez became Tijuana and Mexicali rolled into one. There were casinos and cabarets, dance floors and slot machines. There were high-class joints like the Kentucky Club, the Castle Café, and Big Kids, which served cocktails and prime steak to U.S. politicians, louche writers, and holidaying Hollywood types. And there were rougher establishments like the legendary Hole in the Wall. This was a wooden shack just outside the city perched on the dividing line between the two countries. You could enter from the United States and buy a beer in Mexico. It was the prohibition border in miniature. And it attracted similarly sanctimonious reviews. One American called it "the most immoral, degenerate, and utterly wicked place I have ever seen or heard of in my travels."

There were also drugs. There was marijuana, smoked by Mexican soldiers, Mexican-American workers, and a growing crowd of U.S. hipsters;

there was smoking opium sold to the cross-border Chinese community; and there was morphine and heroin hawked mainly to U.S. addicts.

During the 1920s, concern over drug use grew. In 1922 the local customs official warned that addicts had flooded into southern Texas, as "you can buy morphine, heroin, and opium in Mexico as you buy cigars and ice cream in this country." Fear peaked in the following year, when an El Paso society girl died from an overdose while partying in Ciudad Juárez. (Drug panics in which white men gallantly defend dead white women have a long history.) The subsequent grand jury trial claimed that Mexican smugglers were transferring narcotics to Chinese peddlers, who were selling the drugs to local schoolchildren. (So do drug panics that blame foreigners and minorities.)

At the center of this trade was the person the Americans started to term the "King of Morphine" and the "Al Capone of Ciudad Juárez"—Enrique Fernández Puertas. Fernández was born to a local family in the small village of San Isidro just outside Juárez in 1900. Officially, he started work as a taxi driver. But he and his brothers—Simón and Antonio–also smuggled arms and ammunition from the United States during the Revolution. By the 1920s they had branched out into an array of legal and illegal practices.

Their primary business and the one that provided a steady source of income was smuggling alcohol. The oldest brother, Antonio, owned a liquor store just off the main street. They purchased the booze and then either sold it to independent smugglers or smuggled it over themselves. Contraband generated contacts. And by 1922 the brothers were also working with a gang of American car thieves led by the owner of the Castle Café. These would bring the cars—mostly expensive Cadillacs—to the El Paso–Ciudad Juárez border. The Fernández brothers would pay off the Mexican customs officers to wave them over without a check. Once over, they were stored at the back of Antonio's store and then sold to free-spending local officials.

Both rackets made Enrique a rich man and an eligible bachelor. He married in 1925. According to the rumors, it was his wife who persuaded him to start investing in more legal businesses. (Though it is probably no coincidence that his contact in Torreón, Antonio Wong Yin, was also a master at whitewashing illegal funds. Who said the Mexicans learned nothing from the Chinese?) Whatever the reason, the following year he teamed up with a British-born bartender-turned-rumrunner and launched Ciudad Juárez's most popular bar.

In the eight years it was open the Café Mint Bar became a Prohibition institution. It served fancy cocktails like its famous Special Fizzes (made with egg whites, fruit juices, and spirits) and what one columnist rather generously described as "the best food to be found between New Orleans and San Francisco." In fact, the menu was rather uninspiring faux-European fare; it didn't matter—the patrons were mostly Americans. They were a ragbag of politicians, racists, and starlets. They included Texas governor William Murray, famed journalist (and enthusiastic eugenicist) Henry Louis Mencken, and aviation pioneer Amelia Earhart. It was ersatz Wild West for the border fast set. Around the long bar, the owners placed some of the city's first slot machines next to polished brass spittoons.

The Café Mint Bar was just the beginning. In the following years, Fernández would become one of the city's leading legal businessmen. He opened two shoe shops and bought shares in a silver mine in the mountains near the spectacular Copper Canyon. He also gained the exclusive concession for gambling in the city and opened the Tivoli Casino and then the Gold Palace, a casino and dancehall in the center of the city.

*Ciudad Juárez trafficker Enrique Fernández outside his famous Café Mint Bar.*

But for all Fernández's efforts, he was unable to avoid the allure or, perhaps more important, the profits of illicit industries. He still smuggled booze into the United States but now also brought back untaxed goods that included jewelry and silks. He formed a counterfeiting gang, bought fake plates for producing $50 and $100 U.S. gold certificates, and produced thousands of "the cleverest counterfeits that have ever come under the observation of secret service agents."

Fernández and his brothers also started to traffic drugs. They plugged into the network linking Veracruz, Mexico City, and Torreón. Men like Bernabé Hernández and the Sánchez brothers sent narcotics by post up to Antonio Wong Yin in Torreón, and he transferred them by post to Ciudad Juárez. The Fernández brothers smuggled some over the border. The rest they sold to independent dealers out the back of the Café Mint Bar. Many of these were from the city's Chinese community, who ran a line of opium dens down Calle Colón. (One even stood directly behind the federal health offices.)

The criminal empire depended on a similar protection racket to Cantú's. The Fernández brothers needed to avoid antinarcotics laws. To do so, they made payments to mayors, police officials, tax collectors, judges, and local military commanders. They also got close to the state governor, Luis L. León. He, in turn, used his contacts to link the brothers to important politicians in Mexico City. Their address book included the numbers for senators, congressmen, the number two in the Mexican Treasury, and even President Plutarco Elías Calles's personal secretary.

Where this money went, it is difficult to say. Fernández's supporters claimed that at least some was spent on city improvements. But clearly a lot went into personal bank accounts, luxury homes, and private enterprises. In May 1928 the chief of the municipal police and the head of the state police teamed up to buy the Gambrinus Bar just off the Ciudad Juárez main drag. And in the same year the mayor opened his own joint, El Castillo (the Castle). Locals, annoyed that he had reneged on his promise to extend the city's electrical service, bitterly nicknamed it El Castillo Eléctrico.

Fernández supplemented these graft payments with his own private philanthropy. This had the advantage of appeasing local officials (who could claim some credit), whitewashing his reputation, and gaining further popular acclaim. His focus—like Cantú—was education. Between 1931 and 1934 he paid for the construction of at least four schools in the poor communities to the southeast of the city. He also paid for the teachers' salaries, an open-air theater, and a water pump. Unlike most rural schools, these were not just converted shacks. They had extensive patios and gardens, good ventilation for the days, and even heating for adult classes at night. According to the local newspaper, they were better than "those we have seen in the rural areas of the United States" and cost at least 15,000 pesos each.

If these protection rackets aided social spending, they also had a rather common flaw. They regularly broke down. When new authorities took power, they sought to impose their own protection racket. And they often did so by getting rid of the most powerful existing traffickers and replacing them with their own.

It was something that Fernández would first experience in 1928. A new state governor, General Marcelo Caraveo, came to power. Caraveo was not a man to take orders easily. (He had changed sides on at least four occasions during the Revolution.) He was no fan of the federal government, led by Plutarco Elías Calles. And he wanted to build up funds to keep the state of Chihuahua independent from Mexico City's interference. To do this he tried to hijack the revenue from the state's biggest tax earner—the Ciudad Juárez vice industry. He backed his own candidate for mayor and put a close ally in charge of the city's tax collection. The latter was also charged with controlling local dealers and the cross-border drug trade.

To monopolize the returns, he also managed to persuade someone in federal government (who presumably was also no fan of President Calles) to send a federal agent to the city. The agent, a major Ignacio Dosamantes, was charged with stopping traffickers that were not protected by the state governor. Dosamantes shot at least two of Fernández's dealers and buried their bodies at La Piedrera, a desert wasteland a few miles south of the city. He raided the Casino Chino and shook down Chinese opium dealers for cash. He seized 10 kilos of narcotics worth 300,000 pesos. And he arrested Fernández's heroin-addicted brother Antonio. He then managed to persuade Antonio to confess to drug smuggling and counterfeiting and turn on Enrique.

For Enrique the attack on Antonio was the last straw. He finally tracked Dosamantes to the upscale Río Bravo Hotel. He tried to shoot him but missed; Dosamantes did not. Fernández received a bullet in the leg. He would never walk properly again.

He did, however, find a way out—at least for the moment. If Fernández's criminal associates were a multinational bunch, so were his protectors. Safeguarding drug traffickers in return for money was another shared cross-border pursuit. Soon after Dosamantes fled Ciudad Juárez following the duel, he was shot dead by an El Paso police officer. The rumors were that the U.S. cops were also taking a cut from Fernández's criminal businesses. They were running a parallel protection racket on the other side.

Fernández's second experience of state interference was no less dramatic. But this time it was fatal. During the 1930s a new family had started to dominate Chihuahua politics. They were the Quevedos—a biblically large household of livestock owners from the fertile river valley of Casas Grandes, southwest of Ciudad Juárez. Three of the brothers—Rodrigo, José, and Jesús—had given up cattle ranching for politics. They were well suited to the game and quickly ascended the hierarchy. Within a decade, they had held posts as mayors, tax collectors, city councilors, and deputies. Finally, in 1932–33, they negotiated, bullied, and politicked their way to a clean sweep. Rodrigo was elected governor of Chihuahua; Jesús was elected mayor of Ciudad Juárez; and José was made the city's tax inspector.

At first, the Quevedos had allied with Fernández. They had needed his money and support to come to power. (It was rumored that he had lent them at least 135,000 pesos for their election expenses.) But within a year, they wanted their own protection racket. And they wanted their own followers in charge of narcotics. So they turned on their former partner.

At the outset they went after his legal businesses, burning the Café Mint Bar to the ground and removing Fernández's gambling concession after they "discovered" that he was "the narcotic king of Ciudad Juárez."

Then they went after his illicit ones. This involved more organization and substantially more bloodshed. It also involved two people who would make their mark on the national narcotics industry in subsequent years. The first was a mother, a widow, and a drug trafficker. Her name was Ignacia "La Nacha" Jasso. We shall discuss La Nacha in depth later. Women were no strangers to the drug trade. And she would become a target of the U.S. government, the queen of transnational drug trafficking, and a border legend. But in 1933 she was young and vulnerable. Her husband and business partner, Pablo González, had just been killed in a cantina shootout. She needed support. So when the Quevedos came to her and suggested that they join up and take over Fernández's business, she was unable to refuse. And in the end, it was not a bad deal. She would outlast the Quevedos and rule the city trade for the next forty years.

The second was a lawman and a killer called Raúl Mendiolea Cerecero. Like La Nacha, his notoriety would grow. He would go on to become second-in-command of the Mexico City cops and head of the Federal Judicial Police. But these were just the headlines. He would also be accused of torture, organizing the murder of dozens of demonstrating students, and orchestrating the federal takeover of the Mexican drug trade. But, again like La Nacha, Mendiolea was still young. He was a gun for hire and carried the badge of a Chihuahua state policeman. And in the summer of 1933 the Quevedos ordered him to take out Fernández and his loyal dealers.

Mendiolea and at least another half-dozen hitmen arrived at the border ready for business. They were dressed in black leather jackets and sombreros. They rode in inside a dust-flecked red Ford and cradled Winchesters and .38 pistols. Fernández's associates started to disappear. First to go was Luis Khan, the city's principal smoking opium dealer. He was found bound and shot in the head near La Piedrera. His ears and toes had been cut off. Then it was the turn of Fernández's three bodyguards. Again, their bullet-riddled bodies were all found at La Piedrera. By December 1933 nearly twenty of Fernández's men had been killed.

Then they came for Fernández. In December 1933 they intercepted him in the street. They opened fire from the red Ford and grazed his shoulder. He managed to escape. But not for long. After recovering, he donned a dress and shawl, and began his last fatal journey to Mexico City.

## Chapter 5

---

## Drugs in Depression

EVEN THE DEALERS HAD RUN OUT. IT WAS APRIL 1933, AND LOS ANGELES narcotics agent Harry Smith was down in Tijuana. He was looking for drugs. He had met his American contact in the fleapit Hotel Virginia, just off the main drag. The contact had introduced him to Poncho, a Chinese peddler, who knew the market well. Poncho explained that if the agent wanted heroin or morphine, he was better off buying it back in the United States. He could get him cocaine but only if he wanted to drive a day over to the border crossing at Nogales. Tijuana was dry. Addicts now shuffled over to San Diego to get their fix. The smoking opium situation was little better. You could buy it unprepared at $60 a kilo or prepared at $24 a can. It was more expensive than up north. And it was poor-quality stuff, full of weeds and refuse and grown in the desert in the south of the state. Poncho thought that it was of such poor quality that "it would not under any circumstances be saleable in San Francisco or larger Chinese communities."

During the early 1930s, Mexico's drug market—like the rest of the global economy—was in a depression. Falling U.S. wages played a role. The free spending of the Roaring Twenties, which had propped up the transnational trade and the border vice zones, had now declined markedly. In France and Germany, there were crackdowns on pharmaceutical heroin production. Domestic gang warfare also had an effect. In Ciudad Juárez, the Quevedo brothers were putting pressure on Enrique Fernández. Traditional supply chains broke up. The same year Fernández was murdered, hitmen also killed his wholesaler, the Mexico City pharmacist Félix Sánchez.

But the other reason for the slump in the Mexican narcotics business was supply. For twenty years Chinese immigrants had provided the market, the technical know-how, the networks, and the capital for a big part of the country's drug trade. After the 1929 crash, this came to an end. Anti-Chinese politicians harnessed old-school xenophobia to new ideas of economic nationalism. In the northern states—where most of the Chinese population lived—this led to persecution, pogroms, and mass expulsions.

Feelings peaked in the desert state of Sonora, where the Chinese had worked in mines, on the railways, and as farmers and shop owners. The former president's brother, Francisco Elías Calles, started to enforce an old Revolution era diktat, which demanded that 80 percent of all workers in any business be Mexican by birth. Mass firings followed. Then chaos. Thugs from local anti-Chinese organizations declared a deadline for all Chinese businesses to close down. In some places, like Huatabampo and Arizpe, they dragged shop owners into the street and kicked them out of the towns. In farming communities like Santa Barbara they robbed Chinese homes, raided fields, and pulled up their crops.

At the border, the Nogales authorities chained up Chinese men, beat them with clubs and sticks, and then threatened to shoot them if they didn't cross to the other side. A U.S. journalist followed up the story a few years later. He ingratiated himself with the local police by declaring that he "didn't give a rap whether the chinks were bayonetted out or escorted on soft pillows." He discovered that some had been picked up by U.S. immigration authorities, sent to San Francisco, and then deported to China. Others had been "outright killed." One informant remembered the bodies of the Chinese dangling off the barbed wire of the border fence.

In the Pacific coastal state of Sinaloa, it was little better. At night, gangs of heavies hunted down Chinese residents, locked them in prefab cells, and then loaded them onto cattle carts. They sent them to the neighboring state of Nayarit, or when the Nayarit authorities started to complain, all the way to Chiapas.

Many of those that were not forcibly expelled fled back to China or to the United States. The 24,218 Chinese immigrants who had lived in Mexico in 1926 dropped to barely 5,000 by 1940.

Destroying drug supply has always been a prohibitionist dream. It would become a key component of U.S. foreign policy. Forcing other countries to clamp down on growing and trafficking narcotics was less domestically unpopular and less expensive than sorting out demand. The problem was, it never worked. Drug droughts and spiraling prices looked good on paper but were never more than very short-term. Drugs always found a way. The same was true for Mexico in the 1930s. The supply lines that had been severed in 1933 were back in operation just two years later.

This resurgence of the Mexican drug trade occurred in two ways. Both had their roots in the narcotics business of the 1920s but also provided a roadmap for future developments.

First there was the return of international smuggling operations. It was the Americans who initially discovered this in a series of busts that played out like a movie script. On August 5, 1936, police arrested Maria "Molly" Wendt as she disembarked a steamer at the Port of Los Angeles. They were acting on a tip-off and immediately seized her luggage. Knifing the soft cloth at the base of the cases they found 54 pounds of heroin. Alone, it was worth $100,000. Cut and on the U.S. market, it was worth ten times that amount.

Molly intrigued the American reporters. They salivated over her good looks and her mixed heritage, trying to find the right racial stereotype for the "ivory-skinned young woman ... in whose veins ran the blood of white and yellow ancestors." (She was actually half-Chinese, half-Dutch.) And they were impressed by her bravado. Four days after being caught, she escaped the hotel where the drug agents—for some reason—had left her. She flew to New York and made it onto another ship, where she was eventually recaptured.

A month later another ship was on the way from Havana to New York. The U.S. authorities had found out that the suspected mastermind behind the captured heroin was on board. He was Naftali Loeffelholz Brandstatter, a Polish gangster, a drug runner, and Wendt's former husband. But before the boat docked, Loeffelholz allegedly committed suicide by hanging himself. He was not the last. Two weeks later the source of the drugs, a German pharmacist based in Shanghai, was also found dead. Some newspapers claimed he had also committed suicide. But others declared that the Chinese leaders of the gang had poisoned him to shut him up.

In fact, the tale—with its dodgy suicides, shady European criminals, and exotic molls—was so like a movie that Hollywood decided to make it into one. *To the Ends of the Earth* was released in 1948 and was billed as part documentary, part spy thriller. It had some pedigree. Harry Anslinger, the head of the Federal Bureau of Narcotics (FBN), starred in the film as himself. He used it to promote his assertion that the FBN should be allowed to interfere in other countries' narcotics policies. There were monsters out there after all, and most of them spoke funny. But explicit politics rarely makes for good films. The movie was a hodgepodge of earnest speechifying, square-jawed American heroes, and implausible action sequences. It bombed; Anslinger's acting career was over.

But more important for this story at least was what the film omitted. As the movie's stars crisscrossed the world from China to Egypt to Havana to New York, they left out one crucial link in the transnational trade—Mexico. By 1936, international criminal organizations—like the *To the Ends of the Earth* gang—had again started to use the country as a transshipment point for America's narcotics.

As a transshipment point, Mexico had many advantages. It had multiple ports on both the Atlantic and the Pacific; it had an extensive border with the world's largest drug market; it had only a few poorly paid drug enforcers; and with the expulsion of the Chinese, there was limited competition with domestic traffickers. But perhaps most important, Mexico had recently also become a center for European immigration. Some were refugees escaping the economic depression; others were fleeing authoritarianism; others were keeping an eye on those fleeing fascism and communism; and others still were spying on these.

The most famous was León Trotsky, who moved to Mexico in 1937, escaped one assassination attempt, but fell victim to another three years later. But there were many others. As global tensions increased, 1930s Mexico City was part Ellis Island, part postwar Berlin. Impoverished Poles, Austrian Jews, and Spanish Republicans rubbed shoulders with Russian, German, and British spies. In such a melee, drug traffickers not only got lost in the crowd, they also had ready-made networks of fellow country-men, desperate for work, and relatively knowledgeable about how to move people and products over borders.

The Mexican side of the *To the Ends of the Earth* gang reflected this. It was a truly international crowd and a distinctly 1930s phenomenon. It was a product of the dislocating effects of the Depression and the last wisps of prewar globalization.

The front man for the gang was a mysterious German called Anton Wirthmueller. Though he had a German passport, he bore a striking resemblance to the suicidal Polish gangster, and the police speculated that they might have been cousins or even brothers. There was even a rumor at one point that he and Loeffelholz might be one and the same. He ran an agricultural machinery business called the Machine & Engineering Corporation, based in Shanghai. The operation employed twenty workers and enjoyed at least half a million dollars in capital. It specialized in export-ing German trucks, tractors, and threshing machines to developing nations. In 1935, Wirthmueller had gone to Mexico to "inspect the market" and organize some of the first imports into the country. According to Wendt, he had smuggled over 400 pounds of heroin into the port of Veracruz hidden amid the machinery. If true, it would have been worth a whopping $10 million on the U.S. streets.

Other members included two Mexico City dealers—Judas Furstenberg and Isaac Katz. Furstenberg was Jewish and either from the Ukraine or Poland, depending on whether you believed the Americans or the Mexicans. He was a house painter by trade, but after moving from Poland to Argentina, he got involved in trafficking sex workers into the brothels of Buenos Aires—a crime that got him deported. In Mexico City he and Katz became Mexican citizens and set up a leather goods company. They then estab-lished what was politely called a "theater business"—the Folies Bergère. The place became a key distribution point for the capital's narcotics market.

But the center of the operation and the link between the gang and the Mexicans was a Turkish jeweler called Mauricio Eghise. Here Eghise had a key advantage. He was married to a Mexican woman. She was the daughter of an army colonel named Xavier Ordóñez. Ordóñez was a former revolutionary officer and briefly head of the Mexico City police.

Ordóñez was crucial to the operation. Even for foreigners, the drug trade in Mexico was almost always a family business. He provided Eghise with the necessary contacts in the Mexican customs department to get the drugs in and out. In fact, a Mexican agent who tailed Eghise to the luxurious L'Escargot cabaret just off the Plaza Garibaldi witnessed how this arrangement worked. Eghise arrived at the cabaret with two "sumptuously dressed" women on his arms. (It was unclear whether his wife was one of them.) Here he met a customs agent based in Mexico City. As the evening wore on, the group racked up a huge bill, drinking champagne and cognac. The agent speculated that it was the customs agent who signed the import slips for the German agricultural machinery.

Ordóñez also provided Eghise with the protection. He contracted two former Mexico City policemen to act as Eghise's bodyguards. And he was happy to throw his weight around to protect his son-in-law. When Eghise was first arrested, six weeks after Maria "Molly" Wendt's capture, Ordóñez forced the local cops to let him go. A few months later, he even approached the U.S. consulate to complain that the same police were threatening to extradite Eghise to the United States.

Yet even with Ordóñez's help, the *To the Ends of the Earth* gang was an ephemeral operation. It was the beginning of a pattern. In the following decades, non-Mexican drug rings would be repeatedly drawn to the country's favorable geographical position and its pliable police forces.

In the 1940s a handful of American Mafiosi moved south and attempted to harness Mexico's opium-growing industry. In the 1950s and 1960s, it was the Corsicans and the French who used the country as a heroin transshipment point. And in the 1980s, Colombians moved to the country to try to ship cocaine overland. But these groups never survived long. Negotiating Mexican politics took more than a useful marriage and a few bribes. Protection rackets for international gangs only went so far. And the Mexican authorities always preferred to take down a foreign operation rather than a domestic one. Doing so was good politics. It made the drug trade look like a pernicious import rather than something firmly entrenched.

After Wendt's arrest, the Mexicans started to pursue Eghise. First, they arrested and questioned him. Then, after this failed, they managed to track down one of the gang's stash houses. They arrested the occupants, but they did not have enough evidence to actually prosecute Eghise. Instead, they brought him into the police station and threatened to have him expelled from the country. What happened next is open to debate. The official version was that Eghise on hearing of his expulsion somehow managed to get hold of a razor and cut his neck and wrists. He survived, but only just.

Few people believed that Eghise had slit his own neck. Three suicides in the same gang were too much of a coincidence. Being sent back to Europe in 1937 was bad, but not that bad. More likely those higher up in the gang or in the Mexican government had ordered Eghise to be murdered to shut him up. In the end, it worked. Eghise never testified in a Mexican court but was sent back to Turkey as soon as he recovered.

If international trafficking was one solution to the decline of the Chinese drug networks, the other was the birth of relatively widespread domestic drug production. To look at this, we need to leave Mexico's metropolitan entrepôts and move to the small, dusty farming communities of the country's borderlands.

Sonora is a barren region in northwestern Mexico. It borders the U.S. state of Arizona. For the most part, it is dry, flat, and infertile, with nearly three-quarters of the land desert or arid grasslands. Here, temperatures can often reach into the 40s centigrade. Tilling the earth is not only unproductive; it can be fatal.

Until two hundred years ago Sonora was sparsely populated and remote—home to a handful of zealous Catholic missionaries and migratory indigenous groups. During the nineteenth century, this changed. In a mirror image of American policies of removal and extermination north of the border, successive brutal colonizing wars killed or forced out the indigenous tribes.

Settlers moved in. These settlers came from all over—Mexico's central plains, Europe, the United States, and China. They based themselves around mining towns like Cananea and along the thin strips of well-irrigated lands on either side of Sonora's principal rivers. These places—like Arizpe, Altar, and Ures—became the granaries of the state. Here, peasants grew corn, wheat, chickpeas, limes, and oranges using a mix of old colonial irrigation ditches and new, modern agricultural infrastructure.

They also became some of the first places to experiment with planting opium poppies. No doubt the Chinese led the way. As early as 1923, an informant for the U.S. Customs Service reported that a Chinese cook and a Chinese vegetable farmer were both growing poppy plantations on river-fed lands east of Altar. A year later, he interviewed another Chinese farmer who boasted that this year he would make 6,000 pesos (or around twenty times the average wage) by selling unprocessed opium to buyers in the nearby border town of Nogales.

But other local groups were quick to join in. Sonora's settlers were proud agricultural innovators. Tied to commercial markets rather than farming traditions, they were always willing to try new crops, particularly if they were profitable. (In fact, Mexico's 1920s president, Álvaro Obregón, was not only a pioneer of trench warfare and the Revolution's most formidable general, but also a Sonora chickpea farmer who had invented and patented his own harvester.) Now, some of them moved to opium. The same U.S. agent claimed that as early as 1923 a Mexican local named Alfonso Urice was planting a small test crop. If this was successful, he would move on to more extensive production.

By 1928 many Mexicans had started to join the Chinese producers. According to the U.S. consul, farmers in the region now grew 200 to 300 acres of poppies. It had become a major regional crop and produced around 600 pounds of opium worth 300,000 pesos.

Though a handful of Sonora farmers had taken to opium growing during the late 1920s, the expulsion of the Chinese reduced the local market. It also broke up the old smuggling networks. From 1928 to 1935, production slumped. The farmers were pragmatists and returned to the safer business of growing wheat, cotton, and chickpeas. But in 1936 the price of opium in the United States rose again (principally due to declining Chinese supplies). And opium returned to Sonora's valleys.

Yet, without the large Chinese population, this new version of the Sonora drug industry was also slightly different. Proprietors grew the poppies, extracted the sap, processed this sap into smoking opium, and then sold it. But this time the business had changed location; certain specializations had started to emerge; Mexicans were involved in almost every layer of the production process; and the smoking opium had new markets.

During the 1920s most of Sonora's opium plantations were located in the north of the state. A decade later, the fields had moved south and west. Most of the growers were now based in the steamy, semitropical estuaries of the Yaqui and Mayo Rivers around the towns of Huatabampo and Cajeme. As usual in the drug business, the reason for the move was a mix of risk and reward. Poppies need a lot of water. In the arid north, the fields had to be planted right next to the river or the irrigation channels. As a result, they were relatively easy to track down. Drug agents simply followed the path of the water. In Sonora's southwest, water was much more plentiful. A longer rainy season supplemented the rivers. So opium could be grown away from the obvious waterways. As a result, it was more difficult to discover.

By 1936 the markets had also changed. They were no longer the Chinese populations of Nogales and Cananea. Now farmers either sold to a small enclave of Chinese wholesalers in the coastal town of Los Mochis who had managed to survive the anti-Chinese purges or they shipped it through the ports of Guaymas or Puerto Peñasco to the remaining Chinese population on the border in Mexicali.

Most of the growers were small farmers who used the region's rich, silty soil to grow vegetables for both the domestic and the U.S. markets. Agricultural entrepreneurs, they soon integrated the poppies into their annual growing cycle. One U.S. inspector who visited the area in 1938 remarked that farmers alternated between crops of peas and tomatoes and crops of beans and poppies. Such techniques not only kept the lands fertile; they also put keen-eyed cops off the scent.

If planting the opium poppies was easy, the harvest was not. Once the petals had dropped off, the farmers had to score the remaining seedpod and wait for the sap to escape. Here again, they innovated. They switched from the specially made claws used by the Chinese to common razor blades. To wield them, the farmers attached the blades to short sticks. Even

*Some of the earliest opium poppy fields were located in Sonora. Here a Mexican health inspector examines a small field.*

so, bleeding and collecting the sap, as one U.S. Customs agent surmised, was a "tedious and delicate process." You had to be careful not to snap the seedpod off the plant; you had to make sure the slits you cut into it were exactly the right depth; and you had to scrape off the sap with minimal waste.

Timing was key. The harvest had to be taken in early March just after the rains, the seedpods had to be cut in the late afternoon, and scraping the sap was a morning job. Any time after midday the sap started to sink back into the plant. Traditionally, the Chinese had rolled the sap into small balls and stored it inside leaves. But for ease of transport the Sonora farmers let the sap dry out into quarter-inch-thick slabs, which they then packed into sacks and transported to the buyers.

These buyers were local Mexican merchants. Previously, they had bought up the area's vegetables and sold them in nearby market towns or Pacific ports. Now they used their capital and contacts to traffic opium. For example, in Huatabampo the principal wholesalers were the Otero brothers—Manuel and José María. They had the largest farms in the village, on which they hid substantial poppy plantations. But they combined their crops with those of the smaller farmers, which they also bought in bulk. They were both accomplished smugglers and allegedly ran the village's market in untaxed liquor. And they had impressive political connections. Their uncle was the former governor of Sonora. As such, they were well placed to take advantage of the short boom. According to one U.S. agent, by 1938 they were buying up over half a ton of raw opium worth an impressive 90,000 pesos.

If Mexican farmers had learned to plant, harvest, and buy up the opium, they were still unable to transform it into usable narcotics. For a handful of desperate border addicts, this didn't matter. By the late 1930s, morphine and heroin were so scarce they were prepared to dissolve the raw opium in water and inject it untreated. But others were more discerning. They needed smoking opium at least. Here the Chinese still played a role. It seems that even in Sonora some of the Mexican authorities had preferred profit to prejudice and allowed a handful of specialist opium cooks to stay.

In 1936, Ralph Lane, a U.S. Customs agent, offered a rare glimpse into this delicate process. Lane was, it must be said, a rarity. He not only spoke Spanish, but also had an exceptional sympathy for those involved in the opium trade and a sharp eye for anthropological detail. (He was also, probably as a consequence, immensely unpopular in his own department and keen to change jobs.) While investigating the resurgent trade, he bumped into two Chinese cooks based in a small shack in the Yaqui valley. They seemed unconcerned by his presence and allowed him to stay there and study the method for three days.

They were generous teachers. One in particular was an old man and a "scholarly" fellow who patiently answered Lane's questions and wistfully spoke of the old Chinese traditions. Lane was impressed. "With them it is an art, handed down and must be done just so." First they broke up the blocks of hard opium sap with a hammer. Then they placed the opium in copper bottles with water. These were heated gently until simmering. At this point, the cooks took great care not to scorch the mixture. Then after the opium had dissolved, they strained it through linen into another copper container where it cooled. Here they mixed it with flowers, brandy or even raw sugar to give the drug flavor. Finally, they packed the product into small 5-ounce tins. As traditional copper ones were unavailable, empty cocoa containers had to suffice. The old man was proud of his skills and boasted that even in this humble cabin he could produce smoking opium of the quality he had tasted back in China.

Once processed, the wholesalers delivered the opium to one of Sonora's ports. There was Puerto Peñasco to the north or Guaymas to the south. "Port" was probably too formal a word for what were essentially still fishing villages. Here, opium tins were hidden beneath raw fish or secreted in gallon tins of lard. Small fishing boats then transported the product over the Gulf of California to Baja California. Once there, they were moved by road to the surviving Chinese population in Mexicali. In Mexicali, Chinese dealers either sold the opium to the few remaining dens or to smugglers, who took it over the border.

The new Sonora system was relatively short-lived. By 1940, most production had shifted even further south. But despite its limited span, this Mexicanized version of the opium trade, with its hierarchy of peasants, wholesalers, cooks, and transporters, was an important development. It would provide a template for the future and would reach its full expression a decade later in the neighboring mountains of the Golden Triangle.

## Chapter 6

## The Revolutionary

THIS WAS NOT GOING TO BE EASY. IT WAS JUNE 2, 1939, AND THE WIRY, HOOK-nosed Mexican diplomat Manuel Tello was in Geneva at the League of Nations. He was in the grand council chamber. Dozens of the world's top narcotics experts stared at him, their faces somewhere between blank and irritated. To his left, the tall, thickset figure of the FBN head and U.S. representative, Harry Anslinger, looked particularly incensed. Anslinger already hated the Mexican. They had clashed a few days earlier. Tello had made the mistake of criticizing the American's claims on marijuana. Mexican doctors, Tello had argued, had not found one example of a patient driven to madness by smoking the narcotic in fifteen years of treating users.

But this, he suspected, was going to be worse. Nervous, hands shuffling through his notes, he started to speak. The same Mexican doctors, he explained, had discovered that weaning addicts off morphine and heroin was next to impossible. Prohibition was no help. All it did was create a black market, push up the price of the drugs, and put money in the pockets of the peddlers. Addicts were forced to rob and steal to pay for their fix. Mexico, however, had a solution. The new drug law provided for opening a series of state-run morphine dispensaries. Here, doctors would hand out morphine shots at pharmaceutical prices; addicts would be able to hold down stable jobs; and drug traffickers would be forced out of business. Tello looked up hopefully. Perhaps the sheer logical weight of his argument had won over the crowd?

It hadn't.

Anslinger's pudgy face had gone a deep shade of red. He rose from his chair, collected his notes, and started to address the hall. He was furious. He denied that drug prohibition had been a failure. He claimed that there was evidence that opiate addicts could recover. And he threatened that if Mexico went ahead with the new law, it contravened all the international narcotics conventions it had signed.

Anslinger was right, at least in part. For nearly twenty years Mexico had been at the forefront of drug prohibition. The country had signed on to international conventions, banned the growing of opium, prohibited the sale of smoking opium, and attempted to control the use of hard drugs. In one respect it was ahead of even the United States. A national law against marijuana had been on Mexico's books since 1920. (Anslinger had only managed to pass the U.S. equivalent, the Marihuana Tax Act, seventeen years later. And he did so by repeating the old Mexican prejudices, which linked the drug to insanity and violence.)

The 1931 penal code brought together all Mexican antinarcotics legislation. The code struck against those that "trade in, elaborate, possess, buy, transfer, freely administer and in general engage in any act of acquisition, supply or trafficking of drugs." There were penalties for pharmacists, druggists, and doctors that infringed the laws, and for anyone who imported or exported narcotics. Sentences ran up to ten years in prison.

What is more, police forces did enforce this code, albeit rather selectively. The newly created sanitary police—which was run out of the health department—focused on Mexico City. By the mid-1930s it was arresting and imprisoning nearly 150 marijuana and opiate peddlers a year.

So what changed? What was Tello doing, standing before the League of Nations and renouncing his country's hard line? Did the Mexican authorities go ahead with their proposed law? And perhaps most important, how did Anslinger and the Americans react?

To answer these questions, it is necessary to shift focus. So far, we have examined the mechanics of the drug trade—who took narcotics, who grew them, who processed them, and who sold them. The Revolution, that great social and cultural upheaval that transformed Mexico between 1910 and 1940, has mostly appeared as background. It generalized the smoking of marijuana and pushed impoverished local governors to support transnational trafficking. Its effects on legislation were negligible. In fact, the laws of the 1920s and 1930s relied on ideas about narcotics formulated during the dictatorship.

But in the last years of the 1930s something changed. Revolutionary thinking, which had distributed land to peasants, improved the lives of factory workers, and created a mass schooling system, now started to shift attitudes and laws toward narcotics. At the center of these changes was a group of doctors who believed in creating a just and more equal society through a more socially responsible medicine. And at the center of these was an extraordinary man, Leopoldo Salazar Viniegra.

Salazar doesn't appear in any of the standard histories of the Revolution. Even in Mexico his efforts remain largely forgotten. (Although after his death Mexico City weed smokers memorialized his work by giving marijuana the nickname "Viniegra.") But for two years, as head of Mexico's Campaign Against Alcoholism and Other Drug Addictions, Salazar flipped old thinking about narcotics on its head. His ideas were genuinely radical. They pushed Tello to lecture the League of Nations, they challenged dominant theories about marijuana, and they even persuaded the government to establish state-run morphine clinics.

Yet if Salazar's influence was short-lived, the story of how FBN head Harry Anslinger brought an end to his radical experiment had a much more enduring legacy. It highlighted Anslinger's new role as America's point man not only for domestic but also foreign drug policies. It demonstrated his refusal to accept anything but a prohibitionist legal framework. And it drove home his willingness and ability to bully and blackmail countries that sought to do any different. It was an influence that would cast a shadow over the next eighty years of Mexican drug policing.

*

The Revolution came slowly to the world of Mexican medicine. During the 1920s, race science and eugenics still played important roles in shaping medical thinking. Mexican doctors continued to hold that specific racial and social groups carried certain innate weaknesses. They believed that it was their job to discourage or even prevent the spread of these weaknesses.

This led to some dark places. In 1932, for example, the state legislature of Veracruz passed Latin America's first sterilization law, which required doctors to sterilize patients of indigenous heritage.

For decades, such thinking also brought the clinical investigation of narcotics to a virtual standstill. Medical papers of the time were short on research and long on prejudice. Most simply parroted the same dictatorship-era certainties, which focused on the social profile of the addicts and linked drug use to violence and insanity. They often argued that widespread use risked "degenerating the race" and imperiling the Mexican people. In 1931, for example, Dr. Gregorio Oneto Barenque warned that by smoking marijuana soldiers "let free those ancestral complexes of their warrior race, killing in cold blood and suffering no remorse." To put it bluntly, marijuana made Mexicans act more "Indian." It was a threat that could be averted, he suggested, by punishing drug peddlers the same as murderers.

Yet change did come. During the 1930s, young Mexican medics started to develop what they termed "social medicine." This involved leaving their comfy middle-class neighborhoods and visiting the slums and villages where most Mexicans lived, got sick, and died. But it also involved a dramatic innovation in the way that medicine was done. Doctors were no longer expected to simply transfer their old prejudices from the page to the patient. Instead, they were to use this contact with the public to understand the deeper causes of disease. Poor indigenous peasants died young not because they were poor, indigenous, or had a particular shape of head. They died young because the combination of racism and economic exploitation forced them to work sixteen-hour days, live in draughty, dirty hovels, and drink polluted water.

At the forefront of these changes were Mexico's psychiatrists, who started to embrace a more engaged and surprisingly modern form of psychiatry. Rather than simply locking up and sedating the mentally ill, this new generation sought to understand and alleviate mental illness through education, welfare, and social programs. They called this new approach "mental hygiene."

By the end of the decade, they dominated the country's medical profession. They had their own academic society; they had their own social movement (the Mexican League of Mental Hygiene); and they even controlled the National Academy of Medicine, which up to then had been a fusty, old-fashioned institution run by the country's eugenicists.

The intellectual leader of this movement was Leopoldo Salazar Viniegra. His fellow doctors fondly nicknamed him "Pasteur." It was a fitting moniker. Like the French germ pioneer, Salazar was not only considered the brightest of his generation; he was also a genuine iconoclast. He reveled in shocking the uptight medical establishments in both Mexico and the United States.

Salazar was the Revolution's narcotics freethinker. Though he was born in a small mining community in the mountainous northern state of Durango in 1897, he was from a prosperous family. His father, in particular, did well out of the dictatorship. After moving to Mexico City, he became head of the country's Geological Institute. His son received an elite education, attending the capital's most exclusive school and then doing four years of medicine at the National University of Mexico. Salazar completed his training in Madrid and then Paris.

Education brought prestige. And on returning to Mexico, Salazar divided his time between a popular private practice, a lectureship at the National University, and a position at the capital's largest asylum, La Castañeda. At La Castañeda, Salazar met many of the other pioneers of the "mental hygiene" movement.

It was also here that Salazar started to work on narcotics and addiction. For most of the 1920s, the Mexican authorities had struggled to employ a consistent policy on drug addicts. In fact, even discerning them was difficult. Track marks might have distinguished heroin addicts, but what made an "addict" of smoking opium or marijuana? So some were lumped together with peddlers and traffickers and stuck in jail. Others were given lighter sentences or let off with a fine.

In the early 1930s, things started to change. The 1931 penal code fixed extremely harsh punishments for those who grew, produced, or sold drugs.

But in a series of subsequent adjustments, the country's lawmakers started to shift the treatment of those who could prove they were actually addicts. They even established a drug rehabilitation clinic in the grounds of La Castañeda asylum. By the end of the decade, the clinic was treating hundreds of patients a year.

The clinic provided Salazar and the other followers of the "mental hygiene" movement with a base where they could start to question presumptions about marijuana and opiates. It was also where Salazar started to get a reputation for erratic behavior. On taking a job at the clinic, he moved out of his upscale apartment and rented a small house on site. He repeatedly stole vegetables from the asylum garden. And when he was reprimanded, he and a handful of green-fingered inmates started to grow their own food (and so the rumors went, their own marijuana). The unusual behavior grew. He invited an asylum patient to come live with him; he turned the asylum playing fields into a shooting range; he refused to wear a tie to official functions; he insisted on teaching his students on Sundays; and he graded them not on their exams, but rather on their skills at pistol marksmanship.

Such willful eccentricity brought a certain degree of fame. He was a natural showman and became the national newspapers' go-to head doctor. He offered psychological evaluations of notorious killers, held public demonstrations of medical breakthroughs, and challenged a child prodigy with "telekinetic powers" to a showdown at the National Academy of Medicine. After the kid failed to move anything, he concluded to the assembled journalists that it was a case of fraud.

This unconventional attitude also shaped his investigations into narcotics. He surreptitiously handed out machine-rolled marijuana cigarettes to visiting dignitaries, including, so the rumors went, the members of the Mexican cabinet. Only once they had finished smoking did he declare what they contained. (Visiting American officials were warned, "If Salazar offers you a cigarette, be careful that it is not a marijuana cigarette as he is giving these out to all of his friends to prove that they are not injurious and he may experiment on you.")

This attitude also extended to his formal work. In his laboratory he injected the brains of live chickens with marijuana extract. And in front of a class of medical students, he allowed morphine addicts to shoot up and then discussed the effects. He also left joints around his house and admitted his nine-year-old nephew smoked one, thinking it was just a normal cigarette. Rather than playing down the blunder, Salazar used it as evidence of marijuana's relative harmlessness.

But Salazar's research was much more than just stoner theater. At the time, his work on marijuana was probably the most extensive, in-depth study of the effects of the drug in the world. It was based on nearly a decade of working with narcotics addicts. It included blind tests, extensive interviews, and long-term analysis, which attempted to separate other types of mental illness (particularly schizophrenia) from the effects of marijuana. And it comprised detailed, brilliant, if rather arch, critiques of other medical studies. One study, he pointed out, relied on apocryphal stories drawn from tabloid newspaper headlines. Another was primarily based on the hash-inspired poetry of Baudelaire.

He also employed a doctoral student, Jorge Segura Millán, who did extensive research in parallel with Salazar. Here was engaged, street-level psychiatry. He threw away the marijuana that the Mexican police donated him, declaring it "rubbish." Instead, he worked with pharmaceutical cannabis extract and the finest local marijuana, which he himself sourced from a village just outside the city limits. He then did tests on three groups of people—nonaddicts, addicts, and diagnosed psychopaths; and he constructed a special "smoking box" to do similar tests on dogs. (They ceased fighting and simply ate a lot.)

But what made Salazar's investigations particularly radical was the way he tried to bring together medicine and Marxism. He had been playing with these ideas for some time. In a 1937 speech to the National Academy of Medicine, he tried to blend contemporary neurology, Freudian psychoanalysis, and Marxist economics to offer a strikingly original take on both psychology and modern society.

In Salazar's opinion, "money ... was at the heart" of most mental illnesses. In fact, capitalism itself was a form of insanity. The rich, in their pursuit of money, were suffering a God complex; they became psychopathic in their irrational search for more and more wealth. The middle class abetted this collective delusion by establishing the rules of

*Perro No. 2 normal*

*Perro No. 2 intoxicado*

*Cámara de inhalación para animales*

*During the late 1930s one of Salazar's students investigated marijuana's effects on dogs and even invented a special "dog smoking box."*

the game, including the central rule, which was the "principle of private property." The poor, meanwhile, were left to suffer the very real effects of this mass psychosis "hungry before a table of food" or "freezing outside a clothes shop." The only way out of this, he suggested, was to stop this mass psychosis at its source, eliminate private property, and distribute wealth according to people's needs rather than their irrational desires.

It was communism not as economic inevitability or social necessity but psychological relief.

For a few years, Salazar's ideas simply sloshed around Mexico's medical academy, irritating the older doctors. But in January 1938 he was put in charge of the drug rehab clinic and made head of the country's Campaign Against Alcoholism and Other Drug Addictions. Theory met practice; Marxist psychiatry met the mainstream.

In this new position, his first, rather ambitious undertaking was to change the popular perception of Mexico's most dreaded drug—marijuana. He started by inviting Mexico's leading marijuana "expert," Dr. Gregorio Oneto Barenque, to a debate on the subject at the National

Academy of Medicine. Here, Salazar presented his pathbreaking work "The Myth of Marijuana."

The paper laid out a bold new theory of marijuana's effects. The genuine physical effects, he argued, were minimal. They comprised the drying of the mouth, the reddening of the eyes, and a feeling of hunger. Any further effects were not caused by marijuana's chemical properties. Instead, they were caused by existing psychological disorders (particularly schizophrenia). Or they were caused by the power of suggestion.

Here was the real innovation. Salazar argued that the stories linking marijuana and violent crime were completely untrue. Many were idle rumors. They concerned crimes that were probably caused by alcoholism or mental illness. But others were outright inventions, made up by imaginative, if unscrupulous, journalists. This was bad enough—such stories underpinned the unfair prosecution of marijuana smokers.

But they also had crucial secondary effects. It was these myths—through the power of suggestion—that drove some marijuana smokers to behave in an irrational manner. Smokers acted violently because they believed that was how they should act. It was the myths—not marijuana—that caused murder.

Here then was the first—and to my knowledge the last—Marxist theory of marijuana. For Salazar, what the Mexicans called "marijuana intoxication" and the Americans "reefer madness" was a cultural construct, just like money or private property. It was invented by lawmakers and journalists to demonize and keep down the working class. Furthermore, it was a self-fulfilling prophecy, which simply succeeded in suggesting violent behavior to those who were under the influence.

Such ideas were way ahead of their time. It would take another two decades for the Harvard psychologist and LSD pioneer Timothy Leary to suggest something similar. Leary also believed that narcotics didn't have fixed chemical effects. Rather, he argued, they depended on the drug user's mindset, or "set," and his environment, or "setting." In fact, the only real difference between the two notions was that Leary—the protohippie individualist—believed a person could control both set and setting, whereas Salazar—the Marxist—believed that the bourgeoisie already controlled them.

The public response to Salazar's ideas about marijuana was, at best, lukewarm. At the National Academy of Medicine a handful of psychiatrists applauded his work. And other doctors from the asylum and the federal hospital confirmed his findings. There was also some sympathy for his ideas among government ministers. It was unclear whether they were convinced by his arguments or his spontaneous trials. Whatever the reason, his boss, the head of the health department, quietly backed his work. And there is some evidence that while he was in charge police forces cut down arrests for marijuana possession on his advice.

But in general, the response was horror. Old ideas about marijuana died hard. And Salazar's playful approach was judged arrogant and aloof. His opponent at the academy debate, Oneto, was particularly furious. He really didn't like Salazar. A few months before, he had gone to visit the clinic. There, Salazar had offered him a marijuana cigarette. After he smoked it, he claimed to feel "euphoric and dizzy." Salazar then revealed "in an ironic and mocking fashion" that he had only smoked oregano. Point proven. It was the power of suggestion that had made him feel that way.

Journalists were also overtly hostile. One columnist claimed that Salazar had declared the herb as "innocuous as a drop of distilled water" (he hadn't) and suggested that he should be arrested for infringing the laws on drug distribution. And the conservative broadsheet *El Universal* responded to the debate with the plain-speaking editorial "Marijuana Is Dangerous." It quoted rival doctors who claimed that the drug was as perilous as "heroin, morphine or cocaine" and that the "grifo" (stoner) was as desperate and vicious as a heroin addict looking for a fix.

The Americans were also concerned. They had introduced their first national antiweed legislation—the Marihuana Tax Act—just a year earlier. Their ideas about the drug were explicitly based on Mexican claims that it led to insanity and violence. Now this Mexican doctor, who handed out reefers to unsuspecting visitors, was turning such assumptions on their head. The assistant chief of U.S. Customs described Salazar's papers as the "outpourings of an educated nigger."

Such overwhelming hostility probably ended any hope of changing the law. Though the health department initially claimed that it was willing to entertain an open discussion on the drug, the plan was quietly dropped.

And by the end of the year, even the Americans suspected that Salazar was willing to set aside his findings.

Soon they discovered why. And when they did, their initial pleasure immediately disappeared. Salazar and the Mexican government had shelved plans over marijuana in favor of something even more radical. By 1939 they were preparing the complete overhaul of Mexican drug law.

Like the investigation into marijuana, the new drug law was based on research done at the federal addiction hospital. Rates of recidivism at the establishment were extremely high. Most of the patients had returned to the place four or five times. Salazar claimed that he had only met one heroin addict that had weaned himself off the drug. And he had done so by smoking marijuana. Salazar and his fellow psychiatrists concluded that curing opiate addicts in Mexico's underfunded drug rehab hospital was almost impossible.

But if the evidence was medical, the analysis of the problem was again rooted in Marxism. According to Salazar, capitalism victimized drug addicts two times over. On the one hand, they were already poor, dispossessed, and often suffering physical or psychological pain. In such circumstances, drugs were a release. On the other hand, by taking banned substances they also entered into another, even more exploitative, relationship. Drug prohibition hiked up prices, so dealers could charge them extortionate rates to sate their cravings. And drug prohibition shrouded the act of injecting heroin with an air of attractive mystery. The problem, then, was not so much addiction as an economic and cultural system that—like the myths surrounding marijuana—compounded existing difficulties.

The solution to addiction was neither judicial (lock them up) nor medical (treat them). It was economic. State dispensaries or state-sanctioned doctors would offer morphine to addicts at a nominal price. Here their doses could be controlled and the addicts could be monitored and treated for other diseases. Such a program reduced the amount addicts had to pay for narcotics, allowed them to hold down regular jobs, and lessened the attraction of crime. At the same time, this new system struck at the illegal economy. Forced to compete with the state's low rates, peddlers would be put out of business. Finally, as the business of injecting heroin was forced out of the shadows and into the clinic, it would lose its mystique and allure.

Salazar's economic solution to the problem was novel and drastic. Even today it seems rather neat and farsighted. Other countries, including the United States, had toyed with the idea of treating addicts. But most states paid lip service to some future cure and none sought to undercut peddlers by selling drugs themselves.

Nevertheless, it was probably this last factor that sold Salazar's plan to the Mexican authorities. Under Mexico's radical 1930s president, Lázaro Cárdenas, the state repeatedly established state-run firms to compete with and undercut exploitative private companies. It was a classic economic policy of the Revolution, somewhere between communism and capitalism. By presenting the drug trade as just another form of capitalist exploitation, Salazar pushed radical medical ideas into the mainstream.

In early February 1940, new regulations were introduced based on Salazar's ideas. They permitted both state-regulated doctors and state-run dispensaries to give addicts daily doses of morphine. These were not intended to wean addicts off drugs; they were designed to break the black market and put the dealers out of business.

The next month the regulations came into play. The health department opened a dispensary in the southern area of Mexico City. Here five doctors gave out small doses of high-quality morphine twice a day to addicts. The doses cost 80 centavos each. And to receive a dose addicts had to register and agree to medical advice. By the end of the first week over 500 addicts had visited the dispensary.

The effects were not pretty. Hundreds of junkies waiting for a fix slumped over benches, sleeping on the pavement, and using garden hoses to shower was not one for the postcards. One of Mexico's best journalists did an in-depth study of the clinic and described it as a "terrifying spectacle."

These are the people from the rubbish tips, from the frightening depths of our poorest neighborhoods. Their hair is shaggy and falls over their necks, their beards are straggly and unkempt, their eyes are bloodshot, and their clothes are little more than rags. The women are like shadows, like souls in purgatory, like the witches your grandmother spoke about when she tried to get you to go to

*On Salazar's advice the government established a state-run morphine dispensary in 1940. The Americans eventually forced the Mexicans to close it down.*

sleep. There are many Chinese in line as well, with their almond shaped eyes and their perpetually yellow skin.

Yet, look beyond the disheartening spectacle and the results of the experiment were rather impressive. The addicts who spoke to the journalist commended the trial. They claimed that it had given them a new lease of life. Arturo Muñoz, a Mexican-American former soldier, had become addicted to morphine during World War I. He said that dealers had upped the prices of drugs so much that addicts had to rob to afford them. He ended with a plea.

We only want you to say the truth ... that they dose us according to our physical state so we can reintegrate into society and return to our jobs. Now they are doing this. Tell your readers that we are thankful to the Health Department, very thankful.

Another addict claimed that though he spent 80 centavos on the clinic morphine, this still left him over a peso from his job as a rural laborer. With

*Many addicts applauded the government initiative. Arturo Muñoz, aka Rompepechos, explained to a visiting journalist, "We only want you to say the truth . . . that they dose us according to our physical state so we can reintegrate into society and return to our jobs. Now they are doing this. Tell your readers that we are thankful to the Health Department, very thankful."*

this he could pay for food and rent. On the street, the same amount would have cost him 12 pesos. He would have had to thieve to get his fix. Furthermore, it would have been cut with a dangerous combination of lactose and quinine.

In contrast to the addicts, the dealers were less thrilled. The health department estimated that the capital's heroin slingers were hemorrhaging over 8,000 pesos a day. Rumors circulated that the capital's leading merchant was alone losing 2,600 pesos. She was said to be offering addicts extra narcotics to keep their trade. Or she was trying the radical and, one suspects, self-defeating sales technique of threatening to kill the customers that did not return.

Such results did not go unnoticed. A few middle-class residents who lived near the dispensary complained that the addicts "were extremely dirty and showed signs of contagious diseases." But even they had to agree with the "social need" for the measures. They were in good company. Even old-school eugenicist doctors agreed with the plan. And the snooty Mexico City newspapers weighed in with supportive editorials. *El Universal*, which had condemned Salazar's ideas on marijuana, now boasted the following enlightened stance.

A drug addict is no more a criminal than an alcoholic. Engaging him, registering him and making him submit to medical and psychological treatment can be a fundamental way to combat addicts. In the same way ... the best way to fight the traffickers is to compete with them on the price of the merchandise.

In fact, the whole project was so successful that by May 1940 there were plans to open two further clinics in the slightly less salubrious Mexico City neighborhoods of Tepito and Doctores as well as in the country's second-biggest city, Guadalajara.

Sadly, such optimism did not last for long. On June 7, 1940, the government repealed the regulations. The clinics were closed. The reason given was that morphine shortages caused by the outbreak of World War II made the system unfeasible. The government was simply unable to import sufficient amounts for the system to work.

The real reason, however, was not quite so simple, or so anodyne. Since Mexico had announced the new law at the League of Nations, U.S. officials had been desperately struggling to find a means to shut down the plan. It contradicted the American assertion that addicts could and should be cured. It also risked the establishment of morphine dispensaries on the Mexican frontier. These could generate a transnational black market in Mexico's cheap, state-sanctioned morphine.

Fanning these fears was Mexico's opponent at the 1939 League of Nations meeting—Harry Anslinger.

Bald and eloquent, Anslinger was America's leading drug hawk. For a decade, as head of the Treasury Department's antidrug unit, the Federal Bureau of Narcotics, or FBN, he had successfully publicized narcotics as a serious domestic threat. A shrewd bureaucrat and a master propagandist, he had persuaded U.S. lawmakers to maintain punitive narcotics regulations beyond the end of alcohol prohibition. He had even got lawmakers to extend the regulations to marijuana. Such efforts had generated reputation and power. And by the end of the decade, he was starting to extend the FBN's reach into the field of foreign policy. He now styled himself as not only America's but also the "the world's greatest authority on dope."

Over the next twenty years, Anslinger would expertly weave the drug war into America's foreign policy objectives. Supremely pragmatic and with only a passing interest in the actual facts, he would go on to blame U.S. narcotics addiction on an almost comically incoherent litany of shady conspiracies involving first Axis cocaine smugglers, then Chinese opium peddlers, and then, by the early 1960s, Cuban communists.

But at least initially, he tested his new foreign policy ambitions on an enemy that was slightly closer to home—Mexico. And this time, the strategy was simple—blackmail.

By the end of the 1930s, most of Mexico's medical morphine came from the United States. The U.S. Narcotic Drugs Import and Export Act only permitted sale to countries where the drugs were going to be used for "medical and legitimate uses." And who decided what was deemed "medical and legitimate uses"? Anslinger.

Here he knew he was on slippery ground. In theory, the morphine distributed in Mexico's dispensaries was both "medical and legitimate." In some ways it couldn't be more so. It was handed out by doctors and regulated by law. But Anslinger countered that it was above the levels stipulated by Mexico's own pharmaceutical recommendations and was thus not medical but "gratifying." Addicts weren't just getting a fix; they were getting a hit. And so he used the act to halt morphine sales to Mexico.

The plan worked. By March 1940, Anslinger boasted to the Canadian drug authorities;

We had prohibited the shipment of narcotics to Mexico while the new regulations are in force. Evidently the shoe is pinching the health authorities, as they are using up their small stock for the addicts and do not have enough to take care of the sick and injured and the hospitals, doctors and druggists are putting the pressure on.... They appear to be somewhat shaken by the whole thing.

Mexican hospital patients starved of medication and dying in pain was a small price to pay.

In response the Mexicans tried to save the regulations. They dropped the section that allowed private doctors to prescribe doses to addicts; the regulations were now limited to state-run dispensaries. They agreed to send Mexican law enforcement officers to America for training. They made showy efforts to increase drug policing on the border. And they invited a U.S. representative to inspect poppy eradication efforts. (This was rather undermined when the U.S. representative reported back that when challenged about the upsurge in poppy cultivation "even Mexican officers of a good reputation shrugged their shoulders and said that opium is not used in Mexico.")

Finally, in May 1940, the head of the health department flew to Washington in a last-ditch effort to persuade the Americans. But Anslinger was unwavering.

So instead, they agreed to fudge the issue. The United States would quietly resume morphine exports. Mexico would back away from the regulations, citing global morphine shortages rather than American blackmail. Both would save face. The Americans would look magnanimous. The Mexicans would appear forced into a corner by a conflict they could not control.

Though few realized it at the time, it was a crucial turning point.

Anslinger's intervention foreshadowed what was to come. Over the next decade, the FBN head would use a blend of bureaucratic maneuvering, public grandstanding, and media leaks to shape Mexico's counternarcotics efforts. By the end of the 1940s, Mexico's antidrug laws would be even more punitive than those of the United States. Thousands of peddlers, addicts, and drug cultivators would languish in Mexican jails. Every year, U.S. agents would accompany Mexican soldiers to scour the hills of western Mexico to search for poppy plants and marijuana fields.

Meanwhile, any hope of Mexico embracing a genuinely progressive narcotics policy disappeared. Salazar's dreams crumbled. He was removed from his position and returned to treating patients at the federal drug clinic. More conservative bosses now started to view his eccentricities as provocations. And though his friends occasionally tried to resuscitate his ideas, the moment had passed. The radical stage of the Revolution came to a slow, stuttering close. World War II and then the Cold War forced Mexico into closer and closer alignment with the United States. Drug policy followed in lock step.

By the end of the 1940s, Salazar had left the field of narcotics for that of primary education. But, always an iconoclast, he established an experimental school of open, participative learning for Mexico City's street kids called "The House Without Bars." He died from complications relating to a stomach ulcer in 1957.

# Part II

Coming Up
1940–1960

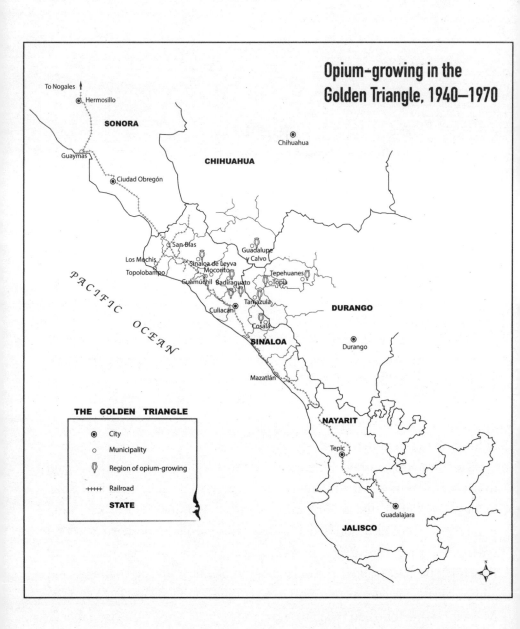

## Opium-growing in the Golden Triangle, 1940–1970

To Nogales

Hermosillo

SONORA

Chihuahua

CHIHUAHUA

Guaymas

Ciudad Obregón

San Blas

Los Mochis

Sinaloa de Leyva

Topolobampo

Mocorito

Guamúchil

Badiraguato

Guadalupe
y Calvo

Tepehuanes

Topia

DURANGO

Tamazula

Culiacán

Cosalá

SINALOA

Durango

Mazatlán

PACIFIC OCEAN

**THE GOLDEN TRIANGLE**

◉ City

○ Municipality

◘ Region of opium-growing

+++++ Railroad

**STATE**

NAYARIT

Tepic

Guadalajara

JALISCO

N

## Chapter 7

## The Golden Triangle

ON MAY 16, 1944, THE U.S. CUSTOMS OFFICER, SALVADOR PEÑA, STEPPED off the train at the end of the line. He had arrived in the hardscrabble mining town of Tepehuanes, Durango, accompanied by two inspectors from the Mexican health department. They were on an important mission. Peasants in the area were planting fields of poppies and harvesting hundreds of kilos of opium gum.

They were also afraid. The highlands were a famously difficult region to navigate—remote, mountainous, dotted with thin valleys and imposing, vertiginous cliffs. Its inhabitants—a mix of miners, peasants, and muleteers—were also notoriously tough. They disliked interfering federal envoys, and they were armed. Thirty years earlier the revolutionary general Pancho Villa had stalked these lands, ambushing military columns, and administering his own justice with a firing squad and a noose. Peña and the Mexican inspectors didn't want to end up as more victims of the highlanders' desire to be left alone.

They had an inauspicious start. The local barracks commander refused to lend them the troops, animals, or supplies needed for the mission.

Eventually, when he did agree, after three days of negotiating, the group was still woefully underequipped for a week trekking through the Sierra Madre Occidental. The animals were old and lame; the fodder provided lasted less than a day; and the guides fled as soon as they left the town. To make matters worse, the poppy growers had been warned of the military column in advance. The inspectors heard rumors that they were digging up their old rifles and preparing an ambush.

The ambush never came. (Though the group was sufficiently frightened that only two soldiers actually pulled up poppy plants. The other twenty-one stood guard.) The early warning was nevertheless enough. It gave the poppy growers time to pull up or burn their crops and then flee to the peaks above. The column arrested a solitary peasant, who made the mistake of forgetting that he had buried a kilo of opium under the dirt floor of his hut.

Despite the lack of arrests, what the inspectors saw amazed them. Poppy was grown in the Durango highlands on a scale they had never seen before. In the three small villages of Los Fresnos, Quebrada Honda, and Metates alone, they saw the charred remains of around 600 acres. The land there was irrigated by a system of raised aqueducts, which directed water down the hills to the fields below. This allowed the growers to pack up to eleven poppy plants into each square meter of well-watered earth. The system, Peña later calculated, could yield up to 3.5 tons of crude opium a year. Sold to American buyers, it would be worth around a million dollars.

During the 1940s there was a sea change in the Mexican dope trade. World War II cut the United States off from traditional European and Asian supplies of opiates. Some addicts went cold turkey, taking advantage of the dearth to clean themselves up for good. Others were less fortunate. In New York, William Burroughs and his fellow Beats, Jack Kerouac and Allen Ginsberg, teamed up (and then fell out) in their desperate scrabble to find new sources of dope.

They were joined by a new subset of addicts: returning U.S. soldiers who had become addicted to morphine while recovering from their wounds. In 1949, Nelson Algren gave the epidemic a voice. His seminal novel, *The Man with the Golden Arm*, told the story of Frankie Machine, a former soldier who had become addicted to morphine while recovering from the shrapnel that was buried in his liver. Returning to Chicago in 1946, he took

*Agent Salvador Peña (left) with his Mexican coworkers.*

up his old job as a card shark and tried to realize his dream as a jazz drummer. But his habit kept on pulling him back in.

Whether they were old hands like Burroughs or novice "hypes" like Machine, the U.S. addicts now had a new supplier—Mexico. Initially, there was only a trickle. But by 1943, U.S. Customs claimed that Mexico was now "the principal source of the supply of prepared opium to the ... United States." The following year, officials reported that they were also seizing morphine and heroin on the Mexican border. The drugs were "definitely of Mexican origin." As the war ended, Mexican opiates were being seized as far north as Chicago and New York. In what would become a long-running affair, Burroughs and his fellow Beats were getting their first taste of Mexico.

The source of the drugs was that corner of the Sierra Madre Occidental that Peña and the two Mexican inspectors had stumbled upon. Poppy growing had shifted south and inland from the tropical Sonora lowlands. The area now covered around ten municipalities. Three were in the state of

Durango (Tepehuanes, Tamazula, and Topia). Two were in Chihuahua (Guadalupe y Calvo and Parral). And five were in Sinaloa (Badiraguato, Mocorito, Cosalá, Sinaloa de Leyva, and Culiacán). Together, by 1947, they produced around 90 percent of the U.S. market in illegal drugs.

The bonanza changed the place forever. It would be home to Mexico's first farm-to-arm opium industry and Mexico's leading opium producer for the next eighty years. Some of its inhabitants would use their skills (and their networks of political protection) to become Mexico's first *narcotraficantes*, rotating among heroin, marijuana, and cocaine depending on U.S. tastes. In fact, by the 1960s the region had become synonymous with the drug trade.

It had also acquired a name: the Golden Triangle.

Even today, the origins of the Golden Triangle as epicenter of Mexico's drug industry are blurry. Some locals maintain that it was the U.S. government that first introduced poppies to satisfy wartime demands for morphine. The story goes back decades but still endures. It has been retold repeatedly by local intellectuals, journalists, and politicians keen to excuse the area's global reputation for narcotics.

Like any rumor, the origins of the tale of U.S. complicity are difficult to untangle. It seems that during the war some U.S. citizens living in the Golden Triangle suggested to the U.S. authorities that the local opium industry could sate official demands for morphine. The authorities turned down the suggestion, but this story soon became intertwined with other tales from the drug underground. At some point in the 1940s, a handful of U.S. fraudsters traveled down to the region and used fake government IDs to buy drugs and sell guns. They were joined by a couple of shady FBN agents who used the story of official morphine demand to lay a trap for a bunch of traffickers from Ciudad Juárez. These three stories, in turn, got bound up with very real tales of the local government protecting the trade. Together, they coalesced into a convenient myth of foreign meddling and Mexican redemption.

Beyond such rumors, there is no evidence of any official U.S. involvement in the establishment of the Golden Triangle's trade. The opium business was homegrown. The real story of why it took hold in this tough and mountainous region of Mexico is a less simple—but more interesting—tale of place, people, and, as the next chapter shows, politics.

When it comes to producing drugs, the Golden Triangle does have some natural advantages. Unlike the Sonora lowlands, the landscape is a mix of precipitous mountain peaks and deep, shaded valleys. As Peña found, getting around was tough. But what was bad for visitors was a boon for opium growers. Peasants could hide poppy fields way down on the valley floor beyond the gaze of nosey government inspectors. Or they could perch them on steep slopes and use ropes to hang over the side and water and weed the plants. Dense pine forests completed the camouflage, casting long shadows over the land below.

The Golden Triangle had a further advantage. Though difficult to traverse, the region was located on the edge of a transport infrastructure. U.S. markets were in easy reach. To the west there was the coastal railway that wound its way up from Guadalajara past the Sinaloa capital of Culiacán to the highland station of Guamúchil. From there the line went north, crossing the border at the dusty Arizona town of Nogales. In 1938 the line was extended from Nogales to Tijuana. There were the roads, which snaked up the coast, following the railway, and also crossed at Nogales. And there were the ports of Mazatlán, Topolobampo, and Guaymas, where a fishing boat or Pacific steamer could take you up to California in less than a week.

If it was the place that made the drug trade possible, it was the people that made it work. Most have been lost to history or remembered for other, perhaps more noble enterprises. It was a surprisingly peaceful initial boom. Teamwork was the rule. The industry did not emerge from the world of organized crime, but mapped over existing links of comradeship and commerce. Most of the novice narcos were friends first and drug traffickers a distant second. Their backgrounds were in farming, trade, or the import-export businesses. Conflict and murder were extremely rare.

As elsewhere in Mexico, the people who first brought the business to the Golden Triangle were the Chinese. Thousands of Chinese laborers arrived in Sinaloa, Durango, and Chihuahua during the first two decades of the twentieth century. But, just as in Sonora, the Great Depression brought mass expulsions and spelled the end of this initial business.

The revival of the region's narcotics business occurred in 1936, around four years after the expulsions. And it was cooperation that generated the surge. To understand how, it is necessary to focus on one of the region's most rugged and remote municipalities, a place that over the years has become synonymous with the drug trade. It is the birthplace of famous narcos like Rafael Caro Quintero, Ernesto Fonseca Carrillo, and Joaquín "El Chapo" Guzmán Loera. Still today it produces more opium than any other Mexican municipality. It is Badiraguato.

During the colonial period Badiraguato was an isolated Spanish outpost on the edge of the empire. But by the nineteenth century it had grown into a major mining center. It was a boom time. Speculators from Mexico, the United States, and Spain flocked to the region to dig out the rich veins of silver and gold in Badiraguato's forty or so mines. The place was described as "an emporium of wealth and an endless font of work." The municipal center swelled. The winners poured their earnings into decorating the local churches with new bell towers and the statues of saints; the losers spent their Sundays drinking away their sorrows in the cantinas that had sprung up to service the crowds.

Then came the bust. Badiraguato's rich reserves started to dry up. The price for silver and gold dropped. And the Mexican Revolution ended further investment. The Badiraguato of the 1930s was a different place from three decades earlier. The mines had closed, the big investors had left, and the brothels and cantinas had shut their doors.

Most of the inhabitants returned to subsistence agriculture, scratching out enough to feed their children by growing corn, beans, and vegetables. A few owned cattle and pigs or made the local moonshine—lechuguilla—from fermented cactus. And a few still panned for gold in the region's streams. But they were the exception. Visitors were shocked at the poverty and malnutrition of the inhabitants. Most lived in dark, airless one-room shacks with palm roofs and dirt floors.

For some, however, the boom times were about to return. This time it was not about shiny metals but what the locals called "black gold," or opium.

The drivers for this change were two men. It was their friendship and the transfer of knowledge between them that made the place the country's first major producer of narcotics. One was a Chinese immigrant called Lai

Chang Wong, a mysterious and semimythical figure who introduced the technology needed to produce opium in the town. The other was more recognizable. He was the man with the connections and the cash—Badiraguato's political strongman and ur-narco, Melesio Cuen Cázarez. Using a mix of official documents, local history pamphlets, and oral testimony, it is possible to assemble their story.

According to locals Lai Chang Wong was "a healer by trade, an adventurer at heart, and a lover until damnation." Born in Canton in the late 1880s, he was forced to leave the country after getting his uncle's wife pregnant. First he arrived in San Francisco, where he trained as a healer. Then, with the outbreak of the Mexican Revolution, he moved south, finding work as a doctor in the army. After catching a bullet in the leg, he moved to just outside Culiacán, where he converted to Christianity and took the name "José Amarillas."

He came to Badiraguato in 1927. Here he set up a small medical consultancy and won over a local girl by courting her Sinaloa-style—on horseback, drum in one hand, tequila in the other, musicians in the background playing his favorite song. He was an exceptional healer. He prescribed effective medicines often imported from the United States. He was a careful surgeon, who would suck out bullets rather than dig into the flesh. But his real talent was dealing with pain. For this he used the opium gum that he collected from the poppies behind his house and cooked up into a soluble paste. He used it as a salve on ulcers, hernias, and even deeper wounds. Those who remembered Amarillas did so with fondness as a "great healer who never charged the poor."

Perhaps no one remembered Amarillas more fondly (or at least more gratefully) than the person who first tried to commercialize his opium technique—his neighbor, Melesio Cuen. Cuen lived a few doors from Amarillas, and they appear side by side on the 1930 census. Though Cuen was about ten years younger than Amarillas, they were clearly friendly. Cuen was godparent to at least one of Amarillas's kids. In rural Mexico such a pledge symbolized a close bond.

Cuen was Badiraguato's political strongman, or *cacique*. The term referred to any rural boss whose charisma, wealth, and contacts made him the de facto leader of a community. Cuen encapsulated all three traits. He had friends in high places, from the big lowland landholders through the revolutionary generals in the governor's palace to the bureaucrats in Mexico City. Such links brought power. He was mayor on three occasions and local deputy once. For most of the 1930s and 1940s he appointed all the local political posts, from the regional prosecutor and the cops down to the person who recorded births and deaths.

He was also rich—a rural entrepreneur who owned shares in the town's two surviving mines and half the property in the town center. He was a showy businessman and loved impressing locals with new modern gadgets. Locals were amazed when he brought the first mechanical tortilla maker and the first cinema to town. Most important, he was well liked by the other townsfolk. Down-to-earth and approachable, he "didn't gauge or exploit," but would lend farmers money at zero interest.

But what really solidified his popularity was his work as a healer and pharmacist. He honed his skills during the Revolution, when he used to patch up Badiraguato's rebels. After the conflict he returned home and established his own consultancy at the back of his shop. Like his neighbor Amarillas, he was a careful and generous practitioner. "With or without money Don Melesio attended a sick person and gave him the right medicine." If he didn't, he also ran a carpentry business, where he could fit the corpse with a coffin.

Two healers in such close proximity might seem strange. But amateur doctors were important in rural Mexico. They ran the full gamut from herbalists and witch doctors through medicine salesmen with pharmacy degrees to unqualified doctors with two or three years of university. The Golden Triangle, in particular, was full of them. Many had been attracted by the money (and the appalling safety record) of the region's mines. Though the mines declined, the healers stayed on.

Sometime around 1936, Cuen and Amarillas's common interests began to bear fruit. The cacique started to combine the Chinese healer's techniques, his own knowledge of medicine and pharmaceuticals, and his political influence. Together they created Badiraguato's first bona fide opium ring.

A Mexican health inspector who braved the journey into the mountains two years later described how the new industry worked. Cuen, he claimed, was mayor at the time. He had surrounded himself with a small group of investors, including politicians, policemen, and merchants. Together they financed the planting of poppies in the well-watered valleys of the municipality. The investors fronted the peasants the seeds, trained them in how to harvest the opium gum, and then paid them a set price per kilo for the dry paste. The industry was so open that many inhabitants of the small village of Santiago de los Caballeros were actually planting the crops outside their front doors and in the main square.

A wannabe local politician also visited Cuen's house in Badiraguato a few years later. He remembered the house was the biggest in the town, with huge porches on which the men would sit, drink, and talk politics. When the politician went to bed, he began to smell a strong, penetrating odor. He got up, wandered over to an outhouse and stumbled upon dozens of milk churns covered with planks. On lifting up one of the planks, he gazed into a gloopy and pungent mixture of freshly harvested gum. He asked Cuen's wife about the smell the next day. She apologized but seemed unconcerned. They had brought the opium to the house because a middle-man was about to buy up the crop.

As global supply fell, the highland opium business expanded, riding the wartime demand for illicit opiates. As early as 1940, one undercover U.S. Customs officer was being offered 300 kilos of raw opium in the center of Culiacán at a discount price. Four years later, as Peña and the Mexican inspectors found, poppy growing had moved out from Badiraguato to cover ten municipalities in three states.

As it grew, the trade also started to develop a distinct division of labor. The names on the rap sheets would change, but the shape would stay the same. In fact—give or take some minor changes—the same hierarchy of producers, intermediaries, and wholesalers still structures the Golden Triangle's drug trade today.

At the bottom of the hierarchy were the peasants. They were called *gomeros* (from the Spanish *goma*, or gum) and were in charge of sowing the poppy seeds around November in time for the torrential rains. They were required to tend to the plants, weed them, water them, and strip out those that were not needed. Around March, after the petals had fallen from the flowers and all that remained was the dry seedpod, the *gomeros* harvested the gum.

Poppy growing in the highlands was a family job. Men tilled the earth and sowed the seeds. Women and children took care of the fields, pulled out the weeds, and collected the gum. It was part of their everyday chores. The local newspaper, which sent a reporter up to the highlands in 1947, reported that the opium trade was a bonanza for the "working class, especially the women who have been employed to collect gum as they used to be employed to pick tomatoes."

The newspaper captured one of the key elements of the early trade. There was no stigma and scarcely any threat of danger attached to it. In the 1940s, it *was* still treated like picking tomatoes. Many of the peasants who were handed seeds or instructed how to extract the sap had little idea what they were doing, and perhaps no idea that it was illegal.

In fact, opium growing was so socially acceptable it could lead to some darkly comic encounters. In July 1946, Paulino Mendívil Salomón, a laborer from the Chihuahua highlands, wandered into the police station in Culiacán. He was angry and was there to make a complaint. He had come down to the city to sell 10 kilos of raw opium that his friend had harvested. But as he was about to make the deal, he was accosted by a cop. The cop waved a pistol at him, grabbed the bag of gum and ran off. After Mendívil finished his statement, he was surprised that the police arrested him. His crime: being, by his own admission, a drug trafficker. It was a felony that up to that point he didn't know existed.

Whatever their attitudes to the trade, what the farmers *did* know was that it was profitable. Most peasants could spare half a hectare of land to grow the crop. A full hectare of poppies produced around 15 kilos of gum. Prices per kilo varied: 100 pesos if you were under contract and needed to sell it back to the intermediary who had given you the seeds, the blades, and the instructions; 300 pesos if you sold it on the rural open market; 500 pesos if you risked going into the city and selling it to the major wholesalers. All this meant that if you were one of the poorest peasants, with a scrap of land and a contract with a local boss, the crop could still make you 750 pesos a year.

Seven hundred fifty pesos might not have seemed very much, but the bar was low. The average wage for a highland laborer was less than a peso a day. And up in the mountains, that kind of money could go a long way. It could buy you a plot of land, a horse, or a couple of oxen. Or it could pay for one hell of a party. In 1947 a Mexican spy decided to go up into the high-lands to investigate the opium industry. What he found surprised him. Gone were the empty streets and the air of decay. Even in the small villages there were overflowing cantinas, brothels, gambling dens, and jerry-built cockfighting rings. By 11 A.M. men zigzagged across the street, bottles of lechuguilla in hand. It was boom time again.

*By the 1940s some Sinaloa growers had built makeshift irrigation networks to water their poppies.*

Above the peasants were the intermediaries. The intermediaries were in charge of handing out the seeds, paying for the collected gum, and bring-ing it to the cities and transport networks to the west of the mountains. In the early years of the trade they also played the role of propagandists who would travel the Sierra Madre to teach old friends and new contacts how to grow and harvest the crop.

The first intermediaries worked for Melesio Cuen. Their names dot the early spy reports. Fermín Fernández, Fidel Carrillo, Ignacio Landell, Gil Caro, Rafael Fonseca. There is a reason their names sound familiar. Many were the fathers and uncles of the generation of narcotraficantes that came to prominence three decades later. Fermín Fernández was the uncle of Eduardo "Lalo" Fernández Juárez, who would go on to perfect the making of Mexican brown heroin. Rafael Fonseca was the father of Ernesto "Don Neto" Fonseca Carrillo, international heroin smuggler and an integral member of the Guadalajara cartel. Fidel Carrillo was Don Neto's uncle.

But those days were yet to come. In the early 1940s they had other things in common. Most grew up together in the small mining town of Santiago de los Caballeros just outside Badiraguato. These were not young men; most were in their forties and fifties. Many were former miners who had shared the experience of trying to eke out a living after the big quarries had shut down. But what gave them a unity, a knack for cooperation and an esprit de corps was that they had all served in the local revolutionary battalion, the Carabineros de Santiago.

The Carabineros numbered around a hundred revolutionaries who had taken up arms against the dictatorship in 1911. Tough, independent mountain men, they knew the hidden paths and shaded valleys of the Sierra. They were famous sharpshooters who—the stories said—could kill two rabbits with a single shot. During the Revolution, they became a de facto special forces unit, helping commanders capture lowland cities and tracking their enemies into the wilds of highland Chihuahua.

Such endeavors made them legends. Their skills and bravery were celebrated in campfire songs. The most popular, "El Corrido de Valente Quintero," told the story of two former Carabineros who shot each other in a duel as the sun rose over a boozy dance in a tiny hillside village in 1922. The song told a true story and captured the brutal infighting that followed the Revolution as well as the bloody-minded machismo of its soldiers. It would become a model for the narcocorridos of the following decades that romanticized similar tales of squabbling friends and heroic, if pointless, deaths.

If the Carabineros were the highest-profile intermediaries, they were joined by another group—the merchants. These had much in common with the former revolutionaries. They were adventurers and smugglers who had often got their break as muleteers ferrying goods away from the taxman's watchful eyes. They knew the secret paths that led up to the isolated hamlets and down to the cities. And as the taxman sometimes caught them, they had the political contacts needed to negotiate a deal. They also had two things the Carabineros lacked, at least initially: ready cash to front the farmers and pay off the authorities, and mules to take the dried gum down from the highlands to the roads and railways below.

The most successful by some distance was Alejo Castro. Like the Carabineros, Castro was there from the beginning and is mentioned as one of Cuen's associates. He owned a shop in the small but fertile valley of El Rincón de los Monzón, about 20 kilometers from Badiraguato center. Here he would buy up local farmers' crops and sell them valuable imports like booze, meat, and soap.

During the early 1940s he used his standing to front money for opium growers and to collect the gum. He was—according to one accusation—"the principal dealer" in the town. And around 1945 he tried to scale the ladder. He moved to Culiacán and set himself up as an opium wholesaler. He bought two plots of land—one north of the city in a small riverside village and another on the road to Badiraguato. He planted them with poppies and then contracted peasants to harvest the gum. Many were from the hamlets around his hometown. He knew they were good workers because he'd used them before to harvest legal crops.

The move pushed him into the big league. He combined his crops with those collected by the Carabineros de Santiago. He employed a team of smugglers to carry small packages of gum by train up to the border cities of Tijuana and Mexicali. He received the payments in money orders sent by telegraph and deposited the money in his bulging account in the Banco de Culiacán. According to the local prosecutor, he was the "Al Capone" of Sinaloa, an overnight millionaire who flashed his cash on properties and parties and bribing the local police.

Castro brings us to the highest level of the Golden Triangle's drug trade—the wholesalers. It also brings us down the mountains to the lush lowlands of Sinaloa state. Lowland Sinaloa was very different from the impenetrable mountains to the east. A thin, flat coastal plain, it was the breadbasket of northern Mexico. Covered by thick fertile topsoil and irrigated by eleven rivers, it was a farmer's dream. A handful of big estates vied for control of the land with dozens of smaller, community-owned farms created by the Revolution. Both groups produced tomatoes, sugar, chickpeas, and wheat for the national and international markets. There was also the state capital, Culiacán, and the two coastal cities of Los Mochis and Mazatlán.

Over the years, Culiacán, like Badiraguato, would become synonymous with narcotics. But in the 1940s it was a modest city of around 20,000 people. Markets and places of worship remained its focal points; it still obeyed the rhythm of the agricultural cycle and the Catholic Church; entertainment was limited to an evening stroll around the city square, a grainy film at one of the city's two cinemas, or, if you were rich enough, a game of tennis at the handful of snobby country clubs.

It was in Culiacán that the opium was packaged, processed, and sent north. Different needs generated a different class of drug trafficker. And though Castro made the move from intermediary to big buyer, most early wholesalers were a distinct type from the mountain growers and collectors. If not elites, they were well-traveled city men, with links to the smuggling points and markets of the north rather than the Sierra's peasant communities. It was their job to buy the gum in bulk from the rural intermediaries and find a way to move it to buyers on the border or, if possible, in the United States.

In the early years there were dozens of these wholesalers. Risks were low and so were entry fees. Anyone with a bit of money and bravado could find a Sierra peasant, buy up some gum, and ship it up to the border. Businessmen, farmers, and professionals flitted in and out of the trade from year to year. There were occasionally opportunistic robberies, but in general there was plenty of business to go around.

Most important among this mass of chancers, opportunists, and curious one-offers was the secretive figure of Roberto Domínguez Macías. Domínguez was an enigma. No one even knew his real name. Between 1943, when he appeared on the FBN radar, and 1950, when he promptly disappeared, the Americans variously called him Manuel Macías, José Domínguez Macías, Roberto Macías, and Roberto Domínguez Macías. Admittedly, they were not very good with names. They also called him Onesimo Rivera (impossible because the real Rivera was in jail, a foot taller, and based in Tijuana) and falsely claimed that he was the nephew of the Sinaloa governor.

But the mystery surrounding Domínguez was not just the Americans' fault. Since arriving in Culiacán, Domínguez had kept his cards close to his chest. A New York businessman who met him at the end of the decade described him as forty-five years old, of average height and weight. He dressed smartly and spoke English well. He said that he attended school in Los Angeles and hinted that his father had been killed in a gang altercation. He also went everywhere with two bodyguards, who would check the customers before he entered a restaurant or bar. But these were the only suggestions of anything untoward. Domínguez was never seen with traffickers or openly mentioned narcotics. He presented himself to the New Yorker as a hotelier who wanted to get into the shrimp-fishing business.

We know for sure that Domínguez first arrived in Culiacán in 1941, but not from where he came. It could have been from Los Angeles; it could have been from Guaymas (where his birth certificate claimed); it could have been from Ensenada (where his rap sheet stated); or it could have been from the border town of San Ysidro (where it was rumored he once lived).

Just like Cuen, his break in the drug business came with contact with the remaining members of the Chinese community. This time it was the Leys, a family of wealthy opium merchants. The Leys owned a shop (the future Casa Ley supermarket chain) and grew a few poppies in a small village just outside Culiacán. According to the FBN, Domínguez first worked for the Leys as a mule, transporting cans of smoking opium to Mexicali for distribution. This may be true. Domínguez spoke English, probably came from the border, and was rumored to have been a smuggler before he was a wholesaler. But one of the Ley brothers claimed that he and Domínguez were partners from the start. Domínguez had the money and owned the land; the Leys brought the tech, grew the poppies, and harvested the gum.

Whatever the origin story, Domínguez clearly realized that the business was a profitable affair, one for which he was allegedly willing to kill. According to the FBN, as he moved up the ladder he got to know some serious San Francisco smugglers. Domínguez was not intimidated. He managed to lure one of these buyers down to the port of Topolobampo just outside Los Mochis, where he murdered him and stole 5 million pesos.

It seems unlikely that any self-respecting mobster would have ventured unprotected to Mexico carrying over a million dollars in foreign currency. But whatever the provenance of his wealth, a newly moneyed Domínguez now peppered U.S. reports. As early as 1943, he was described as the "principal purchaser" in what was already a "soundly established business." Though he lived in an upscale house in Culiacán, he did most of his buying around the station at Guamúchil. He then shipped the opium north by train, hidden in sesame cakes, or preferably, to disguise the smell, guano. The scheme involved serious quantities; around 600 kilos according to one report.

By 1946, the guano cover had gone and Domínguez was now hiding the product under crates of tomatoes, which he sent by truck up to Nogales. Here he had a contact in the tomato wholesaling business who helped him move the drugs into the United States. The scale had increased. A visiting journalist claimed that he was now famous in the region as "the only trafficker who bought drugs by the ton." In just two years, he had transported a total of 5 tons to the United States. If true, it would have been worth over $8 million.

The following year he aimed even higher, attempting to fund the region's first large-scale heroin ring. He brought together the intermediaries from Badiraguato as well as some from further afield in Durango and Chihuahua. It was their job to round up the year's opium harvest and deliver it to a laboratory in Culiacán. Here he had a chemist who was going to convert the opium to heroin. He also assembled a group of Tijuana smugglers who were going to transport the finished product over the border. It is not clear whether the operation ever took off. But discussion itself indicates yet again that it was cooperation, not conflict, that characterized the early trade.

Opium made Domínguez a very rich man. By the mid-1940s he was a millionaire. He owned four hotels in Culiacán, including the upscale Hotel El Mayo. Being known as an opium trafficker seemed to have no effect on his social standing. Sudden wealth was immediate social lubricant. Local elites lent him money at generous rates; they joined him in glitzy tourism projects; and they toasted him at fancy balls. Domínguez—the former mule, the mysterious border smuggler, the opium planter, the faux guano merchant with seven names—was now Culiacán high society.

Domínguez's tale was unusual. Few such outsiders would make their mark on the Golden Triangle's drug trade until the arrival of the hippies in the 1960s. But his story highlights a change in the region's 1940s business—the beginnings of heroin production. It also introduces a new position in the narcotics hierarchy—the chemist.

For the first few years of Mexico's resurgent opium trade, it was an extractive industry. The Mexicans produced the raw materials; the Americans processed them into the finished product. It was an unequal partnership. Morphine and heroin could be sold for around fifty times as much as the same quantity of raw opium. Though in relative terms they were raking in quantities of cash, the Mexicans were only making a tiny percentage of what the Americans earned.

Then around 1943 the dynamics of the industry began to change. Up at the border, Customs officers started to catch a handful of drug mules carrying heroin, not opium. Admittedly, it was a strange type of heroin. It was black or brown rather than white, sludgy rather than powdered. But after sending it off for lab reports, their suspicions were confirmed. It was heroin, albeit a less refined type than that produced in Europe. It was what became known as "Mexican brown."

At first, the Americans thought the American Mafia had produced the product. A handful of mobsters—connected to the California kingpin Bugsy Siegel—had moved down to Mexico in the early 1940s. They had hooked up with corrupt sanitary police and started to buy up some of the country's opium harvest. Yet Mafia influence on the Mexican trade was marginal and short-term. Like other foreign gangs, they lacked traditional links to economic and political elites.

"Mexico brown" was a homegrown product.

Drug traffickers are often at the forefront of economic changes. The combination of high risks and rewards often push them into pioneering new and profitable setups. And, intentionally or not, the shift from producing the raw materials to manufacturing the finished product reflected the drift of the Mexican economy during the 1940s. The government had taken advantage of U.S. wartime production to impose protectionist tariffs on imported goods and initiate a big campaign for consumers to "buy Mexican." The policy (called Import Substitution Industrialization, or ISI)

was a big success. It allowed factories to flourish and provided the founda-
tion for over two decades of industrial growth. Mexico was a mid-twentieth-
century China. A period of construction, urbanization, and stability, the
1940s and 1950s became known as the country's Golden Age.

Heroin "made in Mexico" was of its time. It was the Golden Triangle's
contribution to the Golden Age.

The story of how Mexican brown started to be produced was yet
another tale of knowledge transfer. This time it was between a junior member of the highland opium growers and an esteemed representative of the
Culiacán elite. To make heroin you need chemicals: calcium oxide to refine
the raw opium; ammonium chloride to extract the basic morphine; acetic
anhydride and sodium carbonate to transform the morphine into heroin.
To do this you also need some rough-and-ready laboratory equipment,
including tubs, barrels, pH strips, and evaporators. Perhaps most important, you need knowledge—of the quantities of chemicals needed, of when
to add one to the other, and when and how to filter them out.

In 1940s Mexico, only a handful of people possessed this combination
of skills and goods. One of those that did was Sinaloa's first female graduate and Culiacán's leading pharmacist, Veneranda Bátiz Paredes. Bátiz
didn't fit the traditional narco profile. She was local aristocracy. She was
born into a prestigious landowning family in 1889. Her father owned huge
properties just outside the state capital; her aunt was the governor's wife.
Sr. Bátiz was a relatively farsighted man and wanted his daughters to be as
educated as his sons. So he sent Veneranda to the local university where
she graduated with a degree in chemistry on the eve of the Revolution in
1910.

Such was the Bátiz wealth, the Revolution barely made a dent in it. The
family was still powerful a decade later. Bátiz herself married the son of a
wealthy merchant and also taught at the university before setting up her
own business—a pharmacy.

The pharmacy was called the Botica del Refugio. It was located in the
center of Culiacán on a street it shared with four other pharmacies. Bátiz's
shop, however, was first among equals. Batiz was not only a pharmacist; she
was a wholesaler. She used her family money to buy medicines and chemicals in bulk over the U.S. border in Nogales. She then sold them to the

state's smaller operations. The business made the Botica del Refugio an institution. By the end of the 1940s it had air conditioning, U.S.-style soda machines, and an army of traveling salesmen, each kitted out in a Botica del Refugio uniform.

But the Botica del Refugio's fame was not only the product of business savvy. Sometime in late 1944, the back room of the Botica del Refugio, where Bátiz divvied up the chemicals and mixed the medicines, became Culiacán's first heroin laboratory.

The other instigator, somewhat inevitably, came from Badiraguato. His name was Eduardo Fernández Juárez, or "Lalo" for short. He, like Bátiz, had a lineage. He was born in Santiago de los Caballeros in 1920. His uncle was Fermín Fernández Salazar—a revolutionary who had commanded the Carabineros during the Revolution. After the fighting ended, Fermín moved into mining and then politics, acting as mayor of Badiraguato on three occasions. Like many of his former comrades, he also started to work as an opium intermediary.

When Lalo Fernández hit twelve, the age at which many of his fellow villagers were starting to work the fields or the mines, his family sent him to Culiacán. Here he moved in with an uncle and aunt who were teachers. They found him a job as a janitor at the city's vocational secondary school. The job was fine for a while. But the salary was low and the job boring. At this point Fernández's uncle secured him a job in Veneranda Bátiz pharmacy.

For the next decade he moved up the Botica's pay scale. First he worked as an assistant, helping to clean the shop and fetch medicines for the counter staff. Then he worked behind the counter. Then sometime in the early 1940s he was placed in charge of supplying the pharmacy with the necessary chemicals. The new role was a real step up. He was entrusted with traveling to Nogales and purchasing everything on his boss's shopping list. At this point, he also started to purchase the chemicals necessary to transform opium into the brown heroin that would become the Golden Triangle's standard. And he started to use the Botica's backroom as his lab.

To what extent this was Fernández's idea, Veneranda Bátiz's, or even Fernández's uncle's, we shall never know. Much of the initiative probably came from Lalo Fernández. We shall meet him again and again over the next four decades. He was twenty-four by this time and already had links in the highland domain of peasant opium producers, the Culiacán world of pharmaceutical laboratories, and the border trade in chemicals. Such contacts would serve him well. He certainly had the intelligence and drive. He would go on to be one of Mexico's most successful drug traffickers. Though he never made the headlines, like the really successful drug traffickers, he never meant to. He became the state government's go-to narco, entrusted with negotiating deals on behalf of his fellow traffickers. He ruled Culiacán's drug-producing barrio of Tierra Blanca as the benevolent cacique. He also lived out the drug trafficker's dream and never saw the inside of a jail cell. He died quietly in his sleep.

But it also seems likely that his boss, Veneranda Bátiz, was involved as well. Certainly, she came from another class; she was part of the state's fast set. But in 1940s Sinaloa, the drug business did not carry the stigma that it does today. She also had the technical know-how and the equipment. And it seems extremely unlikely that she wouldn't have known Lalo Fernández's background when she employed him. Or that she wouldn't have noticed the pungent smell of ammonia that heroin production entailed.

Her involvement would certainly explain her business's extraordinary wealth. In 1949 the government took estimates of the worth of every business in the state. The Botica del Refugio was valued at 600,000 pesos. This was over twenty times the amount of the next biggest pharmacy. And this was only the beginning of the elite's complicity in the emergent trade.

## Chapter 8

### The Governors and the Gypsy

RODOLFO LOAIZA HAD ALWAYS WANTED THE TOP JOB. BUT TO ARRIVE THERE had been a grind. Eight years earlier he had risked his career by breaking with Sinaloa's wealthy elite; he had fled to Mexico City and politicked his way close to the new left-wing president Lázaro Cárdenas; he had returned to Sinaloa and brokered an alliance with the state's landless peasants and sugar workers; and he had helped them fight a brutal war against local landowners. Hardened to the realpolitik of regional government, he had even ordered his chief gunman to assassinate his main rival. Finally, on December 1, 1940, it seemed like it had all been worth it. He was inaugurated governor of his home state.

But the state he inherited was broke. The treasury was empty. In fact, it was worse than empty. Wages for state employees were months in arrears; and Sinaloa owed thousands of pesos to the federal government.

At this point, Loaiza made a decision. Rather than request more federal loans or pressure the peasants for more taxes, he opted to take over the drug protection racket from the local authorities. The state government—and not the town councils—would now tax traffickers a certain percentage of their earnings in exchange for protecting them from antinarcotics laws. With these returns, he reasoned, he could finally secure funding for schools, infrastructure, and jobs for his political backers.

Loaiza's decision had far-reaching effects. Borderlands governments had been running these protection rackets for years. But the Sinaloa system was more extensive and more complex than those of Baja California or Chihuahua. This was not one shakedown among many. This was the only game in town; it dwarfed the illegal alcohol and prostitution industries. This was not simply charging a handful of wholesalers and a couple of opium dens. Officials taxed every level of the drug business from the growers, to the buyers, to the chemists and the traffickers. They taxed in cash and they taxed in drugs. And they created an entire state-level police force in order to do so. A lot of the money went into private accounts, but at least some was spent on public works.

It would become the model for how local governments dealt with the drug trade for the next thirty years.

Yet, if Loaiza's protection racket was a guide to future wealth, it was also a warning of what was to come. In these early years, violence connected to the drug trade was minimal. Murders were rare; massacres almost unknown. Compared to the killings of the Prohibition-era United States, Mexican drug violence was negligible. Compared to contemporary Mexican conflicts over land reform, religion, or workers rights—which caused the deaths of thousands—it was nothing.

When there was violence, it came not from the rivalries among the traffickers. Instead, it emerged from shifts in the system of political protection. Growing, trafficking, and refining didn't need monopoly control. It needed cooperation. Protecting the trade was another matter. State governors wanted exclusive rights to tax the trade. To secure them, they needed to take out their rivals for the protection racket. And it was the conflicts over the control of the rackets—rather than the trade itself—that caused the violence. Loaiza would find this out the hard way. His decision would cause Sinaloa's first spate of drug-related deaths, including his own.

Before Loaiza became governor, protection of the Sinaloa drug trade was a localized affair. It was organized at the level of the municipality. The mayors of highland towns like Badiraguato decided what percentage of the opium crop growers had to pay. They then sent their enforcers to review the extent of the fields, check the harvest, and collect the required amounts. These enforcers were usually the municipal cops.

The position of municipal policeman or *comisario de policia* was an important role in rural Mexico. On the surface it didn't seem much. It was honorific and often unpaid. And it mainly involved sorting out tiresome arguments over livestock ownership and public drunkenness. But looks were deceptive; and there were also certain upsides. Perhaps most important, you could carry a gun. You could also bend the law to your own choosing. Smuggling, illegal logging, and running the local still were all perks of the job. It was a role, in short, that allowed local toughs to show a bit of community responsibility while also playing the big man and making a bit of cash on the side. In fact, the position was so prestigious that many of the local police were former revolutionaries from the Carabineros de Santiago.

These local cops were key to the expansion of the trade. In the late 1930s they handed out seeds, pushed local farmers to grow the new crop, collected part of it, and planted their own fields. When U.S. agents visited the region, they found that local policemen owned all the largest plantations. And the other farmers claimed that they had all "been encouraged to grow poppies by the local municipal authorities."

The local policemen were also in charge of protection. This meant paying off any outside authorities that sought to interfere in the trade. They were well placed to do so. The Revolution had brought them valuable contacts, especially in the local military.

One government official recounted candidly how this was done. Immediately after the opium harvest, an army lieutenant arrived in Santiago de los Caballeros. He was "young, pale with chubby cheeks and a couple of gold teeth." He was on a mission: he was there to demand his payoff. The local cops met him and agreed on a deal. In the early years of the trade, cash was still relatively scarce, so they decided to make the bribe in kind. Then they called the opium producers down from the hills.

What followed was a formal and surprisingly public business. As the producers arrived, the local notary took down their names and the amounts they handed over: 150 grams from the farmer Tomás Fonseca; 400 grams from the miner Enrique Carbajar; 200 grams from the laborer Juan Salas.

At the end of the day, the lieutenant left. He carried 6.5 kilograms of opium, worth over 3,000 pesos in the city. It amounted to over three times his annual salary. No crops were burned; no one was shot or arrested; the police had done their job. They had protected local opium growers from the federal authorities.

Quite how much of this early protection money went toward local public works, it is difficult to gauge. No doubt a lot went into (and quickly came out of) politicians' pockets. One secret agent reported that town councilors in Badiraguato "were spending money with open hands"; they had all bought new cars that skidded wildly around the slippery, hilltop streets.

But at least some seems to have been directed toward more communal enterprises. Mocorito, the other big opium center together with Badiraguato, saw a rapid rise in its municipal spending during the period. You didn't have to be a forensic accountant to see something was up. In the 1930s the town had struggled to scrabble together the few hundred pesos needed to employ local teachers. By 1942, it was spending 80,000 pesos a year on public services. In that year the mayor built a market, bought a council car, and even had enough spare cash to spend 6,000 pesos on the disconcertingly vague "unexpected costs." But it was the men who brought in the cash who got the big payouts. A quarter of the council budget now went for police salaries.

It was this money that Loaiza was after. He knew the returns from the trade would not be given up easily. And he knew that the takeover of the protection racket might get messy.

So his first move was to establish a new law enforcement agency—the state judicial police. These were the state's new enforcers. They were drawn from the ranks of former revolutionaries, soldiers, paid killers, and the governor's bodyguards. Officially, they were charged with bringing order to the state's wilder mountain regions by a program of mass disarmament. Unofficially, they were Loaiza's point men in his attempt to redirect the opium revenue from the local authorities to the state government.

It was a task that outlived Loaiza. And over the next thirty years state judicial policemen would take over from municipal cops as those in charge of northern Mexico's drug protection rackets. They would become the main intermediaries between state governments and the drug traffickers. They would be placed in charge of collecting percentages of the profits, protecting growers and dealers from outside interference, and prosecuting or, if necessary, murdering those that refused to pay. By the 1960s they would even become major traffickers in their own right.

Loaiza placed his most trusted hitman, Alfonso Leyzaola Salazar, "the Wild Cat," in charge of the new force.

The Wild Cat deserved his name. By the time he took the job, he was already one of the state's most feared gunmen. (This was no minor accomplishment; at the time, one journalist speculated that Sinaloa had three major exports—tomatoes, opium, and killers.) He was a farmer and a former revolutionary. And in the late 1930s he had helped lead Loaiza's supporters against an alliance of landlords and paramilitaries. Loaiza also used him for off-the-books work; in 1938 he was rumored to have killed his boss's main rival for the state governorship.

As the opium harvest came in, Loaiza immediately sent the Wild Cat and the new policemen to the main source of opium—Badiraguato. Here they demanded that all poppy growers stop paying the municipal government. Instead, they were to now pay state officials for permission to grow their crops. The Wild Cat was ruthless and unforgiving. Peasants that refused were shot; their fields were burned.

The move infuriated the local authorities. So they planned revenge. On March 31, 1941, Fidel Carrillo and other local cops set up an ambush on the thin, winding path up to Santiago de los Caballeros. As his assailants fired from the rocky outcrops above the road, the Wild Cat stood little chance. His men fled. A bullet struck the Wild Cat. He managed to crawl to a nearby shack where he bound his wounds. But he was soon discovered. Carrillo and the local policemen executed him on the spot. They then hung him from a tree outside the village. It was a warning to future trespassers. According to popular legend, they even desecrated his corpse by cutting off his testicles.

The killing of the Wild Cat has gone down in local folklore as a stark lesson in what happened if you messed with Badiraguato's mountain gunmen. It also neatly demonstrated the way shifts in political control—not trafficker rivalries—were the principal cause of early drug trade violence.

But in reality, the Wild Cat's gruesome end did little to slow up the governor's takeover of the drug protection racket. The incentives for some kind of cooperation were just too much. Loaiza and the Badiraguato opium traders soon came to an arrangement.

By 1943, farmers were being instructed to pay state policemen a third of the harvested opium either in cash or kind. In return, state policemen agreed to put federal agents and troops off the scent. They guided antinarcotics forces to fields that had already been harvested and skirted the big crops. The system was so generalized that opium prices increased in accordance with the new taxation.

But Loaiza's agreement did not last long. On February 21, 1944, the governor was holding court at the luxurious Belmar Hotel on the Mazatlán seafront. It was the port's famous carnival and the party was in full swing. Men in Stetsons stumbled and cursed, drank and sang. Women in flowing, pleated skirts swung their hips. A sweating brass band blasted out the popular Sinaloa tune, "El Coyotito."

Loiaza and the rest of the state officials were outside on the patio. It was a VIP area, separated from the rest of the guests by a thick satin curtain. (Loaiza's socialist principles did not, it seems, extend to parties.) In one corner a table overflowed with seafood, sweets, champagne and whisky bottles. Loaiza moved to the music, glass in hand. Suddenly, a silver pistol peaked out from between the curtains, pointed at the back of the governor's head, and fired three times. Loaiza was dead by the time he hit the ground.

Chaos followed. The killer and his fellow gunmen fled the scene firing over their shoulders at the pursuing bodyguards. When they came out onto the street, they called for back up. Another dozen men laid down covering fire. Officials rushed to the hotel phone, but the lines had been cut. "They've killed the governor" went up the cry. Women screamed. By the time the shootout ended, another three men lay dead on the road outside. The gunmen got into two cars and fled toward the countryside.

In postrevolutionary Mexico, assassinating a certain level of politician was relatively common. Mayors were often killed; municipal politics were very much the preserve of paid gunmen. But killing state governors was rare. Only two other state governors were murdered in the twenty years following the Revolution. (In comparison, there were also two assassinations of governors in the United States during the first half of the twentieth century.) Loaiza's murder, then, was big news. And over the next two years the search for the perpetrators and the discovery of a motive became a veritable soap opera. It was played out in the press, the countryside, and the hallways of high office.

In theory, finding out why Loaiza was killed should have been easy. One of the fleeing gunmen was easily recognizable; he was already a celebrity. He was Sinaloa's most famous hitman—Rodolfo Valdéz Valdéz, "The Gypsy."

Though he was a professional hitman who mostly lived in the shadows, we do know a bit about the Gypsy. This is not only because he dominated the front pages in the wake of the murder, but also because a Sinaloa journalist wrote a revealing biography of the killer. The book—*La Vida Accidentada y Novelesca de Rodolfo Valdéz el Gitano* (The Eventful and Fantastic Life of Rodolfo Valdéz the Gypsy) came out in 1949. It was published anonymously. Yet such precautions were in vain. Soon afterward the writer was poisoned in a Mazatlán bar. After his death, copies of the book quietly disappeared; to my knowledge, there are none in the libraries of Sinaloa, Mexico City, or the United States.

But I did manage to track down a single copy in a private collection. Couched in a bizarrely (and in the end pointlessly) respectful tone, the work lays bare the terrifying rise to power of Loaiza's killer. Yet it also reveals the disconnect between the drug trade and the general patterns of violence at this time. The Gypsy may have committed his most famous murder on behalf of the local traffickers. But normally he worked for big landowners. And his real specialty—like most hitmen of his era—was murdering radical peasants.

The Gypsy was born in the tiny hamlet of Agua Caliente in the foothills of the Sierra Madre in 1912. Though the village lay only about 30 miles east of the bustling port of Mazatlán, it was a quiet, rural place. Most of the inhabitants were small farmers who, like the Gypsy's parents, scratched out livings from a few acres of valley land. There were, however, a few exceptions. One of these was the Gypsy's aunt—Margarita Valdéz, who was also nicknamed the Gypsy. Margarita was a local legend. A dusky, dark-haired beauty, she never married. Instead, she did the man's work of tilling the fields, weeding the crops, and harvesting the produce on her own. To complete the look, she rode the region on horse-back, a gun by her side and a fat cigar clamped between her teeth. Strong, independent, and with a fearsome temper, it was Margarita who bestowed her nickname—the Gypsy—on her nephew. It was also Margarita who first taught him how to shoot.

By the time the Gypsy had reached his early twenties, such lessons came in useful. In 1934, the year the radical president Lázaro Cárdenas came to power, the Revolution finally arrived in Agua Caliente. Tenant farmers and sugar workers, who had long pleaded for a more equal division of lands, finally saw their requests met. In a series of decrees, the govern-ment split private landholdings among the landless. Many of these private landholdings were large properties—sugar plantations and wheat farms with their own factories, estate shops, and dependent villages. But state planners were never terribly fussy or exact. And many of their targets were smaller homestead farms like that owned by the Gypsy's parents.

*Rodolfo Valdéz Valdéz, aka the Gypsy (right), famed Sinaloa gunman and assassin of Governor Loaiza.*

In a pattern that repeated itself throughout 1930s, land reform ripped the villages around Agua Caliente in two. On the one side were the poor recipients of government largesse. They called themselves "the Comrades." Tough and driven, they were unwilling to return to lives of hat-tipping subservience and abject poverty. On the other side were the former landlords. They were dubbed "Those of the Mountain." Some—like their leader the lumber merchant and entrepreneur Silvano Pérez Ramos—were frockcoated elites. But others—like the Gypsy—were small farmers of bandit heritage.

Class war quickly descended into outright war. Those of the Mountain waged an increasingly vicious guerrilla campaign against what they saw as the theft of their lands and the usurping of their positions. Meanwhile, the Comrades desperately clung to their newfound possessions.

As the Gypsy's biographer wrote, "the southern region of Sinaloa was converted into a vast graveyard." At the height of the conflict the former landlords were killing up to ten peasants a day. At least a thousand died between 1936 and 1941. So common were the shootings that frightened locals even came up with a new word for "to ambush"—*carraquear*, or to make noise like a rattle. Isolated and rural this violence may have been. But it was murder on a scale comparable to the drug wars of the early twenty-first century.

Horrors were frequent. And it was here the Gypsy found his true calling—murder. With a chubby face and a disarmingly cheery smile, he was an unnervingly cold killer. In 1936 he walked into a rural school and blew away the teacher in front of his class. The teacher's crime—singing a revolutionary song. Two years later the Gypsy dressed up as a soldier, rode into the small community of El Quemado, persuaded the inhabitants that he was there to give them the certificates to their new lands, and then shot them dead. By the end of the conflict he was rumored to have as many as 200 murders to his name.

When Loaiza became governor in 1940, he attempted to end the fighting. Initially, he managed to get both sides to sit down and sign an armistice. They promised to lay down their arms and use the courts to administer justice. But the armistice didn't last. Again, the Gypsy was at the center. In September 1941 his men killed twelve peasants on the streets of Mazatlán; soon afterward he gunned down a union leader; then he killed another eight land reformers in his hometown of Agua Caliente. He capped off his spree by shooting a sex worker in the head in a drunken game of William Tell.

After Loaiza's murder, locals speculated on the Gypsy's motives. Most concluded that the assassination was a continuation of the conflict over land. Loaiza was close to former president Cárdenas and had come to power with the backing of the peasant land reformers.

But in the months following the death more concrete theories emerged. The first was that the official candidate for the next state governor— General Pablo Macías Valenzuela—had ordered the hit. He had a motive. He came from a rival political clique. And when the Gypsy was eventually caught in early 1945, he appeared to confirm the theory. In front of the court he declared that Macías had invited him to his office and ordered that he murder the standing governor.

Yet doubts immediately arose. Was the Gypsy's testimony reliable? Would Macías really murder his predecessor simply to halt a rumored attempt to lever him from power? Why did former president Cárdenas have a private interview with the Gypsy the day before his court appearance? Was he trying to guide the witness and place the blame on this rival political clique? Finally, despite the Gypsy's testimony, Macías was never charged. He went on to become the governor of Sinaloa.

The next theory was linked to the local landowners. It was well known that Loaiza had sent the Wild Cat to kill a rival candidate for governor in 1938. The rival candidate was a former mayor of Mazatlán and an ally of Those of the Mountain. Locals now claimed that Those of the Mountain had clubbed together and paid the Gypsy to revenge their friend's death. In some ways the story added up. The Gypsy worked for Those of the Mountain. But why would they wait a whole six years for retribution? Surely it didn't take that long to drum up the Gypsy's fee?

It was only the final theory that concerned drugs or, more accurately, a conflict over the drug protection racket. Mazatlán's newspapers claimed that traffickers had paid Loaiza 200,000 pesos to lead federal inspectors away from their plantations. Loaiza had taken the money but refused to abide by the deal. In fact, he had helped federal inspectors track down a host of ostensibly protected poppy fields. The paper also asserted that, the day Loaiza was murdered, a group of hitmen had raided the governor's house and taken back the bribe.

Again there were holes in this story. Who were these mysterious traffickers? Were they the Badiraguato merchants who had started to wholesale the drugs? Were they the few remaining Chinese dealers, as one tabloid claimed? If they were, why did they employ the Gypsy, an unhinged peasant-killer from a village far to the south of the opium regions? Surely they had their own gunmen?

But there were also some indications that the drug protection racket theory was real. Loaiza did seem to be increasing the pressure on certain drug traffickers. Opium eradications had grown. And in 1943 he even had Roberto Domínguez Macías and one of his Chinese associates arrested. Furthermore, the Gypsy did have some links to the traffickers, albeit indirectly. The head of Those of the Mountain, the lumber merchant Silvano Pérez Ramos, was long suspected of using his fleet of fishing boats to take opium north from Mazatlán to the California coast. Maybe he had recommended the Gypsy to the traffickers?

Perhaps most damning, however, was the shape of the new arrangement between Loaiza's successor and the local traffickers. Loaiza had always struggled to get Sinaloa's opium producers to pay for protection. His efforts had got the Wild Cat killed. But the next governor, General Pablo Macías Valenzuela, established a much smoother system of state support. If the opium traffickers had not directly paid to have Loaiza killed, they were the beneficiaries of a very lucky break.

The new alliance was not only based on mutual profits but also—like so much of the drug business—personal relations. Macías was much closer to the traffickers than Loaiza. He had fought side by side with the Carabineros. And to cement relations, he put the son of another local revolutionary in charge of his state judicial police. This man, Francisco de la Rocha, controlled the everyday running of the protection racket. To check the traffickers were not being ripped off, the son of the wholesaler Alejo Castro was also appointed Francisco's second-in-command.

De la Rocha's task was twofold. He would send his deputies to collect the payments from the growers and intermediaries. Payment could be in cash or in kind. This part of the job was a family business. One brother ran the Mazatlán police; another brother headed the police just over the border in Durango, and his cousin managed the Badiraguato cops.

In return, it was Francisco de la Rocha's job to lead the annual opium eradication campaign away from protected fields. Every year he would intercept the federal agents when they arrived at the base of the Sierra Madre in Culiacán. Every year he would offer to guide the agents into the opium-growing regions to the east. And every year, without any other alternatives, the agents would agree. They would go up into the mountains, stay there for a few weeks, pull up a few scattered fields, and send increasingly downbeat reports to the federal government. Between 1944 and 1947 the number of hectares of opium poppies eradicated in Sinaloa fell from 200 to barely 30.

Even Mexican agents sent from the capital eventually caught on. "Over time I found De la Rocha's behavior more and more suspicious." When the police chief refused to allow him to inspect a recently discovered heroin lab, he started to dig deeper. Informants eventually handed him a list of all the intermediaries who paid De la Rocha. It was a Who's Who of Badiraguato's major traffickers—Alejo Castro—the wannabe wholesaler, Fidel Carrillo—the man who had killed the Wild Cat, and Miguel Urias Uriarte, the owner of the heroin lab.

Macías's protection racket was open and obvious. He regularly met traffickers in public and was openly hostile to overenthusiastic counter-narcotics agents. By 1947 there were even rumors that he had received so many bribes in kind, he was effectively Sinaloa's biggest dealer. In the same year an intrepid journalist even tried to catch Macías in a sting. He approached Macías's private secretary, explained that he was short of cash, and asked to buy some of the governor's opium. To his surprise, the secretary readily agreed. He offered the journalist 50 kilos of opium and 2 kilos of heroin.

The journalist's exposé was ultimately spiked; his editor feared political repercussions. But, Macías was frequently denounced in the press in more general terms. Such articles contained unsourced allegations that linked Macías with the trade. "Government Agents Are Compiling Evidence

Against the Governor-Trafficker," ran one. "Intimate Collaborators of Macías Sell Opium" ran another.

Yet Macías survived. No doubt international politics played a role. The Mexican president, Miguel Alemán Valdés (1946–1952) was unwilling to confront the governor. To do so would have been to accede to U.S. allegations about Mexican corruption.

But it wasn't all about saving face. From Mexico's perspective, Macías's system worked. In fact, it would provide the model for future relations between state authorities and drug traffickers not only in Sinaloa, but also in many other Mexican states. Sale of narcotics was firmly prohibited; Sinaloa's expanding heroin production never generated a domestic market. And in the short term, outbreaks of violence subsided. The kind of killings that had wracked Sinaloa politics disappeared. More general homicide rates also dropped. What one might describe as the potential social cost of the drug trade dried up.

At the same time, the state budget boomed. Macías completed what Loaiza had started.

A lot of the bribes still went into the state coffers. In fact, it was embedded in the very system. State cops were expected to hand their collections to state tax collectors. And the gains were impressive. From 1944 to 1947 the Sinaloa treasury went from over 11 million pesos in the red to 1.3 million pesos in the black. In the same period the state administration built 130 rural schools, 10 playgrounds, 2 teacher-training colleges, and 2 art schools. In contrast, other state governments faced tax riots, bankruptcy, and declining public services. In late 1947, one Sinaloa official rather brazenly laid out the deal in a confession to a Mexican secret agent. "Do you think that all those new buildings were built with tomatoes? No, my friend, they are made of pure opium."

Even for Mexico's federal government, such achievements trumped the potential public fallout from the racket. Mexican presidents were always looking for ways to grow public services while keeping taxes low. Taking a percentage of the drug profits seemed like a perfect solution. Furthermore, drug earnings were almost entirely in dollars. They paid off Mexico's balance-of-payments deficit, and they propped up the country's falling currency.

In fact, in a private chat with Sinaloa's attorney general, President Alemán seemed to admit as much. Faced with Macías's rather flagrant protection racket, he smiled and shrugged—"at least it brings in a load of foreign currency."

It was an idea that was clearly on President Alemán's mind.

## Chapter 9

## The Cadillac Bust

June 25, 1946, was a slow day at the Nuevo Laredo crossing. By Tuesday even the most earnest Saturday revelers had sloped home. Traffic over the Río Bravo bridge was limited to a handful of rickety produce lorries and a slow stream of poor knickknack sellers. The approaching car looked out of place. Nuevo Laredo's most famous nightspot might have been called the Cadillac Bar, but the name was more aspiration than observation. The man driving the Cadillac looked distinctly uncomfortable as he approached the U.S. Customs checkpoint. His eyes darted around and his hands tapped nervously on the steering wheel.

The car—the two agents decided—was worth a check. They stopped the driver, motioned him out, and started to search. Their instincts had been correct. They knocked the door cavities. They sounded hollow. The agents ripped back the covering. Inside were sixty-three tins of smoking opium. It was Laredo's biggest bust that year.

But it got even better. Lucky find turned diplomatic incident. The driver was not just any old mule; he was Francisco Gurrola, a Mexican immigration agent from the sleepy border town of Naco. And he was connected. His uncle, Juan Ramón Gurrola, was a prestigious Mexico City policeman. Even the car had a backstory. Gurrola had borrowed it from a man named Carlos I. Serrano, then a candidate for the Mexican Senate. More importantly, though, Serrano was also the campaign finance chief and right-hand man of the Mexican president, Miguel Alemán Valdés.

The Cadillac bust was the first sign that the profits from the drug trade were starting to attract those at the top of Mexico's political system.

Miguel Alemán Valdés was Mexico's first civilian president since the Revolution. He was born in the sweltering lowland town of Sayula in the state of Veracruz in 1900. Unlike his predecessors, he was no soldier (though it helped that his father was a famous revolutionary). Instead, he used his contacts, administrative skills, and the rather fortunate (some whispered "planned") deaths of those in front of him. He inherited the Veracruz governorship when the governor-elect was assassinated in 1936. And he secured the presidential nomination after the president's brother and preferred candidate, Maximino Ávila Camacho, died of a youthful heart attack.

Alemán might have been lucky. But he was also one of Mexico's first media-age politicians. He knew how to harness the growing power of newspapers, radio, and even TV. Sharply dressed, with swept-back hair, a neat moustache, and a perpetual grin, he was known as "Mr. Colgate." He represented the smiling face of a more modern, more urban Mexico.

Alemán was also a slick political operator. As minister of the interior, he had studied the competing interest groups that composed Mexico's political panorama. He knew which to ally with, which to pay off, and which to confront. Such skills came in handy. Having harnessed the workers and peasants to vote for his candidacy, he now turned on the Revolution's left-wing supporters. It was, in effect, a counterrevolution. Progressive governors were sacked, land grants were scaled back and independent unions were cowed and taken over. The governing party was transformed into a more effective electoral machine. And he changed its name to capture Mexico's messy blend of social reform and realpolitik. The party was now called the Institutional Revolutionary Party, or PRI. It would dominate the country's elections for the next fifty years.

Central to Alemán's rule were the two *C's*—corruption and coercion. Official graft, of course, was nothing new. His predecessor's dead brother— the little-lamented Maximino Ávila Camacho—had a penchant for bribes that was legendary. For good reason, he was nicknamed "Mr. 15 Percent." But during the first years of Alemán's presidency, corruption reached new levels. It became "grand corruption." It was practiced by those at the apex of power and involved the kind of malpractice and wholesale larceny that endangered the very running of the state.

The practitioners of this corruption were the group of young lawyers, officials, and hangers-on that came to power with Alemán. They were known as his "amigos." Some held official positions. The mayor of Mexico City was a loyal Veracruz ally; the head of the treasury an old university pal. Others simply orbited their friend's newfound power. (Enrique Parra Hernández, for example, was a law-school buddy. Described as "the minis-ter without a budget," he was in charge of Alemán's personal finances and, so rumor had it, his amorous affairs. "[He] steals from the people/Taking whores to the chief/Who after fucking/Thanks them and protects them," went one popular song.)

Whatever their roles, the amigos used their proximity to the president to line their own pockets. Schemes varied. They exploited the government's commercial agreements to sell their own products; they bought up lands and sold them back to the administration at massive markups; and they got inflated official contracts to build public buildings that were never built.

The most important of these amigos was Carlos I. Serrano. Serrano was the other side of the new PRI state. He was the shade to Alemán's sun, the clenched fist to Alemán's beaming exterior. Few people would say it to his face, but he was what one union leader termed "a monster." Even U.S. observers—who were no strangers to backing unsavory Latin American strongmen—were shocked. "I received the impression as I watched Serrano that he undoubtedly represents all that is evil and vicious and dangerous, and that there is nothing that he would not do without a qualm," the U.S. ambassador commented.

Serrano was a fascinating composite of political types—part fraudster, part political fixer, part plutocrat landlord, part mass murderer. His back-ground was obscure. The defense ministry recorded that a Carlos I. Serrano was captain of the Mexican army in 1924. In the same year he joined a failed military rebellion, was arrested and imprisoned. When he reappeared again, he had somehow acquired the title "Colonel," moved east to Veracruz, and fallen in with the Alemán family.

By the mid-1930s he was the politician's friend, backer, and hatchet man. In the meantime, he had clearly made some money, and he fronted Alemán 50,000 pesos during his gubernatorial campaign. When Alemán won, Serrano ran a gang of hitmen who did the governor's dirty work, orchestrating the murder of political opponents and peasant demonstrators. But such favors came at a cost. And over the next few years, Serrano tested the limits of Alemán's friendship. He brazenly dipped into the state funds, paraded his wealth, bought new cars, and a grand hacienda.

The limits, it seems, were never reached. In fact, Serrano's star rose. And by the time Alemán took a run at the Mexican presidency, the colonel was the candidate's closest advisor. In September 1946 he was elected senator and immediately made head of the Mexican Senate. But his real power still lay off stage. During the presidential campaign, he worked as the candidate's moneyman, collecting contributions from politicians and businessmen. And after the election he was put in charge of creating a new secret police, the Ministry of Federal Security or DFS.

The DFS was the coercive branch of the new state. The institution was one of Latin America's first Cold War police forces. It targeted what it termed "subversives" but could be more accurately described as union leaders, peasant activists, and left-wing politicians. It was trained by the FBI. And it was—theoretically at least—an elite unit, initially composed of honor graduates from Mexico's military academy. Though the DFS started small, it soon grew. As one U.S. observer suggested, by mid-1947 it had grown so powerful that it risked becoming "a Gestapo organization under another name."

Though the DFS's principal job was to track, record, and intimidate leftists, the DFS also had another interest—the drug trade. Here, Serrano led the way. Lending his Cadillac to a drug smuggler was only the beginning. During the presidential campaign, he took payoffs from border smugglers imprisoned for narcotics trafficking. And in the first months of Alemán's rule, he bailed out a high-class Mexican City madam caught selling cocaine. Those in the know whispered that Serrano was using her brothel to collect information on political opponents and then blackmail them. The CIA described him as "a man of few scruples, actively involved in illegal business, among which is the trafficking of narcotics."

But Serrano wasn't alone. In early 1947 he extended DFS membership to a group of shady ex-cops. Many were former members of the health department's antinarcotics squad. And many had already been dismissed for overt corruption. "It seems that anyone with a past record as a crooked narcotics enforcement officer needs no other qualification to be accepted as an agent in this group," one U.S. agent wryly observed.

Three of these new agents stood out. They were Marcelino Iñurreta de la Fuente, the former paymaster of the capital's police force and a keen backer of Alemán's political campaign; Colonel Manuel Mayoral, a former Mexico City policeman sacked for narcotics charges and now "in charge of the city's marijuana sales"; and another former policeman and uncle of the Laredo Cadillac driver—Juan Ramón Gurrola. Together these three agents took the three top positions in the DFS. They answered directly to Serrano. And they headed up the organization's push into the drug protection racket.

The plan was relatively simple: targeted repression followed by monopoly control. It was a scaled-up version of the kind of protection rackets that state governments were already operating on the border and in the Golden Triangle.

During the first six months of 1947, the strategy started to take shape. A few token arrests were made. But in general, the arrests were a sham. Most of those detained got out almost immediately. (One Mexican prosecutor complained that "the only results are that the more arrests we make, the more bribes the judges get.")

At the same time, the annual eradication effort in the Golden Triangle was a farce. The attorney general, who was officially in charge of making drug arrests, was paralyzed with fear. The health department's antinarcotics squad refused to turn up, citing insufficient funds. The initial promise of 100 troops was swiftly reduced to 20. And the campaign started in April at least a month after most of the poppy crops had been harvested. Serrano was even rumored to be launching poppy production far from the Golden Triangle, in the Caribbean coastal state of Veracruz. Summing up the new mood, a U.S. agent concluded that "the narcotics traffic is at the highest level ever known. Mexican enforcement measures are at their lowest ebb."

It is difficult to tell how much President Alemán knew about Serrano and the DFS operations. It seems unlikely that he was in the dark. Serrano and Alemán were extremely close. And Alemán was no political ingénue. He was a savvy operator and a fanatical collector of insider gossip on even his closest allies. So it seems that, at least at the beginning of his presidency, allowing federal officials to extort and protect traffickers was good business, especially given the state of the Mexican economy.

When Alemán took charge in December 1946, Mexico was in dire trouble. After the war, the United States was in full recovery and the cost of U.S. imports was rising. By comparison, Mexican exports had stalled. Increased postwar competition and the lowering of demand for raw materials cut into Mexico's industrial and agricultural sectors. Foreign exchange reserves were dropping. And the balance-of-payments deficit was increasing.

At the same time, the returns from Mexico's narcotics business were potentially enormous. The U.S. embassy estimated them at around $20 million; Alemán's private secretary thought they were nearer $60 million. If so, they accounted for around 15 percent of Mexican exports. Without drugs, Mexico would have been much worse off.

It was something that many Americans understood. Mexico—and by extension Alemán—took a laissez-faire attitude to drug regulation because it made good economic sense. In April 1948, U.S. embassy official Raymond Geist came to the nub of the matter.

> The Mexicans realize that the heavy illicit sale of narcotics to users in the United States is a financial advantage to Mexico and increases their dollar reserves, which at the present time is vitally in Mexico's interest. By their efforts to suppress this traffic they voluntarily cut off the flow of dollars into Mexico through the sale of narcotics.

They might have understood the Mexican position. And some in the State Department might have even sympathized with it. But one group did not. And this was a crucial one—the FBN. And more specifically the head of the FBN, Harry Anslinger.

Since forcing Mexico to drop its progressive narcotics treatment program in 1940, Anslinger had kept up the pressure on the country's authorities. He had harped on publicly about the danger of border trafficking, pushed alarmist exposés of supposed narcos, and forced President Ávila Camacho to suspend legal guarantees for drug offenders.

Yet, in the immediate postwar period, such efforts simply weren't enough. Anslinger and the FBN were struggling to keep relevant. Addiction levels in the United States were at a historic low. The FBN's function was drying up. And the U.S. government was more concerned with the stability of the postwar world and the spread of international communism than with a handful of poor heroin addicts.

Anslinger was wise to the shift. He was an acute observer of Washington politics, a savvy bureaucratic entrepreneur, and, above all, a survivor. And so, in response, he speeded up the FBN's transformation from a largely domestic drug agency to an international policing organization.

Supply, not demand, was now the target. The enemy was no longer hooky pharmacists and shady street dealers, but an entire network of drug-producing foreigners. The line played well with a new expansionist American foreign policy and would soon chime with the country's Cold War paranoia. Not coincidently, it also helped with the FBN's ongoing rivalry with the other U.S. institution interested in foreign narcotics control—the Customs Service.

Anslinger—like Alemán—was a media-age politician. He understood the importance of publicizing his message to the broadest possible audience in simple and, if necessary, exaggerated terms. So as well as soberly announcing this move to senators and congressmen, he also outlined it in pulp crime magazines like *True Detective*. The FBN, he claimed, needed to confront a new threat. "With the coming of peace our country faces a foe that can be just as deadly as the enemy on the field of battle ... the opium poppy holds as much potential disaster as an atom bomb."

For a couple of years, Anslinger searched around for a foe worthy of the next fight. There were multiple options; he made a few attempts to target Turkey, Iran, and Italy. But in early 1947 he plumped for Mexico. Mexico was a tempting target. It was a developing nation heavily dependent on U.S. investment that Anslinger had already bullied into changing its drug laws once before. A staged set-to with America's southern neighbor would provide a boost for the FBN's profile, embarrass the U.S. Customs Service (which was nominally in charge of stopping Mexican narcotics), and provide a guide for how other foreign governments should act in the future.

What is more, there was a real suggestion that the Mexican drug trade was actually fairly important. (This—if subsequent actions are any guide— was very much a secondary consideration. In later years Anslinger would jettison any pretense of empirical rigor, play up to Cold War anticommunism, and invent both a fictional Chinese and a fictional Cuban narcotics trade.)

This time, however, Anslinger collected the evidence. He ordered an aerial survey of the Golden Triangle, which seemed to indicate that as many as 5,000 hectares of mountain land were devoted to poppy growing. Then he assessed recent history. There were the embarrassingly poor results from the 1947 eradication campaign. And there were a few high-profile confrontations, including what Anslinger termed with a tabloid flourish, "The Woodbine Check Affair." Here, in May 1947, FBN officials had confronted a group of opium traffickers at the Woodbine border crossing just east of San Diego. They had captured one of the smugglers, but the rest escaped. Later in the evening the surviving criminals had machine-gunned the police chief of the border city of Mexicali.

There was also the increasingly blatant behavior of the DFS. If the FBI had taught them to keep a low profile, it had not done a very good job. In early July 1947 the U.S. military attaché reported that Gurrola—DFS chief and uncle of the Cadillac driver—had recently conducted a conference with U.S. officials about the cross-border narcotics trade. Just as the officials left the room, Gurrola was overheard to brag that he had "found a goldmine of information." He implied that "he would receive information which would assist him in his illicit dope business."

Serrano was no better. He refused to pursue the Cadillac bust in court. He failed to prosecute Gurrola but rather promoted him to one of the key positions in the DFS. But neither did he let the Cadillac incident go. Instead, he "made very strong and rather bare-faced demands on the American Embassy for the return of his car." In fact, he remained so annoyed that when President Truman visited Mexico he refused to attend the official dinner in protest.

Anslinger's strategy to force Mexico to increase its drug regulations was simple. It was one of the things he was good at—theatrical bullying. This time it was on an international stage. After the war he had managed to get the U.N.'s Commission on Narcotic Drugs moved from Geneva to the United States. It was the body that dealt with international narcotics enforcement. And it was located—at least initially—in a temporary base in a former weapons factory on Long Island.

On July 30, 1947, Anslinger got up to address the assembled dignitaries. They were a mix of diplomats, drug cops, and doctors from all over the world. But the American FBN chief was the star. This was his forum. He knew that what he was about to say would cause considerable upset. In fact, he had told some of his most trusted agents to turn up and enjoy the show. "Watch for the discussion on Mexico here, it will be a hot one." But the speech would also be worth it. It would force Mexico to adopt more punitive antinarcotics measures. And it would place Anslinger and the FBN at the forefront of U.S. foreign policy.

First, there was the blizzard of numbers—quantitative analysis of aerial surveys and disconcertingly precise estimates of hectares planted and tons produced. (Anslinger always liked to give the illusion of omniscience.) Then there was the cinematic action sequence. The Woodbine Check shootout was recast. It was no longer a series of massive police blunders that resulted in a dead police chief and a single arrest. It was the intrepid adventure of a daring FBN agent posing as a "Hollywood buyer" who had ensnared a group of desperado traffickers in a carefully planned trap. Then, of course, there was the bullshit. Statistics that touched on the truth were mixed with unsubstantiated guesswork on the number of drug-trafficking airfields (20 to 30) and heroin labs (12). Such figures appeared in no other reports and seemed to have been plucked from thin air.

The initial Mexican reaction was embarrassment. Quietly taking bribes from drug traffickers was one thing; being held up before the world as America's principal source of narcotics was another. Then the Mexican delegation moved on to denial. The Mexican representative at the U.N. claimed that Anslinger's figures were overstated, argued that it was an

American not a Mexican problem, and tried (unsuccessfully) to get a motion passed that would push the United States to deal with its own Mafia gangs.

Back in Mexico the response was muted. Officials paid national newspapers to ignore Anslinger's speech. Meanwhile, they pondered what to do. The growing profits from the drug trade were attractive. On a local level they funded thousands of poor farmers and kept a couple of state economies afloat. On a national level, they offered ample opportunities for payoffs and went some way to balancing out Mexico's falling foreign reserves. But Anslinger's speech was damning. It made Mexico look ineffective and weak and hinted at widespread corruption.

Alemán had to make a decision. Drug profits were useful. But domestic politics was becoming increasingly messy. He needed American backing. The unions were pushing for wage rises; U.S. government funds were the only things keeping the peso afloat; rumors about the amigos' corruption were starting to leak out; and the national newspapers were threatening to reveal them.

So, like President Cárdenas in 1940, he buckled to Anslinger's pressure.

First came the narcotics legislation. Anslinger had suggested a rewriting of the Mexican drug laws in 1946. He even helpfully drafted a template. The proposal suggested a broader definition of narcotics, longer sentences for growers and traffickers, and the seizure of criminals' assets. In an act of abject supplication, the Mexicans adopted Anslinger's model almost wholesale. Drugs were now described as any substances outlined in international drug agreements. Maximum punishments increased to twelve years, and parole for drug offences was banned. The new law even outstripped those of the United States. It was the most punitive law on the continent.

Then came the shift in policing. For over two decades, chasing down narcotics violators had officially been the job of the health department's small, underfunded, and notoriously corrupt police force. The Americans had been pushing for a specialized drug unit, unconnected to the health department, since the early 1940s. The DFS had tried unsuccessfully to audition for the role. Instead, in 1947 the Mexican authorities switched responsibility for drug crimes to the Federal Judicial Police (PJF). The PJF cops were close to the FBN; they had worked cases together before. The PJF would now be in charge of the annual eradication program, the arrest of trafficking networks, and coordination with the Americans. It was exactly what Anslinger wanted.

Finally, the Mexicans launched a rural campaign against opium growing. In 1948, just as the poppy petals were beginning to drop, the PJF launched the official campaign. The crusade went beyond anything even the most optimistic drug hawk had wanted. A PJF agent that had worked closely with the FBN was put in charge. The eradication team included planes, jeeps, radio equipment, a large military force, and fifty PJF agents. Eradication squads were split into nine groups, which scoured the three states of the Golden Triangle as well as the border state of Sonora. Poppy plantations were discovered and pulled up. Peasant growers were located and arrested. The numbers were impressive. (If the Mexicans had learned anything, it was that Anslinger cared about the numbers.) The squads destroyed 663 opium fields, collected 100 kilos of opium gum, and arrested nearly 3,000 peasant growers.

The "Great Campaign," as it was termed, was like nothing that had come before. Launched with a huge press fanfare, it destroyed three times as many opium fields as any of the previous operations. And it arrested more drug offenders than had been arrested throughout the rest of the 1940s. It was drug campaign as military invasion.

There remained what to do with the DFS. Throughout early 1948 the Americans kept up the pressure. In the February U.N. meeting, the U.S. representative threatened that if the Mexicans didn't crack down on corruption the Americans would have "no recourse but to set the record straight at some length with names, dates and places."

And at the end of the month Anslinger—or somebody close to Anslinger—followed through with the threat. News of the Cadillac bust was leaked to syndicated columnist Drew Pearson. The piece was not subtle. "Senator Carlos Serrano is still trying to get his high-powered Cadillac back from the U.S. government after it was seized on the border near Laredo containing 63 tins of smoking opium carefully concealed in built-in compartments in the side of the car."

It was explosive. The Americans had called the head of the Mexican Senate, the de facto chief of the secret police, and the president's right-hand man a brazen narcotics smuggler. Mexican officials managed to limit local reporting of the story. But Alemán was finally forced to act. He responded with a classic PRI mix of suspicious death, effective policy, and ludicrous misdirection.

First, a sacrifice was made. Gurrola, the uncle of the Cadillac smuggler, was sacked from the DFS and sent into exile in Chile. A few months later he conveniently died.

Then the DFS moved out of the narcotics business. No doubt some agents still sold small gram loads on the side (if you wanted to score cocaine for a mid-1960s party, they were your men). But in general, Serrano and his associates backed off their attempt to take over protection of the trade. The DFS was still secretive, brutal, and deeply unpopular. But its plans to move into counternarcotics were sharply dropped. And rumors of its involvement in the drug trade disappeared completely. It would take over thirty years for the DFS to make a comeback.

Finally, Alemán and Serrano cut their ties. Or at least they wanted it to appear this way to the Americans. In April 1948, Serrano approached a U.S. official and announced that he and the president had fallen out. The story he gave was fantastic but memorable. It was designed—one suspects—to put the Americans off the scent. According to Serrano, Alemán's wife had caught the president in flagrante with the Mexican actress María Félix. She now blamed Serrano for setting up the liaison. Serrano and Alemán's friendship was at an end.

True or not, the story was good enough for Anslinger. From May 1948 on, the FBN chief was unfailingly complimentary about Mexican counter-narcotics policies. He used the next meeting of the U.N. to laud the law changes, the role of the PJF, and the Great Campaign. The next year he even did a tour of Mexico.

If Anslinger was a bully, he was also loyal to those that showed contrition. And now he helped the Mexicans clean up the scandals that he had publicized. It was always about control, not the truth.

So in November 1948, Drew Pearson, the syndicated columnist, was forced to publish a humiliating public apology. He now wrote that the story of the Cadillac bust was untrue. He had been taken in by Serrano's unscrupulous left-wing enemies. (Blaming the communists smacked of Anslinger. When in doubt, red-bait the reader.) Anslinger was even quoted claiming the car came from New York and the link to Serrano was a "misunderstanding."

Other journalists were even more unfortunate. A month after Pearson backed down, the émigré Mexican reporter Rafael García Travesi approached the Los Angeles FBN office. He knew about the Cadillac bust. And he had also received a confidential report from a Mexican secret agent that listed the officials protecting the trade. Serrano was at the top of the list. García's story was not only damning stuff, it was real. And the FBN knew it; they had already received a copy of the report. Yet rather than help García, they sold him out. A few days after he had visited the FBN, anonymous American agents bundled him into the back of a car, drove him over the border, and handed him to the DFS. He was beaten, tortured, and then framed for bigamy charges. He would spend the rest of Alemán's presidency in jail.

On the surface, the story of the Cadillac bust, Anslinger's grandstanding, and Mexico's subsequent adoption of stringent antinarcotics measures seems to tell one essential truth. When it comes to drug policy, bullying works. Public humiliation pushed Mexico to stifle federal-level corruption and clamp down on the narcotics business.

There is something to this. Over the next few years, Mexican drug exports dropped dramatically. By the 1950s, Mexico barely supplied enough morphine and heroin for the U.S. Southwest.

But to what extent this was a direct effect of Anslinger's policies is more difficult to tell. The failure of subsequent attempts to get similar outcomes (in the 1970s and 1980s) suggests that it was not the policies that were right but the timing. Anslinger's efforts to put Mexico in its place coincided with Alemán's attempts to overhaul the postrevolutionary system. The counterrevolution needed U.S. support. So the Mexican government ceded control of narcotics policy. At the same time, the policies also coincided with a new overseas supplier. By the end of the decade, European factories were producing most of America's heroin.

In fact, then, if there is one lesson to take from the story of the Cadillac bust, it is that hardline drug policies—even introduced at the most opportune moments possible—don't really work. More precisely, they don't affect consumption rates. It was a transnational example of what experts call the balloon effect, the mechanism by which if you squeeze one source of supply another immediately appears.

By the late 1940s the Mexican drug trade had slumped. But it didn't matter. U.S. demand drove new sources of supply. Between 1945 and 1952 the number of heroin addicts in the United States tripled from 20,000 to 60,000. By 1965 the number stood at 150,000. Mexico had nothing to do with it. It was France.

# Chapter 10

## The New Status Quo

THE YOUNG SAN DIEGO JOURNALIST GENE FUSON WAS BUZZING. THIS WAS going to get him a Pulitzer. January 6, 1952, and he was over the border, looking for narcotics. His editor had sent him south to expose what Californians were starting to term "the youth drug problem." Ten thousand Americans crossed the San Isidro–Tijuana crossing every day; the number rose to 50,000 on weekends. Many were teenagers. Tijuana was the flipside to the uptight, starched-collar puritanism of postwar America. It was sin city. Here they could drink, visit brothels, buy pornography, drop goofballs, and smoke weed. Fuson wanted to find out where.

His first attempt was not terribly successful. Fuson visited a place they told him was called "junkie alley." If it was, the junkies had left. He asked to purchase some H (heroin); the solitary peddler could only offer him a tiny bag of *"secas"* (marijuana).

But this time he was on to something. He was on the outskirts of town in a tumbledown wooden cantina. At the bar, off-duty Americans from the San Diego navy base knocked back tequilas and smoked or, as they allegedly put it, "lush[ed] for a double kick." In a back room a local sex worker entertained a young sailor, and in the bathroom the attendant sold cheap skin mags.

At first, he admitted "business was rotten and the atmosphere matched it; a compound of stale beer, cooking onions, stale smoke." But by 2 A.M., teenagers started to appear. Most were Mexican Americans "dressed in ... Levis, flying jackets with the collars turned up and 'shag' haircuts." Within an hour the place was full, a five-piece jazz band had started to play, and the bar had transformed into a "shouting, struggling, jitterbugging mass of humanity." The dancing was, Fuson concluded, fueled by marijuana. It was sold by "the Duchess," "a cadaverous [man] with acne scars and bushy hair" from the back of a closely guarded booth. Here was the Tijuana Fuson had been looking for. Here was the Mexican Gomorrah.

The following month the *San Diego Union* published Fuson's over-wrought observations. They didn't get him a Pulitzer. But they did make a big impression. In San Diego they helped kick-start a panic over teenage drug use. Parents and civil leaders called for a ban on youngsters crossing the border; sheriffs set up roadblocks and did spot checks; and local prose-cutors held a grand jury inquiry on the subject. Over the next decade, the dread, misinformation, and prejudice traveled northward. By the late 1950s, *Los Angeles Times* writers were trawling the fleshpots of Tijuana concocting similarly alarmist exposés. (They did win the Pulitzer.) And Hollywood directors were producing hysterical border-town titillation like *Eighteen and Anxious* (1957) and *The Young Captives* (1959).

Drug panics, however, had little to do with reality. In the United States—as in Mexico—panics had much more to do with how people per-ceived the racial and social profile of the trade. In this case, Americans feared black and Mexican-American dealers hawking narcotics to their white, suburban kids.

In reality, the Mexican drug trade was at a low ebb in the 1950s. If Fuson had gone down the road and asked the San Isidro Customs officials, they would have told him. In 1952 the agents concluded that the biggest threat to Californians was a $60,000 psittacine (parrot)–smuggling ring. Apparently, American animal dealers were bringing in exotic parrots from South America illegally and selling them to upscale pet owners. Furthe-rmore, this avian trade was dangerous. One agent fell seriously ill due to contact with the birds and was put in isolation in hospital. "It was firmly believed that but for the advent of a miracle cure this service would now be wearing a black armband," the annual report solemnly observed.

By comparison, the supply of narcotics had almost dried up. The same month Fuson issued his missives from "the border hell town," Customs agents reported that the "bottom had fallen out of the opium market in Tijuana. Within the last two or three weeks opium prepared for smoking has been offered for sale in Tijuana at $50 per ... tin and there seems to be no takers." The following year the amount of drugs captured at the border crossing totalled 39 pounds of marijuana, 426 grains of heroin, and no smoking opium whatsoever. The parrots were worth more.

The main reason for the drop-off was economic. You could get better, purer, cheaper heroin from Europe. (You could also get it really easily. By the 1960s the FBN admitted that around a third of its agents were on the take from narcotics importers.)

But Mexico also did its part. During the 1950s, prohibition got heavy. Military forces spread throughout the Golden Triangle. Some were stationed in permanent bases. Others were sent in for the annual eradication programs. These operations did have an effect. Arrests increased and opium production in the Golden Triangle dropped. Outsiders, who didn't come from the region, were prosecuted, killed, or forced to move to other states. And gradually the business that remained changed. The local traffickers that stayed on worked increasingly in the shadows. Persecution pushed what had started as a relatively open commerce toward organized crime.

The early 1950s was the first peak of U.S.–Mexican antinarcotics cooperation. It was Anslinger's project. After his very public attack on Mexican antinarcotics policy, he was keen to firm up alliances. The new Mexican enforcers from the attorney general's office and the PJF were his friends. They exchanged letters and presents—a briefcase and a silver tobacco case for the FBN head and "an unusual evening shawl" for his wife. Anslinger, in turn, supported the Mexican representative's successful push to be head of the UN's Commission on Narcotic Drugs. He rarely missed an opportunity to praise the country's "magnificent steps to curb the opium poppy crop."

What Anslinger liked were two things—the annual eradication campaigns and the sheer quantity of drug arrests.

Every harvest season from February to May, hundreds of troops marched into the Golden Triangle. These were not the rickety, ill-equipped campaigns of the early 1940s. Soldiers were transported in jeeps and trucks; they were supported by the attorney general's new air fleet; and they kept in contact via mobile radio stations. By the early 1960s they were equipped with U.S. helicopters, light planes, and flamethrowers. They raided houses for stashes of opium gum, destroyed runways, arrested peasants, pulled up poppy plants or, when they could, incinerated them. The campaigns grew in size. In 1955, the PJF extended the searches further into the mountain peaks of the Sierra Madre. And in 1959 they started another program to the south in Michoacán.

Arrests also increased. Qualms about arresting innocent peasants waned. There were nearly 2,000 jailed on drug charges in 1951 and another 2,000 in 1952. In fact, from 1950 to 1960 over 13,000 Mexicans were put away under the new punitive drug laws. To put it another way, despite not having a domestic addiction problem, Mexico was putting more people away per capita for federal drug offenses than Anslinger's America.

Military intervention brought violence. And though atrocities were never on the scale of the 1970s, there was a host of bloody encounters. They were signs—early warnings—of things to come.

Some battles pitched the military against the traffickers. In 1955, soldiers confronted the Chavez León brothers in the Durango mountain town of Tamazula. They were traffickers and, as one might expect, also members of the state police. The brothers had been drinking all day. It was opium harvest and they were celebrating. By evening they were firing off their pistols into the bar ceiling. According to the commander, he tried to disarm them. But they refused. A firefight ensued. Two of the three brothers and one of their drinking buddies were killed.

Violence bred its own coping mechanisms. And among the soldiers, a dry humor emerged. It was black ops as black comedy. One 1962 internal military bulletin read: "As for the criminals they can't really complain. Some of them are on holiday with San Pedro [i.e., dead] for having tried to confront our men. Others made the mistake of trusting in their legs to outrun our bullets. They are now enjoying a deserved rest."

Military incursions also pitched traffickers against one another. In general, the soldiers arrived in the mountains blind; they didn't know the growers or where they grew. So they used local informers to find them. Usually, these were villagers press-ganged into offering their help. As one might expect, the strategy undermined cooperation, destroyed bonds of trust, and turned families against one another. It also kick-started tit-for-tat killings. What began as law enforcement quickly descended into blood feuds.

In Michoacán especially, these clashes became endemic. In 1960, for example, Tepalcatepec farmer Don Romulo became an informer. He did so not out of any great sense of duty, but rather to take revenge on other traffickers that had robbed his merchandise. He became the military's go-to source of information and led them high into the Sierra to the most remote plantations. For months he lived well off his new job. He was paid a small commission and was allowed to carry a gun. But when the soldiers left his village, the relatives of the traffickers he had ratted on found him and killed him.

Yet it should be said that during these early campaigns, there were attempts to reduce violent confrontations. This was not the 1970s. The state was no longer revolutionary, but it was concerned with keeping up appearances. And murdering peasants not only looked bad but could also destabilize the countryside. So efforts at conciliation were made. And state-run protection rackets returned. They were just a bit less brazen than the protection rackets of the 1930s or 1940s.

In 1950, for example, the government put General Teófilo Álvarez Borboa in charge of the military in Sinaloa. It was an odd choice. Álvarez was originally from Higuera de los Monzón just outside Badiraguato. After graduating as a teacher, he had joined the Revolution and climbed the ranks to the position of general. Typically, the state avoided appointing commanders to their home turf so as to avoid them building independent influence. But by 1950, conflicts between soldiers and traffickers were getting out of control. So the government took the chance.

On the surface at least, the decision seemed to work. Álvarez met with local representatives, promised to rein in military force, and asked them to report if traffickers were forcing them to grow poppies. In the mountains of the Golden Triangle, complaints of state atrocities decreased. He also attempted to give the area's peasants alternatives to the drug trade. He pushed the state to send agronomists to teach former opium farmers how to make the most out of sugarcane, wheat, and citrus trees. He organized the building of a road between Badiraguato and the federal highway. And soon afterward he got state banks to move to the mountains and offer credit for seeds, agricultural tools, and fertilizers.

Yet, beneath this public effort, he also established another state-run protection racket. Just like in 1910s Baja California, 1930s Chihuahua, or 1940s Sinaloa, this strategy was a double-edged sword and involved a mixture of repression and protection.

Those that were targeted for repression were the traffickers from outside the state. It was a sort of drug policing as regional xenophobia. And between 1950 and 1954 all the major nonlocal traffickers operating in Sinaloa were arrested or killed. In June 1951 it was the turn of José Mendez García, a big Tijuana trafficker who had married into a Sinaloa family and taken over the border trade. He was gunned down in a popular Culiacán restaurant. The following year the authorities finally caught up with the mysterious Culiacán kingpin Roberto Domínguez Macías and charged him with murdering one of his lawyers. Two years later, another border trafficker, Prisciliano "Chano" Cabrera was also shot.

Whether General Álvarez personally instigated this strategy or allowed local traffickers to do it, we don't know. But it certainly happened. And if it was deliberate, it worked. It kept the industry sufficiently small to avoid undue U.S. or federal pressure. It caused limited complaints. (Who would complain if a nonlocal got killed?) And it kept the business low-key by limiting it to groups of tight-lipped, interrelated, local families.

The outsiders that survived the cull fled. They traveled south, dispersing opium growing as they went. Some settled in Jalisco. Cabrera, for example, was a Mexicali-based car thief who moved into narcotics in the 1940s. Before, he had bought his product—like most border sellers—in Culiacán. But in 1950 he shifted to the highlands outside Guadalajara, growing his own marijuana and opium for the U.S. market. Now he consciously bypassed the Golden Triangle. Instead, he trafficked his wares inland and then up through the eastern border towns of Nuevo Laredo and Matamoros.

Outside the Golden Triangle he was relatively safe. But when he briefly visited Sinaloa to buy up the annual opium harvest, he was shot.

Others moved even further south to Michoacán. During the mid-1950s they started to grow opium poppies around the lowland market town of Aguililla. (To this day—like Badiraguato—it remains a center of the drug business.) By the end of the decade, Aguililla resembled Culiacán or Mocorito a decade earlier. Peasants traipsed in from the surrounding pine-topped hills throughout the harvest season, selling small amounts of gum to a group of intermediaries. These then took the gum up to the nearby town of Uruapan, where they had installed small heroin-processing labs.

In contrast, as their competitors died or fled, the Sinaloa traffickers enjoyed a respite from prosecution. As one former grower observed:

> We knew the times to sow, the prices and just how much you could bring forward production. If you broke these rules, that was when there were confrontations. There were accords that had been agreed with the representatives of the authorities and the government, there were accords that everyone knew, the whole community knew … the army knew to burn and cut the plants of the independent sowers but not burn all the fields.

Officially protected or just very lucky, the 1940s traffickers continued to ply their trade. Eduardo "Lalo" Fernández produced heroin in his labs in Tierra Blanca, Culiacán. Another important chemist, Miguel Urias Uriarte got out of jail, returned to his countryside lab outside Bacacoragua, and set up a small commercial runway in the tiny village.

This streamlined, low-profile version of the trade was deliberately discreet. But we can get some idea of it from a couple of extraordinary sources. The first is an extensive account written by the new head of the Sinaloa military zone, J. Jesús Arias Sánchez. Arias succeeded Álvarez in early 1958. When he arrived, he was led to believe that the narcotics business was a thing of the past. He based this opinion on Álvarez's suspiciously optimistic reports. The reality, however, was quite different. Some traffickers were dead; some were in jail. But "poppy cultivation was still undergoing an alarming boom."

On the surface the system resembled that of the 1940s. At the bottom were the peasants. They planted, cultivated, and harvested the drugs. As they often worked on other people's lands, they earned wages as laborers. These averaged 30 to 50 pesos a day. It wasn't bad. It was ten times the official (and often undercut) minimum wage. But as they were stationed near the fields, they also took the major risks. They were the ones the soldiers arrested and prosecuted.

Above the peasants were the intermediaries. These provided the tools and the seeds for the peasants. They were in charge of collecting the harvest and doling out the payments. Finally, at the top were the traffickers. They lived in Culiacán. They fronted the money and brought together the separate parts of the drug network. They never touched the merchandise. Trusted employees would gather the gum from the intermediaries, bring it to the chemists, and then take the finished product to airfields or railway stations for transport.

Yet, something had changed. The threat of state violence had achieved what had not happened organically. Mexico was starting to experience one of the rules of drug prohibition: the more aggressive the policing, the more secretive and violent the trade. No trafficker wanted to suffer a military raid, endure a twelve-year prison sentence, or get targeted for an off-the-books assassination by General Álvarez.

So the trade went underground. What had been done openly was now cloaked in secrecy. It was secured by a code of silence. And it was enforced, if necessary, by force. This shift was distinctly gradual and halting. As usual in Mexico, it was first reflected in the language. The old opium intermediaries and wholesalers were becoming what people started to term *narcotraficantes*.

Thus, Arias observed that when the army actually captured the intermediaries, they never snitched. They said nothing. (Compare this to the hapless Chihuahua peasant we met in Chapter 7 who went to the police station to complain his opium had been stolen.) In return, their families received financial support while they did their time. If they betrayed their employers, they paid for it with their lives. The wealthy traffickers were now completely isolated from the trade. They mixed with the city elites. In fact, "they had such upstanding and official personalities that it was ridiculous to suspect that they were related with illicit activities."

No doubt, many of these traffickers were the old Badiraguato gang, who had started a decade earlier. But there were also newcomers. They were younger, wealthier, and more educated. They were members of the Culiacán middle and upper classes who now moved from occasionally dabbling in the business to full-time work.

Though his name was rarely whispered in public, one of the most important was Jorge Favela Escobosa. By the 1970s he would be known as "the Godfather," famed for being one of the first traffickers to move into cocaine after making his initial fortune in opium. But in the early 1950s, Favela's career had barely begun.

Favela was born in one of the suburbs of Culiacán in 1918, son of a wealthy merchant. He was sent off to school in Los Mochis with a rich uncle. It was here that he most probably picked up knowledge of the trade from the local Chinese dealers. By the time he returned to Culiacán in the early 1950s, he had partnered with another wealthy merchant from Mocorito. Together they started to buy up large quantities of opium and convert it to heroin. Favela bought an upscale hosiery shop as a front. And he wedded Alicia Buelna Avilés, a cousin of another up-and-coming trafficker who would come to prominence in the 1960s—Pedro Avilés Pérez.

Such unions were increasingly common. They linked the old mountain families and the new city crowd; they cemented alliances; and they ensured against betrayal. The ceremonies were a mix of elite traditions and nouveau-riche luxuries. They were held in the city center's grand cathedral, presided over by the bishop and attended by lawyers, hacienda owners, and politicians. But they were celebrated in the city's array of new upscale, U.S.-style hotels with sumptuous seafood buffets, foreign liquor, and big-time bands invited from Mexico City. And they were watched over by the powerful wholesalers who often acted as godparents of the unions. The mob met medieval marriage practices; these alliances were the beginning of the Golden Triangle's narcoaristocracy.

The growing secrecy was also reflected in the way drugs were transported. Gone were the days of stashing a few bags of heroin at the bottom of a suitcase or burying packs of opium under boxes of tomatoes. Smuggling—even inside Mexico—was leveling up.

Planes became increasingly popular. Traffickers now built short runways high up in the Sierra Madre. Sometimes they moved the drugs covertly, sealing them in metal containers designed to carry milk or pig fat. Other times, they just went for bulk. They brought in cropdusters used to spray the state's lowland valleys, pulled out the seats, filled them with plainly packaged narcotics, and then flew them to the border. The use of planes was so common that in 1953 the government suspended all flights from the small rural airports of Sinaloa, Durango, and Chihuahua. Officials also briefly shuttered the Culiacán aviation academy—the training school for a new generation of would-be pilot smugglers.

We can also observe the development of the trade in Mexico's first narco-novel. *Diario de un Narcotraficante* (Diary of a Drug Trafficker) was written by Ángelo Nacaveva and published in 1967. Advertised as cheap pulp fiction, the book garnered scant, generally negative, reviews. It did, however, sell—an impressive 50,000 copies according to the publicity. This was in a nation where print runs rarely went over 1,000. Today it is heralded as the founding text of an entire movement, the original work of what Mexicans term *narcoliteratura*.

Fittingly for a book about an increasingly cagey industry, *Narcotraficante* was not what it seemed. Nacaveva was a pseudonym. In fact, the author was a local journalist named Pedro Serrano. And it was not all the product of his imagination. Serrano learned about the technical side of the business from a master—the Culiacán heroin chemist, Eduardo "Lalo" Fernández. Finally, the book was not about the explosion of the trade in the late 1960s; it was actually based on the development of the business in the 1950s.

The book is long, unwieldy, and frankly a little dull. Characters are thinly drawn if at all. And the story is erratic and prone to go off on strange tangents. But what it lacks in narrative pizazz it makes up for in candor and detail. It is very much the work of a sharp-eyed journalist rather than a novelist. It follows the adventures of a Culiacán journalist and his friend, a lawyer called Arturo. Like many of this new generation of traffickers, they are not poor. But neither are they rich. They are part of Mexico's new precarious middle class. And it is Arturo who suggests that they earn a bit extra by getting involved in the drug trade.

What grabs you first is the relatively ad hoc nature of the business. There is no plan, no grand strategy, no end game. This is still a long way from the efficient, integrated trade of the 1980s. The gang—if it could even be called that—is little more than a group of barflies and acquaintances who each specialize in a particular aspect of the trade.

There is the intermediary who brings the opium down from the mountains; there is the old rural cacique who collects it from the peasants; there is the chemist who converts it into heroin. There is the arms dealer and smuggler who takes it to the border; and there is the car thief who buys up the product for sale in the United States. It is a network of convenience. Arrangements are made on the spot and by chance. When the intermediary fails to deliver the opium, the gang just go up to the Sierra Madre themselves. And when the arms dealer doesn't turn up, Nacaveva decides to brave the border.

Nacaveva also goes to great lengths to describe the sheer tedium of the trade. (This is something for which he has a Proustian talent.) Getting hold of the opium in Culiacán involves long, exasperating waits only occasionally enlivened by drinking and gunplay. Getting hold of the opium up in the mountains is more time-consuming still—weeks of waiting for peasants to come down from their fields in the highland peaks. Converting the opium into heroin is the same. It is a lengthy, smelly, and exhausting process that basically involves stirring a pot of boiling chemicals nonstop for a week. Selling the drugs at the border is another wait. Only this time it's accompanied by the nail-biting anxiety of getting caught.

If it is boring, it is worth it. And like all proficient drug traffickers, Nacaveva is good with the numbers. A kilo of opium costs around 2,300 pesos from the intermediary or 2,000 pesos direct from the peasants up in the Sierra Madre. But converted into heroin, it can be sold in Culiacán for 9,000 pesos. It is 7,000 pesos for three weeks of work; 35,000 pesos when the team get hold of 5 kilos. To put it another way, three weeks of drug work could make the two traffickers five times the average annual wage—each.

A *Nacaveva,* Diario de un Narcotraficante *was Mexico's first narco-novel. It was actually rather thinly veiled nonfiction.*

But by the end of the book what stays with you is Nacaveva's sense of a changing trafficker culture. These are not the forty-something revolutionaries–turned–opium growers of the decade before. These are a new generation, born at the end of the war. These are—as the title suggests—narcotraficantes. They are city dwellers. Their hands are unmarked by work in the mines or labor in the fields. ("Ismael was not educated but had smooth hands which suggested he was a cantina owner, pimp, or smuggler.") When they go up to the mountains, they appear bewildered and afraid. The village fiesta is a cacophony of strange music and distant traditions they find threatening and difficult to understand.

In contrast, their habitats are the cantinas and cabarets of the state capital. Their language is a mixture of Culiacán slang and *calo*, or the language of the urban underworld. (In fact, Nacaveva even includes a useful glossary of terms at the end.) This is the drug trade as commerce, one element in organized crime's portfolio. In fact, even the new term for narcotics suggests this. It is no longer harvested *goma* (gum); it is *mercancia* (merchandise).

There is also a new passion for guns. These are not the long-range Winchester rifles of the Revolution. These are .38 pistols used for close-quarters confrontations. These are for bars and hotel rooms when colleagues turn informers or the police raid. Nacaveva and his friends carry them everywhere and practice shooting whenever possible. When pushed, they use them.

For this new world is one of increasing vigilance and danger.

They buy their chemicals at different pharmacies to avoid detection. Highland inhabitants come down the mountain with tales of the military "going hard" on the peasants. And when they go up there themselves, they see soldiers scouring the other side of the valley. The border is even worse—a threatening place where the gang has few contacts. It is a place where anyone could be an informer, a PJF agent, or an American cop. It is an unforgiving place where, if they are caught, they can expect beatings, torture, or even summary execution.

It is to this world of the border that we now turn.

## Chapter 11

──────────

## Queen Pin

Ruben Salazar had heard the rumors about Ignacia "La Nacha" Jasso since growing up in Ciudad Juárez in the 1930s. Her reputation was formidable. Killer, heroin peddler, one half of a border Bonnie and Clyde, and scourge of U.S. drug agents, she was known as the city's "Dope Queen." She was a fable, a folk hero, and a bogie woman used to scare small kids.

But Salazar, an *El Paso Herald-Post* reporter, hadn't expected to meet her. It was a testament to his tenacity but also, he now realized, to his recklessness. His journey had started about a month prior in July 1955 in the El Paso jail. He had deliberately got himself arrested. (As a Mexican American in El Paso, it was not difficult.) He was on assignment from the newspaper to investigate stories of growing prison narcotics abuse. He was not disappointed. During his brief stint, he saw prisoners chugging amphetamine-filled goofballs, surreptitiously smoking marijuana, and even injecting themselves with heroin.

The heroin, in particular, interested Salazar. One of his cellmates was a young El Paso addict, whom Salazar named Hypo. Hypo explained that the heroin was from over the border in Ciudad Juárez. U.S. prison guards smuggled it in on behalf of a Mexican heroin dealer, La Nacha. Salazar's ears pricked up. He had heard of La Nacha before, but it had been at least a decade ago. He thought by now she must have been out of the business, in prison, or dead. Hypo shook his head. No, she was very much alive. She still sold $5 hits from her house on the other side of the border.

On his release, Hypo agreed to be Salazar's guide. He explained that heroin had taken everything from him. He had sold his furniture, his car, and his apartment. His wife had left him and taken their baby. He lived on friends' couches and on the street. Every day his sole mission was to borrow, scam, or steal the $10 he needed for two of La Nacha's hits.

After driving over the border, Salazar and Hypo crossed the bridge, turned right, and entered the Bellavista neighborhood. Though it stood only a few hundred meters distant from downtown El Paso, it was a world away. The streets were unpaved, the houses were of wood or adobe, and acrid smoke rose from their outdoor kitchens.

The two men left the car and walked down the street, shielding their eyes from the dust whipped up by the wind. Hypo pointed toward a corner plot at the end of Calle Violetas. It was a bigger house than the rest, two stories tall, painted a colonial yellow and with fancy ironwork over the windows. Hypo knocked on the door and waved a $5 note.

They were in. And here she was. At first, Salazar was underwhelmed. Broad-shouldered, overweight, dark-skinned, and with the faint pockmarks of childhood chicken pox, La Nacha (short for Ignacia) looked like thousands of other middle-aged women who had made Ciudad Juárez their home. Dressed in a black skirt and a dark apron, she could have been Salazar's grandmother.

But two things did mark her out. The first was the house. Surrounded by the prefab shacks of one of Ciudad Juárez's poorest neighborhoods, La Nacha's home was a model of Mexican middle-class aspiration. The courtyard was bright, pretty, and flanked by potted plants and climbing vines. The living room was jammed with floral, U.S.-made furniture; beans bubbled on the new gas stove; and a TV blared.

The second were the drugs. La Nacha sat on a bed talking to a younger woman that Salazar soon found out was her daughter. Beside them was a stool with dozens of small strips of white paper. They were neatly arranged in a row. Each contained a $5 shot of brownish heroin. As Hypo later explained, it was what local addicts termed a "dirty load." A mark of the dearth of Mexican product, it was a mix of brown homegrown heroin and stronger white imported stuff.

La Nacha looked at Salazar suspiciously. She eyed his relatively healthy pallor and regarded his unmarked arms. Hypo got the hint. He explained that Salazar wasn't a "mainliner" yet. He didn't inject the heroin. He liked to sniff it. La Nacha nodded. Not all the gringos employed needles, and her product might have been mixed but it was still strong enough to allow for this other kind of use. "All right, he can come anytime." "At night we sell it across the street," added her daughter. It was a twenty-four–hour service.

The deal was done. La Nacha took the bill and handed Hypo a paper. Hypo and Salazar left. Immediately, their fates diverged. Hypo booked into a flophouse and injected the junk. He knew he was screwed. "I've got to quit this habit. For my little daughter's sake. I love her very much. God, I wish I could stop." Meanwhile, Salazar went back to El Paso and wrote up his story. Two days later "La Nacha Sells Dirty Dope at $5 a 'Papel'" was splashed over the front page. And four months later Salazar stood before a Senate committee in San Antonio recounting his encounter with the "Border Dope Queen" to a mass of startled politicians and reporters.

(It was a divergence—it should be said—that didn't last long. In 1970, Salazar discovered the state's general policy toward difficult Mexican Americans when he attended a Chicano civil rights march and was fatally hit in the face by a tear-gas grenade.)

Salazar was not the first person to be surprised by La Nacha. La Nacha had been confounding expectations for decades. And despite Salazar's tes- timony, she continued to do so for at least another ten years. From the 1920s until the late 1960s, she was the alpha and omega of the Ciudad Juárez trade. She was a one-woman syndicate, a multitasker who shifted her role depending on market demands. One day she was hawking small papers of morphine, another she was injecting heroin into the curious, and another she was selling it in bulk to wannabe traffickers. Police attention— from both sides of the border—was ever-present. She survived the violent death of her husband, repeated imprisonments ("she has been in the Juárez jail so many times, it is a second home," one journalist remarked), countless changes of local administration, beatings, extortion, and even conversion to evangelical Christianity. She not only survived; she thrived.

What surprised men like Salazar was not only her perseverance, but also the fact that she was a woman. In theory, the narcotics business was a man's game. Men owned the fields on which the drugs were grown; they formed the bulk of the intermediaries and wholesalers, and most of the traffickers, sellers, and addicts. Yet the masculine world of the drug business can be overplayed. It attracted most of the headlines and fed into both U.S. and Mexican visions of the narcotics business as inherently violent.

In reality, women played—and still play—key roles. Men owned the poppy fields; but women (and children) did most of the harvesting. Their hands were small and steady enough to wield the blade, make the delicate incisions, and extract the gum. Women were also some of the most important heroin chemists. They included Veneranda Bátiz, the upper-class Sinaloa chemistry graduate who teamed up with Eduardo "Lalo" Fernández to produce the first Mexican brown heroin, and Manuela Caro, heroin cook and aunt of future kingpin Rafael Caro Quintero. Women were also the mules. They hid the drugs under their blouses or skirts, took it up by train from Sinaloa to the border, or walked it over into the United States. And they were the women who ran the mules, taught them how to hide the drugs and avoid detection.

This should not surprise us. Women have always done unpaid labor in the house, in the fields, and in the market. Women still do. Drug growing, drug producing, and drug selling were not formal occupations. These jobs didn't have official contracts, hourly wages, and fortnightly paychecks. Compensation depended on the amount produced. So the entire family got involved. Women and children did a large proportion of the work.

But what did stand out was a handful of Mexico's more prominent female drug entrepreneurs. La Nacha was not alone. During the first half of the twentieth century, a handful of women dominated Mexico's local retail narcotics markets. They included Dominga Urias Uriarte, "La Minga," the sister of the Sinaloa chemist Miguel Urias Uriarte, who ran the heroin trade in Tijuana during the late 1940s and 1950s. And they included María Dolores Estévez Zuleta "Lola la Chata," who used a band of female street sellers to supply heroin and morphine to Mexico City's addicts from the 1930s to the 1950s.

*Ignacia Jasso, aka La Nacha, in one of her regular jail stints.*

In fact, Lola's business was so extensive and so long-lasting that she was as famous as La Nacha. By the time of her arrest in 1957, the newspapers called Lola "the empress of crime" and the "queen of drugs." In fact, she was so famous that even the self-obsessed American Beat author William Burroughs realized her importance. Though he never met her, he immortalized her in his particular brand of indulgent prose as slovenly underworld royalty, holding court like "three hundred pounds cut from the mountain rock of Mexico."

These women might have started their careers as the wives or sisters of criminals. And, initially at least, they might have relied on men for protection and enforcement muscle. But they built lasting careers through the employment of extended family, the use of female drug peddlers, the blanket bribery of public officials, and, perhaps most important, the manipulation of the law. Their survival was a mark of how, despite the Anslinger-inspired 1950s crackdown and the arming of the new generation of narcotraficantes, the mid-century Mexican drug trade still remained relatively peaceful.

La Nacha was always evasive about her age. At least she always lied about it to the authorities. She claimed she was 24 in 1925 and again in 1928; she said she was 27 in 1930; and she was somehow still 27 eighteen months later. In reality, she was born in 1900 in the small Durango mining town of Mapimí. During the Revolution, her parents moved to the border city of Ciudad Juárez. Like many urban immigrants, the family still maintained links to their rural roots. (La Nacha's house servants, for example, came from Durango.) But for the rest of her life, La Nacha would be based on the border in Ciudad Juárez or occasionally in the central city of Guadalajara.

Though La Nacha would spend over forty years as an independent dealer, it was her husband that introduced her to the trade. She married Pablo González, "El Pablote," in 1921. El Pablote was a good ten years older than La Nacha. And during their brief marriage it was El Pablote who garnered the headlines. He was also a newcomer to Ciudad Juárez. He had been born south in the agricultural center of Torreón. Like La Nacha, he had washed up in the border town some time around the end of the Revolution. He was a good shot and had started to work for Enrique Fernández's gang. He got into narcotics early. He and Enrique's brother, Antonio, did some of the first trips down to Mexico City to buy up medical heroin and transport it up to border pleasure seekers.

But El Pablote's real passion was violence. Not for him a suffocating life of quiet respectability. While Fernández diversified his assets and moved into real estate and mining, El Pablote stuck to what he knew best—causing chaos. During the 1920s, he was accused of masterminding a prison break, shooting up a hotel, fencing stolen jewelry, and robbing American tourists at gunpoint. He capped this all off in late January 1930 by shooting a policeman in the guts and leaving him to die. El

Pablote bragged that he liked to "breakfast early on owls [the slang for nightshift cops]." The bravado worked; the witnesses were too frightened to testify.

While El Pablote terrified staff at border bars and brothels, La Nacha slowly started to establish her own business. At first, the business involved other petty crime. In 1925, for example, she was caught stealing around 50 pesos of clothes from an El Paso shop and smuggling them back over the border. But soon narcotics started to dominate. Initially, she got the morphine and heroin from Enrique Fernández. Then by 1930 she and El Pablote set up their own network of family members. They bought the product from the capital's pharmacists and sent it up by train to the border.

Over the next five years, her drug business grew. Demand was good. It came from a multinational crowd of border addicts. Most were Americans like Hypo who made short trips into Mexico to buy their personal supplies. Others were an international mix of the desperate and the lost. They included Vicente Scotto, an Italian from Naples who had no home, slept on the street, and got drugs from La Nacha in return for running errands. Finally, a few were Mexico's small band of inveterate users.

But street addicts were problematic. They were unreliable; they drifted from place to place; and they had limited brand loyalty. They got their drugs wherever the drugs were cheapest. The non-Mexicans were the worst. They could snitch on you and then flee up to the United States (as the Italian Scotto eventually did). So by the end of the 1920s, La Nacha had also started to monopolize a rather more static and dependable market—Ciudad Juárez's prison population.

Ciudad Juárez's prison was an imposing building. It had been built during the dictatorship; it was two stories tall and made out of stone and brick; and a turret scored with thin gun slots stood to each side of the entrance. Its location was deliberate. It stood at the corner of the red-light district on Calle Mariscal (also known as the "Street of the Devil"). It was a reminder to partygoers of what the next day might bring if they misbehaved. The prison became an iconic city institution. It was an emblem of Ciudad Juárez as Wild West theme park. Local shops even used to sell postcards of the place.

But for La Nacha, the prison was literally a captive market. And by 1930 she dominated the place's drug sales. Three or four times a week she handed over small packets of heroin, cocaine, and marijuana to two women. They were prison food vendors. They hid the drugs in their baskets beneath their piles of tacos, sweets, and fruit. They brought them into the jail, and then sold them to the prisoners. Beyond the raw drugs, they also sold needles (to inject heroin), foil paper (for heating up the heroin), eyedroppers (to add water to the heated heroin), and even short knives (for sliding the heroin onto the foil paper).

At first, being married to El Pablote helped her evade capture. If addicts were caught and pointed the finger at La Nacha, fear of her husband soon inspired them to recant their statements.

Yet El Pablote's protection did not last long. And on October 10, 1930, he shot up his last bar. This time it was a Ciudad Juárez institution, Café Popular. Café Popular was a cabaret, bar, and brothel at the far end of the red-light street. A giant wooden palace, it hosted politicians and gunmen, business leaders and booze smugglers, journalists and pimps. It was big and brash. The owner, an imposing American woman, boasted that she employed 400 women and that patrons drank over 100 bottles of champagne a night.

The place could also be dangerous, especially when El Pablote was in. This time he entered around 3 A.M. and spied a policeman at the bar. Pleasantries were exchanged; then insults; then El Pablote pulled out his gun and opened fire. This time the policeman was more mobile—or at least less drunk. He hid behind a column and returned fire. A bullet struck El Pablote in the chest. Within seconds he was dead.

Three days later, the funeral was held. The *El Paso Evening Post* wrote it up as gangland drama. "Eyes blazing, black scarf flittering in the wind, La Nacha ... flung her arms wide over the grave as they lowered the coffin containing what had been her husband." "I promise you darling ... I'll kill the one who killed you," she vowed to the assembled mourners.

The aggrieved widow made for good copy but poor business PR. The policeman who managed to rid the city of El Pablote became a *cause célèbre*. Residents raised money to pay for his bail and protected him when he got out. The local newspaper led with the plea "May there be no successor to El Pablote." La Nacha was forced to shelve her planned revenge. Instead, she had to make do with a corrido in celebration of her late husband. Even this revealed a rather lukewarm opinion of the border bandit and a sneaking respect for his killer.

> El Pablote was feared
> All along the border
> Who would have thought
> That he would die this way?
>
> . . . .
>
> And Robles [the policeman] if not a hero
> Handed himself over to the police
> "If I took his life
> It was to defend my own."

El Pablote's posthumous reputation was the least of La Nacha's problems. Without her husband's threatening presence, the thirty-year-old widow was forced to turn to other means of maintaining and protecting her business. In doing so she moved from peddler to entrepreneur, modernizing and shaping Ciudad Juárez's drug market in her own image. By the next decade, she had seized control. She was so influential that by the late 1970s an El Paso Customs officer suggested that La Nacha was not merely an individual nickname, it was a term used to denote an entire organization. "It is like saying the Mafia."

For La Nacha, the employment of family was key. This was a relatively common trafficker tactic. Family members were easy to control and less likely to snitch. And it had the bonus of keeping the money in the family. But La Nacha went further than most, employing her extended family at every level of her organization. In the immediate aftermath of El Pablote's death, she involved her mother-in-law (who provided a useful stash house), her parents (who used their properties to bail her out of jail), two of El Pablote's nephews (who did the sales), and her halfbrother (who transported the heroin from Mexico City).

By the 1940s, her own children took central roles in the organization. They were particularly useful when La Nacha was either in hiding or forced exile. They provided legal business fronts as well as continuing distribution points. One son, Gilberto, bought an iconic border establishment—the

Can-Can Bar—in the middle of the red-light district, which he used to distribute heroin. Another son, Natividad, purchased a Turkish bath—the Baños Jordan—which did the same. And yet another, Ignacio, organized bands of street dealers. Plus, her eldest daughter's son, Hector Ruíz González, "the Arab," also worked as a drug distributor.

Outside immediate family, La Nacha's other employees were almost all women. Many were sex workers. They delivered the drugs from stash house to sales point; they sold the small packets of morphine and heroin; and if necessary they injected the drugs into their nervous clients. Again, the hiring policy made sense. Ciudad Juárez had been the site of a bustling sex trade since Prohibition. But during World War II, it grew. Though there were periodic crackdowns, police enthusiasm usually petered out. Local and state governments needed the money that sex workers paid to ply their trade. (One governor—Óscar Soto Maynez (1950–1955)—was rumored to earn as much as $2,500 in bribes per day.)

La Nacha's ploy of using women—and particularly sex workers—as peddlers worked at different levels. It tapped into a group of Mexicans who had regular contact with potential American clients. It piggybacked on an existing protection racket. And by employing other women, it allowed La Nacha to continue to intimidate sellers who threatened to snitch.

La Nacha's equal opportunity hiring policy revolutionized the Ciudad Juárez trade. A Mexican agent who visited the city in 1937 had seen nothing like it. "The commerce in opiates is scandalous; women and underage children are running about the poor neighborhoods and main cantinas selling little papers of drugs and goofballs." La Nacha, he noted, was at the center of it, handing out packages from her home to an array of American addicts and Mexican peddlers; five of her eight key sellers were women.

This panorama was also borne out by the statistics on drug crime. When the authorities tried to purge the city of drug dealers in 1947, over a quarter of those exiled were women. One in four may not seem like many, but these numbers distinguished the trade from that of other cities. In Tijuana only one in twenty of the sellers were women; in Mazatlán it was one in fifty.

Family members and female dealers formed a ring of protection around La Nacha. But her most important contacts were with the local political and judicial authorities. These started early. A year after El Pablote's death she secured the jail market by paying off (and, so the rumors went, sleeping with) the council member in charge of prisons. Within three years she had forged links with the ambitious Quevedo brothers. By 1934 the brothers not only dominated the state protection racket, they also took out her principal competitor, Enrique Fernández. (After Fernández's death, one newspaper speculated that "primary education's loss was La Nacha's gain.")

Over the next two decades, the political landscape would change. Rival groups would eventually unseat the Quevedo brothers. But La Nacha managed to come to new arrangements. In the 1950s it was with the governor, Óscar Soto Maynez, who supplemented his income from the sex trade with another $5,000 to $7,000 a week from the narcotics business. When Soto was sacked, it was with the head of the city police. And when he was fired, it was back to the governor.

La Nacha's links to state politics were important but not out of the ordinary. Most drug traffickers forged similar arrangements during the period. But what was exceptional was her control over another branch of the government—the judiciary. In particular, La Nacha was a master of getting out of prison by securing what was known as an *amparo*.

The amparo was a distinctively Mexican brand of juridical witchcraft. Originally established in the nineteenth century, the legal procedure was designed to prevent the authorities from obtaining convictions by infringing the constitution. This banned authoritarian policing techniques including torture, harassment, entrapment, and falsifying evidence. Yet what started out as a means to prevent dictatorial rule, soon became the go-to method for criminals to escape imprisonment. It would go on to become the drug trafficker's best friend. It took money and it took contacts. But employ the right lawyer, bribe the right judge, offer the right amount of money, and make the right accusations, and you were free.

Attaining amparos was La Nacha's specialty. Again, she had to learn quickly. In the immediate aftermath of El Pablote's death, the police picked up two addicts and got them to testify against La Nacha. She denied all the charges. She claimed that the witnesses were inveterate addicts (true), had been fed their lines by the police (again probably true), and were lying (probably less true). Nevertheless, the Ciudad Juárez judge decided against her. So instead, her lawyer approached another judge in the city of Monterrey, around 1,000 miles southeast of Ciudad Juárez. He was more flexible, or one suspects, more easily bribed. Within a year, he had decided in favor of her amparo. La Nacha was released.

Over the next two decades the amparo became La Nacha and her family's favored method for escaping prosecution. She acquired them in 1938, 1942, 1947, and 1953. Her daughter, Paula, got one in 1948 and her two sons, Gilberto and Natividad got them in 1956. In fact, La Nacha's manipulation of the legal system was so complete that by the early 1950s she had acquired a kind of super-amparo. It stated that the authorities were enacting a policy of harassment. So arresting her for drug offenses was breaking the law. An official legal notice, signed by a prominent judge, it worked as an effective get-out-of-jail free card. According to the U.S. consul, she carried it around wherever she went.

In many ways La Nacha's control of the Ciudad Juárez drug market was systematic. Other dealers came and went; they rose and fell. But for over thirty years she had the drugs, the sellers, the politicians, and the judges. But survival didn't simply take power and planning; it took innovation and flexibility.

These qualities marked her attitude to narcotics sourcing. Unlike many border sellers who came from the opium-growing areas and were wedded to particular production chains, La Nacha wasn't fussy. She was a retailer first and a wholesaler second. As the journalist Salazar discovered, she kept in close contact with addicts even into the 1950s.

She was also quick to see a bargain and moved rapidly from one supplier to another. In the early 1930s, she brought medical heroin and morphine from Mexico City. By the end of the decade she had moved to Mexican-made morphine cooked up by a small group of Chinese experts in Chihuahua City. At the start of World War II she had secured even better-quality morphine from a former police chemist in Guadalajara.

She was equally flexible and creative when it came to distribution. At first, she combined the captive market of the prison with roving bands of street sellers and sex workers. But soon her methods shifted and she started to open *picaderos*, or shooting galleries. These were small houses or apartments where addicts went to buy heroin, purchase or rent syringes, receive water to mix with the heroin, or even, if necessary, seek assistance from a peddler to locate a vein. Of course, such places had always existed in places with high rates of heroin use. But in Ciudad Juárez, La Nacha began to rely on them in the 1940s as a strategy to deal with evolving market conditions. Increasing numbers of American servicemen needed spaces on the Mexican side of the border to satisfy their needs, while new zoning regulations had closed down the old red-light district and scattered the vice trade all over the city.

La Nacha's female sellers dominated these new enterprises. In 1945, for example, police raided a house in the Bellavista neighborhood. The owners were a thirty-nine-year-old housewife and associate of La Nacha and her two twenty-something daughters. According to their source, the business was not only thriving; it was blatant. "I have seen them inject morphine into innumerable people as the door is open and they don't hide the traffic from anyone."

La Nacha was not only a talented businesswoman, but also a savvy political operator. And she was always shrewd in her dealings with the authorities. In 1942, for example, a new political faction took over the local government and got rid of the ambitious Quevedo brothers. This new group ran on a policy of clamping down on the vice industry. And it allied with the American authorities in order to do so. The new policy highlighted the vulnerability of La Nacha's position. Without official support, there were limits to the protection that family, female traffickers, or outsourced shooting galleries could give you. But the subsequent run-in also demonstrated La Nacha's ability to think on her feet, and, despite the odds, survive.

The first attempt to ensnare La Nacha was by the FBN. Two agents arrived in Ciudad Juárez and managed to track her down. They claimed that they were posing as pharmacists from Oklahoma in need of illegal opiates. According to those arrested, they were actually pretending to be U.S. government employees on official business asking for morphine for the war effort. (This was not only illegal; it was probably one of the roots of the rumor about official American sanctioning of the drug trade.)

Whatever their story, La Nacha was taken in. And in late 1942 she struck two deals. She arranged for the agents to meet her Guadalajara morphine chemist and she agreed to deliver fifteen cans of smoking opium in

El Paso. In both cases, the agents made arrests. The chemist and his associate were caught in San Antonio with 55 ounces of morphine and sentenced to five years in prison. The same month, the agents busted two of La Nacha's mules as they carried the other load over the border to El Paso.

But La Nacha remained free, at least for the moment. She had stayed in Ciudad Juárez and refused to cross the border for either deal. During the 1920s she had been a regular visitor to El Paso; she had even lived there briefly. But after El Pablote's death, she never returned. It was a rule she always followed. Sell to the Americans, but never go onto American territory. The strategy worked. As the local newspaper lamented, "the placid, motherly brains of the alleged gang, had won again."

She had not won, however, for long. The same year, the new Ciudad Juárez authorities raided her house. They found next to nothing—a few barbiturates, a solitary opium pill, and a small packet of morphine, which La Nacha claimed had been planted. But they also persuaded an American addict to testify against her. The situation looked bleak. Busted for possession and distribution, and without the help of the local authorities, La Nacha was looking at two years in prison.

She then did something that was surprising. Knowing she had powerful enemies in both Mexico and the United States, she declared she had converted to evangelical Christianity. She got a small group of fellow evangelicals who lived near her farm on the outskirts of the city to testify on her behalf. They declared that she was now a "religious woman who tries through all means possible to do good to the persons that need her. Yes, some time ago she lived a sinful life, but now her customs and feelings have changed."

She completed the look by inviting journalists into the prison to observe her reformed lifestyle. "I accepted Christ after I heard the Bible message. I have also found through reading the Scripture a consolation and a peace of mind hard to describe." She had become the matron for the female wing of the jail and arranged an evangelical preacher and his "bible prodigy" son to visit the place every Friday.

Perhaps the conversion was real? Perhaps La Nacha was really born again? If so, she would have been pretty unusual. In the 1940s even on the border, Roman Catholicism ruled. Switching to evangelical Christianity was social suicide and, as a result, extremely rare. (Despite considerable American efforts, at this time less than 1 percent of Mexicans converted.)

Whatever her true feelings, the conversion was certainly convenient. At the time, the Mexican president was threatening to invoke wartime emergency measures and send a select group of drug dealers to the notorious prison island of Islas Marías. La Nacha was one of the first on the list. Yet by claiming a sudden rash of religiosity, she managed to persuade the authorities of her good intentions, and to delay the sentence until the measures were revoked. She never went to the island and served the rest of her sentence in the Chihuahua City jail.

Over the next two decades, La Nacha's periodic bouts of piety would serve her well. It became part of her standard defense. When the mayor exiled over seventy peddlers from Ciudad Juárez in 1947, La Nacha pleaded a reformed character and managed to avoid the purge. (Her son, it seems, did not share her spiritual sentiments and was sent away from the city.) In 1954 she made the same claim to avoid new drug charges. And in 1960 she managed to duck charges of running a popular shooting gallery by publicly embracing an Albuquerque pastor. Lies or not, he was at least partially convinced. "I can't say I converted her, but I am hopeful. She promised to use her influence to help me set up a mission near her home. I believe in time that La Nacha is coming to Christ."

In 1982, La Nacha finally did come to Christ. She died. She was still living at her home in Bellavista. She left the house, a small farm, a Turkish bath, and two bars to her children. Her grandson, "the Arab," had already taken over the family business in the 1970s. Yet he had inherited a more dangerous trade than La Nacha had commanded. It was one that federal cops—not state policemen—ruled. And it was one in which violence, perhaps more than bribery, was the organizing principle. Whereas his grandmother had run the trade for five decades, he lasted only a few years. Times had changed.

# Part III

## The High
## 1960–1975

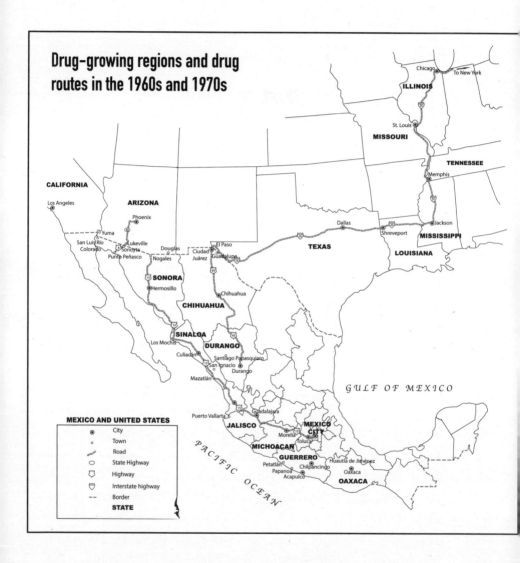

Drug-growing regions and drug
routes in the 1960s and 1970s

CALIFORNIA
Los Angeles

ARIZONA
Phoenix

Yuma
San Luis Rio
Colorado
Lukeville
Sonoyta
Punto Peñasco
Nogales
Douglas
El Paso
Ciudad
Juárez
Guadalupe

SONORA
Hermosillo

CHIHUAHUA
Chihuahua

SINALOA
Los Mochis
Culiacán

DURANGO
Santiago Papasquiaro
San Ignacio
Durango
Mazatlán

Puerto Vallarta
Guadalajara

JALISCO
Morelia
MEXICO CITY
Toluca

MICHOACAN
GUERRERO
Petatlán
Papanoa
Chilpancingo
Acapulco
Huautla de Jiménez
Oaxaca

OAXACA

TEXAS
Dallas
Shreveport

LOUISIANA

MISSISSIPPI
Jackson

Memphis

TENNESSEE

MISSOURI
St. Louis

ILLINOIS
Chicago
To New York

GULF OF MEXICO

PACIFIC OCEAN

MEXICO AND UNITED STATES
⊙  City
○  Town
／  Road
◯  State Highway
⬡  Highway
⬡  Interstate highway
--  Border
STATE

## Chapter 12

---

## The Mexican Stopover

THE FBN AGENTS HAD BEEN IMPERSONATING THE NEW YORK HEROIN dealer for weeks. They had been sending letters to the dealer's contacts in the hope that they might catch his supplier. But it was little more than a fishing expedition and they were about to give up. Yet somehow the supplier had taken the bait. It was December 12, 1953, and a tall, thin man with a French accent was sitting in the dealer's apartment. He was offering the two undercover FBN agents as much heroin as they could buy.

The tall man got the drugs, he explained, from a wholesaler based in Montreal. He deposited money in a Swiss bank account, and three days later he could pick up the heroin. He transported it to New York in specially made false-bottomed suitcases. The heroin was medical-grade stuff produced in labs recently built in the French port of Marseilles. The agents nodded. They knew that a lot of New York's heroin was now coming from Canada and being cooked up in France.

But the route the thin man described was new. Rather than transporting the drugs directly to Canada, his gang brought the heroin into the east coast of Mexico. They then transported it overland to Mexico City and flew

it up to Montreal. It was a route that over the next twenty years would provide nearly a quarter of America's heroin. It was also a route that would
change the scale, nature, and makeup of the both the national and the
international drug business. It was the "Mexican stopover" of what became
known as the French Connection.

The French Connection was made famous by the 1971 film of the
same name. Yet like so much drug war fiction, it told a complex story in a
simple (and racist) way. In fact, even the name—the French Connection—
was a bit of a misnomer. The finished heroin might have been produced in
French factories, but the postwar trade was a global business. The opium
itself came from Turkey. There local farmers siphoned off part of the legal
poppy crop and sold it on the black market. The opium gum was transported to Lebanon, where chemists cooked it down into morphine base.
Smugglers then took the base to Marseilles where Corsican underworld
chemists made it into heroin.

The Corsicans used myriad ways to bring the heroin into the United
States. Just as in the film, they packed it into cars, loaded the cars onto
ships, and then used unsuspecting French vacationers and clueless B-list
celebs to bring the cars to New York. They flew the stuff into Cuba, rested
up at luxury casinos, and then used high-speed boats to transport it the few
hundred miles to Miami. They flew it into Canada and then drove it over
the border into New York State. They also started to take it through Latin
America.

From 1950 to 1972, U.S. agents estimated that the French Connection
moved around 5 tons of pure heroin a year. It was around 80 percent of the
U.S. market. By the 1960s around a quarter of that came through Mexico.
It was big money; by 1970, agents estimated that Mexican contractors were
moving at least $20 million of Marseilles heroin per year.

Of course, using Mexico as a transshipment point was an old game.
Smugglers had been moving drugs from Asia and Europe over the border for at least four decades. But the Mexican stopover of the French
Connection was something new in scale and complexity. It began modestly,
with a handful of French, Canadians, and Corsicans collaborating out of a
Mexico City restaurant, but it soon expanded. By the 1960s, the group
provided heroin for all the border cities as well as much of the American

Southwest. The operation also became Mexicanized. It included notorious Mexico City gangsters, professional smugglers, PJF officials, and even some of the old Golden Triangle traffickers.

Until now, commentators have ignored the French Connection's "Mexican stopover." Mentions have been reduced to a few speculative tabloid stories. Yet it proved crucial to the development of the homegrown Mexican trade. Though U.S., Turkish, French, and Mexican efforts eventually broke the network in 1972, the rise and fall of this international ring of traffickers, local smugglers, and federal cops would shape the Mexican narcotics business over the next two decades.

Madame Hélène Maestri was an imposing woman. Tall, broad-shouldered, chain-smoking, with a booming voice and a thick accent, the French émigré was a star of the capital's demimonde. She had started out serving wine and cakes at the Café Paris in downtown Mexico City. France was hip at the time and the place became the city's go-to literary salon. It attracted many of the capital's up-and-coming authors, poets, and journalists. Mexico's Nobel laureate Octavio Paz remembered her attending tables, cigarette in hand, young lover in tow, and always "smelling of coffee and smoke." She had eyes, another poet remarked, like the statue of Athena at the Acropolis—"deep green, bovine, and shining."

In the 1950s, Hélène moved into the restaurant business. Her place— Chez Hélène—on Río Lerma was just a few streets from Café Paris. It offered a little taste of France—homemade pâté, onion soup, breaded chicken and mustard sauce. Though some of the wealthier writers still came, Hélène had priced out the rest. She now served a new clientele. Among them were French-speaking émigrés, though some spoke the language with a Corsican drawl and others with a Canadian twang. They dressed smart, kept themselves to themselves, and, most important for Hélène, they spent freely. They were the first members of the Mexican stopover.

The head of the operation was Antoine D'Agostino. In many ways he was a throwback to the well-traveled traffickers of the 1930s. Though still in his early thirties, he had been involved in organized crime for nearly two decades. Born to Italian parents in the French colony of Algiers in 1918, he was already committing robberies in his teens. By the time he went to the mainland at the age of twenty, he had been charged with rape and sex trafficking. During the war he moved to Paris. He split his time between spying for the Gestapo, dealing in black-market rations, and running a cabaret. Eventually, his past started to catch up with him. In 1947 he was charged with stealing ration coupons; then he was sentenced for treason in absentia.

On the run, D'Agostino fled to Italy and then Montreal. Here he adopted a new persona, invented a far-fetched backstory (which was not made more plausible when the police found notes outlining his backstory in his girlfriend's purse), and fell in with a group of émigré Corsicans and Canadian gangsters. Together they started to import heroin, first from Italy and then from the Marseilles factories.

The Canadian setup did not last long. In late 1949 the Canadian police started to round up these heroin importers. D'Agostino was forced to run again. By early 1950 he was in Mexico. He had adopted another name, grown a moustache, and started to rent an apartment on the Paseo de Reforma. According to the thin New York supplier, he insisted on wearing dark glasses at all times, and met mules and clients in the comforting setting of Chez Hélène. Within a year he was moving at least 6 kilos of heroin through Mexico per month.

His key ally in this was a man who in time would acquire an even longer criminal record than D'Agostino. His name was Paul Damien Mondoloni, although he also carried passports with four other identities. He was born in 1916 to a relatively well-off family in the beautiful Corsican city of Sartène. Like many of the island's young men, he spent his twenties as a colonial policeman in Indochina. Then sometime in the late 1930s he moved to do similar work in Algeria. The experience was formative. It taught him two essential lessons. The first was how to wield a gun. In August 1949 he and three other Corsicans accosted the wife of the Aga Khan, a prominent Muslim leader, as she left her villa near Cannes. They threatened to kill her unless she handed over her jewelry. They got away with over $450,000 worth.

The second was that narcotics were a good investment. In the aftermath of the robbery, Mondoloni fled France to Cuba and then Mexico. It was here that he met D'Agostino and established the transatlantic network. As early as 1958, the FBN described him as "one of the most important heroin violators involved in the international traffic." Each year he was reported to purchase "the entire output of several heroin laboratories in the Marseilles area and to organize the transfer of this heroin for distribution to American groups."

Professional, well funded, with high-quality sources and a secure distribution network, the Mexican stopover had a lot going for it. Yet it also had one rather glaring weakness. Composed of foreigners and with no Mexican members, it had no local protection. Unlike the 1930s *To the Ends of the Earth* gang, neither D'Agostino nor Mondoloni had family relations in the country. Even their girlfriends were from Marseilles. And D'Agostino spoke only French and Italian.

So after the skinny French dealer had coughed up the network to the New York FBN, their days were numbered. In late 1953, agents arrested one of D'Agostino's Canadian mules in New York. Within a year Mexican cops had tracked down D'Agostino's girlfriend. They followed her to a downtown shop, raided it, and found D'Agostino. Countries lined up to prosecute him. He was extradited to the United States, then Canada, then France, where he was finally imprisoned on charges of treason.

Mondoloni, however, remained free. For the next four years he would base himself in Havana. He lived a life of luxury, organizing the import of tons of Marseilles heroin and then distributing it to an array of Sicilian, American, and Canadian traffickers. But in 1959 the Cuban Revolution put an end to Havana's vice industry. Mondoloni was forced to return to Mexico and rebuild the Mexican end of the French Connection once again. This time he would not make the same mistake of neglecting Mexican protection. From 1960 on, the French Connection would go native.

This new French Connection *a la mexicana* consisted of three broad groups—mules, gangsters, and police protectors. The mules, in particular, were very much of the time. They were no longer sailors on transatlantic cargo ships or shawl-wrapped pedestrians shuffling over border crossings, a couple of ounces of heroin bound around their waists. The 1960s was the beginning of the jet age, the gradual start of mass commercial air travel.

*Paul Damien Mondoloni was the Corsican trafficker who organized French Connection heroin to go through Mexico.*

Drugs were one of the few products with enough markup to warrant the expense of this new form of travel.

As narcotics took to the air; mules moved up a social class. They increasingly became the kind of men who could afford to fly or at least had the confidence to look like they deserved to. Smuggling bought a suit and went business class. Technology shifted accordingly. False-bottomed suitcases—like the ones employed by the thin New York trafficker—became the go-to transport device for the discerning smuggler.

There were plenty of these new jet-setting mules, including pilots, businessmen, and embassy staffers. But the most high-profile was the retired colonel, former Olympic equestrian, and Mexican tourist board employee, Humberto Mariles Cortés. He was arrested in Paris in November 1972 attempting to smuggle 70 kilograms of heroin hidden in four false-bottom suitcases to Mexico on a diplomatic passport.

Whatever Mariles knew, it was clearly too much. Two weeks later, he was poisoned in his French jail cell. His girlfriend—Alma Escobedo

Martínez—returned to Mexico soon after and confessed. Her story was a sad one. It said as much about the limited opportunities for Mexican women as it did about how Mexican traffickers recruited new mules.

Escobedo had started her professional career as a secretary for a series of commercial companies. Her bosses were—to a man—crude and lascivious. Eventually, she left after one of them made, as she put it, a particularly "indecorous proposal." She returned home. But her mother didn't have the money to feed another adult, and she was forced to rent a room in a flophouse in the center of the capital. Here she became a sex worker. It was also here that she got to know a few of the underworld figures involved in the French Connection.

Her madam—a woman she knew as Blanca—could see that Escobedo hated the job. And Blanca suggested a way out. She knew a former john who was doing time for manslaughter in the Lecumberri prison. This was Mariles; he had shot a fellow driver in a roadside altercation. He was lonely and looking for companionship. Why didn't Escobedo go along on a conjugal visit? It was probably a sign of Escobedo's desperation that this seemed like a good opportunity. It was 1968 and she agreed. The relationship took off. Over the next three years Escobedo had two children with Mariles. To pay the bills, he sent her 2,500 pesos a month. Her mother, at least, was satisfied. And Escobedo was allowed back to the family home.

When Mariles left prison, he needed money. So he secured a job at the tourism board through an army friend. But Escobedo also introduced her old underworld acquaintances from the brothel. They suggested that he make a bit extra by bringing heroin from France. It was, they claimed, risk-free. The federal police who ran the Mexico City airport would welcome him when he arrived. (They would even give him breakfast!) Mariles had made three of these trips before he was eventually caught and killed.

Escobedo's confession is not only a depressing insight into the kind of desperation and human wreckage that often accompanied the drug trade, it also introduces two further layers of the Mexican stopover—the professional criminals and the federal police.

The most important of these criminals was the career smuggler Jorge Moreno Chauvet. Tabloids would later dub Moreno the "king of heroin." But he was not your average Mexican trafficker. He was born in the southeastern state of Yucatán to a family of wealthy merchants in the late 1920s. He was brought up in relative opulence in the suburbs of the state capital. His mother was French, his father Mexican, and his uncle head of the state chamber of commerce. He went to a private school, where he learned English and perfected his charm. One U.S. drug agent who met him in the 1960s described him as "a good-looking guy, smart, he acted like a college grad."

Moreno always had options. His siblings went on to become members of the elite. His sister married into another well-off local family. And his brother trained as an engineer and ran his own steel factory on the border. But rather than rely on his social networks, Moreno struck out on his own as a smuggler.

Yucatán had been a center of the smuggling trade for centuries. Lying on the Caribbean coast at the far east of Mexico, flat and with easy access to the sea, it was the perfect spot to bring goods in and out. As early as the 1600s British sailors had been teaming up with local merchants to break Spain's restrictive trade regulations. They brought the goods ashore on the state's pristine white beaches or, by the late eighteenth century, overland through the jungle from British Honduras.

By the mid-twentieth century, smugglers' methods reflected new patterns of global demand. Now Mayan relics were taken out and modern U.S.-made goods were brought in. Planes, not skiffs, did most of the work. In the early 1960s, one particularly garrulous smuggler explained the business to the U.S. consul. "There are 30 clandestine airstrips all over the peninsula from which small planes carried archeological treasures to the U.S. and to which they smuggled American appliances, watches, and guns in return." If relics weren't found, they were invented. Local artists whipped them up with a dentist's drill. "Anything ya want—rain god, corn god, my boys carve it up real good, put strings all over when they put it in the acid bath, like root marks. Sprinkle a little iodine on, like those brown spots on the rocks in the boonies, pee on it, leave it out in da sun a while so it looks like it was layin' around in a milpa [cornfield] somewhere."

Moreno was no artist, and he was not involved in mocking up the faux Mayan treasures. He funded the operations. In October 1956 he was busted for the first time. On raiding a warehouse just outside Mérida, customs officers found "women's dresses, expensive cloth for men and women's clothes, boxes of whisky, toiletries and jewelry." It had all been purchased in America. And no duty had been paid. Moreno was tracked down, arrested, fined 3,000 pesos and given two years in jail. Three years later he was busted again. By this time his business had grown. It now specialized in expensive fabrics and was worth an estimated 3 million pesos. He used airfields along the east coast of Mexico.

In a country where import tariffs were still high and the world's biggest manufacturer lay on the doorstep, being a goods smuggler was not a bad job. The Mexicans even had a name for it—a *fayuquero*—allegedly after an Arab word for a smuggling skiff. The profession was well compensated. By the end of the 1960s the Mexican government estimated that as much as a quarter of a billion dollars of U.S. products were being illegally imported per year.

Yet as Moreno discovered, smuggling untaxed legal goods also had its downside. The balance of risk and reward was good but not great. For a start, the initial investment was big. (In 1956, Moreno had spent 150,000 pesos on buying a plane and renting an airstrip and a warehouse.) Most infuriating, the Mexican customs authorities actually cared about this type of contraband. It was not only illegal, but also disloyal. As state advertising campaigns repeatedly reminded, importing U.S. goods depressed the peso and undermined the Mexican economy.

So, on getting out of prison, Moreno gave up the fabric-trafficking business. He moved to Mexico City and sometime around 1960 hooked up with Mondoloni. He brought in a few underworld figures he had met in prison and turned to smuggling drugs. It was a trade where the risks were not appreciably worse, but the rewards were much greater. And over the next two decades, Moreno's career move—from fayuquero to drug smuggler—would become increasingly common.

Moreno dealt with both sides of the smuggling business. He moved heroin from France to Mexico and also from Mexico to the United States. Professional smuggling had taught him to be flexible. At times, he relied on his old contacts. Associates went to Yucatán, met up with a fishing boat off the coast, brought in the heroin, and transported it to Mexico City. Other times he went to France to arrange the load.

What Moreno was careful to do, however, was not touch the drugs. He was the financer and organizer. The trafficking was left to the mules. In October 1963 a Canadian man, caught smuggling 34 kilograms of heroin over the border in Laredo, described how Moreno worked. The Canadian had been sent to Mexico City by a contact in the Montreal underworld. He was to hook up with a man called George at one of the capital's hotels. George was actually Moreno. The meet was pure underworld theater. The Canadian had been given one-half of a dollar bill. When Moreno walked in, he handed him the other half.

Over the next two days Moreno took the Canadian sightseeing. It was tourism as a trust exercise. "They showed us round the city. We didn't talk any business and in the evening they took us to dine in chic restaurants." George asked the Canadian for the keys to his car. Two days later one of George's associates returned the car. The back seats were packed with heroin and $500. The money was half of the mule's fee.

Moreno was clearly the most important of the French Connection's contacts. His name became shorthand for their operations in Mexico. His heroin traveled up the Eastern Seaboard to New York and across the Midwest to Chicago. In Mexico's border cities, almost all the peddlers bought from Moreno—although they sometimes mixed the product with homegrown stuff. These were what La Nacha would term "dirty loads."

No doubt Moreno had certain advantages. Fluent in Spanish, English, and French, he could converse with all the tiers of the Marseilles operation. As a well-spoken, dapper man, he could persuade higher-class Mexicans to work as mules. It was Moreno, for example, who persuaded Mariles, the Olympic equestrian, to make the runs to France.

But the operation was not perfect. Posh mules were more liable to talk. They lacked a streetwise distrust of the authorities and, threatened with torture, they rarely kept quiet. In the end, this perceived weakness is probably what got Mariles killed. As a result, Moreno still needed two things— muscle and protection.

Muscle he got from two brothers. They were already prolific killers, expert gunmen, and (less successful) armed robbers. Moreno would introduce them to the world of international narcotics smuggling. They in turn would introduce him to the world of Golden Triangle opium traffickers and

*Jorge Moreno Chauvet was a former fayuquero, or smuggler, before he got involved in the Mexican side of the French Connection.*

police protection. It was a coming together that was as important for the Mexican drug trade as the Chinese healer José Amarillas sharing opium production tips with the Badiraguato mayor, Melesio Cuen, or Veneranda Bátiz lending her pharmaceutical lab to Eduardo "Lalo" Fernández. It was a meeting that would shape the trafficking of narcotics for the next two decades.

The two brothers were Arturo and Hugo Izquierdo Ebrard. They were born in Nautla on the Caribbean coast of Veracruz. They were the youngest siblings of a revolutionary general. Though their father had joined the Revolution, they were not radicals or socialists. In fact, they had started their career, like the Gypsy, as guns-for-hire for the local landlords. They came to prominence in March 1948 when they were accused of assassinating a senator on a Mexico City street. Arturo pulled the trigger; Hugo drove getaway.

The murder made a tabloid splash. The two brothers were dubbed "super-gunmen" and depicted as cold-blooded professional killers. There were rumors that they were responsible for the death of over fifty Veracruz land reformers. Arturo—the younger—was particularly vain. Tall, rangy, and with a thin moustache, he would only allow his photo to be taken when he had combed his hair back. Because this was 1940s Mexico, journalists even speculated that the female judge's decision might be impeded by his good looks.

Somehow the judge resisted his charms and sentenced both brothers to the capital's Lecumberri prison. Though they were released around a decade later, they were not out long. In 1958 they tried to rob a Mexican Treasury money truck. They were picked up and thrown inside once more.

At this point the brothers took separate paths. Hugo went to Sinaloa. How he got there was a story in itself. In a move that seemed more Clint Eastwood film than measured public policy, the state governor, Leopoldo Sánchez Celis (1963–1968), invited Hugo to form part of a gang of ruthless—but also rather long-in-the-tooth—bodyguards. They were assembled to run the governor's drugs protection racket. Hugo accepted the offer. So in 1964 the governor had Hugo moved to Culiacán prison and released. He took a new name and married into the family of a Badiraguato heroin chemist.

While Hugo was getting close to Sinaloa's narcoaristocracy, Arturo was still in prison in Lecumberri when Moreno arrived, freshly convicted of heroin trafficking. By the time Arturo was released a few months later, they had decided to go into business together.

Moreno would be in charge of importing the heroin into Mexico, while Arturo would use his brother's contacts in Sinaloa to find buyers and move the substance over the border. Hugo chose two relatively established Sinaloa traffickers—Domingo Terrazas (a Badiraguato native and a neighbor of Hugo's in-laws) and Silvino Guzmán Villanueva (a relative of Joaquín "El Chapo" Guzmán Loera and probably the man who introduced him to the business). Terrazas put up the money—140,000 pesos for a kilo of heroin. Guzmán went down to Mexico City, met up with Arturo, tested a sample, and sealed the deal. He then collected the rest of the heroin and took a plane to Guadalajara, met up with Terrazas, and drove up to the coastal city of Mazatlán. Here, the two traffickers were busted. Police discovered the kilo of heroin in the cavity beneath Guzmán's false-bottomed case.

Hugo and Arturo's initial foray into the drug trade was not terribly successful. But Arturo's three-year sentence did not deter them. And over the next two decades Arturo, in particular, would become one of the shadowy figures behind Mexico's transformation from a relatively small-scale transshipment point to the most important drug-producing and drug-smuggling nation in the Americas. Clearly, the Sinaloa links helped. By the 1980s, Arturo would go into business with another former bodyguard of Governor Sánchez Celis—the 1980s "godfather" of the Mexican drug business Miguel Ángel Félix Gallardo. His Veracruz farms would become key sites for storing cocaine.

But the brothers' ascendance was not simply a result of their ability to link the flashy Euro importers with the Golden Triangle's experienced smugglers; they had family connections as well. Their sister, Graciela, was married to a cop. He was not just any cop, but a PJF cop. His name was Arturo Durazo Moreno. By the 1970s, Durazo, like Arturo Izquierdo Ebrard, would become one of Mexico's most notorious drug traffickers. For now, everyone knew him as "El Negro."

Durazo was born in the northern state of Sonora. His parents moved to Mexico City when he was young. They settled in the central district of Roma. In the 1930s the neighborhood still had that revolutionary air of social mobility. And it was a place where the capital's poor renters (like Durazo's parents) shared the streets with the city's more well-to-do bureaucrats and businessmen.

At school Durazo was not the brightest of students. But he was tough and loyal. These qualities attracted him to two of his rather more bookish classmates. They came from the capital's new middle classes. And they were going places where Durazo never would—high school, university, and the state bureaucracy. Their names were Luis Echeverría and José López Portillo. They would eventually become presidents of Mexico from 1970 to 1976 and from 1976 to 1982.

The two aspiring politicians did not forget the boy that had defended them from the school toughs. And as they climbed the administration, they found a place for Durazo in the state security forces. During the 1950s he worked for the DFS (allegedly using his "special talents" to torture Cuban émigrés like Fidel Castro). By the following decade he had switched to the

PJF, working with one of its antinarcotics units. When his school friend Luis Echeverría was made minister of the interior in 1964, Durazo was put in charge of running security at the Mexico City airport.

We do not know precisely how Moreno's French Connection, the Izquierdo Ebrard brothers, and their sister's husband Durazo came to an arrangement. Hugo always blamed his sister Graciela. She—he claimed— was the brains behind the operation. "You were asking me who was the head. Arturo now has more money, but she always gave the orders. Arturo is only a robot of my sister."

Graciela, by contrast, accused her husband. She and Durazo divorced in 1960. Since then, she claimed, Durazo had a personal vendetta against the Izquierdo Ebrard family. He had arrested Terrazas and Guzmán in Sinaloa, tortured them until they gave up Arturo, and then forced Arturo to reveal his source.

Whether it was the sister, the brothers, or the cop who instigated the association, by the mid-1960s, Durazo ran the protection racket for the French Connection.

American investigators heard about the arrangement as early as 1966. One of their French informers claimed that Durazo was charging Moreno $1,000 a kilo to traffic heroin through the capital's airport. Two years later they picked up another mule who claimed that her boss also paid Durazo for the same service. And the following year yet another trafficker gave the U.S. agents the number of his wholesaler in Mexico City. It was the number for Durazo's office at the airport.

Rumors and traffickers' confessions were one thing. But the Americans soon acquired eyewitness confirmation.

Richard Dunagan arrived in Mexico in 1966. Four years after Anslinger had retired, the FBN had finally set up a permanent base in the country. Dunagan was one of the first operatives. As with many U.S. agents, what he lacked in attention to detail and legal approval he made up for in bluster and daring. And in late 1966, he took this to the limit.

December 24 had been a bad day. His plane made an emergency landing just outside the Mexico City airport. Though no one had died, all the passengers were seriously shaken. And on arriving in the city, Dunagan was filled with adrenaline. So without waiting to change his clothes, he decided to make a case. He had a lead on where Moreno lived and the name of one of Moreno's contacts. He arrived at Moreno's surprisingly humble apartment and rung the bell. Moreno came to the door. Dunagan gave him the name of his contact. "How did you get my address?" Dunagan gave the name of another informer and seller of French heroin from Ciudad Juárez. Moreno slowly opened the door and let him in. Inside on the couch sat two PJF cops.

One, he recognized. It was Durazo.

Sadly, Dunagan's ploy came to nothing. Though Moreno agreed to meet him, negotiated a price, and agreed to hand over a kilo of heroin, Moreno quickly got cold feet. He walked away from the deal, accusing Dunagan (correctly) of being an undercover cop.

Though perhaps it didn't seem so at the time, it was a big miss both for U.S. drug enforcement and Mexican policing. Moreno died young in Lecumberri prison in 1973. (According to Hugo, he was poisoned by his associates.) But Durazo and the Izquierdo Ebrard brothers would continue to organize and protect the Mexican narcotics business for the next two decades.

## Chapter 13

## Acapulco Gold

IT WAS ENOUGH TO MAKE AN OLD SMUGGLER NOSTALGIC. IN JANUARY 1977, Jerry Kamstra was driving down Federal Highway 15 for the first time in five years. It was Mexico's west coast thoroughfare and ran all the way from the border crossing at Nogales, down the Pacific coast, to Mexico City. For nearly two decades, it had been the weed expressway.

Kamstra had first done the trip in 1962, bringing Levi's down, and transporting a dozen kilos of marijuana back up. They were the halcyon days—peaceful, uncomplicated, and well paid.

There was little knowledge, haphazard quality, lots of stumbling around and lots of profit for small investments. The first few trips my partner and I made in the early Sixties were handled in such an incredibly naïve fashion that now I shudder to think of it. We were driving back with weed in the back seat or sending it in a shoe box from Guadalajara.

Then there came the mania—Haight-Ashbury, the long hairs, the summer of love, the music, the celebration of getting high and dropping out. By 1967, it seemed to Jerry Kamstra like all America was moving product.

> Everybody was in on the action, hippies from Frisco with spare bucks and rebuilt Metros, golden boys from Manhattan Beach with hollow surfboards, sailors from Dago on weekend passes, hipsters from Hollywood on to the action taking place behind the [Tijuana] racetrack bleachers.

The weed business, Kamstra mused, had changed fast. Suddenly, marijuana had got "special attention from the Man." There were beefed-up Customs rounds, temporary border closures, roving U.S. drug agents, Mexican police roadblocks, army patrols, and aerial reconnaissance. Now there were diverse brands, superorganized hustlers, smuggler air fleets, and increasing violence. There was also "the complete loss of camaraderie among the few gringos still in the biz."

The 1960s marijuana boom transformed Mexico's drug trade forever. The scale, structure, working practices, and geography of the trade would never be the same again. In fact, in terms of the degree of change, it was closer to an oil boom or the coming of the railroads than your usual mild shift in drug preference.

In less than a decade, the narcotics business shifted from a small, localized operation involving a handful of transnational businessmen, some border peddlers, and a few dozen opium-growing villages to a multimillion-dollar business. As it did so, it spread and it expanded. The number of employees grew from the hundreds to the tens of thousands. They included the peasants who learned to trim the leaves and pull out the male plants and the old-school traffickers and bilingual elites who linked the whole operation to the U.S. buyers. As the money grew, so did the interested parties. And as Kamstra sadly observed, a poorly organized artisanal trade became more integrated, professional, and consumer-driven.

The weed trade was an example of what one observer has termed "deviant globalization." It preceded the reforms that opened up markets and shook up traditional industries in the 1980s and 1990s. It was hyperprofitable, needed relatively low overheads, and was initially at least open to anyone with a bit of money and some contacts. If you could avoid the cops, there were no regulations, no monopolies, no business rates, and no insurance payments. There was just pure demand and supply. It was what one smuggler called "the greatest experience in free enterprise a kid could have." It was outlaw capitalism. It was hippie shock doctrine.

The root of all the change was growing demand. During the 1960s the baby boomers came of age. They were young, moneyed, and eager to rebel against the dull, buttoned-down world of their parents. Marijuana, long demonized as a narcotic for the poorer, browner classes, now became a symbol of white suburban rebellion. And use rose dramatically. In 1962, around 2 million Americans, or 1 percent of the population, had experimented with weed. Eight years later around 3 million Americans were trying the drug for the first time every year. And by 1978, 60 percent of the country's graduating high-schoolers had tried the drug; nearly 40 percent smoked it regularly.

If drugs were at the center of the counterculture, Mexico was at the center of the drugs. The Beat Generation first publicized the idea that Mexico was a place where drugs were widely available and views of them were instinctively progressive. They were completely wrong—as they were about most things Mexican. (Mexico invented reefer madness and locked up more federal drug offenders per capita than the United States.) What was true was that prosecuting white Americans for marijuana was more trouble than it was worth.

During the 1950s, successive Americans came down to Mexico to experiment. Jack Kerouac went on the road, hung out with the locals (or what he described as "the essential strain of the basic primitive"), tried a love affair with a sex worker, got beaten up by her friends, smoked weed, and injected heroin. All the while, he spoke a garbled French-Spanish patois, which he assured readers the instinctively "Beat" Mexicans understood.

There was William Burroughs, who skipped Texas drug charges, took his family down to Mexico City, wolfed down morphine, marijuana, and peyote, shot his wife in the head, and became infuriated when this couldn't be resolved with a bribe. And there were the Beat vacationers—like Allen Ginsberg (sex workers, pyramids, and marijuana), Neal Cassady (marijuana, marijuana trafficking, and dying of exposure besides a Mexican railroad), and Bonnie Bremser (heroin, marijuana, and being sold into prostitution by her American writer-husband).

The literature and legends of these gringo tourists enticed a generation south. By the 1960s, the link between narcotics and Mexico was etched in youth culture. Three of the decade's most iconic drug lore moments happened in Mexico. LSD guru Timothy Leary first enjoyed psilocybin mushrooms by a pool in Cuernavaca. When American surveillance got too hot, Ken Kesey drove the Electric Kool-Aid Acid Test bus across the border. And creepy cultist Carlos Castaneda told his credulous readers that he had seen visions after taking peyote with his (probably fictitious) Yaqui shaman in northern Mexico.

But Mexico's function was not simply to feed the hippie imagination. It also started to play a physical role in the lives of 1960s youths. What had been the place for the Beats to slum it now became the go-to vacation site for millions of young Americans. The sun was out and the peso was 12.50 to the dollar. As one student newspaper reminded its readers, a brief summer job could get you two weeks in the Mexican surf and as many "beaches, beers, bikinis and bargains" as you wanted. It was a "virtual Disneyland of drugs, booze, sex and other assorted vices." Many of these tourists were college students. They borrowed their parents' cars and drove down the coast to bustling holiday resorts like Mazatlán, Puerto Vallarta, and Acapulco.

Drugs became crucial to the experience. In Mazatlán, college students skirted the swanky hotels at the top of town and passed the multicolored shrimping vessels that rocked in the surf. First, they made a line for Mar Vista, an open-air restaurant that was—according to Kamstra—"very popular with the new breed of doper-surfer-longhair." For a few years it became "the headquarters for every freak driving down the west of Mexico, drop zone for dealers and amateur smugglers, shooting gallery for junkies, street corner for spare changers, and stranded drifters." When the local police finally started to clamp down, the tourists just moved further south to the Balneario El Camarón where they could park their VW vans or set up their tents, buy weed, and smoke it away from prying eyes.

Mexico, then, was crucial to the development of both hippie myths and the hippie leisure industry. But Mexico's most important role was as the source of the majority of the counterculture marijuana. If you were American and smoked a joint between 1960 and 1978, the likelihood is it came from Mexico.

The numbers were telling. In 1961, U.S. Customs caught just over 300 kilograms of marijuana crossing the Mexican border. By 1967 this had risen to 22 tons; and by 1970 it was over 81 tons. Officials were finding nearly the same amount in just over a day as they were in a year a decade earlier.

Extrapolating out from Customs seizures is a fool's game. Who knew what percentage of the total they caught? The Customs Service itself made an optimistic estimate of around 5 percent. If this was the case, in 1970, Mexico was producing a low-ball estimate of 1,620 tons of weed a year. If true, this meant drug sales were channeling up to $8 million to Mexican peasant growers and $50 million to the big wholesalers. Just over the border the crop was worth up to $350 million or nearly a quarter of the value of Mexican exports.

The most obvious shift was geographic. Up until the mid-1960s, marijuana growing was limited to certain villages around the big cities. Ten years later, things had changed dramatically. Marijuana growing had spread throughout the republic. Growing zones expanded from the back gardens of small market towns and into the mountains of the Sierra Madre Occidental. The few hippies who made their way to these places whispered admiringly of the swaying dark green fronds of giant marijuana plantations.

One of these more adventurous tourists, mysteriously called "Big D," wrote a small guide to getting high in central Mexico in the mid-seventies. He mentioned some of the traditional planting villages but also newer regions that catered to hippie backpackers and the growing U.S. market. They included the beautiful town of Coscomatepec on the edge of the Pico de Orizaba in Veracruz, where the police were "quite mellow" and grass could be picked up for peasant rates of around $20 a kilo. And they included the fields surrounding the ruins at Palenque, where the police were "very friendly and liberal" as long as you wore a shirt. There was even a dopers hiking route, which ran down from Oaxaca's magic mushroom hotspot of

Huautla to the neighboring state of Veracruz. It was "always full of party people," and locals would sell you milk, mangos, and, of course, weed.

Though marijuana growing was relatively generalized, some patterns did start to emerge. In particular, a lot of the marijuana was grown in the mountains outside American tourist centers. There was a clear logic to this—a balancing out of risk and reward. Mountains hid the crops, at least until the advent of widespread aerial reconnaissance. And high altitudes were believed to produce better-quality weed. Yet growing marijuana near the sale point reduced the risk of seizure (by the cops) or robbery (by the bandits or the cops). Thus, there were concentrations of pot cultivation in the village of San Ignacio just east of Mazatlán, in Los Altos de Jalisco above Guadalajara, and in the hills of Papanoa and Petatlán between the two tourist zones of Acapulco and Zihuatanejo.

If marijuana changed the scale and the geography of the Mexican drug trade, it also shifted the makeup of the business. New groups of traffickers emerged on both sides of the border. As both risks and rewards grew, all of these groups innovated to stay ahead. In just a decade, there were radical changes in quality, packaging, growing processes, and smuggling methods. The speed with which these changes were made and the ruthlessness with which old techniques were discarded were astounding. The kinds of methods and practices that were gospel in 1967 were long out of date three years later.

The drug trade was meeting the rapid churn of mass consumer capitalism for the first time.

The most noticeable of the newcomers were the American traffickers. What marked out many of these new American smugglers were their distinctly elite origins. They were men like Rick Bibbero, who grew up in the exclusive Sea Cliff neighborhood of San Francisco before hooking up with a few other students at the University of the Pacific to transport weed over the Nogales frontier. They were his friends, like the privately educated Ciro Mancuso, who attended Tahoe Paradise College, spent his trafficking earnings on ski resort houses and whose daughter went on to become an Olympic ski champion.

Documentary maker Jay McMullen, who did a program on the scene in 1972, was shocked at how well off most smugglers were. One informant told him, "They come from colleges like Harvard, Yale and UCLA. They are either working on degrees or have degrees in sociology, political science and things like that." "If you want to put a label on them, you got to call them a cross section of Americana, apple pie and the American flag . . . they are from above the middle class."

White privilege met outlaw chic. This was trafficking out of choice, not desperation.

The principal task of the American smugglers was to locate marijuana wholesalers in the border towns. Or, if they wanted to make more money, one of the resorts-turned-pot-markets like Mazatlán, Acapulco, or Puerto Vallarta. They then organized the transportation of this product up through Mexico and over the frontier.

In general, as the San Francisco smuggler Kamstra explained, the profits were impressive. In the early 1960s he bought pot at $8 a kilo in the Mexican interior before selling it at $175 a kilo in San Francisco. It was a markup of over 2,000 percent. Big loads could generate massive rewards. In 1968, Kamstra smuggled 770 kilos in a single load. It was a complex business involving at least a dozen subcontractors, not to mention the peasant growers. But after subtracting the cost of planes, boats, mules, food, petrol, and airfares, he and his partner still earned $184,000 for a few months' work. Even split between two it was a whopping twelve times the average U.S. annual household income.

Smuggling techniques moved rapidly. First, many traffickers traveled by foot. Travis Ashbrook, a surfer-turned-pot dealer from Huntington Beach, remembers buying bulk weed in Tijuana around 1964. He took a taxi east to the quiet border post of Tecate, hiked over the frontier and dumped the weed in a ditch by the side of the road. He then returned to Tijuana, got his car and went back to pick up the marijuana.

As the market for marijuana grew, smugglers began to move hundreds rather than dozens of kilos. So they turned to cars. At first, they tried fitting packets under the seats or in the door panels. But soon Customs officers began searching the obvious hiding places. So they took the bed off Ford Ranchero trucks and added false bottoms. Packed well, the cavity would hold up to 200 kilos. They then added stiffer air shock absorbers so that law enforcement officials wouldn't notice the truck riding low because of the additional weight.

As vigilance increased, so did smuggler ingenuity. Around the border there were garages, which specialized in building "pop-proof" stash cars. In San Francisco it was "Rocky" and "Space," two mechanics who made rigs so secure you needed handmade tools to open then. On one occasion Customs stopped Rocky in a car with 25 kilos of hidden dope. After three and a half hours of searching, they found nothing. The escape went down in hippie lore.

In 1969, the era of car smuggling started to come to an end. Nixon upped the number of border Customs officials and sniffer dogs were introduced. But smugglers adapted again.

Many now took to transporting marijuana by plane. In part, this reflected changes in transport; air travel, like drug trafficking, was undergoing a process of radical democratization. From 1960 to 1980 the number of planes in the United States nearly trebled, rising from 75,000 to 213,000. (By comparison, between 1980 and 2000 they increased by only 3 percent.) So smugglers either got a pilot's license or hired a willing pilot. The circumstances were favorable. Thanks to the Vietnam War, experienced pilots with a sense of adventure and a grievance against the Man were not hard to find.

Planes had big advantages. First, there were the economies of scale. Even smaller, single-engine planes could hold nearly 800 kilograms of weed, or at least four times as much as a Ford Ranchero. Second, there was only a very remote chance of getting caught. In fact, between 1975 and 1977 more weed planes crashed than were actually captured.

The men who sold the Americans the weed were what Kamstra termed the "entrepreneurs." Mexicans called them *abastecedores*—wholesalers. (While it is probably unwise to hang a theory on doper nomenclature, the difference does seem to indicate a division between U.S. and Mexican visions of drug capitalism. For Americans it was about the dream of innovation; for Mexicans it was about the reality of market control.)

Whatever they were called, it was the Mexicans' job to locate the rural weed growers, buy up their product in bulk, organize its transportation down to the sales point, and locate the American buyers. Much like the big

Golden Triangle merchants of the early opium business, they were also responsible for storing and packaging the product.

Gazing back from a contemporary perspective, repurposing heroin networks for marijuana might seem an obvious move. But it was not. The drug trade was still a relatively scattered business. In general, marijuana and heroin sales were organized independently. Wholesalers, dealers, and smugglers were linked by bonds of trust and family to specific growers or markets. So, despite the bonanza, many of the earlier opium traffickers stuck to what they knew. They didn't get involved in the novel, unfamiliar, and more open marijuana trade. The Sinaloa heroin chemist Eduardo "Lalo" Fernández, for example, stayed out of the weed game completely throughout the 1960s and 1970s.

Yet, other old opium traffickers were less cautious. They realized that, even faced with an entirely new market of white college kids, they had certain natural advantages. They already knew groups of peasants willing to take risks for the promise of bigger profits. They had transport links, including trucks and airplanes, which could reach the more remote growing areas. They were based, predominantly, on the west coast near hippie hangouts like Mazatlán and Puerto Vallarta. They had established protection among the state officials. And they had contacts at other border sales points.

From the 1960s on, the biggest smugglers, with the largest clout, have always looked north to the latest opportunities. And they have moved easily from marijuana to cocaine to methamphetamine to fentanyl depending on the market.

The most high-profile of these new multitasking narcotraficantes was Pedro Avilés Pérez. Over the years, Avilés has gained a legendary reputation in both U.S. counternarcotics circles and his home state of Sinaloa. He has inspired a grand nickname (the Lion of the Sierra), a host of corridos (including one by the master, Paulino Vargas), and a film (the slightly less impressive *La Clave 7*).

U.S. agents credit him with bridging the gap between the first and second generation of traffickers, professionalizing the Mexican drug business, and training a new generation of more urban, sophisticated smugglers. In the 1980s they claimed he was the "greedy, cold-blooded organizational

genius" who taught Miguel Ángel Félix Gallardo to group together dispa-
rate smugglers into a cartel-like organization. "Before Avilés you could go
shopping for prices. It was all fragmented. Then Avilés came in and said,
'Lets put it all in one place, deal with one person and set a price.' It was like
the OPEC cartel."

These were exaggerations. The counterculture weed business had no
real price controls; there was certainly no cartel; and Avilés was just one
among many old opium smugglers involved in the marijuana business. In
fact, his demonization was probably more to do with the DEA's desire to
create an obvious public enemy than with any wholesale restructuring of
the drug business. (Furthermore, as we shall see, the DEA had a particular
reason to demonize Avilés; they needed to justify their part in his targeted
assassination in 1978.)

But, like most myths, the legend had a kernel of truth.

Avilés's early life remains mysterious. Some claim he was born in the
1920s and was already running heroin up to the border during the World
War II boom years. The DEA believed he was born around 1940, while the
memorial by the side of the road where he was murdered states he was
born in 1948. His birthplace is equally opaque. Some claim it was on the
Durango–Sinaloa border; others, the small mountain village of Ciénega de
Silva in Chihuahua.

What we do know is that he first appeared on the DEA radar in 1968.
Sometime in the early 1970s he ushered in a key innovation in the trafficking business. Rather than move heroin and marijuana separately in individual loads, Avilés established a series of general narcotics warehouses on the
U.S.–Mexico border.

The warehouses were based in the Sonora frontier town of San Luis
Río Colorado. At the time, San Luis was a small, dusty, out-of-the-way
place. It had no industry except a cotton mill; there was limited agriculture;
it sat opposite the rather uninspiring Arizona town of Yuma; and there was
virtually no tourism, just a few shabby restaurants and hotels. A U.S. journalist who visited the place claimed it had "no reason at all to exist except
for the traffic in narcotics."

It was here that Avilés established his business. First, he built an imposing house on the main drag. It was a huge "fortress-like" building with half

an acre of land, an underground storage cellar, high walls, and broken glass studded in the top. Trucks went in and out of the gates at all hours of the day. He also purchased ranches just outside the city center and constructed storage warehouses and short dirt runways.

Smugglers—particularly from Sinaloa—drove their drugs up and stored them at the warehouses. This was Avilés as narcomentor. One of his young associates was Juan José Esparragoza Moreno, "El Azul." Another was Rafael Caro Quintero. They would both go on to play key roles in what became known as the "Guadalajara Cartel." Clearly, Avilés was still perfecting his training techniques. Both Esparragoza and Caro Quintero were caught bringing weed up to the warehouses and imprisoned.

Beyond providing storage, Avilés also provided contacts and transport. Contacts came in the form of the new generation of hippie smugglers. According to U.S. Customs, San Luis Río Colorado was "the score center for California dopers." The meeting place was the Rancho Motel near his house on the main drag. With a swimming pool, the Rivera Club bar, and over fifty bedrooms, it was a place to relax in as well as a place to make deals.

Transport was provided by trucks or planes. Here again, Avilés innovated. Traffickers had used planes before, but Avilés expanded the practice. He had U.S. pilots steal planes from small airports, take them to his ranches, load them with marijuana, and then fly them over the border. By 1973 he had at least a dozen aircraft, including large twin-engine Lockheed Lodestars. U.S. agents described it as a "fleet." Mechanics serviced the planes to make sure they worked, and spare parts were flown in every few months.

But the key to Avilés's success was integration. Offering storage, contacts, and transport to both heroin and marijuana peddlers all in the same place a few miles from the U.S. border was something new. It allowed Avilés's business to grow far beyond earlier trafficking operations. This was a long way from Lalo Fernández cooking up heroin in his kitchen or La Nacha selling wraps of heroin out of her front door.

Officials on both sides of the border soon got some understanding of the scale of the operation. Arizona drug agent Phil Jordan had been aware of the Avilés stash houses for at least a couple of years. And in 1973 he finally got clearance to organize a joint U.S.–Mexican mission against the trafficker. The mission was a mark of America's new power over Mexican drug policy. It was run out of Phoenix and manned by U.S. agents, Yuma County police, and a select group of PJF cops. It was called Operation Cactus.

In late February 1973 the Americans got word from an informer that Avilés was on his ranch. They descended on it in force. What they found amazed them. The gunmen who defended the ranch were equipped with the latest weapons. "It was like a firefight in Vietnam." When they eventually gained entry, they found a staggering 24 tons of marijuana hidden beneath one of the barns. In all, over the next two weeks, the agents discovered another 45 tons of marijuana hidden in stashes around the town. They also confiscated 39 airplanes. At the time, it was the biggest dope bust in Mexican history. Even if they were poor-quality, the loads would have been worth over $12 million in Los Angeles.

Avilés himself escaped, but only just. He had been tipped off and sped off just as the police arrived. The U.S. agents found coffee and breakfast on the table and still warm.

What happened after the San Luis Río Colorado bust is hazy. Rumors abounded. Avilés had become a recluse and got addicted to heroin; he had moved down to Guadalajara and undergone plastic surgery; he had offered $10,000 for the head of any American drug agent.

More likely, he returned to Sinaloa and went underground. His brothers—Francisco and Carmelo—became the public faces of the family business. Francisco's La Pitayita ranch just outside Culiacán became the base of operation. It was a big place, used nominally for cattle farming. But there were also heroin labs, marijuana stashes, and two airstrips. American smugglers now paid money upfront into a U.S. bank, flew down to the ranch, and picked up as much marijuana as they had paid for. Carmelo moved northeast to Ciudad Juárez, where he linked up with local smugglers to move the marijuana over the border into Texas.

In the long term, Avilés may have been the most influential of these new entrepreneurs. But he also shared the expanding trade with a host of newcomers.

One group that moved in quickly were the border smugglers. After Prohibition, they had diversified. They now moved certain valuable, untaxed commodities out (including spirits, coffee, lumber and *candelilla* wax—a vital ingredient in chewing gum and shoe polish). And they moved other untaxed goods in (including cars, electrical goods, gold, and jewelry). Many of them had become de facto fayuqueros. But with the growth in the marijuana market, they saw new opportunities. And like the old opium dealers, they had certain initial advantages. They had links to U.S. communities; they knew the unguarded routes over the border; and many of them already had political protection. All they needed to do was find some marijuana and get to know some hippies.

The other large group of entrepreneurs was based in the new hippie tourist resorts. Here smuggling experience was less necessary. Many of the American buyers shifted the product. Instead, you needed three qualities— English language skills, capital, and connections among the mountain growers. Being bilingual was especially crucial. Despite their college educations, most U.S. smugglers did not speak Spanish. (This should come as little surprise. Still today there are U.S. professors of Mexican history whose Spanish is limited to shouting restaurant orders.) In fact, one U.S. pilot admitted that of a hundred or so smugglers he knew, only two knew the language. "They don't go to the ranches as they don't speak English. Instead they go to the intermediaries."

Because of these essentials, many of these tourist-zone wholesalers came from the elite. One pot smuggler, Richard King, had a source in Acapulco called Manuel Mendoza. He was half-Uruguayan, half-German, and spoke three languages fluently. He had married into a Mexican family, sent his son to a posh private school, and managed to marry him off to a senator's daughter. Contacts gave him clout. And when he made the move from fayuquero to drug smuggler, he was confident he was well protected. In fact, Mendoza was so elite, that he hadn't even tried the herb. "He believed that it was only the poorer lower-class Mexicans that smoked it."

The entrepreneurs, like the American smugglers, were also pioneers. First came the changes in packaging. During the early days, marijuana was bundled into burlap sacks. It was bulky and stank. By the middle of the 1960s, even the more naïve Customs inspectors could pick out the odor of the herb. So the entrepreneurs modernized. They started to soak the mar-ijuana in sugar solution or Coca-Cola, box it into 1-kilo blocks, and then press it down with a hydraulic jack. These blocks (dubbed "Telephone Books") were then wrapped in cellophane. Blocks could be secreted easily in car doors or stacked simply in planes. And the cellophane hindered—at least somewhat—the ostentatious smell.

Perhaps the biggest change was in the quality of the weed. The pres-sure came from up north. During the early 1960s most consumers didn't care about quality. Weed was so scarce, they smoked anything. But as mar-ijuana went on the mass market, concern for quality grew. In part, then, this was a question of taste. Some wanted a brief buzz, others a prolonged, trippier experience. And no one wanted to spend their time picking out sticks, seeds, and stones. But it was—although few admitted it—also a question of prestige. What better way to prove your counterculture creden-tials than having the best weed?

The drug trade was bumping up against those emerging signifiers of consumer capitalism—choice and status.

By the late 1960s the concern for quality had hit the market. Mediocre weed sold cheap or simply didn't sell. American buyers disparaged it as ditchweed, Culiacán Garbage, or Tijuana Regular. Instead, they started to search for more rewarding highs.

Distinctions started to be made. Michoacán pot was held to be darker in color and stonier because of the damper climate in the state's coastal hot lands. Nayarit marijuana was more psychedelic as it was grown at high altitudes. Different types of weed started to acquire different names. Most famously there was Acapulco Gold, which was popularized by a dreadful 1967 song and a tedious 1973 guerrilla documentary. But there was also Zacatecas Purple, Guadalajara Green, and Yucatán Red.

The most desirable weed, and the one that could get entrepreneurs the best price, was *sinsemilla*, or "seedless," marijuana. It was the name given to the unpollinated fluffy tops of female marijuana plants. Stacked with resin and particularly potent, by the end of the 1960s it had gained the reputation as the gold standard of Mexican weed, golder even than Acapulco Gold. By 1969 a kilo of the best sinsemilla would fetch four times the price of regular weed.

To this day, legends about the origins of sinsemilla abound. It was only grown in Oaxaca and had to be harvested by female growers. It was grown in the mountains outside Puerto Vallarta by an unspecified group of "Indians." It was first popularized by a counterculture supernetwork that included protohippie Tom Newman, California rock band the Byrds, and a DEA fink and inveterate bullshit artist, David Wheeler.

Stripping fact from the mess of weed-addled memories and self-mythologizing is like doing archeology in a tar pit. But we can be sure of some things more than others. First, Mexicans knew about the properties of unpollinated marijuana plants for at least half a century. There was even a local term for it doing the rounds since the 1910s. It was "sheep's tail."

Second, sinsemilla was popularized and first sold in bulk by a fabled Jalisco-based weed entrepreneur. The American buyers knew him only as "Papa Grande." It was Papa Grande who sold his product to the weed-funded LSD cult the Brotherhood of Eternal Love. It was Papa Grande who provided the marijuana for Lake Tahoe dope entrepreneur Ciro Mancuso. And it was Papa Grande who started the fad for specialized packaging.

His "sheep's tails" were immaculately stacked in colored cellophane wrappings. A sticker on the front showed a cartoon of a peasant. In one hand he grasped a wad of dollars; in the other, a few branches of marijuana. Underneath was the boast "Papa Grande: No Hay Mejor" (Big Daddy: There's No Better). At Christmas he would even cover the product in seasonal wrapping paper.

Papa Grande's identity is still a matter of debate. He was the Keyser Söze of Kush. Some claim that it was just a stock name used by an array of different weed dealers. Yet the stories about Papa Grande seem too consistent to be a generic marketing myth. Others assert that it was Pedro Avilés Pérez or Ernesto Fonseca Carrillo. But neither was based in Jalisco in the 1960s.

However, by triangulating half-a-dozen former trafficker testimonies together with available published information, it is possible to make an educated guess. Most probably, Papa Grande was another former Golden Triangle wholesaler. His name was Ruperto Beltrán Monzón.

Though Beltrán is now all but forgotten, for a moment during the 1960s, he had a reputation akin to that of Joaquín "El Chapo" Guzmán Loera with a story full of savvy business sense, daring prison breaks, outlaw heroics, and the occasional murder.

Beltrán was born sometime in the late 1920s in the tiny hamlet of Milpas Viejas, Badiraguato. He was slight, with a moustache and a single gold tooth. With his wife, another Badiraguato native, he started buying and processing opium during the 1940s. Various siblings and cousins operated as the couple's agents.

In the early 1960s, Beltrán started to move into marijuana. Initially, he bought his product from the hills between Puerto Vallarta and Guadalajara. He then moved it by train up the coast to Baja California. Trouble, however, soon followed. In 1961 he was accused of killing a federal transit cop who had stopped him when he was transporting drugs through Mexicali. He pleaded not guilty. His lawyer claimed that he was an illiterate simpleton set up by vicious police thugs. The supposed witnesses had been so badly beaten they would have "confessed to their guilt in the deaths of Christ, Abraham Lincoln, and Mahatma Gandhi."

Despite the lawyer's claims, Beltrán was sentenced to thirty years. Yet prison didn't hold Beltrán. For a supposed simpleton, he was pretty slippery. He escaped in 1964 by hiding in a piece of prison furniture. He was caught, but escaped again in 1965, this time by organizing a mass prison break.

Wanted and hunted, he moved his entire operation permanently to the marijuana-growing region to the west of Guadalajara. Here, according to his hippie buyers, he set up in a large hacienda, most probably somewhere near the small village of Las Navajas. He continued to work with his family.

His wife continued to buy opium and process heroin; he moved into producing high-quality weed. It was, according to one buyer, "well cared for, manicured, sinsemilla, without any waste and picked at the right time." It was purplish in color with greenish rich buds. The dope came from up in the Jalisco Sierra or from down south in Michoacán. Deals were done in nearby campsites or down by the coast outside the port of Manzanillo.

Around 1970, Beltrán assumed an increasingly low profile. The military moved into Guadalajara and arrested many of the gang. The soldiers claimed, at first, to have captured Beltrán himself. But two days later they stated that they had made a mistake. Whether this was a genuine error—or more likely they had released him after the payment of a bribe—it is hard to say. But after the run-in, Beltrán ceased to trouble the tabloids.

Nevertheless, his legacy lived on. Members of the Brotherhood of Eternal Love transported his pot from Mexico to Hawaii. Here it mixed with native strains and fueled the island's surfer hangouts. It became known by the cognoscenti as "Maui Wowie" and by the alarmist tabloids as "superpot." It even received that most coveted of posthippie accolades: the "warm smell" of Papa Grande's *"colitas"* was commemorated in the Eagles' "Hotel California."

Yet such fame was rare. Few Mexicans involved in the weed business acquired transnational legends. The majority of those involved—and the people from whom men like Avilés and Beltrán bought their product— were the weed growers. They were at the bottom of the bonanza. In general, they were Mexico's poorest peasants. They lived in remote villages up in the mountains.

For Mexico's peasants the marijuana boom arrived at an opportune time. It was a classic meeting of U.S. demand and Mexican desperation. By the 1960s the rural economy was in decline; poverty was worsening. Increasing birthrates were annulling the benefits of revolutionary land distribution; local elites were struggling bitterly against any further allocation of their lands; the government was keeping prices for agricultural crops artificially low; and rural wages remained pitiful. In 1975, for example, the government estimated that of the 8 million Mexicans involved in farming, nearly three-quarters earned less than 300 pesos ($24) a month.

By comparison, peasant weed growers could get paid a minimum of $2 a kilo of weed. Most peasants could probably afford to give up around half an acre to the new crop, often interspersed between corn plants. At best this could produce around half a ton of marijuana—or at least $1,000 worth. No doubt the peasant cut of the drug business was woeful. (This was raw, untrammeled capitalism after all. In San Francisco the same amount would be worth at least a hundred times more.) But it was better than the alternative. Six months of work on a hardy, relatively labor-unintensive crop paid you over four times what most peasants could earn in a year picking tomatoes or harvesting corn.

Such rewards drove thousands into the emerging industry. In some places it even took over from traditional subsistence agriculture. In San Ignacio, Sinaloa, just outside Mazatlán,

[t]here arrived a moment in which the principal crop, more than corn, beans and squash, was marijuana. No one even bothered to hide it. There was a competition between the peasants to see who could sow and produce more. I remember that there was an enthusiasm among the sowers. Although it had been grown a little in the years before, it was not until then that it reached its peak. It was like discovering something similar to gold.

*By the 1960s, growing marijuana among the cornstalks was a common way to disguise the crop.*

In fact, marijuana growing became such a part of everyday peasant life in certain communities that it soon developed its own customs and traditions. Angel del Valle published a fascinating snapshot of weed growers in an unnamed town near Mexico City in the late 1960s. He observed how peasants planted the seeds on the side of the ridge that got most sun and was least likely to flood. He saw how they disguised the plants with foliage or by growing it between corn stalks.

Around harvesttime he claimed that local *curanderos*, or healers (presumably the descendants of the herb vendors of the late nineteenth century), went to check that the plants were ready. They did this by walking the field in a white smock and seeing how much resin stuck to their costumes. If they came back covered in the stuff, it was time to cut. In fact, there were even fiestas to mark the beginning and the end of the marijuana season.

In Mexico, culture moved fast. Marijuana had gone north and been converted into a consumer product. Yet back in the villages, it was already being reincorporated into the peasant way of life.

In the end, the demise of the Mexican peasantry would take another half century. And peasants would go on to employ a series of strategies to stave off the end. Some took up arms and joined left-wing guerrilla insurgencies; others fled to find uncertain but slightly better paid work in the cities; others, still, fled up to the United States.

But others turned to drug growing. It was—and still is—the opposite of white-collar weed smuggling. It was not a choice; it was a necessity. And perhaps even more than guerrilla insurgency or mass outmigration, it would shape Mexican peasant relations with the outside world for the next fifty years.

Unlike dying in abject poverty, it attracted the attention of the Mexican and U.S. governments.

# Chapter 14

## Mexican Brown

MEXICO'S 1960S MARIJUANA BOOM WAS FOLLOWED ALMOST IMMEDIATELY BY another drug bonanza, this time for heroin.

In early 1973 after a smattering of high-profile French Connection busts, President Richard Nixon proudly announced that America had "turned the corner on drug addiction." By the end of the year, U.S. drug agents grimly joked, "Yeah, we turned a corner, and there was an army coming."

On the streets, desperation bred innovation. Just twelve months earlier, most U.S. addicts had been injecting white heroin. Produced in Marseilles heroin factories, the French Connection product was usually around 5 to 7 percent pure. The U.S. drug agents who collected heroin samples from throughout the country found that an average of 72 percent was cooked up in Europe. Only 28 percent was the brown-colored Mexican product. But by November 1973, the numbers had reversed. Now 45 percent of samples were white; 55 percent were brown.

By 1975, agents found that 90 percent of 300 samples taken in fourteen U.S. cities were Mexican brown (if powdered and good-quality) or Mexican mud (if poor-quality, gooey, and darker). In cities like Chicago and Los Angeles, all the narcotics came from south of the border. In cities like New York, where the French stuff had dominated, Mexican product now comprised over 80 percent of smack. "Everyone is doing business with the Mexicans today. There's practically no other way to deal in heroin," declared one DEA investigator.

Furthermore, it was stronger—much stronger. On average it ran at 17 percent pure. Some of the samples in New York's East Village were over 30 percent. A lot of 1970s addicts were not just getting high; they were getting dead. In 1971, only 29 heroin addicts had expired from overdoses. By 1975 it was 1,789.

Just like the marijuana boom, the heroin rush transformed the Mexican trade. It cemented the geographical dispersion of the trade. Peasants outside the Golden Triangle started to grow poppies as well as weed. Smugglers in eastern border towns like Reynosa and Nuevo Laredo started to move heroin as well as marijuana.

The structure of the opium business also changed. Consumer capitalism hit heroin; the artisanal turned professional. Chemists tested, innovated, and traced out changes in U.S. tastes. And there was a new focus on U.S. sales. Such shifts allowed old-time Golden Triangle traffickers like Eduardo "Lalo" Fernández and Jorge Favela Escobosa to shore up their enterprises. But it also encouraged a new generation of traffickers to enter the trade.

By the early 1970s, America was going through one of its periodic opiate crises. In part, it was generational. Counterculture youths had no recollection of the harmful effects that heroin had wrought on their grandparents' generation. But it was also a question of circumstances. Rebellion had become associated with drug taking. And some young Americans were taking it to its logical conclusion. One Baltimore high school student described the journey. Around 1966 "I started on Thunderbird wine and then sniffing glue." The next year he moved on to marijuana and pills. In the counterculture economy, narcotics were prestige; they were the markers of cool. "The more serious drug I used, the more status. To me, marijuana was status because it was illegal ... I was completely on Quaaludes most of eleventh grade." By 1968 "everyone had moved up a notch ... The drinkers were into pot and the pot smokers of the previous years were into acid." This student was now on heroin.

At the same time, young U.S. soldiers were fighting a brutal war in Vietnam. Most smoked marijuana and many started to take heroin. "Fourteen year old girls were selling heroin at roadside stands on the main highway from Saigon to the U.S. army base at Long Binh. Saigon street peddlers stuffed plastic vials of 95% heroin into the pockets of GIs as they strolled through down town Saigon," claimed one eyewitness. By 1971 half of all enlisted men had tried the drug.

Heroin had, in the words of one historian, left the ghetto and crossed both the "suburban" and the "military firewalls." Heroin had become a drug for white middle-class kids. One 1974 study claimed that 6 percent of men between twenty and thirty had tried heroin and half of these were hooked. The same historian estimated that as many as 3 in every 1,000 Americans were addicts.

At first, American addicts used French heroin. It was dependable and easy to acquire. Ten to twelve tons were imported per year. But, during the last years of the 1960s, the authorities started to squeeze supply. It was an international effort. In Turkey, the authorities reduced the number of officially registered poppy cultivation areas. And in mid-1971, they agreed to a complete ban on the crop. In the United States, drug agents began to make high-profile busts.

Finally, France started to crack down. In part, it was U.S. pressure. But mostly it was the growth of France's own heroin problem. "It exploded on us. Now kids here are going straight to mainlining heroin with no waystops, no hash or LSD, along the way." The authorities came down hard. In 1972, narcotics cops raided the Marseilles labs and arrested the major chemists. The French Connection had come to an end.

Mexico's own role in the French operation was also rapidly wound up. In Mexico there was rather less fanfare. In April 1972 the PJF shot dead a Corsican trafficker, Lucien Sarti, in a Mexico City street. Six months later the former Olympic equestrian, Mariles, was killed in a Paris jail. And soon after that the Yucatán smuggler Moreno met a suspicious end in Lecumberri prison.

Yet even after the killings of 1972, the heroin business continued to grow—perhaps even faster than the marijuana boom. One laid the groundwork for the other. The knowledge, the infrastructure, the routes, and the protection rackets were already in place. Enterprising narcos realized those same routes could be repurposed to move Mexican brown. So, between 1972 and 1976, Mexico went from producing around a ton of heroin per year to producing between 5 and 10 tons. At the border each kilo was worth a low-ball $30,000. Together, it produced annual revenue of $150 million to $300 million. Potentially, it was worth up to 15 percent of Mexican national exports.

By the 1970s the heroin business had moved way beyond the Golden Triangle's mountain villages. It now sustained many of Mexico's struggling peasants.

Quite how many, no one really knew. No doubt a lot of U.S. intel was guesswork used to generate funding for counternarcotics institutions. (In August 1975, in a rare moment of honesty, the DEA admitted that its knowledge of opium cultivation in Mexico was "so lacking in detail and documentation as to handicap any detailed analysis.") But nonetheless the DEA tried. And what it claimed was a lot. A DEA report estimated that by 1976 a minimum of 217,000 laborers worked on planting, thinning, weeding, and harvesting the opium poppies. If further stages of collecting, processing, and trafficking were taken into account, the number was nearer 500,000 or a somewhat incredible 1 percent of the Mexican population.

As demand increased, opium production spread. From the rural villages around the Golden Triangle, poppy cultivation extended to places like Choix in the foothills to the north of Culiacán, which had never grown poppies before. After returning to Pacific coast states with intermittent traditions of opium production like Michoacán and Jalisco, the crop spread further into the mountains of Guerrero, Oaxaca, and Chiapas. Finally, it moved east to the highlands of Veracruz and Puebla. By the middle of the 1970s there were reports of opium plantations on the Guatemalan border and in the hills overlooking the port of Veracruz. The U.S. authorities confirmed that it was being grown in at least ten of Mexico's thirty-one states.

Technical expertise followed. At first, the big buyers contracted skillful poppy scorers from the mountains around Badiraguato. The skilled workers fanned out to the newly opened fields, where they earned a day wage to extract the gum from the poppy bulbs. But they also ended up teaching local peasants how to do so themselves. So, by the second half of the 1970s, most scorers were from the villages where the poppies were grown.

Money also followed. Most poppy fields were relatively small enterprises, around a quarter to half a hectare in size. Any bigger and a field risked detection. But even a quarter of a hectare could produce 2 kilos of opium worth a minimum of $3,000 or about five times the average annual wage

Initially, this sideline cultivation simply put food on the table. "Yes, I planted opium poppy and marijuana fields. You do what you must to eat. We're poor in my village. We grow drugs to buy food," confessed one Sinaloa peasant. But some started to earn enough to take part in Mexico's new commercial economy. In 1976, Salvador Díaz, from an unnamed village in western Mexico, explained that he had started growing poppies four years ago. His crop wasn't large, just enough to earn $1,000 a year. But it was five times what he got from producing potatoes or melons. It pushed him from subsistence farmer to consumer. He had already bought his first car, a 1955 Ford. And he was eyeing a new TV and a sewing machine for his wife.

For most peasants, the new crop paid for a handful of electronic goods, a car, or as counternarcotics campaigns increased, an imported U.S. gun. Others looked longer-term and invested in a small bit of agricultural land, urban property, or a university education for their children. (In Oaxaca, quite a few teachers and engineers admitted that their parents briefly dabbled in drug production to pay for their university fees and living expenses.)

In some villages, particularly in highland Sinaloa, the combination of opium cultivation and work as poppy scorers produced serious profits. The British agronomist Paul Yates was treated to a brief vision of one of these surreal, high-spending booms.

Yates had been doing a report on irrigation projects in the coastal town of Los Mochis for nearly a year. In early 1974 one of his Mexican friends invited him to take a tour of the Sinaloa Sierra. The trip up was an uninspiring moonscape. "Occasionally I caught sight of a patch of maize among the rocks, a little barley in a gully, a few uncouth, rough looking locals, until we came to a village." The village looked tiny—a handful of small adobe houses, a public square and a single brightly painted church. But initial impressions were deceptive.

> We strolled along the one and only street. There were shops with the latest hi-fis and electrical equipment, there were shops with dishwashers and deep freezers, there were shops featuring expensive gowns and ladies underwear. There were two car dealers, one with in its window a Lincoln Limousine, the other showing an Alfa Romeo Sports. What was going on here?

His guide had one word. "Poppies."

They went to one of the village bars and took a table. A spit-and-sawdust cantina this was not. They ordered a bottle of Dom Pérignon and two fat Cuban cigars. His guide started to explain.

> This is poppy country. You may not have noticed coming up the hill a movable barrier at the side of the road. It is electronically controlled. They know me, but you would not have been allowed in. Had you persisted you would have been shot, and the incident would never have been reported.... These people look like peasants. They affect that appearance deliberately as a disguise. But make no mistake; each of them is a peso millionaire. Several are dollar millionaires. They tolerate me here because they know I will keep my mouth shut. By the way don't mention in your report what you have seen here. It would not be healthy for you.

No doubt the guide was exaggerating. Most opium growers were far from peso millionaires supping Dom Pérignon in hilltop cafés. Yet Yates's observations ring true. He certainly had no reason to lie. Until recently, they remained buried in his unpublished diaries.

The heroin boom, like the marijuana bonanza, also spawned a new generation of smugglers. Most were limited, freelance operations. They bought up small amounts of opium from the farmers, paid for chemists to process it into heroin, took it up to the frontier, and then moved it over the border. Even small amounts made big money. One trafficker told documentary maker Jay McMullen that he could make 2 kilos of heroin for around $13,600. On the border he could sell this for $60,000. The profit was over $46,000.

In some crossings, these smugglers dominated the economy. And they transformed the look and the layout of towns. Between 1970 and 1974, for example, the population of Nogales doubled to around 100,000 people. Here one U.S. journalist claimed,

> Narcotics traffic [was] so blatant that on the border hypes from Arizona can cross through the checkpoint and go to a long line of cabs parked on the Mexican side of the fence. The cabbies are fully equipped with the works and bags of heroin. For a $15 cab ride the hypes can shoot up in the cab within rock-tossing view of the Customs headquarters.

But Nogales didn't offer only dime bags. If you wanted a bigger score, there were the dealers. Mid-level sellers moved product out of the bars in the red-light district of Canal Street. They included Hector Ojeda Miller Jr., who ran La Posta cantina, cooked a mean steak, and reserved the upstairs room for drug deals. He was wanted in the United States but was protected by his father, a customs inspector.

But the really big transactions were done at the La Roca restaurant. A cavernous place, carved out of the side of a cliff, it had a courtyard and a fountain out front "illuminated by discreet electric bulbs and flickering torches." It was a luxurious joint. According to one U.S. journalist who visited the place, "its opulence mocked the poverty surrounding it."

Meanwhile, drugs were stored in the Buenos Aires district on the outskirts of town. U.S. agents dubbed it "the junk warehouse." A decade earlier it had been a mix of cardboard and corrugated-iron shacks. Now there were small houses made of brick or concrete. Locals paid for their construction by guarding small quantities of heroin and cocaine. "This is an entirely new area whose new (although low in comparison) affluence is entirely due to the dope traffic," surmised a visiting reporter.

The wealthy traffickers had moved on from Buenos Aires to a new development perched on a hill above Canal Street. It was called the Colonia Kennedy. Here lush new homes cost up to $300,000. Lincoln Limousines were parked in the driveways. "I went up to a house there not long ago. I've never seen anything like it. It had a library as big as a three-bedroom house. It's all dope money up there. That's the only way anybody in Nogales can afford homes like that," reported one Nogales old-timer. They even had a name for it—Dopers' Row.

Because the amounts needed to make a profit were so small, most of it was brought over by individual smugglers. There were hundreds of them and most were contracted per haul. It was what locals called an *operación hormiga*," or an "ant job." Whereas Customs had caught shipments of over 300 kilograms of French heroin, by 1974 the most Mexican brown they had ever captured was 8 kg. Some walked, others traveled by horse, but most smuggled by car. As weed smugglers took to the air, as much as 94 percent of heroin was still packed into door cavities or secreted by expert mechanics inside the engine.

Though the heroin industry was fairly dispersed, there was also a handful of wealthier and more powerful trafficking clans. Over the past thirty years they had formed trafficking networks and cemented them with ties of blood, intermarriage, and friendship. Many were still from the Golden Triangle and included the pioneer of brown heroin Lalo Fernández and the 1950s businessman-trafficker Jorge Favela Escobosa. To stay ahead, they started to innovate in the fields of drug production and sales.

Fernández, in particular, had expanded his influence. His base was Tierra Blanca, a suburb to the north of Culiacán just over the Humaya River. Visiting journalists described it as "a sprawling disarray of one-storey homes and shops, unpaved streets and noisy cantinas." A traditional first stop for many of the city's rural immigrants, it had a reputation for lawlessness and was the location of many of the state's prefab heroin labs. Locals still remember their strong vinegary smell pervading the streets.

Here, Fernández was in charge. He was the cacique, or strongman. He adjudicated disputes between residents, dished out money to the poor, and handed out presents at Christmas. His wife also did extensive charity work, purchasing beds for the hospital and buying books for schoolchildren.

Meanwhile, those directly involved in the business got rich. When documentary maker Jay McMullen flew over Tierra Blanca in late 1973, he noticed new California-style homes replete with gardens and swimming pools.

But Fernández's influence stretched beyond Culiacán's poorer neighborhoods. He also had strong political connections. Multiple sources—from U.S. drug cops through Mexican secret service agents to government employees—testified to the links between Fernández and Leopoldo Sánchez Celis, the governor of Sinaloa (1963–1968). Fernández's wife and the governor grew up in the same small Sinaloa village. The governor's rather cloyingly positive biography ends with the following cryptic but revealing lines.

In the Colonia Tierra Blanca, the chief [presumably Lalo Fernández] continued to manage the big business with complete security … [Sánchez Celis] had friends in the business but no one could prove his links … but the horse rides didn't stop nor the presence of the friend in the parties of Tierra Blanca, because the concept of Friendship that Don Leopoldo had was too great to break up these situations.

The bonds between the trafficker and the governor went beyond shared leisure activities. The governor's administration even agreed to rename one of the main streets of Tierra Blanca after Lalo's grandfather, the revolutionary hero also called Eduardo Fernández.

For the U.S. narcotics agents, Fernández was "like a ghost." Though they knew he was Culiacán's most important heroin trafficker for at least fifteen years, they never managed to get an informant in his organization. He rarely left Tierra Blanca. And U.S. agents rarely—if ever—went in. In fact, he was so mysterious, the Americans didn't even know what he looked like.

Culiacán's other major trafficker was Jorge Favela Escobosa. He was a merchant's son from a suburb of Culiacán, with an elite background. Journalists portrayed him as surprisingly refined, a fan of horse racing but also classical music. They also claimed he was extremely rich. There were rumors of Swiss bank accounts, bribes in excess of $10 million, PEMEX gasoline franchises, construction firms, and seaside tourist complexes.

*Eduardo "Lalo" Fernández (circled) among his neighbors in the Culiacán suburb of Tierra Blanca. They are attending the ceremony for renaming Tierra Blanca's main thoroughfare after Lalo's grandfather, the revolutionary hero also named Eduardo Fernández.*

*Eduardo "Lalo" Fernández with his wife. She came from the same town as Governor Sánchez Celis.*

According to the DEA, he had such good contacts that he could pull together a 100 kilograms heroin deal in a matter of hours. Like Lalo Fernández, Favela was also obsessively discreet. His organization comprised close family members. His wife (a cousin of Pedro Avilés Pérez) took an important role. And he almost always traveled under an assumed name. When he was arrested briefly in 1976, he was carrying ten false IDs.

During the 1970s heroin boom, Lalo Fernández and Favela cooperated. The Americans thought Fernández was the "godfather" and Favela an important lieutenant. The Mexicans tended to describe Favela as the senior partner (principally because they caught him). They were probably more-or-less equal associates who worked together on some of the Mexican drug trade's major innovations.

The first change was to the quality of heroin. Growers and processors started to notice that poppies grown in different soil types and at different altitudes had different concentrations of opium. It took around 10 kilograms of Sinaloa opium to make 1 kilogram of heroin; by contrast, it took only 6 kilograms of gum produced in Guerrero to make the same amount. Ageing the opium also helped concentrate its narcotic properties. As a result, big purchasers like Fernández and Favela increasingly bought better-quality opium from the southern states. They also started to store and stockpile the gum, often for as much as six months.

At the same time, they also improved the heroin processing. Labs were moved from the villages down to the city. They became more permanent and were now based in brick houses rather than wooden shacks. Better gear was bought; it was even rumored that some traffickers were buying job lots of old U.S. university chemistry equipment.

The younger generation of Sinaloa cooks took chemistry and pharmacy courses at the local university to improve their skills. New foreign chemists also arrived. There were rumors of French Connection chemists fleeing to Mexico as early as 1972. And over the next five years dozens of American heroin cooks came down to Culiacán and worked in the family labs.

By the mid-1970s, the Mexican heroin market—like the Mexican marijuana market—was diversifying. Consumer culture was hitting smack. There was faux French Connection white, grainy Mexican brown, gooey Mexican mud, and pretty much everything in between. Colors ranged from white to light beige to dark brown; consistencies from large grains to small dog kibble; and purity from a low-grade uncut level of 45 percent to French Connection levels of around 90 percent.

Big dealers like Favela and Fernández encouraged their chemists to come up with the better product. "It was necessary to hand over quality, we competed amongst each other for who sold the best. Purer drugs meant better earnings and was more attractive to the traffickers and those that could pay for it," explained one chemist.

Chemists shared knowledge together with tips of the trade. They learned to add novocaine to the mix to increase strength. Fernández and Favela's light beige heroin "made in Culiacán" (although often using opium from Guerrero) got the reputation as the best Mexico had to offer. In fact, it got so good that some Culiacán chemists even started to dye some of their well-processed white heroin brown in order to give it an authentic look.

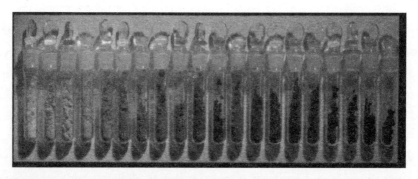

*During the 1970s, Mexican chemists produced many different varieties of brown heroin.*

If heroin was the big earner, traffickers like Fernández and Favela also started to move into another highly addictive hard narcotic—cocaine. Quite how this came about is still unclear. No doubt the U.S. market played an important role. During the early 1970s, demand for cocaine started to grow; it was a glam drug, taken by rock stars, actors, and the higher echelons of bohemia. (It was cocaine that the two bikers smuggled in from Mexico in *Easy Rider.*) But soon it started to move down the social hierarchy. And between 1969 and 1974, U.S. seizures of the drug increased sevenfold.

The Sinaloa traffickers were there almost from the beginning. According to those close to Fernández, he had been in the business long enough to realize that drug fads came and went. It was heroin now, but soon it would be cocaine. At the same time, his daughter married into a Colombian military family. They allegedly provided the link between the cocaine wholesalers and the Mexican traffickers.

Favela was also an early adapter. In 1976, his brother-in-law, Jaime Buelna Avilés, confessed that Favela had been selling him cocaine for at least four years. He would buy a kilo for around $12,000. He either sold it to Ciudad Juárez smugglers who took it over the border, or carved it up into smaller loads and sold it to a Culiacán peddler who peddled it around the city's upscale bars and nightclubs.

Cocaine soon started to rival heroin in terms of weight, if not quite value. As early as 1975 the DEA claimed that Mexico was trafficking 35 to 40 percent—4 to 5 tons— of America's cocaine. If true, it was worth another $60 million.

Furthermore, there was some evidence that traffickers like Fernández and Favela were using their chemical know-how to make even more money. By the mid-1970s, they were importing coca paste, or *basuco*, from Peru. They were then using their own labs to transform it into cocaine. Basuco could be bought at a fraction of the cost of the finished product and converted into cocaine in a one-to-one ratio, but only with the right chemicals. In 1977 the Americans got confirmation. A cocaine chemist told Peruvian police that his boss, one of the country's biggest traffickers, had sold 2 tons of coca paste to a Mexican trafficker the previous year. His name—Lalo Fernández

As well as experimenting with new drugs, the big Golden Triangle traffickers also tried to secure U.S. distribution networks.

Fernández and Favela looked at two groups. In the Southwest they focused on experienced Mexican-American dealers. In Los Angeles, for example, Favela's biggest customer was Arthur Martinez, a forty-something peddler originally from New Mexico. As early as 1967, he was rumored to receive 2 kilos of Favela's heroin and ½ kilo of his cocaine per month. Quickly, the business grew. By 1970, Martinez boasted to one informant that he had over 100 sellers on the Los Angeles streets. And the following year, one of his moneymen claimed to U.S. agents that he was delivering $100,000 to Favela's stash house in Tijuana every week.

In 1972 the Americans started to investigate Martinez in earnest. They discovered that Favela's men would hide the heroin in a small cavity between the radiator and the frame of a car. They would drive it from Tijuana to Los Angeles and park it somewhere on Beverly Boulevard. The deliveryman then phoned Martinez, who ordered his own employee to pick up the car. It was taken to a garage, the product was removed, the radiator put back in place, and the car returned to Favela's deliveryman. The heroin was then divvied up into 10-ounce lots for Martinez's dealers. These lots were distributed in dead drops in telephone booths and restrooms, disguised in rolled-up newspapers or even cereal boxes. Every week, Martinez would also take a slice of his profits and send it back to Tijuana to pay for the next load.

Investigators also discovered that Martinez, like Favela, was careful to launder his profits through legal businesses. He had a clothing store, an appliance store, a car-leasing store, a shoe company that sold Mexican-made shoes (and was also allegedly used for smuggling), and two Sizzler restaurants. Hawking cocaine had even got him contacts in the movie business. This was, after all, L.A. He had set up a production company with a former Hollywood weed dealer. He had even started to use the house of the star of a cooking show as a stash house.

The other distribution network was the American Mafia. Evidence for this was much weaker. Of course, there were always rumors. An anonymous heroin wholesaler told filmmaker Jay McMullen that a lot of the product was sold in advance to U.S. Mafia buyers.

But there were also more solid leads. In early 1977, DEA sources reported that the Mafia head Joseph "Joe Bananas" Bonanno had flown from his new residence in Tucson to Culiacán. Favela's brother, Victor, met him. He was driven to one of Mazatlán's most upmarket hotels, the Camino Real. Here, he discussed business with the Favela brothers and a Bogotá-based cocaine trafficker for four hours. The report concluded, "The Bonanno meeting with Favela Escobosa is extremely significant since it puts the shrewdest of all the U.S. mafia bosses and one of the most

experienced of the mafia dope traffickers in league with the top drug supplier in Mexico."

In fact, U.S. distribution networks were now so important that they
formed the basis of a new group of Mexican traffickers. They were the
clans with extensive extended families north of the border.

The biggest and most notorious of these new cross-border trafficking
clans were the Herreras. The patriarch of the family was Jaime Herrera
Nevárez. In many ways Herrera was an archetypal Mexican farmer. He
was born in the late 1920s in the small town of Santiago Papasquiaro,
Durango, on the eastern side of the Sierra Madre Occidental. Like many of
the Golden Triangle's opium wholesalers, he came from one of the town's
wealthier families. And before he got involved in narcotics, he had made
money in timber, cattle ranching, and commerce. Buying up raw opium,
processing it, and then selling the refined product was simply an extension
of his commercial enterprise.

While traffickers like Fernández and Favela relied on technical know-
how and product innovation, the Herreras' advantages were rather more
circumstantial. First came the roads. During the 1940s, most of the opium
grown in Durango went west. Trucks and mules took it down to the Sinaloa
lowlands and up the Pacific coast. But during the following decade the
state built a network of roads that ran east. These linked Herrera's hometown to the state capital of Durango and the crucial crossing point of
Ciudad Juárez. From there, you could get to Chicago in just over twenty-
four hours. And as the Herreras found out, when the French Connection
collapsed, Chicago was the doorway to the East Coast heroin market.

Second, there was the migration. Chicago had been a center of Mexican
migration since the Revolution. But with expansion of the steel and meat-
packing industries, the movement grew. And by 1960 there were over
50,000 Mexicans spread over the two western neighborhoods of Pilsen and
Little Village. Many were from Durango and had fled during the religious
conflicts of the 1920s and the droughts of the 1940s. The Herreras discovered that the community provided a ready-made protection and distribution network.

The circumstances might have been favorable, but the Herreras also
played them well. They moved from transporting to processing. Durango

gum was no longer shipped off to Sinaloa to be cooked up. It was now boiled down in labs in small villages near Santiago Papasquiaro as well as in Durango City.

They also focused on smuggling the heroin to the United States in new and interesting ways. It was packed in wheels of Chilchota cheese; it was hidden in metal pipes and fed to cows that were then shipped to Chicago slaughterhouses. But mostly it was smuggled by car. It was another "ant job." A couple of kilos were stuffed in the metal sleeve surrounding the driveshaft. Covered in road grime, it was almost impossible to find. The technique was so successful and so prevalent it even got a name—the Durango driveshaft.

But the Herreras' real strength was distribution. The difference between the price for wholesale and street-sale heroin was enormous. During the mid-1970s, you could get a kilo of heroin for around $30,000 on the border. In Chicago, cut with additives and milk powder, that same heroin kilo was worth over $200,000.

The big markup persuaded the Herreras to move into sales. Dozens of members of the Herrera organization started to arrive in Chicago. Many were family members. They included Jaime's brother—Reyes Herrera Sr.—who bought the El Centenario restaurant in the South Side Kensington neighborhood. They included his son, Reyes Herrera Jr. who orchestrated street sales. They included Jaime's son, Efraín, shot dead in a Chicago bar in 1974. And they included two cousins, Jesús Herrera Díaz and José Ramón Herrera, who were arrested in 1973 for selling 1-ounce bags of heroin on the corner of 122nd Street and Halsted.

The move changed the geography of the U.S. heroin trade forever. As the *Arizona Republic* pronounced in 1979, "For decades Chicago has smarted under the epithet of America's second city. But in one area, Chicago takes second place to none. Heroin trafficking." Now most of America's heroin came through the city. And a lot of it stayed there. By the second half of the decade, the DEA claimed that there were now over 400 dealers and nearly 60,000 addicts. If true, the city had an addiction rate of around 20 per 1,000, seven times the most pessimistic national average. But a lot was also distributed to eastern cities like Boston, Pittsburgh, and, most important, New York.

For the Herreras, it was a boom time. By the end of the decade, the DEA claimed that the Herreras were delivering as much as 8 tons of 5 percent heroin to the city per year. After expenses, this gave a profit of a staggering $155 million. The U.S. agents surmised that as much as $100 million was sent back to Mexico. No doubt it made the Herreras extremely wealthy.

But it also paid scaled-up state protection rackets.

## Chapter 15

### The Rackets

AL GAY OWNED THE DUST-BOWL BORDER TOWN OF LUKEVILLE. ADMITTEDLY, there was not much to own. There was a trailer park, a motel, a mall, a gas station, and an airfield. Out of season, the population barely hit double figures. The bank had foreclosed on the last owner. Big overheads and minimal traffic had sunk the venture.

Despite Lukeville's shabby exterior and limited potential, Gay had gone out of his way to purchase all the property in the area. The owner of charter air services in Alaska and Phoenix, he had bet his existing companies on his ability to make the place work. He had persuaded the local bankers to sell the bank to him, built a new grocery store, refitted the airfield, and bought 150 acres of extra land.

But the desert hamlet did have one advantage. It rested on the Mexican border. Just a few hundred meters south lay the town of Sonoyta. Here Route 2 from Baja California met Route 8, which ran up from the coast at Puerto Peñasco. It was a drug-running thoroughfare. Customs officers called it "the hub." And Gay knew it. According to the DEA, the entrepreneur had made his money trafficking marijuana from Mexico into the

United States. He was a daredevil pilot and still proudly demonstrated to visitors how he flew below the Customs radar.

Now he was establishing a more stable business. It was a cross-border venture. Drugs came by fishing boat into Puerto Peñasco. They were transported to Sonoyta and then up to the grocery store at Lukeville. Trucks then drove the narcotics, hidden under piles of fresh fish, to Gay's air charter service in Phoenix. From here they were distributed to the rest of the United States. At the same time, guns were smuggled south. This part was not even subtle. The grocery store had an annex at the back with "wall to wall machine guns." Gay himself was obsessed with them and would pick off wildlife with a handgun at family picnics. The guns were taken to Sonoyta and then either driven west to Tijuana or south to the coast.

To do this, Gay had got close to the Sonoyta mayor. Parties on both sides of the border were frequent. He had paid for the mayor's daughter to attend the University of Arizona and forked out for his son's medical bills. The mayor now used his own fishing fleet to help bring in the narcotics.

The rapid growth in both the marijuana and heroin trades transformed the shape and scale of protection rackets on both sides of the border. In most of Mexico, state police forces continued to play an important role. They charged growers, producers, and traffickers to move narcotics and arrested (or occasionally killed) those who refused to pay.

As had happened in Baja California under Esteban Cantú, some money was still channeled to social projects, including schools, irrigation, and roads. But increasingly, state police moved into the trafficking business themselves. The move had several, probably unintended, side effects. The social distribution of drug money declined. There were fewer schools and more police officers. The thin line between crime and law enforcement dissolved even further. And other institutions—like the municipal cops, the federal police, or even the military—saw their power recede.

The 1970s war on drugs relied on the myth that corruption stopped as soon you crossed the Río Bravo. But in the U.S. there were also borderlands protection rackets. They were run by Customs patrols, sheriff's departments, powerful local families, and men like Gay.

Effective protection rackets were designed, at least in part, to minimize violence. Violence was bad for business. It generated federal crackdowns.

The rackets were not, however, infallible; there were problems. First, changes in authorities often generated intense upswings in violence as new state police forces attempted to rewrite the arrangements. Expected payments rose; some traffickers were kicked out; others were let in. Conflicts ensued. Then there was always the danger of exposés. Occasionally, state authorities came down hard on journalists or members of civil society who tried to unmask the system.

State governors operated most Mexican protection rackets. Lalo Fernández's friend and the governor of Sinaloa, Leopoldo Sánchez Celis, ran the most notorious. The first civilian governor in decades, Sánchez Celis was a classic mid-century Mexican politician. A charismatic and proud Sinaloan with an encyclopedic memory for names and faces, he had risen through the ranks of the state bureaucracy. But he knew his audience. And he knew how to play a role. Part rural strongman, part party apparatchik, he wore "a bandana round his neck, ankle length boots, and a moustache that was half Zapata half city slicker. He moved like a man who could do you a favor but could also do you harm."

The traffickers, who often sported the same look and performed the same ambiguous role, loved him. As early as 1962, an American writer based in Mazatlán wrote to a friend in the Los Angeles Police Department that "Sánchez Celis was the poppy growers' candidate."

As the 1963 election approached, the Mexican president, Adolfo López Mateos, knew he had little choice. The traffickers were too rich and too influential. They wanted Sánchez Celis, and López Mateos had no desire to "throw this part of the country into a civil war." So, Sánchez Celis became the official PRI party candidate and won without opposition. It was, the writer opined, "a humiliating shellacking for President López Mateos and a serious disappointment for American officials." But the Americans were also ill equipped to complain—"after the way we screwed up the Cuban invasion we're in no position to get snooty with the old man."

The effect, the writer claimed, was "an expanded and officially protected poppy agriculture." It was the old protection racket mix of protection and repression. For a fee, the state authorities protected certain fields and laboratories. There were no raids, no public burnings of crops, and no arrests. By contrast, Sánchez Celis used the state judicial police to target the independent producers or lead the soldiers to them.

The innovation of the state judicial police, however, was to move into the drug trade themselves. No doubt a few local cops had skimmed and sold product in prior years. Who was going to miss a few ounces of opium or a few pounds of weed? But this was large-scale and systematic. And it relied on contacts with American smugglers. Increasingly, the police didn't simply protect the trade; they headed the trade.

William Estes, a law student at the University of Oklahoma and book-keeper to a gang of midwestern dope runners, explained how this system worked.

> On one of our trips into Mazatlán we ran into Mexican officials and entered into an agreement with them. We had to pay them $5,000 for protection and from that point on we had to buy our marijuana from them. Then we could land anywhere we wanted to.

The arrangement was a winner.

> It was a lower price, better quality and better quantity and our people could go to the official fields and pick out the marijuana that we wanted. Every time we landed they [the state police] were there with their uniforms and cars and they handled pick up and delivery. They would barricade the road to make sure that no stranger came down the road. They had big hay trucks, large trucks, 4 ton trucks and no one could get by them.

It seems likely that this was an official policy. U.S. smugglers often heard rumors that the governor of Sinaloa effectively "ran" the state's drug industry. And Sánchez Celis was certainly not shy about recruiting renowned toughs to enforce his protection racket. Veracruz hitman Hugo Izquierdo Ebrard was given a state police badge; so was another famous gunman, Antonio Aramburu, "The Bat." Perhaps more remarkably, so too was Rodolfo Valdéz Valdéz, "The Gypsy," and so too was Miguel Ángel

Félix Gallardo. The first had murdered Sánchez Celis's predecessor two decades earlier. The second would go on to become Mexico's leading cocaine smuggler.

In fact, with its mentors, its connection to growers, chemists, and U.S. smugglers, there was probably no better training program for future traffickers.

The drug boom and the protection racket made a lot of cops very rich. Culiacán policemen were spotted spending thousands of pesos at some of the city's nightclubs. Some even bought homes next to the big traffickers in the new upscale neighborhood Lomas del Boulevard (now popularly known as "Gomas del Boulevard"). And the Mazatlán chief used his wealth to buy up one of the resort's most luxurious hotels; it became a safe spot for smugglers and dealers to meet.

But the system was more than simple personal corruption. At least some of the money was distributed. Sánchez Celis was certainly one of the few Mexican governors of the 1960s who had the cash to do more than perform ribbon-cutting duties. Via Sánchez Celis's "Sinaloa Plan of Peasant Improvement," the state government built 500 sports fields and over 400 communal farms.

Sánchez Celis also managed to combine the racket with a deliberate and, it seems, rather effective effort to keep down violence. As the American writer who first flagged Sánchez Celis's drug connections observed, the drug trade was not only "organized," it was "disciplined." By tacit agreements with the traffickers, Sánchez Celis signaled that he would not interfere with business in Sinaloa. In return, they would settle their differences outside the state. "Don't fight here. Go away and fight. Here just work and I won't disturb you," he was rumored to tell them. Those who disobeyed were banished. (This is probably why trigger-happy sinsemilla smuggler "Papa Grande" ended up in Jalisco.)

Sánchez Celis also undertook a broad, state-level antivice campaign. In just 1965 he claimed to have closed down over 1,500 unregistered bars and brothels and decommissioned over 8,000 guns. Such assertions were probably exaggerations. Governors' annual reports allowed a lot of space for specious statistical bragging. Yet murders in the state did drop. Nineteen sixties Sinaloa was the center of Mexico's drug trade. But it was also twenty-fifth out of twenty-nine states in terms of homicides per capita. Twenty years earlier, at the height of the land conflicts, it had been second.

Indirectly perhaps, but drugs had brought peace.

Many state governors—consciously or not—attempted to copy the Sánchez Celis system. By 1974 the U.S. State Department claimed that "corruption" was "the single most inhibitory factor in the entire anti-narcotics effort." They were precise about its locus. "It is known to exist at high levels in state and local governments and police organizations." The DEA was in agreement. It described state police forces as "nothing more than organized criminal organizations that conducted their nefarious activities from behind a police badge."

Oscar Flores Sánchez, for example, was the governor of the border state of Chihuahua between 1968 and 1974. Like his Sinaloa counterpart, he was a middle-class professional, but with a knack for playing the rural populist. He was all linen shirts, firm handshakes, and veiled menace.

Under Flores, the state police ran the local narcotics protection racket. The chief received $20,000 to $30,000 a month from Ciudad Juárez traffickers alone. If other law enforcement agencies caught these favored traffickers, he quickly engineered their release. According to a 1974 secret service report, any seizures from groups that didn't pay protection were handed over to the chief's friend and associate, a merchant called Isauro Medina. He would then arrange for the narcotics to be transported over the border.

To what extent Flores knew about this, it is hard to tell. But if he didn't know, he was in the minority. The control of the drug trade during the boom years gave state police forces an enormous step up in scale and power. They went from small, relatively limited units, attached to a particular governor and based primarily in the state capital, to sprawling moneymaking machines with thousands of personnel and a presence in every municipality. By the early 1970s, state police forces effectively ruled large swathes of northern Mexico.

Other law enforcement groups quickly grasped the new limits of their authority. On August 22, 1974, for example, three marijuana smugglers went to the municipal police in Chihuahua City. They complained that they had been beaten, extorted, and robbed by the state police. The municipal police took down their grievance and started to investigate. The following day the deputy chief of the state cops arrived at the city police station and warned them off "anything relating to drug trafficking." It was not a frivolous threat. The head of the city police was petrified about reprisals. The only institution he thought could protect him was the military. So he went straight to the local battalion commander to put his story on paper. But even this was not enough. Within days he was sacked.

But nowhere was the arrangement more flagrant than in Sinaloa, where by the 1970s Sánchez Celis's restricted mentorship scheme for aspirant drug traffickers had grown into a police-run drug-trafficking enterprise.

Accusations of corruption were now frequent. In 1969, the police chief of Mazatlán was charged with shaving the heads of rowdy hippies, running an illegal abortion racket, and directing his own marijuana drug ring. In 1971 the head of the state police was sacked and arrested on drugs charges. It took less than a month for rumors to start about his successor.

In early 1973 seventeen officers put in a complaint about the head of the state police's special ops unit. It was a measure of how far the ethical expectations of the job had fallen that they only mentioned his marijuana protection racket and penchant for underage girls in passing. They were more incensed that he was late with their wages.

Money not only bred impunity, it also raised numbers. And by the time Sánchez Celis's successor had stepped down in late 1974, the state police of Sinaloa totaled over 5,000 members. To put this in context, this was fifty times the number of state police that failed to marshal the murderous land conflicts two decades earlier. It was over ten times the number of federal police *for the entire nation*.

Unsurprisingly, the state police of Sinaloa were so powerful by the mid-1970s that they could even intimidate the federal authorities. When an American agent asked the Mexican attorney general why he didn't do more about the local rackets, he received the reply: "I couldn't go in there with less than a brigade of normal strength. Before I got out of the airport I would be killed."

Even the Americans had their authority curtailed. U.S. drug agent David Wilson recollects following an American trafficker in a Cessna 206 from the airport in Sacramento to a dirt airstrip to the west of Culiacán. He was accompanied by a handful of Mexican PJF agents. They circled overhead and saw the Cessna land. Dozens of men met the plane and started loading it with bales of marijuana. The pursuers then landed and blocked the smugglers' escape. They arrested four traffickers and seized nearly half a ton of weed.

At this point the trouble started. The PJF agents explained to Wilson that there was no time to question the captives. "We needed to leave as soon as possible." They got into a truck and sped to Culiacán. The agents started to explain. They were from Mexico City. "They had no authority here." Here, the state police were in charge. The handful of PJF agents stationed in Culiacán rarely left their HQ. They could not assure their colleagues' safety. Wilson and the visiting PJF men "spent the night under armed guard at a local hotel." They left the next day.

If the drug boom extended and strengthened local Mexican protection rackets, it did the same in the United States. The incorruptible U.S. law enforcement officer was a powerful myth; it was repeated in countless films and TV shows. Local American journalists were often rather less aggressive and more in hock to local potentates than their Mexican counterparts. And exposés of corruption were often quietly buried or explained away as the acts of individual malfeasance rather than systemic malpractice.

But the protection rackets were as extensive north of the border as they were south of it. They had to be. In the late 1960s, Nixon tripled the number of Customs agents on the border; and he increased the number of counternarcotics agents nearly tenfold. Unlike local Mexican police officials whose primary job was to keep down levels of socially disruptive crime (like theft or murder), it was the U.S. agents' explicit and sole task to prevent the trafficking of drugs. Yet still tons of heroin and thousands of tons of marijuana got through.

The smugglers certainly knew these U.S. protection rackets existed. On being arrested in 1974, the Mexican-American trafficker Roberto Hernández claimed that the American police "knew perfectly all the movements of the traffickers on the frontier. Yes, they work with them, they exploit them." If big loads were caught, they forced traffickers to hand over bribes of up to $300,000. In case the Americans doubted Hernández's honesty, he even named the culprits, including Customs officials. "They don't just shake down traffickers but also *braceros* [Contracted Mexican workers]."

Another 1970s smuggler used to boast that he had a U.S. cop that worked for him at one of the border crossing stations. "American cops like money as much as the Mexican cops and they are cheaper to buy," he used to say. The smugglers even had a name for it. Being let through by a compliant Customs inspector was termed "a $50,000 wave."

Richard Blum—who was sent to the border to investigate corruption by the Nixon administration—admitted that there "was corruption in the U.S. Customs." One PJF official told his rather shocked DEA associate: "We take bribes, you take bribes. We admit it, you don't. Which is more honest?" For a fee, Customs agents would help certain selected border retailers hook up with prospective big-city buyers. These selected retailers would then snitch on their competitors. It was win-win. Officials made big showy busts; and they made money on the side.

In 1974, El Paso Customs official George Hough was caught with 11 kilos of cocaine. During the trial he explained that he was only following local protocol. For years he and his fellow officers had been crossing over to Mexico illegally, staking out known trafficking zones, kidnapping the dealers, and stealing the drugs. The drugs would then be taken back to the United States. Some was handed over to the authorities and portrayed as another high-value Customs seizure. The rest was sold to local U.S. dealers.

Hough was hazy on what happened to the kidnapped dealers. Some were caught, tied up, and left to the elements. The more valuable targets were handed over for ransoms to the Mexican federal cops. But some, at least, were killed outright. Hough recounted that his supervisor had ordered him to murder one particularly difficult New Mexico trafficker called Jim French. "The Frenchman is a psycho, armed and dangerous. If you see him, blow his shit away."

In the end, Hough's accusations were quietly hushed up. Hough was given bail and ran away. The trial was sucked into a grand jury investigation, which was not open to the public. And the three principal officers were sacked but not prosecuted. However, the message was clear. The U.S. Customs officials at El Paso were not simply infringing Mexican national sovereignty. Like the Mexican state police, they had moved into drug running.

Arizona was as bad as Texas. Here influential families and local police forces moved into the trade. And we would have known nothing about it had it not been for an extraordinary investigative effort, albeit one that has now been almost completely forgotten.

On June 2, 1976, *Arizona Republic* reporter Don Bolles twisted the key in his Datsun's ignition. The car was engulfed in flames. Bolles survived the initial attack, but succumbed to his injuries eleven days later. He had been looking into the links between the Arizona vice industry and some of the state's prestigious families. In the subsequent months, thirty-six of Bolles's fellow journalists teamed up to try to pursue the investigation. They called it the Arizona Project. They fanned out across the state, interviewed dozens of law enforcement officials, staked out bars and brothels, and even went over the border to Sonora and Chihuahua. They collected thousands of pages of interview transcripts, notes, and classified official documents.

The resulting work was, unfortunately, sidelined. Many of the big East Coast newspapers—like the *New York Times* and the *Washington Post*—refused to print the accusations. They argued that the claims were excessive and driven by a desire for vengeance. Others thought the exposé too provincial. "I really have to wonder whether our readers would regard 80,000 words on the state of Arizona as a real service," declared the *Chicago Tribune*.

Yet, the documents, now collected at the State Historical Society of Missouri, paint a damning picture. By the early 1970s, diverse groups and individuals on the north side of the border were starting to muscle in on the trade. Some were entrepreneurs like Al Gay, the businessman who took over Lukeville.

Many were border law enforcement officials. There was the border sheriff, who mixed shaking down Mexican immigrants with moving marijuana over the border in the trunk of his car. And there was the Douglas police chief, Ronald "Joe" Borane, who was accused of drug trafficking and money laundering. Though he managed to beat the charges, suspicions remained. Notoriously, one local rock group (T and The Boys) is believed to have lampooned him in a popular frontier hit—"Joe Cocaine." And one DEA agent even accused him of planning to murder his brother's rival for mayor.

But most were linked to important political families. They used their sway to make embarrassing accusations against their trafficking relatives go away. The north had its own caciques.

In September 1972, for example, the nephew of Republican giant Barry Goldwater was arrested for selling 80 pounds of weed to an undercover officer. The trial became a long-running farce. It was delayed six times and three judges stood down. The fourth acquitted him even though the nephew had handed the drugs directly to an undercover agent.

But the most serious scandal and the one that national newspapers refused to touch concerned senator Joseph Montoya from the neighboring state of New Mexico. He was suspected of being one of the links between the U.S. Mafia and the Sinaloa heroin traffickers. In April 1970, for example, a plane landed at Tucson airport. It was carrying the senator. U.S. drug agents had been informed that it was also carrying drugs. So they attempted to search it. Montoya, however, immediately phoned the drug agents' boss and convinced the agents to stand down.

Two years later, American agents told a similar story. This time they were informed that traffickers were moving 50 kilos of heroin inside a 40-foot pleasure cruiser. It was being transported by land from the Pacific coast port of Guaymas up through Nogales and to Albuquerque. The Americans had asked a group of PJF cops to search the boat. As soon as they started the search, the driver called Senator Montoya. He called the PJF head in Mexico City and the search was stopped. "Bingo, like that their problems are over. They even get a police escort from Hermosillo to Nogales," one DEA man wryly reported.

These local protection rackets were designed to keep down or at least disperse or disguise outbreaks of violence. But occasionally the systems broke down; killings spiraled. Before the PJF and the American DEA agents arrived in force in the mid-1970s, the reasons were usually twofold—a change of local government or an attempt to unmask the racket.

In 1969, for example, Alfredo Valdés Montoya took Sánchez Celis's place as governor of Sinaloa. A dapper, fastidious intellectual with a degree in economics, Valdés had none of Sánchez Celis' easygoing bonhomie. And he found the kind of backroom deals—cemented over drinks at boisterous Tierra Blanca parties—not to his taste.

Valdés first mistake was to employ an outsider, Ramón Virrueta Cruz, as his chief of police. Virrueta came from Tijuana and was either ill informed about existing arrangements or commanded to go after them. Whatever the reason, his men compounded their error by firing on and killing the nephew of Eduardo "Lalo" Fernández. Fernández or one of his relations decided to take revenge. Virrueta was gunned down on June 6, 1969, in the middle of a Culiacán street. It was an urban rerun of the killing of the Wild Cat almost thirty years earlier.

But the killing didn't stop with Virrueta. In what would become a familiar pattern, the investigation into the murder broke down alliances between trafficking families. The PJF, which had been brought in to handle the inquiry, forced one trafficker, Domingo Terrazas (arrested as part of the French Connection in 1964), to rat out two others (Fernández's relatives) for the murder. The relatives were arrested and flown immediately to Mexico City.

The arrests generated a tit-for-tat blood feud. On July 8 former Sinaloa state policemen shot up Terrazas's car as he was driving through Guadalajara. He was hit in the arm and back but somehow survived. A couple of months later Terrazas hit back. He got police to pursue one of Fernández's allies, the governor-killer Rodolfo Valdéz Valdéz, "The Gypsy." He was shot, injured, and arrested. Kilos of heroin were seized.

Finally, in December 1969, Terrazas's luck ran out. The same former state cops shot both Terrazas and his son as they left their farm just outside the city. The killers now used a U.S. Army issue M1 carbine. The son's head was shot completely off.

The other principal causes of violence were the sporadic attempts to unmask these protection rackets. These attempts were made by everyday citizens and by journalists. Yet perhaps the best example involved a crusading, if naïve, local politician.

Oscar Venegas Tarín was a bit of a prodigy. A graduate of Chihuahua University with a degree in animal science, he had been elected the mayor of his hometown of Guadalupe in 1971. He was just twenty-eight. For decades Guadalupe had been a quiet farming community, but the drug trade had changed it. It lay on the border, about 20 kilometers southeast of Ciudad Juárez. Just to the north was U.S. Highway 10. Here the Río Bravo was shallow and Customs officials were sparse. Geography had damned it. By the early 1970s, Guadalupe had become a crucial drug crossing point.

Venegas was keen to change this. He was concerned that many of the farmers' sons were increasingly attracted by drug profits and had run his campaign on promises to clean up the town. But he was no cop; his strategy was negotiation rather than confrontation. He approached the local trafficker, an old associate of queen pin La Nacha named Alfonso Antúnez Ceniceros. And he asked him to stop trafficking. Antúnez agreed. Trafficking was radically reduced.

This was when things started to go wrong. Three state policemen arrived in Guadalupe. They dragged Antúnez out of his house and beat him to a pulp. He was taken to Ciudad Juárez hospital for treatment. Concerned, Mayor Venegas immediately went to see the dealer. Antúnez explained that the state cops had beaten him because he had neglected to pay them their regular 75,000 peso monthly bribe. Getting out of the drug business had angered the dealer's bosses—the police.

Venegas, who somehow still seemed to believe in the essential fairness of the system, went to complain to the state prosecutor. The state prosecutor dutifully listened. But the following day he published accusations in the local newspaper that Venegas was himself a drug trafficker.

At this point, it started to dawn on Venegas that "the mafia is protected by the high authorities of the state." But his problems didn't end there. New traffickers now moved into Guadalupe and started to ply their trade. They confronted Venegas's brother in a local bar. Venegas's brother shot one dead. The remaining traffickers then took their associate's body and propped it up outside Venegas's brother's house. It was a warning: his death would be avenged. With a gift for understatement, Venegas claimed that the move "had a depressing impact on my family."

Venegas then decided to go public. He took his story to the local newspaper, which published it on the front page. By making a stand, he effectively signed his own death warrant. Especially since his enemies—and the power structure that backed them—were about to obtain immense federal power. The state protection racket was going national.

In 1976 the former governor of Chihuahua, Oscar Flores Sánchez, was made national attorney general. One of his first acts was to put Venegas on the list of most wanted traffickers. He was made a "class 1 violator." And on September 19, 1978, PJF officials shot him dead.

# Part IV

## The Comedown
## 1970–1990

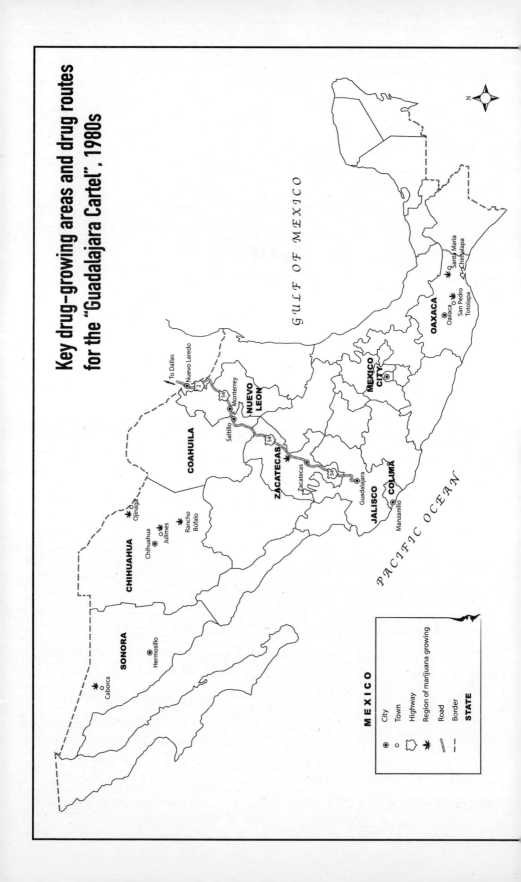

# Key drug-growing areas and drug routes for the "Guadalajara Cartel", 1980s

GULF OF MEXICO

PACIFIC OCEAN

To Dallas
Nuevo Laredo
Monterrey
NUEVO LEON
Saltillo
COAHUILA
CHIHUAHUA
Ojinaga
Chihuahua
Julimes
Rancho Búfalo
SONORA
Hermosillo
Caborca
ZACATECAS
Zacatecas
JALISCO
Guadalajara
COLIMA
Manzanillo
MEXICO CITY
OAXACA
Oaxaca
San Pedro Totolapa
Santa María Chimalapa

**MEXICO**

- ◉ City
- ○ Town
- ⬡ Highway
- ✳ Region of marijuana growing
- ▮ Road
- ---- Border
- **STATE**

N

## Chapter 16

## Narcs

MARK WAS LYING PROSTRATE AND NAKED ON A PLASTIC PONCHO. THEY HAD been working him over for hours. He'd been slapped, punched, kicked, and beaten with the butt of a gun. Sweat and blood sloshed in a puddle around him. There were ten agents in there with him—six from the DEA, four from the PJF. It was a collaborative effort. But the Americans were in charge—"they took names, identification, wallets, everything."

One agent stood on his hair. Another four held his limbs. Then another man approached. In his hand he held a dirty plastic cord. The two wires at the end fizzed with electricity. "They put the shock to my balls and held it there until I convulsed and just couldn't do anything anymore. You get to the point where you can hardly even talk."

There was worse to come. In the afternoon they returned. They put him on a chair and bound his mouth shut with duct tape. Again, four men grabbed hold of his limbs. Another pulled his head back and started to pour soda pop up his nose. The sensation was unbearable. "You're drowning. You're trying to cough and you can't." His muscles tensed; he fought and struggled, but the four agents held firm. After about a minute it was too much; he passed out. They splashed water over his face and started again. "They fucked with me for about three bottles' worth."

It probably didn't occur to Mark, but he was enduring a niche form of torture. It was waterboarding Mexico-style. By the 1970s, it had become such a popular tactic that Mexican agents had even come up with their own name for it. They dubbed it the Tehuacanazo after the Tehuacán brand of mineral water that they employed.

After being dragged out of his camper van in Mazatlán with a bag of marijuana, Mark endured Tehuacanazos and other cruelties for nine days. But he lived; American weed dealers were rarely killed. Mexicans caught with drugs were often not so lucky. There were frequent stories of small-time farmers being hurled from helicopters into the Pacific Ocean. And locals whispered that the deserts outside certain border towns were littered with the graves of missing dealers.

The counterculture drove the massive expansion of the cross-border drug trade. It also launched the corresponding counteroffensive—the war on drugs. Though U.S. weed smokers often complained about Nixon's heavy-handed domestic policies, in reality the war was much more unforgiving south of the border. Pushed by a foreign power, backed by foreign money, and buoyed by domestic prejudices, Mexico's 1970s drug war was terrifying and brutal.

Its foot soldiers were PJF cops and U.S. drug agents. They were the narcs. And as Mark and many others found out, it was the narcs—and not the drug traffickers—who introduced widespread, frequent, and ruthless violence to the world of Mexican narcotics. It was also the narcs that started to take over the old locally run drug protection rackets.

The declaration of war came from on high. In 1969, Richard Nixon became president of the United States, pushing a law-and-order agenda. Fighting crime—and particularly drug crime—became a cornerstone of U.S. policy. Nixon considered it a war. During his campaign, he had promised to "make a frontal assault on the narcotics, marijuana and dangerous drug traffic across the Mexican border." And in September 1969 he was true to his word. He ordered Customs officials to search every vehicle crossing the border.

It was called Operation Intercept. (Though it soon got other names. Hippies called it the "world's largest dope grope" and Mexicans dubbed it "the grass curtain.") It was presented as a public health measure, a means to seize narcotics. According to the official press release, it was designed to "reduce the volume of narcotics … which are smuggled into the U.S. from Mexico, thus cutting down the supply available to addicts and users."

But in reality, it was blackmail. The real aim was to sink the cross-border economy and coerce Mexico to adopt more stringent counternarcotics measures. Future Watergate protagonist Gordon Liddy was clear about this. "For diplomatic reasons the true purpose of the exercise was never revealed … it was an exercise in international extortion, pure, simple and effective, designed to bend Mexico to our will."

The stop-and-search program caused vast traffic backups. On the first weekend in Tijuana there was a six-hour wait to cross the border. Radiators boiled over, batteries failed, and many had to push their cars to the United States. Border tourism crashed. Within a week, business owners in Ciudad Juárez reported that earnings had dropped 80 percent. Tijuana's racetrack reported that its "parking lot" was "deserted."

The point had been made. Mexico needed to intensify its counternarcotics measures or America would cripple its border economy. On October 12, Customs officials halted the operation. And two weeks later U.S. and Mexican representatives met to hammer out a joint drug policy—Operation Cooperation.

Over the next five years, the Nixon and Ford administrations held the Mexicans to the plan. Generally, the Americans used financial inducements. As early as March 1970, the U.S. donated five helicopters and three Cessnas worth nearly a million dollars to the Mexican counternarcotics effort. By 1975, they had given $35 million for training and equipment. Over half of America's international counternarcotics budget was going to Mexico.

America's efforts to launch a drug war were accompanied by two home-grown incentives. The first was a growing official understanding that drug money allowed certain regional governments to assert an unsettling degree of political independence. The state police forces of Sinaloa, Durango, and Chihuahua not only protected local drug businesses, but also limited federal interference. Even Mexican secret service agents were wary of going there.

A drug war—armed and funded by the Americans—was a cheap way to reassert central control.

The second incentive was a domestic panic over marijuana use. This was not difficult to drum up. And it was politically useful. It protected the Mexican government from accusations of diplomatic submissiveness and channeled the program against out-of-favor groups. Government ministers, tabloid journalists, and suggestible doctors linked long-standing suspicions over the harmful effects of pot smoking with a hodgepodge of contemporary fears over student protests, left-wing radicalism, U.S. cultural influence, and (because this was Mexico) declining machismo.

In form, the campaign recycled the fears of old marijuana panics. There were the massive exaggerations. In December 1971, newspapers reported that half of Mexico City's street kids were addicted to the drug. (Subsequent research found that paint thinner—not marijuana—was a much more common street narcotic.) There was the claptrap pseudo-science. In March 1972, neurologists from Leopoldo Salazar Viniegra's former university claimed that marijuana caused "psychosis, hallucinations, and disorientation" and that in terms of risk it was "akin to heroin." And there were the alarmist stories. "Drugged with Marijuana He Stabbed His Mother," ran one headline. "Marijuana Leads to Homosexuality and Suicide," ran another.

Bolstered by these homegrown concerns, Operation Cooperation comprised three elements—a tightening up of Mexico's narcotics laws, strengthened eradication efforts, and intensified policing.

First, there were the legal changes. In early 1971 the authorities banned any bail for drug offenses. And later that year they started to refuse amparos for drug cases. The drug traffickers' traditional get-out-of-jail-free card was revoked. The following year they passed a law that effectively confiscated lands on which drugs were grown. In 1973 they added peyote and magic mushrooms to the list of banned substances. Finally, in 1974 they overhauled the drug laws completely. Penalties for traffickers were upped to a maximum of fifteen years. A new section of the law also introduced penalties for public officials who protected the drug trade.

The changes closed off legal loopholes and ensured that traffickers that were caught were harshly punished. You could no longer pay bail or apply for favorable amparos and escape into the mountains. Unless you had a lot of money and serious political protection, capture now meant a long time inside. As one U.S. narcotics agent remarked, "tucking three marijuana cigarettes into your shirt pocket is about as smart as hanging three hand grenades around your neck."

The second strategy was to beef up and extend the annual eradication program. There were more troops, more guns, more comms, and more tech. By 1974, planes tracked down prime growing areas with new multispectral photography. They were followed up by troop-carrying helicopters, which flew the soldiers on search-and-destroy narcotics missions from Chiapas in the south to Tamaulipas in the north.

But the most important strategy, at least during the first five years of the effort, was increased policing. On the Mexican side this involved the PJF. Ever since Anslinger had first pushed for a stand-alone federal drug squad in 1947, the PJF had been Mexico's principal counternarcotics cops.

Yet, over the years the PJF's reputation had declined. By the late 1960s, there were only 264 agents of whom barely 10 percent specialized in narcotics. The majority rarely ventured outside Mexico City. The Americans described the force as "woefully lacking communications and ground equipment ... understaffed and undertrained." Pay was low (around $200 a month) and corruption rife.

The new war on drugs, however, proved a boon for the institution. Many of the older agents were released and a new generation of young recruits was brought in. By 1974 there were 360 agents and by the following year over 530. Add to this the numerous informal employees (termed *madrinas*) who often carried a badge and a gun and did a lot of the group's dirty work, and there were probably over 1,000.

These recruits now got training, first by the American drug agents, and then at a special PJF academy. They also got equipment. Instead of knock-off weapons bought cheap, they now carried AR-15s and AR-18s and had .45s and 9mm pistols stuffed beneath their belts. They also got transport. By the middle of the decade, the PJF boasted a fleet of thirty-nine planes and helicopters.

But perhaps the biggest change to the PJF was in terms of deployment. PJF agents no longer sat in Mexico City waiting to be called upon. Hundreds were now stationed throughout the border cities. There were bases from Tijuana in the west through Nogales and Ciudad Juárez to Matamoros in the east. There were also additional bases on main thoroughfares like Highway 15, which ran through the Sonora capital of Hermosillo.

In 1972, the U.S. and Mexican authorities also combined to create a special antinarcotics unit within the PJF. The members were carefully vetted and specially trained. It comprised around fifty agents, who were allowed to roam throughout Mexico busting drug crime with only limited oversight. They were led by the counterinsurgency veteran Florentino Ventura Gutiérrez.

Described as "cold, cruel, and relentless," the Americans loved Ventura. If they wanted suspects tortured or killed, he was their man. One DEA agent remarked.

> He is the most brutal man I have ever met. And efficient. Efficiently brutal. I have no doubt at all in my mind that if you got in the man's way you would be out of the way, either alive or dead, but you would be out of the way. . . . Torture to him was no more shocking than violent weather. . . . I found Ventura to be a classic. He's one of my favorite people.

The Americans and the Mexicans were keen to portray these recruits as a new breed of police official—youthful, driven, and impervious to bribery. By the mid-1970s, the new cops were dubbed the "Mexican Gangbusters" or the "South of the Border Untouchables."

Yet beyond the headlines, the reality of the PJF was markedly different. Researching the true history of the institution is a tough job. The organization was famously closed off; journalists called it "hermetically sealed." We still have little idea about recruitment procedures or personnel. But what we do know hardly inspires confidence. The purge of the older generation was not entirely effective. There were still cops, like the president's school friend Arturo "El Negro" Durazo, who managed to hold on to their jobs despite copious charges against them.

Moreover, the new breed was little better. They included former drug traffickers like Armando Martínez Salgado. He was the brother of a large-scale weed wholesaler from southern Guerrero. They dubbed him "The Vampire" because of his resemblance to Christopher Lee, who played the role of Dracula throughout the late 1960s and early 1970s. One DEA agent who worked with him described him as "openly corrupt." "He was only interested in collecting money for his self enrichment and to pay off superiors to maintain his position in a highly lucrative area." He also had a furious temper. Once he got into a fight with one of his colleagues, tracked the man down to his house, and then fired a clip from his .45 into the pavement outside. He was "totally impervious to the fact that bystanders could be killed by ricochets."

They included the menacing figure of Francisco Sahagún Baca. The son of a well-off family, he had a taste for the finer things in life. Wherever he was posted, he always insisted on staying in the most upscale lodgings. He was a dapper dresser, a "perfumed dandy" who would only wear one color from his shirt and socks down to his watch and rings. He was also terrifying. One of his agents described him as "irascible, whether drugged or not, violent, and aggressive. When he got angry, he used to throw things out of the window. Just his presence could instill fear. He was just very sinister."

Sahagún would go on to run drug rings up on the Sonora border, down in Guadalajara, and finally side by side with El Negro Durazo in Mexico City. In Hermosillo, residents remember that his grand residential pad doubled as a torture center. They thought it tainted and used to drive blocks out of the way just to avoid it.

The new breed also included out-and-out psychopaths. Durango-born Gustavo Tarín Chávez was a secret service agent before being sacked and imprisoned for murder. After a stint in jail, he got out, changed his name, and bought his way into the PJF. He was then sent down to the tourist resort of Acapulco and arrived with three of his brothers. Together they worked as the government's goon squad and were charged with arresting, torturing, and then disposing of the bodies of left-wing insurgents and drugs traffickers.

He was taciturn and vicious. Even the general who employed him was unnerved. "He seemed normal, he was quiet and had few friends. However sometimes he let slip his temper. On one occasion I observed that to get the attention of one of his brothers called Manuel, he made him get down on his knees and then slapped him." Manuel, it seems, got off lightly. He would eventually gun down another of his brothers in the street.

Though they came from all over the country and had diffuse (and often disturbing) backgrounds, these new PJF officials started to develop a distinct institutional culture. It was reflected in their pitch-black humor. Methods of torture were given jokey nicknames. Waterboarding was the Tehuacanazo; the cattle prod was the *chicharra* (cicada) because of the clicking noise it made; and torture centers were dubbed "the opera house where everyone sings." They also shared a way of dressing, or what one DEA agent termed "Mexican federale couture." It was all tailored leisure suits, ostrich-skin cowboy boots, and gold bracelets with their names engraved in diamonds. It was a dress code that would soon become associated with traffickers themselves. The PJF were not only inventing narco-violence, they were also pioneering narcoculture.

Armed, supported, and partly funded by the gringos, they were now some of the most powerful men in Mexico. At the end of drunken get-togethers, they would demand that the mariachis play José Alfredo Jiménez's macho ballad "El Rey." And they would all croon along: "With money and without money, I do what I want. I have neither a throne nor a queen nor anyone who understands me. But I am still the king and my word is law." It became their theme song.

The PJF's allies in this war were the U.S. narcotics agents. Most worked for the successors to Anslinger's FBN. Initially, they were members of a short-lived Nixon-era drug force called the Bureau of Narcotics and Dangerous Drugs, or BNDD. Then, from 1973 on, they were folded into a new organization called the Drug Enforcement Administration or DEA.

Following Operation Intercept, increasing numbers of these agents were stationed south of the border. There were now offices in Mexico City, Monterrey, Culiacán, Mazatlán, Guadalajara, Uruapan, and Acapulco.

Add to these the private contractors, border Customs agents, border DEA agents, and the State Department's Narcotics Assistance Unit, and there were probably as many as 200 American narcotics officials working in conjunction with the PJF at any one time.

American newspapers liked to portray U.S. drug agents working abroad as the smiling, noble, and incorruptible faces of a benign empire. Journalists quoted agents earnestly explaining that "the combination of foreign service and law enforcement is unique. We are a unique corps of professional people who've combined these two professions. It appeals to your pride to be part of an elite group." They were described as "crusaders for the American way of life."

Yet, the American agencies, like the Mexican ones, had their own problems. For a start, they emerged from the wreckage of Anslinger's FBN. The bureau had eventually been shut down in 1968 after spiraling accusations of corruption. (Off the record, one former agent claimed that at least a third of the agents were on the take.) But the trouble didn't go away. Similar accusations dogged the BNDD and the DEA, where many former FBN agents found refuge.

Corruption now mixed with the old rivalry with Customs. And this in turn overlapped with new internal rivalries between the different agencies, which had been merged together into these new counternarcotics bodies. Former cops, FBN, Customs, CIA, and other agents all now struggled for recognition. Finally, there was the strong whiff of institutional racism. Just as in the FBN, white bosses, or "suits," continued to order around black or brown undercover agents. They called Hispanics "pepper bellies" or "cage agents." ("Because any monkey can buy dope," one agent was informed.)

These divisions immediately soured working practices south of the border. Factions abounded. There were the former CIA toughs who had trained in undercover ops in Vietnam and were rumored to be setting up assassination squads to take out high-profile targets (including San Luis Río Colorado weed entrepreneur Pedro Avilés Pérez).

There were ambitious blowhards like Joe Arpaio, who had saved his FBN job by snitching on his colleagues and who was rewarded with control of the Mexico City BNDD office. He was loathed, it seems, by everyone. And he was nicknamed "Nickel Bag" Joe for his habit of favoring small

buy-and-bust operations and then greatly exaggerating their importance.
"He never told the truth. He also falsified nearly every report that came out
of there concerning progress. Most of the cases that came out of there, he'd
make pretty good but it was bull, pure bull," a fellow agent remarked. In
fact, there was even a special agent in the Mexico City office whose sole job
it was to scan the Mexican newspapers, find the names of arrested suspects, and simply claim the bust as the BNDD's own.

Then there were the ostentatiously corrupt. Joseph Baca, for example,
started his career as an Albuquerque cop. A cousin of the PJF commander,
Francisco Sahagún Baca, Joseph used his influence to free his family members from drug charges in New Mexico and was rumored to bring back
loads that his cousin had seized as early as 1964.

In the late 1960s, he joined the BNDD, linked up with some former
New York FBN agents, and was moved to Southern California. Suspicions
about his conduct continued. He was recorded making a deal with a notorious Mexican-American trafficker held in the Tijuana prison. He was even
rumored to have persuaded other DEA agents to take trafficker bribes.
Internal affairs launched investigations against him in 1969 and 1973. Yet
the cases were dropped, principally because a lot of the evidence came
from rival Customs officials.

Other agents were not so fortunate. Sante Bario was a former Treasury
investigator who joined the BNDD in 1972. Four years later, he was moved
to the DEA's Mexico City office, where things didn't go well. He was
stressed and beset by night terrors; his hair started to fall out in clumps. At
best, he showed a stunning lack of judgment and got close to the notoriously corrupt new head of the PJF and former Ciudad Juárez hitman Raúl
Mendiolea Cerecero. At worst, he started to take payoffs himself. And at
the end of 1978 he was accused of handing over 5 kilos of cocaine to one
of his informers.

He was arrested and jailed in San Antonio. After a week, he choked on
a peanut butter sandwich, had an allergic reaction, and went into a coma.
He never recovered, and died a month later. Doctors who inspected the
sandwich claimed that it was laced with strychnine.

Whether he was murdered or just supremely unfortunate, the affair
stank. And the DEA was keen to draw a line under the matter. The response

to a Freedom of Information Act request for his file bluntly declared that "all documentation on Sante Bario has been destroyed."

Mexican and American agents may have distrusted one another, but they had much in common, including shared couture. (When one DEA wife visited the embassy offices, she saw that the "corridors belonged to men in cowboy gear and leisure suits.") Soon they began socializing. U.S. agents supped tequila at PJF parties and learned the words to "El Rey." They also needed one another. The Mexicans needed American intel, American money, and American-looking agents to pose as buyers. The Americans needed Mexican backup and firepower.

In the wake of Operation Intercept, both groups descended on the border towns of northern Mexico. Initially, under Arpaio, they used buy-and-busts. The American agents posed as buyers and then tried to set up deals with marijuana and heroin wholesalers. When the dope was handed over, the PJF agents pounced. This was not only a legal grey area (under Mexican law, it could be viewed as entrapment); the results were also underwhelming. Few wholesalers wanted to do major deals with Americans they had only met on a couple of occasions. And the kind of upfront money the Americans could offer (the so-called flash roll) was often too small to tempt the really big dealers.

More effective, but also more calamitous, was the use of informants. As both the DEA and the PJF's intelligence networks grew, they increasingly resorted to this way to make cases. One U.S. agent who worked south of the border estimated that as many as 80 percent of cases were made with CIs, confidential informants.

CIs roles varied. Sometimes they simply picked out potential mules at police roadblocks. And sometimes they approached the cops with specific intel on a particular airstrip, delivery, or stash house. Informants came from all walks of life. Many were forced into it. They were drug couriers or small-time peddlers who had been caught, turned, and persuaded to work for the police in return for favorable sentencing. Others came to the work voluntarily. The DEA paid especially well; American agents were often inundated with offers of information in the run-up to Christmas.

But the most important CIs were the drug traffickers themselves. They had essential information and an incentive to share it. In what would become an increasingly common pattern, they started to use the police to protect their own businesses or to exact revenge on rival traffickers (who might in turn have snitched on their network).

This widespread use of informants ripped up nearly half a century of cooperation. It pulled apart old alliances and agreements, bred distrust and paranoia, and set traffickers against one another. In short, it created competition where they had been none. While some traffickers moved to an arrangement with the state, others—fearful that betrayal would now lead to a long sentence or worse—tracked down and assassinated suspected informants. South of the border, DEA agents in the 1970s would regularly lose a dozen or so CIs to death or disappearance.

Beyond the use of buy-and-busts and informants, Mexican and American agents also employed a host of unsanctioned methods. They were illegal, brutal, and their principal effect was to exacerbate the violence. Traffickers now not only feared long sentences, but also torture, death, and the persecution of their families.

The first of these tactics was murder. The PJF, in particular, was well known for using ruthless force against traffickers. There were few U.S. agents working south of the border who did not witness at least one fatal shootout or cold-blooded assassination. Richard Blum, for example, a special U.S. envoy working in Hermosillo in 1972, remembered the color-coordinated PJF commander Sahagún stopping a caravan of trucks filled with pot. He ordered his men to kill all the drivers and then seized the drugs. Out of courtesy, Sahagún also offered Blum a share of the loot.

Another U.S. agent who worked on the Arizona–Sonora border in the late 1970s, recalled something similar. After traffickers kidnapped a local Mexican prosecutor, PJF agents were flown in from Mexico City. They started to perform raids and searches. After five days, the prosecutor was released. "But the bodies of many drug traffickers began appearing in dark alleys and on roadsides leading out of Nogales. It was a message that was heard loud and clear." Another prosecutor explained, "If the traffickers kill one of us, then we will kill forty of them in order to teach that they cannot do this—they will pay and pay heavily for their actions."

It became a border horror story, something to strike fear into traffickers and visiting journalists. One local cop gave a U.S. reporter the following advice. "Don't ask the Nogales Federal Judicial Police anything, don't investigate anything, and never, ever, go to their base. The fields behind them are full of the people they tortured to get information."

Some U.S. agents even took part in the killings. One BNDD agent, who worked down in Mexico under Arpaio, described one such incident in his evidence to the grand jury. One of his colleagues, while working in Ciudad Juárez, ordered another colleague to shoot a fleeing suspect in the back. The colleague refused. So the first agent "emptied the gun into [the suspect] ... until he was shot to pieces." He claimed that Arpaio asked his superiors not to investigate and they agreed. No charges were brought against Arpaio.

In addition, the use of torture was extremely common. No doubt in Mexico (as in the U.S.) law enforcement officials had regularly relied on force to secure prosecutions. But the demands of the drug war exacerbated its employment. They pushed it from an occasional, last-resort strategy to the go-to method to assure jail time.

The logic was as follows. The Americans wanted arrests. Yet drug crime, unlike other felonies, had no direct victim. Cases could rarely rely on the testimony of witnesses or complainants. So even if Mexican investigators found narcotics, they also needed confessions. To get these quickly and effectively, they employed torture. And the judiciary acquiesced to the practice. In a series of landmark decisions, the Mexican Supreme Court gave confessions "full probatorial value" regardless of how they were obtained.

There were few U.S. agents who did not at least witness torture. Many encouraged it and many—as the hippie Mark discovered—got involved. The ex-BNDD grand jury witness described his shock at the prevalence of the practice.

Down there, I really got an eyeful. They [BNDD agents] actually participated in the torture—anybody, it didn't matter a shit who it was. They would actually participate in the torture of these god damn people. I got caught up in a god damn gun fight there myself and killed men. Now we were running into this kind of stuff constantly, all the time

The most common method was the beating. Again, the ex-BNDD agent described how both Americans and Mexicans treated one unfortunate Italian-American trafficker.

We arrested him and took him off to the holding cells.... . The Mexicans started getting a bit rough with him and one of the American agents jumped in and started battering the hell out of the guy too. The guy was making lots of noise, you know hurting. They never gave him a chance to answer a question, they were really giving him hell, stomping him, kicking him. He was hurting pretty bad, so this agent took a pair of socks out of the guy's suitcase and crammed them in his mouth so he couldn't scream and he couldn't answer the questions either.

But beating was just the beginning; agents called punches and kicks "the light treatment." Harder stuff included the Tehuacanazo (waterboarding); plunging prisoners' heads into shit-filled water; hanging prisoners from the ceiling by their thumbs and their scrotums; and electrocuting suspects in the balls, anus, and on the soles of their feet.

There were also more devious psychological tortures. One American prisoner described agents hanging a frozen corpse from a meat hook inside his cell. It was a grotesque sight. "First his eyes started thawing and as the water trickled down it looked as though he was crying. As he thawed out the hole where the meat hook was inserted pulled his ribs apart and I could see his liver, heart and lungs."

But most of these more focused psychological tortures involved suspects' families. It was the state—not the traffickers—who first infringed the unstated agreement of "no women, no children."

At times, the threat was enough. When Mexicans captured Rafael Díaz, with cocaine, they warned him that if he didn't confess they would force his pregnant wife to give birth without medical treatment. Unsurprisingly, he signed immediately.

But they also employed rape. Four traffickers that were caught in Tijuana described their experiences to an American journalist.

> They brought [my wife] here and did it to her. There was nothing I could do. I was all tied up. She cried and cried. "If you're not gonna tell, we're going to kill you and your wife. Now, where's the [stash]?" Then they took the belt and tied it around here [he pointed to his genitals] and began to pull tighter and tighter asking me all the time about something I didn't even have.

At the end of the ordeal one of the prisoner's wives was so distressed that when she saw a nail sticking out of the wall she ran over to it and tried to cut her throat open.

The blend of intensified policing and unchallenged brutality produced significant results. In these circumstances, who wouldn't snitch or confess? There were big raids on Pedro Avilés Pérez's San Luis Río Colorado house in 1973 and on his brother's Sinaloa ranch three years later. There were high-profile arrests of members of the Durango-based Herrera clan and the Culiacán trafficker Jorge Favela Escobosa. And if you believed the figures, there were also major seizures—69 tons of weed in the Avilés warehouses, 25 kilos of heroin and 30 tons of weed in a single bust in Tijuana.

The sheer number of Mexican drug arrests also rose dramatically. They grew from just over 1,000 throughout the 1950s and 1960s to nearly 9,000 by midway through the 1970s.

But this kind of no-holds-barred, hyperaggressive policing also radically accelerated the violence connected with the trade.

At best, U.S. and Mexican cops were brutal but honest. At worst, the newly arrived cops were openly corrupt. And they used their newfound power to link up with certain traffickers and take out the opponents. In doing so, they broke the local protection rackets with their stress on distribution and nonviolence. And they started to establish more powerful, federally backed rackets.

Nowhere was this escalation of violence clearer than in the northeastern border town of Nuevo Laredo. Nuevo Laredo had never been a drug
town. There was no big vice district. On the other side of the border was
the sleepy settlement of Laredo, Texas. And production areas were hundreds of miles and two mountain ranges to the west.

But during the 1960s, this changed. What Laredo did have was connections. It lay on Highway 85. The road linked Texas to the major Mexican
metropolises of Monterrey and Guadalajara. If you wanted to bring weed
grown in Jalisco or Guerrero to the big markets on the East Coast of the
United States, you went through Nuevo Laredo. By the end of the decade,
it was a thoroughfare to match Highway 15 in the west. The Americans
estimated that as much as $1 million worth of drugs passed through the
city each week. If true, it would have accounted for a quarter of the nation's
narcotics.

Initially, multiple family-based gangs ran drug smuggling in the area.
There were former booze runners-turned-fayuqueros like Juan Nepomuceno Guerra; there were the Texas-born Mexican Americans like Federico
Gómez Carrasco; and there were local newcomers like the Reyes Pruneda
clan. In general, the business was fairly peaceful. Cooperation rather than
competition was the rule. And the enterprise was protected by a network of
local cops and customs officials.

In late 1970 this ended. Two new PJF officials arrived in Nuevo Laredo.
If you believe the locals, they started to shake down the local smugglers; if
you believe the U.S. and Mexican officials, they finally started to make
major seizures. Whatever they did, it angered some of the traffickers. And
Refugio "Cuco" Reyes Pruneda, the head of one clan, gunned down both
the cops as they ate by a taco stand.

The killing was the beginning of a bloodbath. Without question, the
traffickers were responsible for some of these murders. On July 28, 1972,
traffickers shot another PJF agent; in September 1972 they killed a suspected police informant outside his car showroom; and in December 1972
they attacked two soldiers who were traveling in a requisitioned car.

But the violence didn't travel in only one direction. Sixty PJF cops
arrived in the wake of the initial killings. In August 1972 the authorities

sent one of its top prosecutors along. Together they descended on the town "like an army," according to locals. They dragged in smugglers, tortured them on nearby ranches, and forced them to give up other traffickers.

Some suspects they murdered. In February 1972, for example, a farmer found the body of the leader of the Reyes Pruneda clan tossed by the side of the road. He had been shot eight times, three times in the head at close range. In August 1972, the PJF launched a raid on the Reyes Pruneda ranch, killing two of the cousins in the process. In fact, by March 1973 only two of the seven Reyes Pruneda brothers remained alive. Five had been killed in what newspapers euphemistically called "duels with the police." The cops also started to take out the smugglers' protectors. PJF agents also killed as many as five customs officers and a dozen municipal policemen.

Getting traffickers to rat out their competitors also generated conflicts between the drug gangs. They killed suspected informants in advance or in revenge over the capture or death of their fellow gang members. The authorities not only knew about the rivalries; they encouraged them. "It is plausible that various gangs in Nuevo Laredo area have long worked in alliance. Now that the heat is on, there might be some falling out amongst them. This, of course, would be a useful development as far as law enforcement efforts are concerned," wrote the U.S. consul. Dividing traffickers was just good drug policing; the consequent bloodshed just collateral damage.

By the middle of 1973, the PJF's campaign had pushed the homicide rate in Nuevo Laredo to the highest in the country. It was a rate of nearly 100 per 100,000 or nearly four times the national average. "People see the movie *The Godfather*, and they think there's a lot of killing in it. That's nothing compared to this," one local remarked.

Over the next few years the situation in Nuevo Laredo was repeated throughout Mexico's major wholesaling or smuggling cities. PJF cops moved in; smugglers and local cops started to turn up dead; murders increased. The pattern was most noticeable and most extreme where the PJF took over the local protection rackets and then cooperated with certain traffickers to eliminate others.

This, for example, was the case in southern Sinaloa. Here in February 1974, Mazatlán PJF officials teamed up with the charismatic San Ignacio weed dealer Manuel "Crazy Pig" Salcido Uzeta, and they decided to take out a group of competing wholesalers. They kidnapped six of them, took them to a ranch nearby, butchered them with machetes, shot them in the head, and then burned their bodies.

The authorities tried to cover up the crime, claiming that Salcido had "forced" the officers to commit it. But locals knew better. They claimed that the PJF chief had originally ordered the killings. The local newspaper claimed that he had "confused Mazatlán with a place to be invaded." Protesters declaimed that he had handed his officers a "carte blanche to attack, humiliate, or torture the inhabitants of this region and imprison people without orders of apprehension and without any guarantees."

In Ciudad Juárez another notoriously corrupt PJF commander, Daniel Acuña Figueroa, employed similar tactics. He arrived in the city in early 1973. Immediately, there were charges that he was protecting certain smuggler factions, particularly those linked to Pedro Avilés Pérez.

At the same time, Acuña also took out the more independent factions. Roving PJF patrols ran the popular smuggling routes between Ciudad Juárez and the farmlands to the southeast. They tortured couriers and peasants indiscriminately. They murdered traffickers, often in secret. They even killed La Nacha's grandson, "the Arab," though they disguised the murder as a car crash.

Occasionally, Acuña's men worked more openly. In March 1975, for example, they raided a suspected trafficker's house. When the son of the suspect returned home, they forced him to lie prone on the ground and then shot him in the head. The PJF claimed that the son was armed and had tried to escape. But the Mexican secret service, which performed an in-depth report on the incident, concluded:

It has now become a custom for agents of the PJF to take part in shootouts causing multiple deaths and injuries as part of their investigations against the trafficking of drugs. They have become a scourge and a threat not only for those individuals dedicated to this illegal commerce, but also to the citizenry in general, peaceful families, and innocent people.... The fact that an individual is involved in drug trafficking doesn't mean to say that his family is involved as well. And it doesn't give the right to the federales to enrage these families and stamp all over their homes.

Though it was well known, the DEA ignored it. In fact, "they cooperated with Acuña despite the controversy stirred in Juárez over the presence of armed U.S. agents in Mexican territory." The Americans were even rumored to have taken part in some of the killings.

## Chapter 17

## The Atrocities

"DID YOU SEE THAT?" THE SERGEANT ASKED HIM. THE FARMER, BALTASAR Ayon Ayon, could hardly have missed it. It was late afternoon on September 19, 1980, and he was just a mile or so from his home in the small Durango highland village of Los Remedios. He had been sitting, head slumped, hands tied behind his back by the side of a stream for over half an hour. In that time a dozen soldiers had been taking turns to duck his cousin's head beneath the water. He would struggle and kick as they held him down. Every few minutes they would yank him out and scream questions in his face. "Where are the drugs? Where's the fucking weed?" As he spluttered and coughed, they would punch him in the face and chest. This time, when they pulled him above the water line, he no longer made a sound. Even the rasping struggle for breath had gone. He was dead. Now it was Baltasar's turn.

Baltasar nodded. "Then stand over there." The sergeant motioned Baltasar to the center of the stream about 15 meters from the soldiers. He covered his mouth and whispered to his colleagues. "When I tell you to shoot, shoot." Then he turned to Baltasar and shouted, "Run!"

Baltasar knew this game. It was the *ley fuga*, or the law of flight. Suspects were instructed to run. Soldiers shot them in the back and then claimed that they had been killed attempting to flee. It was an old trick. The authorities had been using it to administer cowboy justice for over a century.

Baltasar didn't want to play. "I've got no reason to run. If you've got anything on me, you can put me in front of a judge." The sergeant shrugged, turned to his men, and ordered them to open fire anyway. As Baltasar turned, bullets whizzed past his ears and kicked up the water on either side. Suddenly his legs gave way. He collapsed; his body went limp; around him the water turned red; and he floated downstream.

The soldiers thought he was dead. And so, for a bit, did Baltasar. He had been hit five times, three times in the calf, once in the testicle and once in the thigh. He floated downriver for a while, drifting in and out of consciousness. When he was out of sight of the soldiers, he managed to pull himself out of the stream and dragged himself to a nearby shack. He had been amazingly lucky. The bullets had gone straight through. At the shack, friends patched him up and lent him a horse, which he rode further up into the Durango hills.

In late 1975, the war on drugs hit the opium- and weed-growing regions of Mexico with force. Gone was the stress on borderlands policing. Now Mexicans and Americans focused on rural eradication. They launched the world's first large-scale herbicide campaign to target narcotics and sent the military to occupy growing zones from the Golden Triangle in the north, down through the Sierra Madre Occidental to the southern states of Guerrero and Oaxaca. The catchall term for the campaign was Operation Condor, but DEA agents knew it as "the atrocities."

Operation Condor was a turning point for Mexican counternarcotics policies. For decades, the Mexicans had run military eradication campaigns. For at least five years, they had also employed a heightened degree of violence against narcotics traffickers. And though they didn't like to admit it, they had been testing the effects of herbicides on drug crops since the late 1960s. Yet this was the first time that they had brought together all three strategies and extended them throughout most of western Mexico.

According to both the American and the Mexican authorities, Operation Condor was an unparalleled success. It radically reduced the volume of Mexican narcotics hitting the U.S. market. Military officials from Latin America, Asia, and the Caribbean were invited to inspect the efforts. And over the next three decades, the combination of strategies would become a model for militarized counternarcotics measures throughout the globe.

Yet the cost was enormous. The soldiers of Operation Condor shot up villages, ransacked houses, and stole valuables. They raped women, beat children, and tortured and killed certainly hundreds and possible thousands of Mexican farmers. The effort resembled a Cold War counterinsurgency more than a traditional counternarcotics campaign. And like the counterinsurgencies of Central America, the Southern Cone, or parts of rural Mexico, it was pushed, supported, and applauded by the Americans.

Furthermore, its success was widely overstated. Initially, the numbers looked good. No doubt Operation Condor briefly reduced the amount of Mexican heroin and marijuana crossing the frontier. Yet this had little or no effect on U.S. addiction rates; other countries quickly picked up the slack, just like Mexico had a decade earlier. Perhaps more important, the effort disrupted Mexico's local protection rackets, clearing space for corrupt PJF cops to assert control over the country's remaining narcotics networks. Between 1976 and 1985, the Mexican drug trade effectively became a politically approved, federal-level business.

Since Nixon's presidency, the authorities had channeled millions toward America's counternarcotics agencies. First, they established the BNDD and then, when that failed, the DEA. They filled both organizations with old agents and new recruits. And they gave them free rein to roam south of the border. Yet results were disappointing. Heroin addiction rates were up, and drug overdoses were at their highest level ever. By 1975, Senate inquiries and press exposés described the DEA as not only ineffective, but also racked by infighting, stuffed with CIA loons, and with mob affiliates in some suspiciously senior positions. In May 1975, the attorney general demanded that the head of the DEA resign. There were even rumors that the Justice Department was about to get rid of the entire project.

Fortunately, at least for the DEA, they had a scapegoat: the Mexicans. To be fair, the evidence was not hard to assemble. In early 1975, the DEA started to use multispectral aerial photography to identify poppy fields and review Mexico's eradication effort. The report was damning. The claims of escalating eradication efforts were at best misleading and at worst a deliberate lie (although one that the Americans had happily repeated when their federal budget was secure).

The 1975 report claimed that over half the poppy plants had already been harvested before they were cut down; it suggested that many areas now grew two or even three crops per year; and it confirmed that poppy growing had extended outside the Golden Triangle and down through the western mountains of Mexico. The eradication campaign was little more than a "vicious circle of incompetence, apathy, and corruption."

The solution, they surmised, was to spray the drug crops with herbicides. This had long been a dream of American drug hawks. Anslinger had toyed with the policy as early as 1946, and Nixon had put the measure on the table yet again. In theory, pesticides were cheaper than soldiers. And pesticides were also something the Americans knew a lot about. If Vietnam had taught them anything, it was that even if they weren't any good at fighting in jungles, they were pretty good at defoliating them.

Now the key was to persuade the Mexicans to roll out the strategy on a massive scale. The classified 1975 paper—"Potential for a Forward Strategy Against Heroin in Mexico"—suggested that if the Mexicans were reluctant to support "intensive poppy eradication using helicopter-borne herbicides … and punitive action against opium cultivators" the U.S. would have to fabricate some "external" or "induced" incentives. The incentives the paper proposed were a textbook Anslinger combination of public humiliation, manufactured panic, and diplomatic bullying.

First came the public humiliation. The Mexican authorities—as Anslinger had discovered as early as 1947—were extremely sensitive to external criticism. U.S. censure risked trade, put off international investment, and in the mid-1970s endangered the reputation of Mexico's jet-setting, peacemaking president, Luis Echeverría. So in late April 1975 someone leaked details of official corruption to the *New York Times*. The story was really embarrassing. It claimed that at least one "high official of a major ministry" was a major drug trafficker and revealed that "high Mexican police chiefs" were becoming millionaires by selling their protection to big dealers.

Then came the panic. Persuading the Mexican government to come down hard on rural opium growers had always been tough. The trade provided money, employment, and social services for many of the country's poorest communities. And though there had been U.S. efforts to play up Mexican domestic heroin addiction, it was a difficult sell. Most assessments concluded that, despite the big upsurge in production, homegrown addicts were incredibly rare.

Instead, the Americans started to play on a more realistic Mexican fear—left-wing guerrillas. Inspired by the Cuban Revolution and pushed by the harsh reprisals against Mexico City's 1968 student movement, such organizations had started to grow. In the southern state of Guerrero small rural forces were combating local landowners, state gunmen, and federal soldiers. And in the big cities of Guadalajara, Monterrey, and Culiacán, another organization, the Communist League 23rd September, had begun to perform shocking, high-profile operations that included kidnappings, assassinations, and bank robberies.

To firm up the link between the drugs and the guerrillas, the Americans pushed the idea that traffickers were exchanging narcotics for high-caliber weapons which were then being sold to the insurgents. The Americans knew that the Mexicans were concerned about this possibility. The Mexicans had already conducted their own secret service investigation into the drugs-for-arms trade in 1974. They also knew that the links were tenuous. The investigation had concluded that most of the guns were actually bought by poorly equipped state cops. But the reality didn't really matter. As the "Forward Strategy" paper commented, "Whatever the truth about the relationship between the arms traffic and the drug traffic, the US could possibly play upon the concern of the Mexicans over insurgency by linking US efforts to check the arms flow to the Mexican drug efforts." In other words, *you stop the drugs and we'll stop the guns.*

To cement the argument, in July 1975 the DEA announced the breaking of a vast, humiliating, and at least partially fictional drugs-for-arms conspiracy. The case involved a Cuban-American trafficker called Alberto Sicilia Falcón.

Though Sicilia was clearly involved in the drug trade, the case was overblown. He fit the stereotype of a drug lord almost too well. Sicilia had the tastes of a James Bond villain and had constructed a huge hilltop residence outside Tijuana replete with chintzy décor, surreptitious listening devices, two pet lions, and an underground shooting range hidden behind a sauna. He was close to some high-up—yet eminently disposable—Mexican public figures including Irma Serrano (the lover of the former president), Gastón Santos (the idiot son of an out-of-favor regional politician), and Dolores Olmedo (a left-leaning Mexican society lady). He was even what the newspapers could term a "sexual deviant." He was a playboy, purportedly a bisexual, and had a U.S. conviction for perversion.

But for the DEA, Sicilia's big attraction was that he was allegedly the crucial intermediary between the worlds of international trafficking and left-wing insurgency. This Ian Flemingesque premise was the least convincing part of the whole charade. According to one U.S. witness, Sicilia had tried to buy a U.S. made "super rifle" with which he intended to arm conveniently vague "Central American guerrillas" and "possibly organize a coup." According to another, he was moving arms to Guerrero's insurgents in return for "100 plus tons of marijuana." The claims—which were only uttered behind the closed doors of a San Diego grand jury trial—were quickly leaked to U.S. and Mexican newspapers.

Job done. Now drugs weren't just killing Americans; they were funding Mexican terrorists.

The final piece of the strategy involved another Anslinger tactic: diplomatic bullying. Again, the DEA's hands were all over it. In late October 1975 they invited the Democratic congressman Charles Rangel to Mexico. As the representative for Harlem, he was concerned about New York's spiraling addiction problem. He wanted to know where the drugs came from; so the DEA decided to show him. Flying him over the mountains outside Culiacán, they pointed out the fields of pink, red, and purple flowers. It was a shock, Rangel claimed, even to some of his Mexican handlers. They had assured him that most poppies were harvested from January to March. These crops revealed that the traffickers were securing two or even three

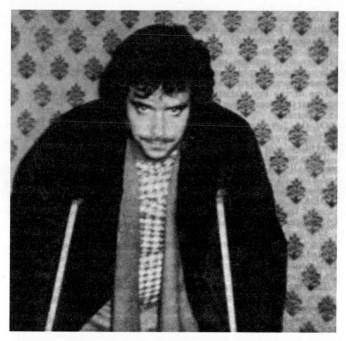

*Alberto Sicilia Falcón was a drug trafficker. But the United States pushed his prosecution in order to persuade the Mexicans that there was a link between drug traffickers and sales of arms to guerrillas. Here he is photographed after his arrest. He is on crutches because he "fell off a horse."*

*Alberto Sicilia Falcón in better times. With Irma Serrano, the former lover of President Diáz Ordaz.*

harvests a year. It also suggested that the annual New Year eradication campaign was insufficient for combating the growing problem.

Incensed, Rangel immediately sent an alarmed letter to President Ford, published the letter as a press release, and cajoled nearly a hundred fellow congressmen to demand action from the authorities. It was a clever move. Now it wasn't simply the DEA and the Republican drug hawks that were pushing herbicide spraying; bleeding-heart Democrats had taken up the cause.

By November 1975, Mexico was in a corner. It had been publically execrated for corruption. It had been blamed for the U.S. heroin epidemic. And it had been partially persuaded that drug money was purchasing some guerrilla weaponry. So on November 13, Mexico's attorney general held a press conference. He announced that Mexico would start to use airborne herbicide spraying to kill drug crops. Unsurprisingly, given the rushed nature of the policy change, he was light on the specifics. But he assured journalists that they would "not be using napalm" or any other chemicals "that damage ecology." And he claimed—even less credibly—that Mexico had not been pushed into doing this by U.S. pressure.

Over the next year, the authorities began mapping out what would become Operation Condor. Initially, it covered most of Mexico's west coast from Sonora in the north to Oaxaca in the south. It would last—in one form or another—for the next decade. And gradually it would be extended to new growing zones to the south in Chiapas, to the east in Veracruz, and to the north in Coahuila.

At the center was aerial spraying. From November 15, 1975, on, Mexican planes would use a mix of multispectral photography and old-fashioned observation to track down poppy and marijuana plantations. They would mark crops on a map and then hand those maps to the helicopter pilots. These would then spray a chemical called paraquat on the marijuana fields and another called 2,4-D on the opium poppies. The following day, soldiers would be flown in to inspect the results.

Around 1,600 soldiers split into over 100 small platoons were now stationed in advanced bases up in the mountains. In the Golden Triangle there were bases in Badiraguato (Sinaloa), Choix (Sinaloa), and Topia

*In late 1975 the Mexican government started to use DEA pilots to spray opium
and marijuana fields with herbicides.*

(Durango). In early 1977, they increased the numbers still further, sta-
tioning 2,400 troops in Sinaloa and up to another 7,000 in the other
drug-producing areas. The general responsible for the 1968 student killings was given command of the operation.

It was the army's task to check the spraying zones, destroy any remaining
plantations, track down and seize harvested crops, arrest suspected growers
or traffickers, and hand them over to the PJF. By 1977 the Mexican army
was effectively working as America's largest counternarcotics police force.

The Americans provided much of the funding for Operation Condor,
along with most of the chemicals and all of the aircraft. They also provided

key personnel. These comprised DEA agents as well as privately contracted pilots, mechanics, and communications specialists. At first, there were around 70 of them, based principally in the Golden Triangle. They flew the big Bell 212 helicopters, acted as visual spotters, and verified the destruction of the plantations. And though there were new regulations, which tried to limit DEA participation, Americans still got involved in both the arrest and the questioning of suspects.

But most important, Americans provided the legitimacy. They denied the frequent accusations of torture and justified the violence. "People were getting machine gunned. You don't eradicate that kind of crime by walking in and being extremely polite about it," claimed the DEA head in 1978.

On the surface the results—or at least the declared results—were impressive. Spraying herbicides radically accelerated the process of eradication. One plane could kill 55 hectares of opium poppies a day. In comparison, an entire platoon of soldiers equipped with machetes and sticks barely covered 3 hectares. At the same time, the permanent military occupation of great swathes of Mexico's mountains led to a rapid upsurge of drug seizures, lab raids, and arrests.

The campaign posted huge numbers. Before the advent of aerial spraying, the Mexicans had struggled to eradicate over 3,000 hectares of opium and marijuana plantations. In the first year of spraying, they stated that they had eradicated over three times as much. And the following year the results were even more impressive. In just one year, they had destroyed over 9,000 hectares of poppies alone.

Beyond the optimistic stats, the campaign did actually make inroads into the price and availability of narcotics north of the border. Between 1976 and 1978, heroin purity dropped from 6.2 to as little as 3.5 percent; and the price per milligram almost doubled, going from $1.26 to $2.19. In the same period, overdoses declined markedly from a high of nearly 2,000 a year to less than 500. By 1978 the Mexican share of America's heroin market had allegedly fallen from 90 percent to 50 percent.

The numbers, however, came at a price. And for Mexico—if not for the United States—it was high.

The authorities always claimed that their pilots were scrupulously careful. Herbicide spraying only targeted drug crops. And any accidental spraying caused no long-term damage to the soil, food or the health of peasant farmers.

Experts were less convinced. A confidential State Department report concluded that, if imbibed, paraquat in particular was extremely toxic. "It has probably caused more deaths both purposeful and unintentional than any other herbicide I know of," the writer claimed. The doctor in charge of Mexico City's biggest children's hospital was equally concerned. He pointed out that inhaling the chemical or consuming vegetables covered in it could cause agonizing death through pulmonary fibrosis.

Those who experienced the spraying knew the damage the toxins could do. First, there seemed to be some confusion over what chemicals the pilots were actually using. Though they always claimed that they were exclusively employing paraquat and 2,4-D, witnesses claimed that they were also spraying the much stronger herbicide DMA 6. Second, whatever they were spraying, it was having an effect on more than just the drugs. Villagers claimed that land that was sprayed could no longer be used to grow crops. And one DEA agent who worked on some of the early paraquat tests admitted that "the liquid got into the water supply ... by the end of the week it had killed everything down the mountain."

The chemicals also harmed anyone who came into contact with them. Journalist Craig Pyes remembers trying to photograph one of the spraying helicopters as it flew overhead. He got covered in either paraquat or 2,4-D. "They didn't know which." "I got into the helicopter and started vomiting and vomiting. I had rashes all over my skin." Peasants up in the Guerrero mountain village of Xixila told a similar story. Where the government had sprayed, "nothing grew." And several villagers, including a couple of children that were caught in the chemical mist, quickly got sick and died.

But if the effects of the chemicals were officially uncertain, the military occupation of large swathes of western Mexico had more tangible consequences. The brutality of the counternarcotics campaigns of the early 1970s now moved from the cities to the countryside. State-sanctioned violence came to the Sierra.

Just as up on the border, murders were frequent. Some were outright massacres. On November 2, 1976, soldiers attempted to enter the mountain village of Santiago de los Caballeros. A gunfight ensued that left at least twelve dead. A year later there was another shootout between the military and villagers just outside Mazatlán. This time gunfire claimed fourteen victims. Though in both cases the army claimed that they were fired on first, these accounts seem unlikely. On both occasions, only one soldier was among the dead. And in Santiago de los Caballeros, witnesses claimed that the soldiers had simply opened fire on a village dance. "They ran and fell like flies. Dead and dead and dead. How many? Dozens."

But mostly the killings were kept low-profile. As the farmer Baltasar discovered, they were committed away from settlements; they were often covered up by accusations that suspects had fled or opened fire first; and soldiers often tried to intimidate witnesses into silence. In November 1978, for example, peasants complained that soldiers had attacked their small village of Pino Gordo, beaten one of them to death, and forced the others to flee. As soon as they reported this, the soldiers returned, tracked them down, and compelled the farmers to say that they had lied.

Despite these measures, complaints still litter the army's files. April 27, 1976, PJF cops and soldiers descend on a marijuana field just outside the Chihuahua town of Guadalupe y Calvo. Farmers "open fire" and four are

*From 1975 on, thousands of soldiers descended on the drug-growing regions of Mexico as part of Operation Condor.*

killed. April 9, 1978, the soldiers at a checkpoint also in Guadalupe y Calvo shoot and kill Daniel Rivera de la Rocha. They claim he had inexplicably "taken out his gun" and tried to run the roadblock. February 14, 1979, soldiers open fire on a runway outside Culiacán, killing a pilot and two others.

It seems the more remote the population, the more extensive the violence. Up in the indigenous regions of Chihuahua, where news rarely got out and Rarámuri Indians had long attempted to escape state interference, the army was particularly brutal. In November 1979 the priest of the small enclave of Sisoguichi claimed that he knew of at least one villager shot, another beaten to death, and another so brutally tortured that he later died of his injuries.

Beyond the murders, there was also the widespread use of torture. Soldiers followed a three-step process. First, they grabbed suspected peasant growers and subjected them to a field inquisition. This involved beating or a Tehuacanazo-style waterboarding.

Often this initial treatment was done en masse. In San Ignacio, one farmer's son remembers troops arriving just after the rains. They made all 200 of the village's men lie down face-first in the mud. They proceeded to beat them with the butts of their guns, kick them in their stomachs, plunge their heads into the water, and waterboard a select few. Eventually, one broke. He coughed up the names of twelve supposed marijuana growers, who were then dragged away.

After the initial questioning, suspects were then taken to the forward army bases. There, soldiers and a scattering of PJF agents continued the torture. Again, there were beatings and near drownings and even more vicious versions of the Tehuacanazo that used Alka-Seltzer or chili powder mixed with water. Up in the Rarámuri region, there were also reports of castrations and needles being inserted under the fingernails of victims.

Such violent interrogation normally lasted around a week. Those who survived described the process as truly terrifying. In fact, it was so brutal that at least one pilot decided it was too much. After the usual beatings, he eventually promised to show the troops where he went to pick up marijuana. Instead, he plunged his plane and its three military occupants into the side of a mountain. Anything was better than returning to the camp. "They've beaten me but they're not going to torture me anymore. And now they're going to die with me," he shouted defiantly over the radio as the plane went down.

The final stage, however, was at the police base back in Culiacán, where the PJF took over from the army. It was their job to elicit the confessions. Prisoners were kept in the cells for two to three weeks. During the ordeal around a dozen agents would take turns brutalizing the suspects.

In 1978 a Sinaloa lawyer was also tossed into the cells with the drug suspects. He started to take their testimonies and compiled a report. It made for disturbing reading. In all, he listed eighteen distinct types of torture. Some were well known. There was frequent use of the Tehuacanazo (although—blame the U.S. influence—they had now branched out to using Pepsi-Cola), the cattle prod, dunking in shit-filled latrines, and beatings with rifle butts. But there were also some novelties. Cops found that if they beat the sides of prisoners' heads with the palms of their hands they could break their eardrums and cause extreme pain. Cops also discovered that if they tied prisoners' hands behind their back sufficiently tightly, they could cut their circulation and make them pass out.

The eventual effects of these tortures were horrific. A prosecution rate of nearly 100 percent came at the cost of dozens of cases of partial or total deafness, kidney failure, abortion, severe mental trauma, the breaking of multiple bones, and at least eight dead, three disappeared, and one poor man who was forced to have both his legs amputated. "I thought I was in hell rather than a federal agency of the Mexican government," the lawyer later remarked. And this was only what he found during his brief stay. There were rumors that during the first eighteen months the Culiacán PJF alone had killed at least sixty suspects.

Beyond the most egregious examples of murder and torture, there were the usual cruelties one might associate with an occupying army. There were multiple reports of beating, threatening, and terrifying young children. And the army files are full of complaints of rape, sexual abuse, and the kidnapping of young girls.

Robbery was also common. In fact, it seems it was the norm. Few complaints didn't include some mention of troops purloining the peasants' scant possessions. Soldiers stole livestock; they stole food; they stole money; they stole radios and TVs; and they stole jewelry. One enterprising commander

even stole cars and established a chop shop near his base to fix them and
sell them.

One DEA agent who accompanied troops on a raid remembered capturing a pair of opium smugglers;

> The soldiers took the couple to the stream and interrogated them
> by dunking them in the water. In less than 20 minutes they admit-
> ted being gomeros [opium farmers] and provided information on
> traffickers who would be purchasing from them. The soldiers took
> all stuff from their house. I saw one of them carrying a large mat-
> tress on his back

In theory, the DEA agents were meant to report any incidents of torture to their superiors. Yet in three years of intense cooperation with the
Mexicans, not one single complaint was made. Instead, the higher-ups
repeatedly denied any knowledge of malpractice. The U.S. embassy's narcotics advisor stated that there was "no reason to believe that prisoners
have been mistreated by the Mexican police."

Yet it was clear that the DEA knew very well what was going on. It was
a conspiracy of silence.

Agents not only nicknamed what was happening "the atrocities," they
even joked that Jaime Alcalá García, the head of the PJF in Culiacán, had
"killed more people than smallpox." One DEA agent, who was stationed in
the city in 1977, went into some detail:

> Alcalá immediately started to purge the criminal element by
> torturing and killing them. It was known he had created un-
> marked cemeteries in remote areas where he buried hundreds of
> violent criminals. His right hand man, Gerardo Serrano, carried
> out Alcalá's orders to the letter.... Serrano looked like a harmless
> college student but in reality he could kill without hesitating or
> flinching.

Furthermore, the U.S agents didn't just know about it; they used the
information that the brutality elicited. According to one PJF agent, they

would stand in the background taking notes while the Mexican cops beat the suspects.

Beyond these unsanctioned methods, Operation Condor also extended the widespread use of informants into the mountains of western Mexico. Soldiers, the PJF, and the DEA had an army of small-time opium planters and marijuana growers that they had spared and set free in return for snitching on their neighbors.

The effect was exactly the same as at the border. It destroyed trust, divided affiliations, and sparked tit-for-tat killings. One DEA agent recounted employing a couple of old peasants to trace marijuana plantations just outside the Chihuahua town of Ciudad Madera. After two weeks up in the hills, they managed to locate numerous fields. Together the DEA and the PJF raided the place and arrested a relatively important local politician. But there was a leak. And within a month the two peasants had been tortured, killed, and their truck pushed off a cliff. It took days to find their remains.

In fact, in the mountains the effects were probably worse than at the border. Here divisions created by the employment of informants piggybacked bitter existing rifts, particularly over land. Soldiers often forced poor peasants to rat out the predatory landlords who had stolen their lands to grow opium poppies. But after the soldiers had made a few arrests or pulled up a few fields, they left. "The indigenous peasants are offered no protection. They are between a rock and a hard place and constantly suffer reprisals, attempts on their lives, and threats," one report admitted.

Quantifying the death toll of Operation Condor is a tough job.

Mexico's counterinsurgency drive against leftist guerrillas, which ran in parallel to the counternarcotics campaign, has elicited substantial academic inquiries, journalistic investigations, and at least one official review. And historians and activists have estimated that as many as 3,000 leftists were killed and another 7,000 tortured by the state. But there has been no comparable attempt to measure the drug war dead of the 1970s. Peasant dope farmers have never elicited the same sympathy as communist students.

Furthermore, to do so now—with any degree of accuracy—is probably impossible. Both the army and the PJF were experts at hiding bodies, tampering with evidence, and menacing witnesses. They were the lessons of the counterinsurgency repurposed for counternarcotics. They buried the corpses in the hills in unmarked graves and shot them in the back of the head and pushed them out of helicopters into the Pacific Ocean. If they needed to get rid of a lot at one time, they stuffed them into canvas sacks, loaded them onto a transport plane, and dumped them into the sea. Often the efforts were not entirely successful. One American, who lived on the Guerrero coast during the 1970s, said that he used to buy fish on the beach at Playa La Angosta. "I used to buy there every morning and every morning I'd go there, there'd be a fucking body floating there."

Based on my research, I would estimate that during the first three or four years of Operation Condor the state certainly killed hundreds and probably thousands. Incidents of torture—from beatings to more extreme forms of violence—certainly numbered in the thousands. These atrocities were focused in the Golden Triangle and the southern state of Guerrero. But there were also reports of killings as far south as Oaxaca. (In early 1978, for example, a handful of indigenous peasants from the town of Ocotlán complained that a helicopter gunship had open fire on local farmers, leaving over twenty dead. If it was a lie, it took deep roots. And talking to locals forty years later they repeated the accusations.)

If so, counternarcotics killings were probably around the same as those committed by state counterinsurgency forces.

# Chapter 18

## The Barbarians of the North

WHEN JORGE VILLALOBOS BEGAN RECEIVING BULLETS IN THE MAIL, HE knew his time was running out. Then a smuggler opened fire on him in the street in front of a group of local cops. The cops did nothing; they simply turned away. Now he kept a semiautomatic rifle in the corner of his office. It was loaded and ready. And every day he walked to work, he clutched a revolver close to his chest. But he knew he was just prolonging the inevitable. "If they want to kill me badly enough, they will do it, despite every precaution."

It was December 1976 and Villalobos had been the government's prosecuting attorney in Nogales for four years. During that time, he had put away hundreds of smugglers. They included high-profile traffickers, gun-running members of the city elite, and a cabal of local pharmacists arrested for amphetamine and cocaine smuggling. In December 1975 he even detained the head of the Sonora state police for hijacking eighty sacks of marijuana.

Villalobos was an unlikely legal hard man. Short, slight, and rather bookish, those who met him described him as humble and unassuming,

with a limp handshake. He had grown up in Mexico City. There he had
come to admire his godfather, one of the capital's more respectable police
officials. Villalobos was hardworking and ambitious, and initially he had
balanced a job as a beat policeman with training as a lawyer. When he
finally gained his degree, he moved into the Attorney General's Office (the
Procuraduría General de la República, or PGR). Here he was known for
being scrupulously honest. Sent to work in Tijuana in the 1960s, he had
banned PJF agents from torturing suspects and raided the infamous La
Mesa prison and jailed its director. He had even put one of his own men on
trial for extortion.

Such actions generated quite a reputation. In Mexico, civil leaders heralded him as a hero. Over the border in the United States, agents nicknamed him "Mr. Clean," claimed that he was "super straight," and
commented that he always "did things the right way, the legal way."

In the end, they did come for him. But it was not the enemies Villalobos
expected. On December 3, 1976, the new attorney general, Oscar Flores
Sánchez, sacked the Nogales prosecutor. He immediately ordered his successor to compile a case against him. Within ten days it was ready. Two PJF
cops now accused him of taking bribes from drug traffickers.

The charges were baseless. No one in Nogales believed them. The two
PJF cops were known to hold a grudge against Villalobos. And even his
successor eventually dropped them. But Villalobos was ruined. He heard
rumors that his former employers had ordered local PJF agents to apply the
*ley fuga*. He escaped over the border to the United States. Here he would
die anonymous, penniless, and separated from his family. Yet before he
fled, he recounted his story to one of his few remaining supporters—the
poet, journalist, and intellectual Oscar Monroy Rivera.

The story he told was scandalous. In fact, it was so shocking that even
an outspoken troublemaker like Monroy was too scared to publish it. And
until now it has remained buried among his private papers.

According to Villalobos, during the 1970s a group of corrupt officials
had infiltrated the PGR and the PJF. In return for ample payment, this
group had agreed to safeguard a select crowd of Sinaloa and Chihuahua
traffickers. Villalobos had long irritated this group. He didn't play along. He
refused to take bribes; he sacked corrupt cops; he arrested protected

traffickers; and he even prosecuted dodgy judges. The only reason he survived so long was his connections. For four years, his boss—the attorney general, Pedro Ojeda Paullada—had protected him.

But, in December 1976, José López Portillo became the president of Mexico. He immediately moved Ojeda to another ministry. And he put the group of corrupt officials in charge of the PGR and the PJF. They were the former governor of Chihuahua, Oscar Flores Sánchez, who was made head of the PGR; former Ciudad Juárez hitman Raúl Mendiolea Cerecero, who was appointed head of the PJF; and the former head of Mexico City airport security, Arturo "El Negro" Durazo Moreno, who was made head of the capital's police. Since they were all born on the frontier with the United States, government insiders soon dubbed them "the barbarians of the north."

The barbarians' accomplishments were dramatic and far-reaching. Over the next six years they attempted to centralize the country's scattered drug protection rackets. Eventually, the new arrangement would become known as "the plaza system." The plazas were just the old protection rackets. But they were now under federal rather than local control. It was a major turning point in the relationship between the Mexican state and the drug trade.

The takeover itself was a complex and violent undertaking. The barbarians had to remove scrupulous officials (like Villalobos), destroy local rackets, cow traffickers into paying, and then protect them. At the same time, they had to arrest (or murder) uncooperative traffickers, keep journalists and the DEA at bay, and also shift the trade from marijuana and heroin to a new drug—cocaine.

José López Portillo was not your average Mexican president. An intellectual and a university lecturer, he had got into public administration late. He had scant experience of the messy world of party politics. His school friend, Luis Echeverría, had originally promoted him to finance minister in 1973 and then nominated him as the official PRI presidential candidate. Initially, the selection seemed to suggest Echeverría's desire to keep acting as the power behind the throne.

Preening and arrogant, but with none of the political savvy of his predecessors, in fact López Portillo proved to be his own man. Or perhaps more accurately, he proved to be incompetent in his own way. His term was marked by two things. The first was an enormous oil boom, which lasted from 1977 to 1981. It ended with the collapse of the international oil price, the massive extension of public debt, and the devaluation of the peso. The economic catastrophe ruined middle-class Mexicans and led to the suspension of debt repayments and the nationalization of the country's banks. It also gave López Portillo the unfortunate moniker "the devalued president."

The second was corruption. Like President Alemán three decades earlier, López Portillo presided over a significant change in what one commentator described as both "the quality and quantity" of official corruption. Buoyed by the oil boom, insulated by an increasingly autocratic party, and protected by a supremely overconfident president, corruption moved up a level once again.

Those close to the president no longer skimmed percentages and passed on some of the rewards to those further down the hierarchy. They now hijacked department budgets, employed entire administrations as personal corvée labor, and flaunted their wealth by building mansions overlooking the capital. López Portillo led the way. According to a leaked CIA report, while the economy sank, he salted away between $1 billion and $3 billion. (His grandsons claim that his direct family saw none of this. Most, they claim, went to his second wife—an Italian-born sex-comedy actress. Such penury—it should be noted—did not prevent the younger grandson from employing a manservant while at Oxford University.)

Nowhere was López Portillo's poor management, political tin ear, and tolerance for graft more apparent than in the world of law enforcement. Here he ignored multiple warnings. Instead, he appointed the barbarians of the north.

The least provocative appointment was the head of the PGR, Oscar Flores Sánchez. At least the Americans liked him. They had known him for some time. He had helped lead the joint U.S.–Mexican foot-and-mouth campaign in the late 1940s. He was charming, well educated, and spoke good English. And their initial reports praised him as "self-confident ... able and extremely active despite his age."

But perhaps the Americans were not the best judges. Locals in Chihuahua knew him as "the king of chatuma [the local slang for opium gum]." And the Mexican secret service had concluded that, as governor of Chihuahua, Flores had presided over a vast drug protection racket. "Although we do not have evidence that demonstrates that Flores has been directly mixed up in this commerce, we do have evidence that some of his closest collaborators were and actually are mixed directly or indirectly in the drug trafficking business. We think that it is impossible that Flores does not have knowledge of these activities."

Furthermore, Flores's first moves as PGR head didn't inspire confidence. He sacked the scrupulous Villalobos and pushed for his imprisonment; he put the whistleblower and former Guadalupe mayor Oscar Venegas Tarín on the list of most-wanted drug traffickers; and he promoted a notoriously corrupt lawyer—Samuel Alba Leyva—to head the government's antinarcotics campaign.

Appointing Mendiolea as head of the PJF was more controversial. Since orchestrating the massacre of Enrique Fernández's Ciudad Juárez drug gang in the early 1930s, Mendiolea had forged what one might politely describe as an up-and-down career. He moved to Jalisco, where he headed up the police reserves and helped protect local heroin traffickers. He worked in the state food company, where he was accused of grifting over 250,000 pesos a month in expenses. Finally, he went to Mexico City, where he rose from head of special ops to deputy head of the capital's police. Here, he was accused of running the capital's prostitution racket, extorting street sellers, backing a quasi-fascist student organization, and organizing the repression of urban squatters, railway workers, and political opponents. He capped this off by allegedly orchestrating some of the most vicious attacks on protesting students in 1968.

Even for a corrupt Mexican cop it was quite a record. And between 1970 and 1976, Mendiolea was banished to the political wilderness. But there is a saying in Mexico: "In politics, no one is ever fully alive or completely dead." And in 1976 the balding, thickset septuagenarian captain made a surprising come back. López Portillo—on the advice of Flores—resurrected Mendiolea as head of the PJF.

Gruff and authoritarian, Mendiolea had none of Flores's easygoing charm. Visiting journalists—used to the niceties of Mexican politics—were surprised that he offered them neither a handshake nor a seat, but simply scowled, demanded their credentials, and proceeded to lecture them on his official duties. U.S. officials were similarly unimpressed, noting that he had immediately taken over PJF recruitment and hired a group of new cops, described as "with criminal antecedents" and "little education."

Even the Mexican secret service noted that something was up. They reported that Mendiolea had also ordered commanders to avoid arresting drug traffickers without his explicit approval. The move, they concluded, not only centralized counternarcotic enforcement, but also "as traffickers knew of this decision, allowed them to transport, distribute, process and export their product with complete impunity throughout the republic."

Mendiolea set a new low, but perhaps the most surprising appointment was Arturo "El Negro" Durazo Moreno as head of the Mexico City police. Since Durazo had survived the overhaul of the PJF in the early 1970s, his penchant for graft had, if anything, grown. During Echeverría's presidency, he had continued to both protect traffickers and transport narcotics. The Americans built an extensive file on him. In April 1972 he organized the import of 400 kilos of cocaine and ran it up to the United States in refrigerated trucks. And in June 1974 he received $60,000 from Culiacán trafficker Jorge Favela Escobosa in return for protecting another 32 kilos of white powder.

By 1974, the Americans even managed to get an informer inside the Mexico City airport. He described exactly how Durazo's protection racket worked. Traffickers would send drugs to the airport with three separate mules. Two would be carrying kilos of product; the other would be holding only a few ounces. Durazo would get his men to bust the small-time mule. He would announce a major seizure and inflate the bust with a few kilos of milk powder. At the same time, the other two mules were rushed through customs and delivered their briefcases to one of Durazo's men. He got the plaudits for good police work and he got the payoff as well.

Durazo's graft had got so egregious that by January 1976 the Americans were ready to bring formal charges. A Miami grand jury heard how he had helped transport at least five loads of cocaine into Florida in the early 1970s. The prosecutor even issued an arrest warrant for Durazo.

The warrant was passed on to the U.S. State Department, the Mexican minister of the interior, the attorney general, and both Echeverría and

López Portillo. Yet nothing was done. As one journalist later noted, "Durazo not only escaped prosecution, he was promoted." The accusations were dropped and the arrest warrant quietly forgotten. (In 1981, Durazo returned to Miami as the special guest of the city police force. With either a great sense of irony or a quite supreme lack of self-awareness, he pondered in his Miami speech why the media "glorified criminals and rubbished the police." At the time, he was using most of Mexico City's cops as unpaid laborers at his two huge residences.)

Quite why the accusations were buried remains uncertain. Personal relations clearly played a role. In August 1976, López Portillo explained to the American ambassador that he had known Durazo for nearly forty years. Their friendship went deep. Durazo had always helped him "in the playground and in physical confrontations." He owed him. And his loyalty could not be questioned. So he had decided to reward him with a prestigious job. Yet he assured the ambassador that he was not naïve. He knew his friend was a "wild one," and he promised the American that Durazo "would operate only under suitably controlled circumstances" and "would be giv[en] no official functions in any narcotics-related fields."

But some whispered that the CIA was also involved. Only a few institutions had the power to make a DEA file, a grand jury warrant, and a State Department protest disappear almost overnight. The CIA often used narcotics corruption to blackmail foreign politicians. Durazo clearly moved in counterinsurgency circles and was involved in some of the state's shadier operations (including a particularly brutal counterinsurgency kill squad called the Jaguar Group). And when he finally fled Mexico in 1982, CIA operatives helped him get a visa to stay in the United States. It was not the first time the Company would sacrifice drug policy for national security. And it would not be the last.

Whatever the reason, U.S. observers soon got a sense of the limits of López Portillo's assurances. He refused to allow Durazo to run for governor of the border state of Sonora. (When Durazo complained, his old friend replied, "Don't fuck around, fucking Negro, you're going to get me into a fight.") Instead, he made him head of the capital's police force.

Within a month of his promotion, Durazo had persuaded the authorities to drop corruption charges against the notoriously crooked PJF commander, Francisco Sahagún Baca. He invited him to return from his exile in Spain. And he promptly appointed Sahagún head of his special investigations unit. By early 1977, the U.S. embassy had received verifiable intel that Durazo was now "recruiting personnel for Mexico City police department primarily consisting of those commandants that have well documented past[s] in narcotics involvement."

They weren't wrong. Durazo's hiring list was a Who's Who of the PJF's dodgiest borderlands commanders. They not only included Sahagún Baca, but also Rafael Chao López (based in Culiacán in 1973) and Daniel Acuña Figueroa (based in Ciudad Juárez from 1973 to 1975).

With their jobs secure and their own staff in place, the barbarians now set about controlling the country's drug rackets. Until now, no commentators have managed to trace the emergence of this new, centralized protection racket. But they have given it a name. It is known as the "plaza system", and it was first popularized in journalist Terrence Poppa's extraordinary account of the rise and fall of Texas borderlands smuggler Pablo Acosta. Now it is very much part of narcosociology, wheeled out in Netflix series and crime thrillers to describe Mexico's deep-seated and enduring corruption.

The evocative shorthand refers to the zone of influence of PJF commanders. And it suggests the practice of charging chosen traffickers a fixed percentage to move their product through the zone or plaza. According to insiders, every month these local commanders sent at least part of this money back to the barbarians in Mexico City. U.S. intel sources claimed that border traffickers were paying the PJF commanders as much as $80,000 a year.

Yet calling the barbarians' project a system suggests a degree of top-down control, unruffled order, and trafficker subservience that was simply not there. In fact, the barbarians' attempt to assert power over the country's protection rackets was less of a system and more of an unstable and bloody putsch.

Getting the traffickers to pay, for example, was a savage business. In each border city or production zone there were dozens—perhaps even hundreds—of traffickers. (In just the northeast, in the 200 miles between Ciudad Camargo and Matamoros, one PJF agent listed at least fifty smugglers that he knew about.) Some traffickers were paying other police forces; some the military; some were trying to get away with not paying at all.

So ensuring payment initially resembled a brutal extortion racket. In the midst of Operation Condor, Culiacán's PGR prosecutor, Carlos Aguilar Garza, and the PJF commander, Jaime Alcalá García, would beat and torture traffickers until they agreed to cough up. Off the record, state officials concluded that "Operation Condor is a way for some federal authorities to make themselves very rich. They have their own jail—nobody knows who comes and goes but them. It's a closed system. And once inside they torture people to see who has the money and who doesn't."

Aguilar continued to employ this strategy after he was moved to Tijuana in 1978. According to a revealing *San Diego Union* series, Aguilar employed a nephew of the Matamoros trafficker Juan Nepomuceno Guerra as his chief PJF agent. Together they tortured local smugglers, shook them down for money and narcotics. The paper managed to track down at least ten local traffickers who had been extorted between $10,000 and $100,000. Some had even moved to the United States and risked jail time to escape the racket. As Aguilar and his agents were the top lawmen in the city, they had complete impunity. Complaining was not only useless; it was dangerous.

> Before filing a lawsuit I would want to ask where can I complain? Where will my words find an echo? Who will listen to me? ... Who will protect my children? Where will the lawsuit go to and will the persons be punished and not just transferred to another place? And I will be here subject to others and I will be, as they say, marked down in their book. So I consider it impossible to file a lawsuit against anyone.

Aguilar and Alcalá were not one-offs. This kind of behavior was generalized. Similar accusations of PJF agents brutally extorting traffickers and smugglers litter the period. Up in the border town of Ojinaga, the commander subjected the local trafficker to three days of intensive torture. The trafficker was almost drowned, strapped to a bench and jabbed with a cattle prod and punched in the ribs, kidneys, and head. Such treatment not only ensured regular payment, it was an extended hazing. At the end of the torture, the PJF commander slapped the trafficker on the back, commended him that he had "balls," and said that he expected $10,000 a month.

Beyond extortion, both PGR and PJF agents regularly used their influence to get favored traffickers released from prison. This type of protection was a rather shrewder trick. On the surface they were fulfilling the American demands for arrests. But after a short time inside and the requisite payments to the police and the judicial authorities, the traffickers were let out. Officials did their job and got paid.

Yet at times, this catch-and-release strategy could be risky. If the Americans wanted the traffickers badly enough, they tended to keep an eye on them. In 1978, for example, the PJF arrested one of the top Durango smugglers, Rodolfo Herrera Nevárez. They had copious evidence, including Herrera's confession and a banking executive who was prepared to go on the record saying he had laundered Herrera drug money. Yet within a week, the case was dropped on a technicality. The Americans found out only because the head of the PGR, Flores, mistakenly mentioned the incident to embassy staff. He then claimed—to the consternation of the Americans—that it was not worth bringing Herrera to trial. "Once before the Mexican judge the defendant would be set free simply by stating that the declarations made to the PJF were not true and made under duress."

The Herrera case highlighted the thin line the barbarians walked. They were in constant struggles not only with the traffickers, but also with other institutions. They ranged from the DEA (which wanted arrests) through the Mexican press (which wanted a degree of judicial rectitude and transparency) to the military and the other law enforcement agencies (which wanted kickbacks or arrests). Give too much to any of these and you could upset a rival group.

The Herrera incident, for example, risked a diplomatic incident. So, to smooth over relations, the PJF decided to give the Americans their top trafficker target. The target was the old San Luis Río Colorado wholesaler, Pedro Avilés Pérez. Journalistic accounts, popular corridos, and thinly fictionalized treatments (including one in the Netflix *Narcos: Mexico* series) have long speculated on the demise of the Lion of the Sierra. Vague accusations of trafficker betrayal abound.

Until now the details have remained firmly under wraps. In a series of interviews with DEA agents, however, I finally managed to get the actual story. In reality, there was no betrayal. The PJF takedown was a government hit; it was a blood offering to the drug hawks of the north. It not only underlined the rather obvious game of institutional give-and-take; it also demonstrated—once again—the collusion of Americans and Mexican agents in the violence of this early drug war.

The Americans wanted Avilés bad. After the 1973 raid, Avilés had put a $10,000 bounty on the head of any DEA agent. And they had responded, somewhat childishly, by putting a $10,001 bounty on his. For five years, Avilés had managed to remain below the radar. But just two weeks after Herrera's release, PJF commander Alcalá lured Avilés into a trap. He asked to meet the trafficker on a road just outside Culiacán on the evening of September 15, 1978. They were going to negotiate a payoff. But it was Mexican Independence Day and Avilés turned up ready to party. He was accompanied by bodyguards, friends, and at least three teenage girls.

On arriving at the meeting spot, they were met by a barrage of bullets. Avilés and his companions died almost immediately. But just to make sure, Alcalá unloaded an exploding round into each of their heads. He then collected Avilés's payoff money, declared that Avilés had fired first, and demanded the bounty from the Americans.

To be fair to the Americans, they had learned to be rather wary of the PJF's claims. So they decided to get proof. They paid a worker at the local morgue to snap a photo of Avilés as he rested on the slab. The photo was the first picture that the Americans had ever got of Avilés. And as Alcalá's claims were verified, they duly paid up.

Killing traffickers was a standard plank of the barbarians' policy. As Avilés learned, PJF protection was conditional. It depended on a matrix of factors, from levels of payment through international pressure to relations with other traffickers and other Mexican institutions. To Flores, Mendiolea, and Durazo, murder had had little, or no, downside. It appeased the Americans, who—as we have seen—were unconcerned with legal niceties south of the border. It punished the uncooperative. And any money that was squandered could be made up by the more cooperative traffickers. These were also now much more likely to pay on time.

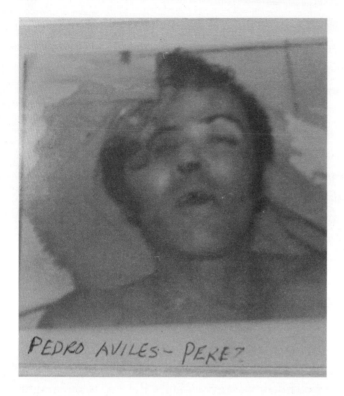

PEDRO AVILES- PEREZ

*Pedro Avilés Pérez,
on a mortuary slab,
with half his head
missing. After he
was assassinated,
the DEA tried to
get confirmation. So
they paid a mortuary
assistant to take this
photograph.*

Similar—if lower-profile—incidents scattered the crime pages particularly during the first two years of López Portillo's rule. In Oaxaca, for example, PJF commander Armando Martínez Salgado, "The Vampire," was an expert at these motivational killings. In July 1977 he was alleged to have tortured, murdered, and then burned three Americans and three Mexicans who were involved in a drug deal near the indigenous village of San Dionisio Ocotlán. It is also alleged that he stole $60,000 and that a few weeks later his men shot dead another unarmed American trafficker on a Oaxaca City street.

The Vampire tried to explain away the first murders as a feud between traffickers. But local villagers told a different story. They pointed out that the man the Vampire accused was actually one of the dead. They repeated the coroner's report that the six dead smugglers had been tortured with the hot blade of a military bayonet. They also claimed that in the aftermath of the killings the PJF had raided their village, burned the house of a suspected drug trafficker and kidnapped his teenage son.

But such accusations didn't matter. Just as the incident risked generating a scandal, Mendiolea, the head of the PJF, arrived, declared the Vampire innocent and the case closed. The American authorities didn't seem to care. Friends of the dead smugglers whispered that it was the DEA that had actually passed on the names of the dead smugglers to the Vampire. The blend of power, presidential protection, and U.S. support bred almost complete impunity.

On occasions, journalists attempted to unmask the PJF's protection racket. Such attempts were infrequent. Most Mexican newspapers were run by conservative oligarchs and heavily subsidized by the state. And unmasking corrupt officials, especially in a way that might attract U.S. criticism, was rare. Furthermore, cops had their own spin doctors. These were former journalists who would pay their former colleagues for positive coverage. Durazo was famously keen on upbeat—if entirely fictional— news stories. He even employed a well-respected journalist from the big national *Excélsior* as his PR specialist.

But occasionally it did happen. In early 1978 the Sinaloa journalist Roberto Martínez Montenegro threatened to expose Aguilar and Alcalá's takeover of the local protection racket. In response, four gunmen sprayed his car with bullets as he drove back to his house. He passed away the next day.

Aguilar immediately tried to pin the killing on his rivals for the racket— the state police. And to make sure that the charges stuck, he arrested a Sinaloa police chief, who was then subjected to particularly brutal torture. He was slapped, beaten, and pistol-whipped. He was then tied to a bench and had electric cables wound around his penis and inserted in his anus. Then came the Tehuacanazos—twelve bottles in all. Then after three days, they brought in his wife and children. They attached electrical cables to his seventeen-year-old daughter's nipples, took off his blindfold, and made him watch as they tortured her. Finally, inevitably, he confessed to a crime his torturers had committed.

If journalists were an occasional nuisance, the PJF also faced some rather sturdier opponents. The first were the traffickers themselves. These occasionally took matters into their own hands. They either sought to defend themselves or to wreak revenge on their tormenters. Gunmen—suspected to be working for Sinaloa weed smuggler Manuel "Crazy Pig" Salcido Uzeta—eventually killed Alcalá in his Guadalajara

offices. Insiders whispered that it was comeback for the killing of Pedro
Avilés Pérez.

But more often than not, it was other Mexican state officials that challenged the PJF's monopoly of the narcotics business. Conflicts between the
PGR, the PJF, the state police, and the army were frequent. Such struggles
ended any notions of a stable or agreed-upon system.

The most intense competition came from the Mexican secret service,
or DFS. During the 1970s the DFS had waged an increasingly brutal counterinsurgency against radical students, opposition politicians, and urban
guerrillas. To do so, it had expanded, recruiting new agents from the army,
local police forces, and organized crime. But, by the end of the decade,
their role in the counterinsurgency was coming to a close. In 1978 the president had even announced an amnesty for political prisoners.

Sidelined but still powerful, the DFS increasingly turned toward extortion and organized crime. One gets the sense that in theory there was a
division of labor. The PJF had drugs; the DFS had everything else. And
during the late 1970s and early 1980s, spooks seemed to focus on extorting
human traffickers, squeezing fayuqueros, and car theft. The car racket was
a particularly good earner and took hundreds of high-value vehicles from
California and then sold them to rich Mexico City politicians.

Yet, occasionally, the two organizations clashed over control of the narcotics business. In July 1978, newspapers reported that PJF and the DFS
agents were fighting for control of the trade. They had engaged in a shootout in Culiacán, which had been quickly hushed up. Now both groups had
established roadblocks on the exits to Nuevo Laredo and were forcing traffickers to pay. The following year there was a similar conflict in Guadalajara.
DFS agents shot and killed the PJF commander in the city. It caused such
a scandal that Mendiolea was again forced to turn up in person. He claimed
that the PJF commander had actually been sacked a week earlier and tried
to make the case that the killing was the result of "personal issues" rather
than any inter-institutional beef. Few were convinced.

If the PJF's takeover of the drug protection rackets introduced a new
level of brutality and violence to the Mexican drug business, it also introduced a big shift in the geography and the mechanics of the trade.

For over a decade, Mexico had specialized in the peasant production of marijuana and opium. But intensive herbicide spraying—with DEA oversight—radically reduced these growing zones. By the late 1970s, red and deep-green fields no longer covered the hillsides of the Golden Triangle.

Nonetheless, Mexico continued to produce. By 1980, marijuana crops still yielded 750 tons, and opium plants still provided over a third of America's heroin. Some was still grown in tiny fields hidden away down deep ravines or secreted amid swaying corn plants in the traditional growing zones of the Golden Triangle, Michoacán, or Guerrero.

But a lot—particularly of the better-quality sinsemilla—was now produced in nontraditional growing zones, particularly in the southern state of Oaxaca. The place had some distinct advantages. It was relatively far from Operation Condor bases. (The closest one was on the coast in Acapulco.) It was famously mountainous and difficult to traverse. And it had some of Mexico's poorest and most desperate peasants. (By the late 1970s, barely 10 percent could afford milk, meat, or eggs on a regular basis.)

It also had a few families that were well placed to take advantage. The most prominent were the Díaz Paradas, a biblically large clan of farmers and merchants from the tiny highland village of San Pedro Totolapa. By the mid-1970s the four Diáz Parada brothers were handing out marijuana seeds and fertilizer to many of the local families. These, in turn, were planting the crops in the mountains surrounding the village. Some of these plantations were huge. In 1977, for example, soldiers found thirty workers harvesting weed from a field of over 600 acres.

By 1981, newspapers were announcing that Oaxaca was Mexico's top marijuana producer. They estimated that it produced 7 billion pesos more than the state's legal crops. In fact, the trade was now so prevalent that even the state's religious authorities had started to take note. The local bishops issued a public letter that summarized the business. It was the first time that the country's Catholic Church had explicitly dealt with the narcotics trade. And it revealed that the Díaz Parada empire now reached over 100 miles from their hometown of San Pedro Totolapa, across the Isthmus of Tehuantepec, and down to the jungle town of Santa María Chimapala on the edges of Chiapas.

> There is a perfectly organized network which advances seeds, credit, fertilizers and other inputs; it technically supervises the sowing, the weeding and the harvest and even attacks possible plagues; it collects, packs and stores the product. There is a system which transports the herb with trucks, trailers, and even hidden airstrips where private planes land.

> A sign of changing modes of drug production, it was now a fully integrated agricultural operation, similar to the coffee or the tropical fruit businesses.

*By the early 1980s, the Díaz Parada clan had started to grow marijuana extensively in the east of the state of Oaxaca. Here is a bust from 1984.*

Yet, under the PJF, Mexico was increasingly a transportation rather than a production zone. Narcotics grown elsewhere were brought into the country and then delivered over the border. The move made perfect sense;

it achieved the balance the PJF was looking for. Cutting down on the big rural plantations reduced the risk of U.S discovery. It also cut out the need to survey and control swathes of Mexico's countryside. Instead, it played to the PJF strengths. They already controlled the airports and the ports, and had agents stationed along Mexico's border crossings. Charging traffickers for moving merchandise through these places was easy.

*During the 1980s, soldiers still sprayed and pulled up poppy crops. Yet, the effort was perhaps taken rather less seriously than before.*

Even weed was now increasingly imported and moved through Mexico. One American wholesaler explained how this worked. He purchased potent Thai Stick from Thailand. He organized the transport of up to 30 tons of the produce into the western Mexican port of Manzanillo every harvest season. Here a Mexican border smuggler—whom he had originally met in Las Vegas—paid off the PJF and the army to let the weed through. The army even agreed to transport the stuff in military trucks up through Mexico and over the border for a 30 percent cut of the profits. If you were lucky enough to smoke top-end Thai Stick between 1976 and 1981 (the year the wholesaler was busted), most likely your product came through Mexico.

But the big earner was now cocaine. Again, it was a question of demand. During the late 1970s, cocaine gradually percolated down the hipster hierarchy. It moved from West Coast bands through Wall Street bankers to become what *Newsweek* described as "the status symbol of the American middle class pothead." Ads for cocaine spoons and silver cocaine holders dotted the back pages of *High Times,* and by 1979 nearly 10 percent of eighteen-to-twenty-five-year-olds had tried the drug. In fact, it had become so widespread that even President Carter's drug advisor snorted it at a Washington, DC, party—and had to resign afterward.

And it was here that Durazo really got involved. Drugs, admittedly, were now only part of his portfolio. As police chief of Mexico City, he had moved into prostitution, armed robbery, kidnapping, and the wholesale appropriation of government funds. His was a huge enterprise, which allowed him to buy a fleet of luxury cars, build an outrageous mansion on the edge of Mexico City, and force the capital's cops to work on the construction of a mock Greek palace (dubbed El Partenón) in the seaside resort of Zihuatanejo. And though most of his money was squirreled away in

*El Partenón, Arturo "El Negro" Durazo's luxury beachside complex in Zihuatanejo is now abandoned.*

Switzerland, American agents speculated that by 1982 he was probably worth $1 billion.

But drugs were still a big part of the business and Durazo continued to protect shipments of cocaine that came into the Mexico City airport. By the early 1980s, a Honduran smuggler named Juan Matta Ballesteros was organizing many of the imports from Colombia. As we shall see, he would later move to Mexico and build links to the Guadalajara cartel and, perhaps most important, the CIA. (Whether he had them in 1981 or 1982, it is uncertain. But it might have explained Durazo's connections to the Company when in exile in the United States.)

However the drugs arrived at the airport, workers lugged suitcases of the stuff past customs and to waiting police vehicles. From here, most of the narcotics were shipped to the northeast border at Matamoros. Here he had managed to engineer the appointment of one of his close associates as PJF commander and another as local head of the DFS.

The rest was sold to his officers to distribute. In fact, according to an extraordinary exposé by one of Durazo's former agents, Durazo and Sahagún ran it like a franchise operation. They would call in the commanders and force them to purchase an ounce of the stuff for around 60,000 pesos. "There's too much *perico* [slang term for cocaine], you bastards, the chief Sahagún wants you to collect together the money and buy it." They could either sell this in the capital, where it would fetch around 90,000 pesos, or club together and organize its transport up to the border.

The same agent claimed that under Durazo cocaine use among Mexico City police officers also rose. "You often heard in the halls of the police department 'How goes it, chief, do you fancy a snort?'" Similarly, President Luis Echeverría's lover, Olga Breeskin, confessed that Durazo often called her into his office with the words, "Hey, beautiful, do you want a taste of the good stuff?" "It was always the best, I never had to pay."

The barbarians' federal-level protection racket changed Mexico's drug trade forever. It robbed local governments of funds and funneled payoffs to an increasingly distant and corrupt Mexican City administration. It shifted the trade away from homegrown drugs and toward the transportation of imported narcotics. But most important, it increased the violence associated with the trade. Maintaining such a protection racket was a brutal

business. It not only involved pushing local cops out of the trade and forcing traffickers to pay up. It also involved defending the whole operation
from pressures from U.S. drug agents, inquisitive journalists, and other
state institutions eager for a cut of the payoffs. And this brutal business was
now on a national scale.

# Chapter 19

## The "Guadalajara Cartel"

DEA AGENT CHARLES LUGO COULD JUST MAKE OUT THE PURPLE TOPS waving in the wind, buffeted by the chopper's airstream. It was November 6, 1984, and as the helicopter approached, the Chihuahua desert gave way to rows of deep green. His informant knew the fields were big, but he wasn't expecting 500 acres of sinsemilla. On the edges stood a complex of wooden sheds, which were used to dry the marijuana. And in front of them stood hundreds of Mexican farmworkers, all dressed in standard-issue jeans, shirts, and palm hats. He had arrived at the Búfalo Ranch. At the time, it was the world's biggest weed seizure. *Time* magazine called it "the bust of the century."

As the helicopter landed, Lugo got out. Over the next two days he would join up with Mexican soldiers to inspect the property. They reconnoitered the Búfalo Ranch outside the town of Jiménez as well as other marijuana fields discovered around Julimes. The scale was astonishing. In all, there were thirteen pot farms, eight separate workers' camps, and between 2,000 and 4,000 tons of pot. And this was just the beginning. There were dozens of drying sheds, tons of sinsemilla seed, and an irrigation system based on a network of wells. There were tractors and helicopters and thousands of laborers, who had been employed as marijuana trimmers, dryers, and packers. They had been bused in with promises of big wages and easy work.

And there were the guards. They were well armed. They carried semi-automatic rifles slung over their shoulders and pistols stuffed in their waistbands. And they used them. They shot workers that attempted to flee; they beat those that tried to take a rest; and they dunked a handful in barrels of freezing water to incentivize the others. To complete the look, at least three of them carried badges from the secret service, the DFS.

What Lugo witnessed was the first public demonstration of the power, scale, and financial might of a new kind of narcotics operation. Soon DEA officials had given it a name: the "Guadalajara Cartel." By the end of the decade, the term had moved into general use. The Americans had invented another enemy. Again, it was useful shorthand. It was a simple way to refer to a definable foe. The term "cartel" immediately brought to mind OPEC, price controls, and the perversion of good-old, fair-minded, Anglo-run capitalism. And it promised victory. Destroy the cartel and you demolished the drug trade.

*The burning of the Búfalo Ranch, 1984.*

*The living quarters for the workers at the Búfalo Ranch, 1984.*

In fact, the Guadalajara Cartel was not really a cartel. It had no formal structure, no set of rules, and no prescribed operating procedure. It certainly didn't attempt to control prices.

Instead the Guadalajara Cartel was a volatile group of old-school Sinaloa traffickers, kidnappers, and former paramilitary hitmen. When President López Portillo left office in 1982, a new federal protection racket attempted to control this unstable alliance. The barbarians and the PJF were no longer in charge. Now it was the turn of the DFS. Traffickers, gunmen, and spooks came together to service the spiraling U.S. demand for both cocaine and sinsemilla marijuana.

To do so, the group expanded, developed, and became more vertically integrated. Drug gangs met big businesses. Labor was now brought in-house. Traffickers no longer scoured the hillsides for a few tons of peasant weed. As Lugo discovered in the Chihuahua desert, they bought up fields, dug wells, distributed seeds, and paid the peasants to work the land. And they no longer squirreled their money away in a few lavish houses, top-of-the-range cars, and thoroughbred horses. Banks now became central to hiding and moving around drug money.

Yet, the DFS-run protection racket, like the barbarian system that preceded it, soon became mired in conflicts. There was no pax mafiosa. These conflicts for protection racket profits now pitted DFS agents against rival groups from the army, the PJF, state governments, and local administrations.

At the center of the Guadalajara Cartel was a group of Sinaloa-born traffickers. The three most high-profile—at least after 1985—were Ernesto "Don Neto" Fonseca Carrillo, Rafael Caro Quintero, and Miguel Ángel Félix Gallardo. Fonseca was second-generation narco aristocracy. Born in Badiraguato in the early 1930s, he was the son of one of the first opium intermediaries. But it was his uncle on his mother's side—the Wild Cat's murderer, Fidel Carrillo—who got him involved in the business. Carrillo bought a house in Tijuana and ran opium and heroin over the border during the 1950s. They were both busted in a police sting operation in 1955. Carrillo received a five-year sentence. Fonseca got off, although not until after enduring "a beating in his noble parts." He learned his lesson: always pay off the cops. And by the early 1970s he had gotten involved in smuggling cocaine from Ecuador, through Mexico, and into the United States.

If Fonseca was a Sierra aristo, Rafael Caro Quintero was narco royalty. He was a third-generation trafficker. His age remains a mystery to this day. Born in 1953 or 1956 (according to the newspapers), 1954 (according to his 1985 confession) and 1952 (according to the DEA), he was even better connected than Fonseca. In fact, there were few members of his family that were not involved in the trade.

First, there were the blood relatives. His father was a trafficker; his paternal aunt—Manuela Caro—was a preeminent heroin chemist; his maternal uncle Lamberto Quintero was a famous 1970s trafficker. So were his brothers—Miguel and Hector (until he was killed in a bloody shootout in Culiacán). Then there were the connections by marriage. His first wife was a member of the Elenes trafficking clan and his wife's sister was married to Fonseca's nephew. When he tired of her, he moved on to Sylvia Fernández, the daughter of Lalo Fernández and the former wife of Fonseca's son. One of the first things DEA agents did when they arrived in Mexico was compile family trees; in Sinaloa, genealogy made good counternarcotics.

Caro Quintero got involved in trafficking young. As early as 1971, he was busted moving weed up to Avilés's warehouses in San Luis Río Colorado. When he got out of jail, he moved to the stunning old desert mission town of Caborca on the Sonora coast. Here, he bought over 80 hectares of land and set up a new business growing high-grade "sheep's tail" marijuana. By the early 1980s he effectively ran the town. And as befitted a narco princeling, he bought a huge livestock estate, the Rancho El Álamo. Named after Mexico's most famous military victory, the spread resembled a medieval palace. Locals dubbed it "the Castle."

The last of the trio was Miguel Ángel Félix Gallardo. Félix Gallardo was not raised in the business. He was born in 1946 in a small village to the west of Culiacán. Initially, his parents labored on a local estate. But they worked hard, purchased a small part of the land, and had grander dreams for their children. His sister, who was interviewed in 1989, boasted the fine-grained snobbery of the up-by-the-bootstraps petite bourgeoisie. She clearly wanted to distinguish their upbringing from the majority of Sinaloa's mountain traffickers. "We come from a decent, well brought up family. We're not huarachudos [sandal-wearing peasants]. My mother was left with nine kids and kept working on the land to help us move upwards."

Félix Gallardo embodied this go-getter attitude. He finished secondary school and then did a stint at a local business college. He worked briefly as a traveling salesman before joining the Sinaloa state police under Governor Sánchez Celis. The job made him. He got close to the governor's favored heroin chemist, Lalo Fernández. And he got close to the governor himself. He worked as the governor's private bodyguard and would go on to become godfather to one of the governor's sons.

Described as "astute, discreet, refined and unusually austere," Félix Gallardo was one of a new breed of Sinaloa trafficker—a very modern mix of narco, cop, and businessman. He was the Stringer Bell to Caro Quintero's Avon Barksdale. He forged links to the state's prestigious families. He married into a wealthy local clan, and his sister—at least so the rumors went—had a son with future Sinaloa governor Antonio Toledo Corro. He moved to the exclusive Colonia Las Quintas neighborhood next to the city zoo, bought the hacienda where his parents had worked, filled it with ornate artwork, and purchased a seaside pad just west of Culiacán. He also moved

effortlessly between licit and illicit businesses. Accused in 1976 of trafficking cocaine, within months he was buying up real estate in Culiacán.
Three years later, he was listed by the DEA as "Mexico's principal mover of
cocaine." But it didn't matter; with his contacts, nothing stuck. And in the
same year, he was put on the board of a state-owned investment bank. He
was even rumored to have adopted an alias and moved to La Jolla beach,
San Diego.

*Miguel Ángel Félix Gallardo started out, like many traffickers, as a policeman.*
*In fact, he was one of Governor Leopoldo Sánchez Celis's bodyguards. He is the*
*tall, slender man on the right of this photograph, next to his boss, Sánchez Celis.*

Though the trio grabbed the headlines, they were not alone. The
Guadalajara Cartel included many other Sinaloa-born traffickers. There
was Caro Quintero's brother—Miguel—who ran the weed fields in
Caborca. There was Fonseca's nephew, José Antonio "Doctor" Fonseca
Iribe (killed by the police after a wild Guadalajara car chase. "Perhaps it
was a coincidence, perhaps it was an execution," sang the Tigres del Nortes
in their corrido in his honor). And there was Manuel "Crazy Pig" Salcido
Uzeta, the San Ignacio weed wholesaler who had famously butchered his
rivals in league with the Mazatlán PJF.

These had their own contacts, their own fields, and their own gunmen. Sometimes they teamed up; sometimes they went it alone. Some were wealthier than others; some were better connected. But there was no one boss or kingpin. An informant who worked for Fonseca throughout the early 1980s described their relations as follows:

> There was a group of people who like him were from the same state. They spoke to each other on a familiar basis. They each had their own retinues of people, they were bosses in their own right. They did not take orders from each other, but gave orders to their own personal bodyguards and sometimes to the retinues of other bosses, and they met together to make decisions without allowing other people to be physically present or close to them.

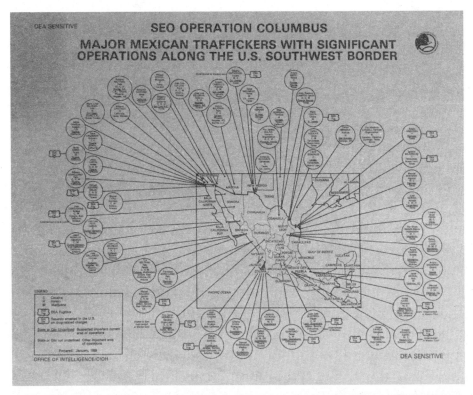

*The DEA called Mexico's 1980s drug traffickers "the Guadalajara cartel." But as this map of major traffickers demonstrates, this shorthand failed to capture the multiplicity of independent, geographically dispersed smugglers.*

Pushed out of their home state by Operation Condor, the Sinaloa traffickers arrived in the western city of Guadalajara in the late 1970s. Though a stuffy, heavily Catholic place, it had some clear advantages. There were roads and railways to the northwest crossing points of Tijuana and Nogales; and Highway 54 ran north to Zacatecas, then Monterrey and then the border at Nuevo Laredo. As the hippies knew, there were weed-growing areas northwest of Guadalajara in the hilly region bordered by the towns of Tequila, Hostotipaquillo, and Magdalena. It was dubbed Jalisco's own Golden Triangle. There were good poppy-growing valleys toward the coast. And the city itself had flourishing pharmaceutical and chemical businesses. Getting the materials to process heroin or cocaine was easy.

Guadalajara also had another advantage: a ready pool of other criminals. Many were originally from right-wing student groups. During the 1970s counterinsurgency, the government had employed them as professional assassins. They had been charged with killing left-wing students and suspected guerrillas. And they had been dedicated to raising funds through kidnapping, robbery, extortion, and shaking down small-time weed dealers. No doubt drug traffickers had moved in the same circles as counterinsurgents and organized criminals before. But it was here in Guadalajara that all three became firmly intertwined.

The most high-profile of these killers was Javier Barba Hernández. Barba was a Cold War killer, a kind of big-collared, shaggy-haired version of Sinaloa's "Gypsy." He grew up in the Lomas del Paradero neighborhood, just next to Guadalajara's public university. A charismatic street brawler, he came to prominence as the head of a student goon squad in the early 1970s. In 1973 his gang shot a local left-wing activist and then ran the escape vehicle over his body for good measure. Two years later, Barba was suspected of assassinating the powerful head of the university's student organization. It was a measure of the rather politicized academic expectations of the time that a year later he graduated as a qualified lawyer.

But it was crime rather than credit that brought him to the attention of the Mexican security services. They had arrived in Guadalajara in the wake of a series of public guerrilla attacks (including the rather embarrassing kidnapping of the U.S. consul). But they were understaffed and ill informed.

"The DFS didn't know shit, it hadn't worked here before," claimed one local policeman. So, to glean knowledge, they decided to link up with some of the more trigger-happy right-wing students, including Barba. And by the late 1970s, Barba and his gang carried official badges and did the government's work.

In reality, it was not a great change; it was more of the same. They kidnapped suspected guerrillas, tortured them in DFS "safe houses," forced them to give up their comrades, murdered them, and then secretly disposed of their bodies. In 1977 alone they disappeared at least twenty-two leftists.

As the left-wing threat subsided (or, perhaps more accurately, was killed off), Barba continued to work for the security services. But now he turned to straight-up crime. By 1979 he ran a unit of agents who kidnapped rich merchants and farmers on the highways of rural Jalisco. They were not subtle. They rode around in government vehicles, busted one of their members out of Nayarit state prison, shot a local mayor, and killed two local cops who were transporting their payroll.

Such work opened doors. And by the early 1980s, Barba started to get close to the exiled Sinaloa traffickers. Gangs merged. Retinues blurred. Favors were exchanged. They shared the same protectors and they partied in the same places.

At the center was Barba's frequent hangout, the legendary nightclub Guadalajara de Día. A vast former cantina in the center of the city, it was stacked with red velvet booths, gaudy lighting, and suspiciously young sex workers. It attracted mayors and governors, police chiefs and secret service heads, narcos and right-wing assassins. Sahagún Baca had been a regular and declared the owner "like his sister" (presumably if his sister had dealt in underage sex workers); so were Fonseca, Caro Quintero, and Félix Gallardo. The drinks were watered down, but the coke flowed freely. And the live soundtrack was provided by a very 1980s Mexican mix of rancher balladeers and camp pop icons.

A new protection racket now presided over this motley crew of Sinaloa traffickers and former state gunmen. With the election of a new president, Miguel de la Madrid, in 1982, the barbarians' reign was over. Flores and Mendiolea left office. And to demonstrate a clean break with the López

Portillo administration, Durazo was tracked down and prosecuted for corruption.

The DFS now replaced the PJF. Secret service agents now ran the federal drug protection racket. In some ways, it was the beginning of a global trend. Over the next twenty years, as the Cold War wound down, many of the soldiers of the world's authoritarian regimes and undeclared dirty wars found new opportunities in organized crime. They had the contacts; they had the experience; they had the moral flexibility; and they knew how to surf the limits of state support. The move spanned East and West. KGB agents joined the mafia free-for-all of postglasnost Russia. Guatemalan death squads moved into shifting cocaine across the thin isthmus between South and North America.

But it was also a move rooted in the politics of Mexico's security forces. By 1982, there was what one U.S. agent called a "revolving door" between the PJF and the DFS. Agents from the former frequently moved into the latter. There was the former Ciudad Juárez PJF commander Daniel Acuña Figueroa, who headed up the DFS in Tijuana. And there was the PJF cop Rafael Aguilar Guajardo, who became the chief DFS agent in Ciudad Juárez.

Formally, the system was similar to the one established by the PJF. DFS commanders ran the "plazas," and favored traffickers gave them monthly payments. Fonseca, for example, paid the local DFS commander between 50 million and 60 million pesos a month. Some of the money, at least, went toward fitting out local DFS offices and paying and equipping DFS employees. It was all that really remained of the old distributive protection rackets.

A lot now went into private bank accounts. Rafael Chao López—another former PJF agent turned DFS commander in Matamoros—owned a mansion in Mexico City's exclusive Pedregal neighborhood and two more in McAllen, Texas. He also owned a Chinese restaurant, a big import-export company, an apartment complex, a tourist development, and a private jet. (The jet was painted with the DFS symbol and Chao's favorite animal, a tiger. Even the narco fashion for big cats actually emerged, it seems, from the state.)

But a lot of money now went to Mexico City and the head of the DFS, José Antonio Zorrilla Pérez. Regional commanders arrived every month, walked into Zorrilla's office with suitcases of money and left empty-handed. Chao confirmed this.

> On the instructions of Zorrilla Pérez, the commanders in charge of the plazas of Monterrey, Nuevo León, Matamoros, Reynosa, Miguel Alemán and Laredo used to get together eight to ten million pesos. The money was handed over in person in his office in the DFS. He knew that the money came from drugs and illegal workers. I personally did about twelve handovers of the mentioned amounts with this system to Zorrilla Pérez.

In return for the payments, the DFS offered the traffickers impunity. This was now a VIP service. It involved distributing DFS badges, securing individual drug traffickers personal protection, and offering protection to drug fields and stash houses. DFS agents stood guard around the Búfalo Ranch and kept the workers in line; they did the same in marijuana fields in Zacatecas; and they surrounded the runways north of Guadalajara that brought cocaine in and out. They even provided the guards for frozen-fish warehouses in Mexicali, where workers secreted small packets of cocaine. Finally, it also involved escorting the drug loads through Mexico and over the border.

DFS protection changed the scale, the makeup, and the mechanics of the Mexican drug trade. In the most basic terms, the DFS was much larger than the PJF. There were at least 3,000 formal agents as well as thousands more paid thugs, paramilitary goons, and unofficial *madrinas*. By the early 1980s, many of these were already involved in other forms of crime, including kidnapping, bank robbery, car theft, and extortion. They now imported these into the drug business. The DFS also had much greater geographical reach. It had agents throughout Mexico. It allowed the drug trade to spread further into states like Zacatecas, Veracruz, and Puebla, where its influence had been negligible.

Together this alliance of traffickers, gunmen, and spooks started to service America's shifting drug demands.

In particular, they moved into the growing market for cocaine. Between 1981 and 1984, U.S. cocaine imports doubled from 70 to 137 tons per year. And with the creation of a new affordable version—crack cocaine—it was becoming the drug of choice for America's increasing numbers of jobless and poor. As it did so, cocaine crept up the Eastern Seaboard from Miami to Washington and then to New York. Between 1984 and 1986 the percentage of Manhattan offenders that tested positive for cocaine increased from a disturbing 42 percent to a staggering 83 percent.

At the same time, trafficking patterns changed. A massive law enforcement effort—called the South Florida Task Force—squeezed the traditional entry point for South American cocaine. Big traffickers now shifted from running the drug on powerboats through the Caribbean to moving it by air or land through Mexico.

The cop-turned-trafficker Félix Gallardo was at the center of the increasing cocaine business. Initially, he employed Eduardo "Lalo" Fernández's old South American contacts. In the early 1980s he was still importing coca paste and transforming it into cocaine using Fernández's recipe. Even then it was a pretty large-scale enterprise. One informant stumbled in on at least 600 kilos of cocaine drying in the sun outside a corrugated-iron warehouse.

But around 1983, Félix Gallardo attempted to move up a level. He made contact with a bulk cocaine dealer called Juan Matta Ballesteros. Though Matta Ballesteros had grown up as a street kid in the small Central American country of Honduras, over the years he had acquired cast-iron drug contacts. He had trained as a cocaine chemist; his wife was from the Colombian city of Cali; and his airline—SETCO—was supported and protected by the CIA. During the early 1980s, his principal Mexican contacts had been the police officials Arturo "El Negro" Durazo and Sahagún Baca. But when the two cops fled, Matta Ballesteros turned to Félix Gallardo. He even moved to Guadalajara and started to organize the shipments.

Product arrived by plane on rural airstrips north of Guadalajara. Félix Gallardo would take some of the product and send it north. Loads of up to a ton would arrive by van at suburban San Diego stash houses every month. Félix Gallardo would divide the rest among the local trafficking gangs. Fonseca would take some; so would Barba. Sometimes they would team up and move product together using tankers or planes. Others would use their own routes and their own employees.

Though Félix Gallardo was clearly at the center of the Guadalajara cocaine trafficking, the system of DFS protection allowed for plenty of other major Mexican importers. The ageing underworld hitman Arturo Izquierdo Ebrard bought Matta Ballesteros's product and flew it to remote jungle airstrips in Veracruz. By 1985, the Durango-based Herrera family was also involved, transporting 250-kilo loads through airfields in Campeche and into the United States.

Unquestionably, cocaine was important. It was easy to hide, simple to ship, and at the time, the Americans were still focused on Caribbean rather than Mexican routes. And its importance was accelerating. In 1985 the Mexican authorities seized 2.5 tons of cocaine. It was as much as they had seized in the previous decade. It was fast replacing heroin and marijuana as the lifeblood of the Mexican drug trade.

But during the early 1980s the everyday business of most Mexican traffickers was still marijuana. More specifically, it was high-grade sinsemilla. Again, it was a question of American demand. Quality Thai and Colombian product had boosted the taste for sinsemilla. And by the mid-1980s, a pound of sinsemilla cost as much as $2,500 or over four times the price of standard weed. Yet an eradication effort, focused in northeastern Colombia (and based on Operation Condor), cut into supply. So again, Mexico picked up the slack, rebuilding the market position it had lost at the end of the 1970s. Even before the eye-opening Búfalo bust, the U.S. authorities estimated that Mexican marijuana had jumped from 6 percent to 20 percent of the domestic market in just one year.

Rafael Caro Quintero and his brother Miguel were at the center of the sinsemilla industry. They had been experimenting with producing crops in irrigated farms to the south of the Sonora town of Caborca since the late 1970s. From 1980 to 1984, they cultivated between 40 and 100 acres at any one time. The product was moved in multiple ways—hidden in trucks under boxes of eggs, stashed in petrol tankers, or flown directly to the United States by plane or helicopter. They brought in U.S. pilots to move the loads and U.S. weed specialists to improve yield and potency. One, a former marine, described his role.

> I'd explain to growers how to grow, how to space the plants, how to pick the branches so they split, how to prune the branches we didn't want. I got some resistance at first but I had their trust because I was moving more product than anyone else.

It was the high point of weed's transnational green revolution.

After the Caborca experiment, Caro Quintero and his partners expanded. Around 1982 they moved to the state of Zacatecas. At the time it was a narcotics tabula rasa. A quiet state of grand colonial churches, semiarid plains, and cactus-strewn mountains, even the hippies had stayed away. But it was perfectly placed; it lay on Highway 54 on the way from Guadalajara to the border. So they used their DFS connections to team up with local landholders and buy a series of ranches in the dry flatlands in the east of the state. They purchased the ranches as small cooperatives, splitting the costs of the land as well as the drilling of wells, the purchase of expensive pumps, tractors, and tons of sinsemilla seed. Here they planted a variety of high-value strains, including Michoacán Verde Limón and Sinaloa Sheep's Tail. Within three months, the brown desert turned a deep green. Locals started to call the network of farms "Colombia." It was the test run for the Búfalo complex.

*By the early 1980s, traffickers were building sophisticated irrigation systems to grow sinsemilla marijuana in Mexico's drier states, like Zacatecas and Chihuahua.*

The combination of state protection and market demands generated massive profits. As usual, these are no more than ballpark figures, but the most reliable estimates suggest that by 1985 Mexican drug profits had even outstripped those of the mid-1970s. Together, cocaine, sinsemilla weed, and the remaining opium fields produced profits of somewhere between $2 billion and $6 billion per year.

Some of this money still percolated down. If you were lucky enough to live in a growing zone, like Caborca, or one of the border's transport hubs, like Ojinaga, you might get a fancy primary school, a new church, or a generous tip from one of the visiting narcos. But most did not. They still lived up in the Sierra. They now shared their villages with military barracks, spray helicopters, and rowdy soldiers. They got counternarcotics, not narcotics profits. And to benefit at all from the trade, they now had to leave their villages, take a bus to these new intensive growing zones, and earn day wages as trimmers, packers, or warehouse workers.

These wages ranged from $13 to $20 a day. And as purchasing power plummeted after the 1982 peso crash, they were still attractive. In Badiraguato, for example, 3,000 young men, or a tenth of the population, left every year to work on the new Zacatecas and Chihuahua plantations. The fields even got a name; they became *el norte chiquito* (the little north). This was the narcotics business as agro-industry.

And like agro-industry, the big profits now went to the men who owned the lands and had the contacts: the traffickers. As usual, these spent money on cars, on clothes, and on real estate. But such were the rewards, they also started to launder the money through banks. In fact, banks became crucial to the international expansion of the Mexican trade. Again, it was a major technological change. It was as important as learning how to grow sinsemilla or cook up high-grade heroin. Banks allowed traffickers to transfer money quickly and efficiently between countries. Gone were the nail-biting days of carrying around cash-stuffed suitcases, exchanging two halves of a dollar bill, and waiting in bars and hotels for tense handovers.

Bankers now became as central to the narcotics business as chemists, agronomists, or lawyers. In 1982, for example, the DEA did a rather thorough investigation of Félix Gallardo's operation. It worked as follows. First, cocaine wholesalers in California collected his share of the profits. To avoid U.S. money-laundering regulations, they trucked the money in bulk south of the border. Once in Mexico, the money was transferred to Félix Gallardo's personal banker at the Multibanco Comermex in Guadalajara. The banker would pay out small chunks to Félix Gallardo's bodyguards, his warehouse workers, and his DFS security. Meanwhile, Félix Gallardo's accountant would withdraw money in the form of cashier checks of $10,000 to $50,000. He would then wire these to a Bank of America branch in San Diego. Félix Gallardo's banker there then forwarded the money by check to cocaine dealers in Peru and Colombia. Apart from moving the money south, it was a closed circuit.

In recent years, commentators have harked back to the 1980s as an era of limited conflict. It is powerful political nostalgia. But it is poor history.

No doubt, under the DFS some alliances were made. The secret service and the Mexican military, for example, seemed to have come to some sort of agreement. The crossover of personnel and shared concerns brought alignment. Other pacts were more impromptu. One Jalisco DFS official explained that he had an ongoing dispute with the PJF chief in Oaxaca. Whenever he sent down his agents to pick up weed, his men were disarmed and his loads were seized. Gunfire was often exchanged. So eventually they reached an agreement. They would split control of the roadblocks between the two organizations. The DFS got three days a week; the PJF got the rest.

But in general these alliances were rare. All the DFS takeover really meant was that the secret service now joined the military, the PJF, the state police forces, and the local cops in the struggle to control the protection rackets. The kind of small-scale, localized conflicts that had accompanied squabbles over which institution received the bribes now scaled up dramatically.

They escaped the confines of the Golden Triangle and spanned much of Mexico. And they became increasingly frequent. It was not only a new governor that could now spark off these disputes; it was the appointment of a regional DFS chief, a new PJF commander, or a local police head. There was no clear hierarchy or order. Alliances shifted and changed. Each new appointment necessitated a fresh reordering of forces and reallocation of bribes. As these institutions were almost entirely insulated from official prosecution, violence became the sole approach for winning these struggles.

Between 1982 and 1985 alone there were bloody confrontations in Ojinaga (PJF/DFS vs. state police), Veracruz (PJF vs. DFS/local police),

Baja California (PJF/military vs. DFS), Coahuila (DFS vs. local police), Matamoros (PJF vs, DFS), Ciudad Juárez (DFS vs. local cops), and even Mexico City (DFS vs. PJF).

But the most explosive conflict occurred in Guadalajara itself. In March 1983, a new governor, Enrique Álvarez del Castillo, came to power. He appointed a new state prosecutor and a new state police chief. And they tried to take over the protection racket from the DFS agents. They set up roadblocks throughout the city, disarmed smugglers and federal agents, and seized 1-ton loads.

On the surface, it looked like counternarcotics. But they were simply trying to squeeze a bigger slice of the bribes. What's more, the effort soon caused a division within the alliance of DFS agents, paramilitary hitmen, and Sinaloa traffickers. Some wanted to come to an arrangement. Others resisted what they saw as unnecessary demands. It even, allegedly, caused a rift between the old Sinaloa allies. Félix Gallardo favored peace. Fonseca and Caro Quintero opposed any arrangement. And soon the disagreements turned bloody.

The Guadalajara murder rate skyrocketed. Just in 1984 there were shootouts between DFS badge holders and state police, between state police and traffickers, and between DFS agents and fellow agents. In February 1984, gunmen—including former paramilitaries and DFS badge holders—burst into the DFS head office and shot the regional commander. In April, state police arrested the head of the local branch of the secret service for kidnapping and murder. And in November, Fonseca's nephew and his wife were gunned down after running a state police checkpoint. Early 1985 was even worse. Traffickers allegedly declared the first two weeks of the year "the fortnight of firing on the police" and regularly sprayed state cop cars with bullets.

Members of the so-called cartel were at each other's throats. It was so bad even the DEA started to take notice. In November the station chief reported with unusual alacrity:

> The violence previously reported has increased drastically without any serious consequences for the traffickers. The local govern-
> ment is completely compromised and unwilling to cope with the

deteriorating situation.... . The traffickers commonly travel the
street and highways armed with automatic weapons and usually
carrying credentials from the DFS or some other federal law enforcement agency.

But the report was ignored. It was traffickers killing traffickers. Who
cared?

The Americans soon would.

## Chapter 20

## The Martyr and the Spook

It was March 7, 1985, and the DEA's chief Mexico agent, Ed Heath, was in the morgue again. He was staring at what remained of a heavyset Hispanic male. Since he first arrived in Mexico nearly twenty years earlier, Heath had gotten used to seeing what violence could do to a body. In the 1960s, he had teamed up with PJF agents, adventured into the hills above Acapulco, and shot chunks out of peasant weed smugglers in sweaty, nerve-racking shootouts. When he returned in 1973, he had watched his friend the PJF commander Florentino Ventura's savage interrogation techniques at firsthand. He had even gone out for drinks with him afterward.

But this was different. At least it felt different. The body was that of DEA agent Enrique "Kiki" Camarena. The dirt-flecked corpse was now in such a state of decay it was difficult to tell exactly how he had died. It was certainly a few weeks ago now. Three ribs were broken. So was his right arm. There were bruises, cuts, and burns all over his body. And his rectum had been violated by a stick. But doctors reassured Heath that what finally killed Camarena was the deep indentation on the left side of his head.

The drug war was a numbers game. Its success or failure was measured out (and manipulated) by endless graphs of arrests made, kilos seized, and purity affected. Heath knew this better than most. He was one of the few field agents to have risen through the ranks to become an administrator. And he had done it by encouraging DEA support for Mexico's numbers-focused effort.

Yet, occasionally, the scale of the war narrowed. Budgets, policies, and in the final analysis, lives could be shaped by a single public scandal, unfortunate overdose, or grisly death. Such events had the power to drive panics and direct governments. As Heath stared at Camarena's remains, it occurred to him that this was probably one of those moments.

Camarena's murder was a turning point for the Mexican drug trade and the American war on drugs. Some of the effects, even then, Heath could have imagined. The subsequent investigations broke up the Guadalajara Cartel and brought an end to the DFS. It also provoked a rapid rise in Mexican narcotics arrests, a rearrangement of federal and local protection rackets, and an increasing wave of drug-related violence.

Back in the United States, Camarena became the drug war's first martyr, the poster boy for the DEA. His sacrifice bolstered the department's budget, its personnel, and its political standing. Money and plaudits finally brought what administrative overhauls could not. And it finally shook off its reputation for shoddy fieldwork, institutional racism, ruinous infighting, and criminal collusion. By the late 1980s, it spearheaded America's increasing focus on international counternarcotics.

The empire had a new enemy. And the empire's face was now a dead Mexican-American drug agent.

But over the years the Camarena story became much more than a prop for U.S. drug hawks. As the investigations rolled on, a motley gang of difficult DEA agents, intrusive journalists, and ageing academics started to poke around at the inconsistencies in the official case. They questioned the killers' motives. They connected it to a rash of other suspicious murders. And they found a whistleblower—a 6-foot-7 American spook named Lawrence Victor Harrison. He told another story, one of U.S. corruption that involved the CIA and its plans to fund Nicaraguan paramilitaries with Mexican cocaine money.

And so what had begun as a simple morality tale started to resemble the drug war's JFK assassination. A solitary murder was now overlaid by so many myths and theories that gleaning the truth was not only impossible but also kind of missing the point. What had happened to Camarena was now less a question of evidence and more a question of belief.

Around 2 P.M. on February 7, 1985, four men bundled Camarena into the back of a car. They drove him from the U.S. embassy to a quiet suburban house in the western district of Guadalajara. The same day they also seized a pilot, Alfredo Zavala Avelar, who had worked with Camarena on several weed cases, and took him to the house. Here, secret agents and traffickers brutally beat and tortured the two men. They burned them with cigarettes, poured gunpowder into their wounds and set it on fire. They were questioned about everything, from the identity of DEA agents and confidential informants to what they knew about traffickers, policemen, and politicians. Within two days they were dead or at least near it. Bodyguards put a tire iron through Camarena's head to make sure, dumped them both in the back of a car, and then buried them at night in the Primavera Park west of the city.

Around three weeks later, federal cops instructed the killers to dig up the bodies and dump them on El Mareño Ranch in the neighboring state of Michoacán. They wanted to frame the trigger-happy congressman who lived on the farm or the corrupt cop who allegedly owned it (Durazo's former right-hand man, Sahagún Baca). At the very least, it would confuse the investigation and put the gringos off the scent.

But years of complete impunity do not breed organizational discipline; and coordination was not their forte.

On February 28 a PJF commander showed the DEA an anonymous note. It claimed the bodies were on El Mareño Ranch. It was one of many tip-offs that the office had received. But for some reason, the PJF took this one seriously. On March 2 the PJF organized a raid on the ranch, were allegedly met by automatic gunfire, and killed all four inhabitants, including the congressman. A full three days later they allowed the DEA agents to conduct a search of the place. The DEA found nothing.

The next day, however, a local farmworker spotted a couple of plastic fertilizer bags dumped by the side of the road outside the ranch. One was

ripped and two discolored legs jutted out. One of the traffickers later confessed that he had been ordered to dump the bodies but had arrived too
late. He saw the place was already surrounded by cops and so decided to
dump them nearby.

This was how Ed Heath found himself in the morgue of Zamora Red
Cross Hospital peering over Camarena's month-dead corpse.

The Americans had lost agents in Mexico before. In 1969 they lost the
head of the Mexico office in a mysterious drowning off the Acapulco coast.
In 1974 traffickers shot two agents in bungled stings in a single year. And
there were numerous tales of wild firefights, drunken bar brawls, and near
misses. But these were quickly covered up. They were embarrassing. They
revealed that U.S. officials were doing some pretty sketchy things, at best
incompetently and at worst illegally.

This time it was different. The American government made it clear
that they expected the Mexicans to find Camarena and his murderers.
Their tactics were from the traditional drug war playbook—a mix of economic blackmail and public humiliation. In mid-February, Customs officials organized a weeklong stop-and-search at the border. In a nod to the
notorious Nixon-era strategy, it was dubbed "Operation Intercept II." Next,
the U.S. ambassador gave a press conference in which he declared that
Guadalajara was the center of the Mexican drug trade. He also first floated
the story that Camarena's kidnapping was probably revenge for the 1984
Búfalo bust.

Soon afterward the head of the DEA started to name names, going on
prime-time TV to accuse Félix Gallardo, Caro Quintero, and Fonseca of
orchestrating the murder. He further claimed that Mexican police officials
were protecting the traffickers and that they had even helped two of them
(Caro Quintero and Matta Ballesteros) escape overseas.

The Reagan-era New Right of the Republican Party eagerly joined the
pile-on. They rarely missed an opportunity to blame other countries for
spiraling U.S. drug use. And they were keen to extract other Mexican concessions over trade, oil, and immigration. Camarena's death proved a lucky
windfall.

So in a series of Senate subcommittee meetings, they added the governor of Sonora to the growing list of corrupt officials. And they voiced a

completely unsubstantiated (and false) rumor that one of President Miguel de la Madrid's relatives was a key contact between the Mexican and the Colombian cartels.

Such accusations were embarrassing and threatening. And they started to push the Mexican authorities to make arrests. In March 1985 the Mexicans placed the DEA's go-to torturer, Florentino Ventura, in charge of the investigation. He moved to Guadalajara and rounded up trafficker bodyguards and associates. He brought out the Tehuacán bottles and the electrical cables once again. And he started to innovate, partially cooking suspects' feet in specially adapted microwave ovens. Some started to talk. Not coincidentally, they echoed the Americans' accusations. They blamed the murder on revenge for the Búfalo Ranch. And they pointed the finger at Caro Quintero, Fonseca, and their official backers.

The interrogations started a flurry of activity. On April 4, Ventura arrested Caro Quintero at a beachside resort in Costa Rica. And three days later, his men seized Fonseca in Puerto Vallarta. The following day the Ministry of the Interior canceled all DFS credentials and effectively closed the secret service down. Some agents were folded into a new intelligence-gathering organization. But Zorrilla was gone; some were arrested; 400 agents were expelled; and warrants went out for leading DFS commanders.

After this initial burst, progress slowed. U.S. investigators met a mix of indifference, vested interests, and a grindingly slow judicial system. But little by little, they took down many of those involved. The right-wing hit-man Barba was shot along with a handful of Fonseca's bodyguards; DFS agents were arrested and imprisoned.

In December 1988 a new, U.S.-educated president, Carlos Salinas de Gortari, came to power. And he announced his willingness to work with U.S. drug hawks by arresting Félix Gallardo (in April 1989) and former DFS head Zorrilla (in June 1989). Both received heavy sentences. Whether they were involved in the murder or not, by the end of the decade, most of what the Americans now termed the Guadalajara Cartel were either in prison or dead.

It looked like success. Or at least it looked like success to the DEA.

In the early 1980s the DEA had stumbled from one disaster to another. The glory years of Operation Condor seemed long ago. In 1980, U.S.

support for Bolivia's cocaine-funded coup reminded the organization of its position in the Cold War pecking order. In 1981 the appointment of a former FBI agent as acting director added another set of tensions to existing conflicts. (In a break from tradition he even banned agents from attending the topless bar located below the DEA offices.) The following year a massive class-action lawsuit, which compensated 200 African-American agents, laid bare the institutional racism of the place. Also in 1982, the department's budget dropped to its lowest level since 1974.

In contrast, Camarena's killing made the organization. It gave it a narrative—a founding fable. It was the story of a border-born Mexican who had moved to California and become a U.S. citizen and a go-it-alone narcotics agent. He had pitted his wits against a gang of devious, coke-crazed criminals and managed to score the largest marijuana seizure in history. But his former countrymen had sought revenge, tracked him down, and ended his life in a brutal and vindictive fashion. They had done so with the open support of a squalid and crooked political administration.

The story was simple, persuasive, and played nicely to a host of U.S. anxieties. It conveniently cleansed the DEA of accusations of corruption, torture, and prejudice; it succinctly divided the world into good cops and bad traffickers; and it did so in a way that tiptoed delicately around the United States' changing racial makeup. No doubt there were good Mexicans. They came to America and they adopted American values of honesty and integrity. But there were also a lot of bad Mexicans. They lurked over the border; they poisoned your kids; and they were propped up by a corrupt, antidemocratic regime.

The story became a drug war archetype (a narchetype?). It was repeated in prime-time news slots and countless adulatory press pieces, which culminated in *Time* magazine's iconic November 1988 "Death of a Narc" front page. It was recounted with exuberance in the true-crime bestseller *Desperados*. And it was laid out in Michael Mann's proto-*Narcos* miniseries *Drug Wars: The Camarena Story*.

It also became wrapped up with the DEA's new family-friendly self-image. Camarena became the face of Red Ribbon Week, an alcohol, tobacco, and drug awareness campaign. His sacrifice provided a bridge from the no-nonsense DEA hard men—still in mourning for their topless bar—to the pious parents organizations at the other end of the antidrug alliance. In 1988 it even got the ultimate "Just say no" endorsement. The Reagans presided over the national rollout of the campaign.

Camarena's death gave the DEA a story; what's more important, it gave it money. Stamped with a new blood-soaked relevance, backed by the New Right, and directed by a Washington-savvy FBI management team, the DEA budget skyrocketed. In 1987 alone, the DEA's funding more than doubled. Suddenly, an organization that had struggled to put together the cash for convincing flash rolls had money to burn. Hiring increased. Between 1985 and 1988, DEA personnel grew from 4,000 to 6,000. So did the money available for operation costs. When Hector Berrellez was put in charge of the Camarena investigation in 1989, he demanded a half-dozen agents and at least $200,000 for informants. In the end, he was given twenty agents and a budget of $3 million.

Even soft benefits increased. Gone were the days of slumming in out-of-town hotels. When Berrellez was posted to Mazatlán in 1987, he admitted he "lived like a rock star." The house the DEA rented for him was a "5000 square foot mansion on the water with an Olympic sized pool, and a full-time staff that included a chef, maid, chauffeur, a crew of gardeners and a zoologist." Now DEA agents didn't only have to hang out with traffickers, they could live like them.

But beyond reputation and money, what the DEA agents really got was power. More specifically—international power. Overseas drug enforcement officers had always felt like second-class U.S. officials. They lacked the Harvard degrees and economic muscle of the State Department diplomats. And they didn't have the political cachet of the CIA spooks. (One suspects it was why the head of the DEA in Mexico used to prowl the embassy corridors with a tie that read "Fuck You" in day-glow orange letters.)

And after the freewheeling heyday of the Nixon era, overseas DEA agents had repeatedly complained that they were forced to hold back. They were hobbled by the niceties of diplomatic protocol, by repeated State Department interference, and, in particular, by the 1976 Mansfield Amendment. The amendment had effectively banned agents from helping to secure arrests on foreign soil.

But the murder ended such reservations. In 1986 the United States started the drug certification process. It was a vast annual review of countries' antinarcotics efforts. It placed counternarcotics policies at the center of U.S. foreign policy, and it demanded the massive expansion of DEA operations overseas. And, it added a stick. Failing the review meant decertification. And decertification meant the loss of U.S. aid, U.S. trade incentives, and multilateral banks loans. It was a macro, bureaucratic, rolling version of Operation Intercept. It was drug policy as economic blackmail.

But there were also more goodies. In the same year, Congress passed the Drug Interdiction and International Cooperation Act. This cut congressional oversight for international drug ops, extended asset forfeiture to properties owned by suspected foreign drug traffickers, and made it easier to deport narcotics violators. And Congress passed another act, which while it didn't entirely repeal the Mansfield Amendment, made any violation of the amendment effectively impossible to prosecute.

The DEA was off the leash.

No doubt the way this played out still depended on individual country circumstances. But in Mexico this meant not only repeated public reprimands for the Mexican government; it also translated into kidnapping and targeted assassination. Who said the DEA never learned from the Mexicans?

Kidnapping, in particular, became the go-to method to avoid the tedious rigmarole of extradition. In January 1986 the DEA paid $32,000 for local cops to kidnap Tijuana weed trafficker René Verdugo Urquidez. They bundled him into the trunk of a car, smuggled him over the border, and then—with a keen sense of irony—held him for arriving in the United States without the right paperwork. Two years later they flew into Honduras, grabbed Matta Ballesteros, tortured him with a stun gun, and then took him north to the United States. Then, they paid Mexican police another $50,000 to kidnap, torture, and then fly the doctor Humberto Álvarez Macháin to El Paso. All three were eventually prosecuted for their parts in the killing.

And although no DEA agent will explicitly state this, it is also pretty clear that the old 1970s strategy of extrajudicial execution was reinstated. Sometimes, the Mexicans didn't need much encouragement. In 1987 one DEA agent—who wished to remain anonymous—helped a Mexican army general track down and seize Félix Gallardo's uncle. The general was furious, apparently, at the murder of one of his friends. He suspected that the uncle knew the location of the perpetrator. After a rather rough interrogation, he walked the uncle into a sugar-cane field and shot him in the head. He yanked off the man's Presidential Gold Series Rolex and tossed it to the DEA agent.

But occasionally, the Americans decided to take matters into their own hands. In 1991, Mexico's CIA station head invited the same DEA agent for a meeting in what insiders termed "the bubble." It was the U.S. embassy's secure operations office. Here they planned the assassination of a major narcotics violator. At this point, the DEA agent refused to elaborate. But he hinted that the target was another of the Camarena suspects, Manuel "Crazy Pig" Salcido Uzeta. Salcido certainly died soon after in suspicious circumstances, gunned down by unknown masked men in a busy Guadalajara street.

The return of DEA agents as pistol-wielding enforcers clearly pleased many in the United States. But the effects in Mexico were the same as usual. No doubt, the figures looked good. Between 1984 and 1991, prosecutions for drug crimes nearly quadrupled, moving from under 3,000 to over 11,000 per year. Leading traffickers saw the inside of a jail cell, or, if not, a coffin.

But the unrelenting pressure drove up drug-related deaths. Just as in the early 1970s, the more brutal the drug war, the more likely traffickers were to turn on one another, snitch on their competitors, and kill their associates when they suspected them of snitching.

This new round of violence centered on Sinaloa. In the months following Camarena's murder, many of the Guadalajara traffickers returned to their home state. Initially, they were welcomed. It was not surprising. As the Americans were keen to point out, the governor had a son with Félix Gallardo's sister. The governor also knew his narco history and had appointed an ageing member of the De la Rocha family (responsible for the Sinaloa protection racket in the 1940s) as head of the state's mining and forestry commission. And he made a famously brutal cop head of the state police. By 1985, Amnesty International had awarded the Sinaloa cops the hard-fought title of the "most repressive police force in Mexico." De la

Rocha was the smiling link to the Sierra farmers; the state police chief was the muscle. Together they were charged with collecting the state's drug revenue.

But the homecoming also brought a new wave of murders. DEA and PJF investigators used small-time busts to recruit an army of informers. If they were discovered, they were dealt with brutally. In Mazatlán and Culiacán, drive-by shootings returned. Tortured bodies started to appear in the fields outside the cities. By early 1986, there were an average of fifty-eight murders a month in Culiacán alone. It was a homicide rate of over 150 per 100,000 or over seven times the national average. One DEA agent who worked in the region confessed that he personally had lost twenty-three informants to revenge attacks.

Yet Camarena's death also had other, less intended consequences. By the early 1990s, it had become clear to those investigating the killing that the DEA's story was dubious. It was mythmaking as murder inquiry. They also discovered that other mysterious government agents moved in the same circles as the suspects. They were the CIA.

Over the past three decades, CIA involvement in Camarena's death has gained considerable traction in Mexico. It culminated in a series of exposés in the immediate aftermath of Caro Quintero's release in 2013. There was a front-page write-up in Mexico's leading news magazine, a bestselling book (J. Jesús Esquivel's *La CIA, Camarena y Caro Quintero: La Historia Secreta*), radio interviews, and online follow-ups. Ask most news-savvy Mexicans who killed Camarena and they will now claim: "It was the CIA." And if they are really clued in, they will list another half-dozen or so high-profile murders with CIA fingerprints.

In comparison, most Americans have resisted the idea. To stick, conspiracies need to be comforting, and the CIA drugs-for-arms racket is not. So the U.S. journalist who originally broke the story was rubbished by the mainstream press and hounded to an early grave. The 2013 investigations were briefly covered—somewhat strangely—on Fox News. But they were almost immediately dropped. Fox invited on a delusional conspiracy nut to undermine the serious accusers. The Mexican journalistic exposé was never translated; an American version of the tale was quietly published online and quickly forgotten. And the whole dubious story of DEA heroics and Mexican corruption was restated for a contemporary audience in the Netflix series *Narcos: Mexico.*

So beyond the fact that Camarena's story still sells, what do we know?

We do know that the original investigation into the Camarena case was deeply flawed. Inquiries were made at pace; crime scenes were systematically destroyed; and confessions were elicited by torture. Unsurprisingly, these confessions followed exactly what the Americans wanted. As the ambassador had speculated a few days after Camarena's disappearance, the confessions claimed that his death was revenge for the Búfalo bust. It was a simple, comprehensible tale that made the DEA look good and the Mexicans look bad.

Yet the Búfalo revenge story is improbable. First off, Camarena had nothing to do with the Búfalo bust. The informant was an escaped ranch worker. He had approached the DEA's office in Hermosillo, not Guadalajara. And it was Hermosillo's agents that approached the PJF to coordinate the bust. Furthermore, according to one of Caro Quintero's pilots, the police who raided the ranch returned most of the captured marijuana to the traffickers within weeks of confiscating it.

In subsequent years there have been other versions of the revenge theory. Camarena was involved in two operations that might have raised the traffickers' ire. The first was the discovery of Caro Quintero's Zacatecas weed fields. This seems unlikely. Camarena's discovery generated few arrests and limited seizures. The PJF seem to have deliberately bungled the raid. The second was Operation Padrino—a program aimed at confiscating traffickers' U.S.-based funds. Here Camarena's work did lead to big financial losses. But he was far from the center of the operation. All he had done was stumble on a few bank accounts. And if they just wanted revenge, why had they bothered to blindfold Camarena, torture him, and question him for two days?

So where now?

It was a question that the DEA agent Hector Berrellez had also started to ask himself. In 1989 the DEA put him in charge of running the Camarena case. Berrellez was a Vietnam vet with fifteen years in the service. He had worked undercover in the United States and Mexico. He knew traffickers and knew that they could be violent. But the Camarena killing didn't add up. Why had an alliance of fabulously wealthy traffickers, right-wing thugs, and secret service officials opted to kill a DEA agent? Why had they risked their wealth, their freedom, and their families? For revenge? For a few million dollars' worth of pot? That they probably got back?

Berrellez had heard rumors about the CIA's involvement in the cocaine trade before. He had seen U.S. cargo planes landing on a Mazatlán ranch. He had been told that they were bringing in guns for the CIA. And he had been ordered to stay away. "I'm a good soldier. It was a government operation, so I left it." A Guadalajara DFS agent—who had fled to the United States—told Berrellez that his job had been to protect Mexican and Nicaraguan traffickers. They were moving drugs north and shipping weapons south. He said that they were working on the instructions of the CIA.

And in the year Berrellez took the Camarena case, the U.S. Senate released the Kerry report. The report stated that the Nicaraguan Contras were funding their civil insurgency against the left-wing Sandinista government with cocaine money. They were in what the report politely termed a "symbiotic" relationship with drug traffickers. And the CIA knew all about it.

The CIA was, of course, keen to deny this. And it did so repeatedly. But over the next decade, the connection between the CIA and the Contras became increasingly transparent. CIA insiders, shady contract pilots, disillusioned DEA agents, and a handful of traffickers all testified that the Company had sought to get around the U.S. Congress's ban on Contra funding by establishing a drugs-for-arms racket. Traffickers would bring drugs to CIA-protected airstrips in the United States. They would exchange cocaine for repurposed Vietnam-era assault rifles and cash, then return with their haul and split it between the Contras and the Colombian cocaine lords.

The question was what role the Guadalajara gang played in all this. The Guadalajara DFS agent suggested that if Berrellez really wanted to get to the bottom of it, he needed to bring in the traffickers' radio specialist. He was nicknamed "White Tower."

It was a fitting moniker. In a story full of mysterious characters, "White Tower" was the most enigmatic of all. He was not your average Guadalajara tough. For a start, he was a 6-foot-7 American. His real name was probably George Marshall Davis. However, there was considerable confusion. In

1990 the court transcriber misheard his name and took it down as George Marshall Leyvas. And throughout most of his time in Guadalajara he was known as Lawrence or Lorenzo or Larry Victor Harrison.

From what we now know, it seems that Davis was born in Pasadena in 1944. His father died when he was young and Davis grew up in 1950s California as a rebel, but a smart one. Despite a brief stint in foster care and a reputation for using his fists, he earned his high school diploma and in 1964 moved to San Francisco. It was the swinging sixties. And Frisco youths were already smoking Jerry Kamstra's Mexican draw.

But it was also the Cold War. And Davis—the rebel—took another direction. He became a conservative. He worked on Nixon's failed presidential campaign; he sat in on classes at Berkeley's law school; and he got close to oilman and diplomat George McGhee. It was probably McGhee who got Davis a job in the CIA. By the end of the decade Davis had changed his name to Lawrence Harrison, moved to Guadalajara, and was working with DFS agents tracking down left-wing insurgents.

Over the next decade he continued to work undercover for the Company and the DFS. At the time, the two were tightly intertwined. They had the same enemies—foreign communist agents, Marxist students, and real or suspected guerrillas. For the more paranoid of America's Cold Warriors, Mexico was the buffer between an increasingly liberal United States and a mass of communist-sympathizing, Cuba-inspired Latinos. Mexico had to be kept stable at all costs. So it was a close arrangement. DFS chiefs were CIA assets; and CIA agents worked out of DFS offices and carried DFS badges.

In a 2013 interview, Mexico's former undersecretary of the interior confirmed the relationship:

> The DFS was entirely at the service of the CIA.... It even had some of its agents assigned to the agency full time. There was a house ... where [those agents] lived. The Americans paid them, dressed them and gave the orders.

While undercover, Lawrence Harrison took on various jobs. He taught English to Guadalajara students, passed the names of those with guerrilla sympathies over to the DFS, and never saw them again. He moved briefly to Acapulco, got close to Mexico's counterinsurgency specialist General Mario Arturo Acosta Chaparro, and saw the bodies of traffickers and guerrillas wash up on the surrounding beaches. And he worked briefly as a legal advisor for Guadalajara's PRI organization.

As the threat of left-wing insurgency diminished, Harrison's role changed. By the early 1980s he had moved from law to tech. And he started to establish radio networks for the DFS and their gang of right-wing paramilitaries and Sinaloa-born traffickers. It was in this job that he got close to Fonseca. He even moved briefly into one of the drug lord's lavish suburban houses.

By 1984, however, the relationship started to sour. The conflicts among traffickers, state government officials, and secret agents grew. Fonseca and Caro Quintero, in particular, were increasingly paranoid. And Fonseca decided that Harrison was a threat, or a rat, or a thief, or all three. He ordered his gunmen to give the American "a bath." The term was short for a "bath of bullets." On September 11, gunmen dressed as PJF cops tracked down Harrison and shot him and his companion.

Harrison survived but only just. He convinced Fonseca or at least one of his DFS colleagues of his reliability. And for the next five years, as the fallout from the Camarena case brought down the Mexican secret service and locked up even the best-protected traffickers, Harrison kept his rather tall head down.

But he was tired, scared, and increasingly distrustful. By 1989 the new Salinas administration had arrested Félix Gallardo and DFS head Zorrilla. Loose ends were being tied up. Maybe he would be next? As a result, when Berrellez tracked him down and offered him protection in return for testimony, Harrison agreed. After two decades living undercover in Mexico, the lanky spook finally came home.

Until his death in November 2018, Harrison would only occasionally speak on the record. He was questioned by Berrellez at length; he testified at a handful of grand jury investigations; and he gave cryptic interviews to a few journalists and academics. He was clearly a difficult interviewee. Sworn to secrecy and twenty years a spy, he was always careful what he said. He never, for example, directly admitted that he worked for the CIA.

Though it was pretty clear that he did. His patter was often convoluted and opaque. It was short on direct accusations and big on hints and inferences. It needed prior knowledge and begged for triangulation.

But, in essence, what Harrison claimed was as follows. Following Congress's 1982 ban on funding the Contras, the CIA had sought to use cocaine money to buy them guns. Oliver North, a member of the White House's National Security Council, led the effort. He was helped by the Cuban-American covert ops specialist Félix Rodríguez, who organized the day-to-day running of the operation. But as news of CIA involvement started to leak, North and Rodríguez were joined by members of Mossad, the Israeli secret service. The Israelis now started to front the program.

Together the American and Israeli agents worked with Central American cocaine smugglers, such as Matta Ballesteros. And when Matta Ballesteros hooked up with Félix Gallardo and moved to Guadalajara, the Americans also started to work with the Mexicans. They now shipped the narcotics and the guns through Mexican airstrips. They also, Harrison claimed, started to train Contras on the traffickers' ranches in the Caribbean state of Veracruz. Harrison said he had even met two of the American instructors. They were former mercenaries who had worked putting down left-wing rebellions across the world, from Africa to Uruguay. Now they worked exchanging guns for cocaine and training wannabe Contras.

The system was not, however, foolproof. And the CIA and its Mexican allies constantly feared detection. Illegally running guns through Mexico was bad enough. Buying them with cocaine money as the crack epidemic took off risked setting America on fire.

So they dealt ruthlessly with possible discovery. In 1984, for example, a Veracruz journalist started to investigate rumors of the Americans running military training camps in the state. He passed on the rumors to the well-connected and combative Mexico City journalist Manuel Buendía. He, in turn, probably asked the DFS commander, Zorrilla, about the matter. Zorrilla told the CIA. And on May 30, 1984, gunmen shot Buendía and the Veracruz journalist dead. In a none-too-subtle hint, they sewed the Veracruz journalist's lips shut with wire.

Harrison suggested that it was this drive to cover up the training camps that resulted in the shocking—and again poorly explained—massacre of twenty-two PJF cops in the Veracruz village of Hidalgotitlán in September 1985.

Harrison speculated that similar motives also explained the DEA man's murder. Camarena, like the Veracruz journalist, like Buendía, and like the federal cops had stumbled onto the drugs-for-arms operation. This was why he was killed.

Many—including some members of the DEA—have dismissed Harrison as a crank. But those who personally met him, from Berrellez to the veteran border journalists Charles Bowden and Molly Molloy to two University of Wisconsin academics, were convinced by his story. Berrellez even sent him for a lie detector test, which he passed on three separate occasions.

And a lot of his story rings true. It indicates why traffickers like Fonseca and Caro Quintero seemed so confident of their own impunity. It chimes with the confessions of other U.S. operatives involved in the drugs-for-guns scandal. It explains why someone recorded tapes of Camarena's interrogation; it explains how the CIA managed to get hold of these tapes; and it suggests why one of the tapes ends with Camarena's interrogators asking him about a ranch in Veracruz.

But there are also holes. Big holes. And because it is about the CIA, there are conspiracies. And there are conspiracies within conspiracies. They are enough to fill another book. (In fact, if readers are interested, there is an exhaustive and occasionally paranoid study by the two Wisconsin academics.)

The first concerns the supposed Contra training camps in Veracruz. Despite repeated reference to these, no one has any idea where they were. Instead, there are multiple unproven theories. Some claim that they were in northern Veracruz on the ranch of the ageing hitman and heroin trafficker Arturo Izquierdo Ebrard. Others claim that they were established somewhere in southern Veracruz near the location of the 1985 PJF massacre. (But the locals I spoke to maintain that Mexican weed smugglers killed the PJF officials and deny any knowledge of covert military camps.) And the only published mention the dead Veracruz journalist made of CIA-run sites was not even in Veracruz. It was on the foothills of the Sierra Negra volcano in the neighboring state of Puebla.

The second concerns the DEA investigation. In the two years following Berrellez's encounter with Harrison, the agent managed to secure more witnesses to the Camarena murder. Their evidence helped put away half-a-dozen other alleged culprits, including Verdugo (the kidnapped Tijuana weed smuggler) and Álvarez Marchaín (the kidnapped Guadalajara doctor). Some of the witnesses' statements rang true and backed up Harrison's claims.

But there were problems. Despite coming from unschooled memories, the witness statements were disturbingly consistent. They named the same names; they focused in on the same incidents. Furthermore, they alleged the direct and flagrant collusion not only of CIA operatives, but also of high-up Mexican government officials. They claimed—incredibly—that these officials, including the secretary of defense and the secretary of the interior, openly planned the Camarena killing and visited the house while he was being tortured to death. Such accusations not only undermined their statements, they called the whole investigation into question.

The third issue concerns the role of Camarena's DEA colleagues in Guadalajara. In Esquivel's 2013 exposé, one of Berrellez's witnesses claimed that he recognized one of Camarena's DEA colleagues at the trial. The colleague was not there in his official DEA capacity. Instead, he was there to give evidence on behalf of one of the defendents. The witness intimated that this colleague had always been in the pay of the Guadalajara traffickers.

It is a claim that has refused to go away. Over the last few years more former cops have backed it up and offered some salacious (and unrepeatable) details. It is also a claim that may explain why on the tapes Camarena's interrogators repeatedly asked him about the money traffickers were paying him. (It is something Camarena repeatedly denied.)

Did—as some now speculate—one of Camarena's DEA colleagues take a bribe, claim that he had passed it on to Camarena, and then blame Camarena when the traffickers' fields were raided and their bank deposits seized? Was the DEA as involved in Camarena's death as the CIA?

As any reader that has followed these claims and counterclaims up to here may be starting to realize, the Camarena case is still a deep, dark hole.

And it is one that is still getting deeper. The DEA investigation continues to this day; it is now thirty-five years old and counting. Fiction and reality are firmly intertwined. In 2019 the DEA recruited *another* alleged witness; series 2 of *Narcos: Mexico* was released; and *USA Today* hinted at new prosecutions. In 2020, Amazon Prime Video's documentary on the investigation—*The Last Narc*—was announced, delayed, and then released. It was cut for legal reasons and then sued anyway.

Parsing all the evidence, reading through all the testimonies, and comparing them to similar accusations of CIA-backed drug running in Southeast Asia, Afghanistan, and Central and South America, it seems likely that U.S. agents were using the Guadalajara traffickers to move cocaine and guns. The stories of training camps are unproven but plausible. Secret services—working with no oversight and complete impunity—have always gravitated toward money and resources. And I would be extremely surprised if some of the DEA agents in Mexico were not on the take. They had been in the past. And they would be again.

What we do know is that what started off a rather simple tale of perseverance and sacrifice has become a vortex. It sucks in all the drug war's murderous grievances, political feuds, and hypocrisies. It has come to embody the blurred lines separating mythmaking, counterinsurgency, drug trafficking, and policing. What you think about the Camarena case now doesn't reflect what happened to the murdered DEA agent. It signals what you think about the drug war. It signals what you think about Mexico and the United States.

# Part V

---

# Into the Abyss
## 1990–2020

## Chapter 21

### The Takeover

DRAGO REMEMBERED THE MEETING WELL. HE WAS IN AN UPSCALE Argentine restaurant in Mexico City. He was playing bodyguard. He sat at a table next to his boss, the head of the Tijuana cartel—Benjamín Arellano Félix. The boss was there to meet one of the heads of the Mexican Attorney General's Office, the bureau nominally in charge of prosecuting drug crimes. An enormous fat man, stuffed into a dark suit, sat opposite the cartel chief.

Drago immediately dubbed him "the Whale."

Slick and needy, the Whale clearly wanted to impress. Earning regular bribes from Arellano Félix would be enough to retire on. He asked the boss if he could choose the wine to accompany the meal. "All I need to know is your favorite fruit, the season of the year you like most, and where you might want to live, France, Italy, Chile or Australia."

The boss was silent. He stared at the Whale. The Whale started to sweat. Arellano Félix held out his finger and beckoned the lawyer to come closer.

Do you think I flew here to talk to you about the fucking weather? Fucking fat faggot, fucking son of a whore ... you can stick your

favorite fruits up your arse. Stick a fucking pineapple up there if
you want. But if you don't want me to stick a bullet up there, stop
this fucking messing around and pay me some fucking attention. I
don't live in France, in Italy or in Chile, nor in fucking Australia. I
live here, and it's here that I have my business.

The Whale's smile disappeared. The boss continued.

You know what my business is about, so let's save this fucking bottle of wine, actually let's save this whole fucking meal, so I can save
seeing your fucking Mongol face. You work for me now. You hear
me? You're mine. I'm letting you meet me now just so you know
who's the boss. I'm letting you meet me so you know who's your
fucking daddy, you fucking chilango faggot. I know my people
spoke with you and told you what to do. I know that my people gave
you money. That money was from me, you fucking shitty faggot.
Don't forget. Now you eat from my hand.

A cultured wine connoisseur the Whale might have been. But a savvy
observer of the shifts in narco power he was not. The Mexican drug trade
had changed. More specifically, the relationship between the drug trade
and the Mexican authorities had changed. And it had changed radically.
Political dealmakers no longer held sway.

The Whale would learn this lesson the hard way. A few years later he
reneged on his agreement with the boss. He sold out the cartel to their
rivals. Drago, the bodyguard, now got new instructions. "Now don't go and
pay him, put him six feet under," the boss ordered. Within a week, it was
done.

For nearly eighty years the Mexican authorities—first local, then state,
then federal—had protected drug traffickers from prosecution. The power
dynamics of the protection rackets had stayed constant. Drug traffickers
had to minimize violence, avoid U.S. scrutiny, and not sell drugs south of
the border. Crossing those lines got you arrested, killed, or handed over to
the gringos. Enrique Fernández had found this out; so had Pedro Avilés
Pérez. Less ostentatious traffickers like Eduardo "Lalo" Fernández had not.

The Camarena murder suggested that these rules could be tested. But the subsequent investigation reinforced the reality that the Mexican state— and the U.S. drug cops—would come down on offenders brutally and effectively.

But during the 1990s the system—such as it was—broke down. Power dynamics reversed. Increased drug profits and declining state power put the narcos in control. And they—not the cops or the secret service agents— now took over running the country's drug protection rackets.

The principal reason for this change was the money. During the 1980s, Mexican traffickers had transported around a third of Colombia's cocaine into the United States. They earned big rewards. They charged the Colombian cartels between $1,000 and $2,000 per kilo. Pablo Acosta, for example, charged $1,250 to deliver the product over the border at Ojinaga. Usually, he moved around 5 tons per month. It made him $75 million a year.

But by the turn of the decade the Colombians were feeling the heat. U.S. officials had managed to shut down the Florida trafficking route almost completely. Navy patrol vessels and low-flying planes now kept a keen watch on the thin strip of sea Colombian powerboats had used to smuggle in the loads. U.S. and Colombian agents were working together to dismantle Pablo Escobar's cocaine empire. In December 1993 they completed their pursuit, shooting Escobar dead on a Medellín rooftop. And in the same year, they took down the Cali Cartel's Florida distribution network, arresting three lieutenants in quick succession. Two years later, the Colombian government reintroduced extradition for drug criminals. Getting directly linked to U.S. smuggling now risked an interminable U.S. prison sentence.

The blows were heralded as vital victories in America's overseas drug war. Yet cocaine prices never wavered. All they did was change the way the Colombians and the Mexicans did business.

The Mexicans would now take most of the risk for transporting cocaine north of the border. A Cali Cartel accountant, who gave evidence in a Miami court in 1997, explained that the new system was called "one for one." Half the cocaine now went to the Mexicans; half remained with the

Colombians. By the end of the decade, the DEA estimated that the Mexicans were now moving somewhere between 80 and 90 percent of America's coke.

DEA agents, who started to pick up on the move, were impressed by the smooth, businesslike way in which the change was made.

> [The Colombians] were thinking, "How do I diminish my exposure to potential extradition? Why don't I just hand the whole thing to the Mexicans? I still make a huge amount of money and I lower my exposure to potential extradition as its no longer my kilo. I get out of the business because it is getting too much pressure to do this in the U.S. And concurrently I've still got the European market. I'm making hand over fist money in Europe, I'm making tons of money in Mexico. Let the Mexican cartels deal with the DEA and the FBI and the U.S. Customs."

The move toward wholesale cocaine trafficking coincided with shifts in transport. At first, traffickers used planes. Big planes. Former weed smuggler Amado Carrillo Fuentes got rid of his fleet of go-fast Learjets and started to buy old 727 passenger planes. He ripped out the seats and loaded the plane with 3 to 5 tons of cocaine. It soon earned him the nickname the Lord of the Skies. If a plane crashed, it was no big loss. Each cost $300,000 or the value of around 12 kilos of cocaine—less than 0.3 percent of the next load.

But, with the signing of the North American Free Trade Agreement (NAFTA) and the removal of trade restrictions, the traffickers also returned to moving product by land. For two years, the Americans observed the traffickers getting ready. Mexican traffickers bought up warehouses and trucking companies in the border cities. Some even hired trade consultants to work out what products got through the new border inspections more quickly. One DEA agent remarked: "They have specific issues. Does a perishable get through quicker than a load of steel? What kind of cargos gets through faster than others?"

Drug trafficking was no longer about marshaling peasant growers, perfecting sellable strains, and secreting a few kilos of sticky heroin in a car drive shaft. Things moved so fast that one PGR official even mocked the sinsemilla producers of the 1980s as hippie "narco-ecologists." The modern drug business was now about riding the explosion of globalized trade, gaining comparative advantage, securing warehousing facilities, and refining transport logistics. Narcos' kids now pursued degrees in international business, not the old favorites like chemistry or agronomy.

When tariffs were removed and the border was finally opened on January 1, 1994, the traffickers were ready. Tracking down drug loads went from tough to nearly impossible. In 1995 in just Laredo, Texas, over 6 million trucks and cars crossed the border in a year; 18,000 per day. The cocaine needed to sate America's appetite could be transported in just thirteen trucks.

Together the changes transformed the Mexican drug economy. In a stroke, they added a zero to Mexican drug profits. For every 2 kilos traffickers crossed over the border, they no longer got two $1,000 crossing fees. Now they got the wholesale value of a kilo of cocaine on the American side. By the mid-1990s, this was around $25,000. If they could cut it and distribute it through their own networks in U.S. cities, they could make nearly $200,000. Two zeros more profit.

In macroterms, the effects were even more startling. During the 1980s, experts estimated that the Mexican drug trade brought in between $2 billion and $6 billion a year. Ten years later, the Mexican authorities now put drug earnings at around $30 billion. It was—as they admitted—an estimate. But it valued narcotics as worth 38 percent of Mexican exports and over four times the value of the biggest legal export—oil.

The traffickers who profited from these changes were those that survived the Camarena roundups. They had some familiar backgrounds. (The new drug capitalists, like the new neoliberal capitalists, usually drew from the same small pool of elite families.)

Some were second- or third-generation smugglers from the Golden Triangle. They included weed specialists like Ernesto Fonseca Carrillo's nephew Amado Carrillo Fuentes, Pedro Avilés Pérez's nephew Jesús Labra Avilés, and the Culiacán landowner–turned–heroin dealer Ismael "El Mayo" Zambada. Others were former fayuqueros and border smuggling professionals like the Matamoros kingpin Juan García Abrego or the

Tijuana-based Arellano Félix brothers. Others still were ex–government officials, like the old Operation Condor torturer Carlos Aguilar Garza.

The Americans grouped them together into geographical zones, gave them leaders, and called them cartels. This taxonomic, name-and-shame strategy had worked in Colombia, so why not Mexico? By the early 1990s, there was the Juárez Cartel, led by former DFS agent Rafael Aguilar Guajardo and then by Amado Carrillo Fuentes. There was the Tijuana Cartel, led by Pedro Avilés's nephew Jesús Labra Avilés and the Arellano Félix clan. And there was the Gulf Cartel, led by Juan García Abrego.

Cartels were shorthand, a convenient fiction. They gave a name to what was a fluid, amorphous, and (though they dared not say it) unbeatable marketplace ecosystem. In its classified files if not on its press releases, the DEA's own intelligence arm admitted that the Amado Carrillo Fuentes organization had been called many things—"the Mexican Mafia, the Mexican Corporation, the Sonora Cartel, the Jalisco or Guadalajara Cartel." The Juárez Cartel was just the last in a long line of expedient badges. But it was not a cartel and it had no rigid hierarchy. "It functions more as a loose federation of trafficking organizations than a regimented, organized mafia group or cartel."

No doubt only a few high-level members of the organization had really firm links to the Colombians. These individuals brought in the cocaine and smuggled some of it into the United States themselves. But they also sold a lot to smaller smugglers. They linked up with other groups to organize transport, protection, bribes, and the actual act of getting the stuff over the border. There were dozens of these small groups. The DEA, in its drive to bring order, split the Carrillo organization into five *"patrones,"* or bosses "responsible for decisions affecting all aspects of the federation"; nine family-run "divisions" "responsible for specific geographical, logistical or special responsibilities"; twelve border gatekeeping groups and dozens more of what the DEA called "family syndicates," contracted out for specific jobs and paid per kilo.

Together these so-called cartels were a strange blend of the very modern and the very traditional. They were both flexible post-Fordist businesses and old-school mafias glued together by kinship, friendship, and extravagant parties.

Americans rarely penetrated these organizations. Mexicans rarely revealed them. In fact, in comparison to the Colombian cartels, we still know relatively little about them. Myths, drug war hype, and exaggerations abound. (Good network analysis tends to make poor narcocorridos.) And even those enmeshed in the everyday smuggling often remained in the dark about what other groups were doing.

But, in recent years, Mexico's foremost investigative journalist, Anabel Hernández, has managed to use a combination of court testimonies, mob lawyers, and an extraordinary jailhouse confession by the son of Ismael "El Mayo" Zambada to map out the new geography of the Mexican drug trade as well as how one of these smuggling networks actually worked.

In the late 1990s, Zambada had managed to secure a link to the Colombian cocaine producers. He contracted a maritime specialist and the brother of one of the old Guadalajara Cartel bigwigs to go to Colombia and bring up 10-ton loads by boat to the Caribbean coastal town of Chetumal. Two other contractors then brought the cocaine overland to Mexico City, where Zambada's brother stored the stuff in warehouses near the city's rail depot. Here, the cocaine was divided up. One contractor, Tirso Martínez Sánchez, "the Footballer," arranged to have the drugs shipped by train from Mexico City through Nuevo Laredo and all the way to New York. Between 1999 and 2003, Martínez admitted that he moved at least 50 tons of the stuff. (The DEA claimed that it was nearer 80 tons.)

Around 2003 this system broke down. (Martínez said in a Brooklyn court that his daughter became distressed at the bloodshed the cartel was causing.) So Zambada employed another transport expert, who stashed the cocaine in secret compartments in gasoline trucks. This contractor then subcontracted out the actual moving of the stuff through the border at Mexicali and to Los Angeles.

Each stage of the route was priced differently depending on the mode of transport, the police presence, and the levels of bribes necessary. It cost $6,000 to get a kilo of cocaine from Colombia to Culiacán, $4,000 to get a kilo from Culiacán to Los Angeles, and $9,000 to get a kilo from Culiacán to Chicago. The U.S. police and Customs inspectors in the Midwest—it seems—charged a heavy premium to look the other way.

If the money from the Colombian cocaine business changed the nature of drug smuggling, it also changed traffickers' relationship with the state. This wasn't inevitable. Had the Mexican state been financially buoyant, ideologically coherent, and politically formidable, perhaps it could have controlled the rush of cash. In the midst of another drug boom during the 1970s, it had crushed independent marijuana and heroin smugglers and forced favored traffickers to shift their drugs through the PJF-controlled plazas. The policy was brutal. Yet it had enforced a degree of control.

But by the mid-1990s, the state was markedly weaker. The economy was tumbling even before the signing of NAFTA. Real wages nearly halved over the decade.

The PRI, which had previously survived rifts and scandals with minimal political fallout, began to fracture. In 1987 many left-wing supporters left the party and followed Cuauhtémoc Cárdenas, the son of 1930s president Lázaro Cárdenas, to form a rival party. Over the next few years, economic nationalists faced off against free-trade neoliberals; political democratizers fought old-school authoritarians for the control of the PRI; and tight, elite bands waged desperate struggles to install and protect individual presidents.

These feuds spilled over into public exposés and political assassinations. In the final two years of President Salinas's reign (1988–1994) and the first two of President Zedillo's (1994–2000), there were two guerrilla uprisings, the devaluation of the peso, the shooting of the pope's representative in Mexico, the assassination of the PRI presidential candidate and the secretary general of the party, and the arrest of President Salinas's brother on both murder and money-laundering charges.

For decades, PRI operatives had lived by the code of *"disciplina,"* knowing when to politick and when to shut up. In the 1990s this code went out the window. Mexico's security forces, in particular, became increasingly fragmented. By the end of the decade they were a tangle of half-measure reforms, forgettable acronyms, and bitter rivalries. There were over 1,600 state and local agencies. There was the new intelligence agency, brought in to replace the DFS (and including many of its former agents). There was the principal antinarcotics bureau, the PGR, and its agents from the PJF. There was the army, which was increasingly pulled into antinarcotics operations. And there was the litany of short-lived specialist antinarcotics forces.

Even inside the individual institutions, there were divisions. Under Salinas, the PGR had five separate directors, ranging from hard-nosed counterinsurgency torturers to the head of Mexico's human rights agency.

The PRI was not only losing control of its institutions, it was also ceding control of its territory. In 1989, the rival National Action Party (PAN) won the state governorship of Baja California; in 1992 it took Chihuahua: in 1995, Jalisco: and in 1997, Nuevo León. By the middle of the decade the PAN also controlled 225 municipalities, including a lot of the big border cities like Tijuana and Ciudad Juárez and many of the big drugs hubs like Guadalajara and Monterrey.

Flush with cash, and faced with a one-party system in decline, Mexico's traffickers now paid off great swathes of the Mexican state and its security forces. Corruption increased in scale, reach, and political aspiration. This was no longer about gaining the protection of the local cops or the drug police *commandante* or a nearby army commander. This was a level above even grand corruption. This was about gaining control of whole sectors of the state. It was what some political scientists termed "state capture."

The step up in the amount of money involved was eye-watering. One 1993 study estimated that the new cocaine traffickers spent nearly $500 million on corrupting state authorities per year. This was up from $1.5–$3.2 million a year just a decade earlier. Like most drug statistics, it was a napkin calculation, but it was a believable one. When federal authorities finally arrested the Matamoros trafficker Juan García Abrego in 1995, they discovered his little black book of bribes. A million dollars for the national commander of the PJF; $500,000 to the force's operation chief; $100,000 to each PJF agent stationed in Matamoros. And this was just one city and one police force.

The money now got everywhere. A lot, of course, went to the counter-narcotics bureau, the PGR. Here, El Mayo Zambada's lawyer claimed that "99 percent of the officials are corrupt. There's not one that doesn't take money." (This had increased—it should be said—since the early 1990s when it was thought to be only 95 percent.) And the money went to their police enforcers, the PJF. In fact, as the DEA observed, "smuggling organizations in the northern states of Mexico are hesitant to transport their loads within Mexico without the security of protection purchased from the PJF."

Payoffs also overwhelmed state and local police forces. When one Ciudad Juárez smuggler joined the city's police force at the end of the decade, he found that at least a quarter of the new recruits were already members of the cartel. The local police academy was effectively a cartel training camp. You got a badge, a gun, and weapons instruction. And now you could travel to cartel hits in a squad car.

Beyond the police, the traffickers also started to pay off new groups as well. They included the military. In early 1997, Mexico's new drug tsar, General José de Jesús Gutiérrez Rebollo, was arrested after just three months on the job. He was found to be living in one of Amado Carrillo Fuentes's properties in Mexico City. Prosecutors revealed that they had recordings of him discussing bribes with the drug lord. More revelations followed. Someone leaked internal Ministry of Defense documents, which discussed open meetings between Carrillo and high-ranking military officials. The Americans claimed that they had evidence that at least thirty-four other officers were taking cartel money.

Traffickers expanded their payroll to include members of leading political families. It was rumored that traffickers had managed to reach the upper echelons, when since the early 1990s the DEA had started to notice unexplained sums of money in offshore bank accounts of President Salinas's brother, Raúl. Suspicions were waylaid, at least temporarily, when Raúl got a gig at the University of San Diego.

It appeared, however, that Raúl was unrepentant. He penned a ditty on the comparative ethics of corruption. ("If you rob from the many 100 per cent/There could be a moral offense/A few points more, a few points less/ Morality is a question of percent.") And when he returned to Mexico more unexplained payments supplemented his civil service salaries. Finally, in 1995, Swiss police captured Raúl's wife trying to withdraw $84 million from one of his bank accounts. Over the next few years they found $250 million in 289 separate accounts. He was eventually sentenced to 50 years in 1999 for murder. (However, he continued to protest his innocence and his conviction was quashed after serving less than a decade of his time. Soon after his release all the money was returned to him.)

What the traffickers got for these payoffs was the usual—protection. Just on a grander scale. Local cops blocked entire stretches of rural roads to allow cocaine-packed 727s to land. Federal cops lifted roadblocks to allow smugglers' trailer trucks to pass through. Generals gave traffickers warnings about imminent raids and attempted arrests. (Most famously, in March 1997, Amado Carrillo Fuentes escaped from his sister's wedding just minutes before state forces arrived.)

But the amount of money involved also started to upend the relationship between the traffickers and the state employees. Eduardo Valle Espinosa, a former student radical pulled in to cleanse the PGR under Salinas, witnessed the system up close. He concluded that, in 1993, "Politicians are at the service of the drug traffickers" rather than the other way around. He called it not a protection racket but a "narco-democracy."

The term is probably a bit strong. The takeover was never complete. Even as the PRI crumbled, most of Mexico's institutions functioned fairly well. There was water, electricity, and schooling. Per capita income continued to outpace most developing countries. The transition from single-party dominance to competitive multiparty elections was comparatively smooth and peaceful.

The narco takeover was also gradual and uneven. Some claimed control passed to the cartels as early as 1989, when Félix Gallardo allegedly got together his fellow traffickers at a mafia meeting in Acapulco to divvy up Mexico's drug plazas. That year the PAN won the governorship of Baja California Norte, and key crossing points like Tijuana and Mexicali were now out of PRI hands. Yet Félix Gallardo always denied that he did this. He claimed that the government still allocated the plazas.

Whether narcos or the government led the allocation, it was clear that by early 1993 a radical realignment had occurred. There was a cull of the former PJF and DFS agents that had moved into the drug trade. Plaza bosses, like former Operation Condor torturer Carlos Aguilar Garza and Ciudad Juárez kingpin Rafael Aguilar Guajardo, were murdered. So were other major traffickers and a bunch of Félix Gallardo's relatives. The shift also tied in with politics. In 1992 the PRI also lost control of the governorship of Chihuahua and the crucial crossing corridor of Ciudad Juárez.

Whatever the exact timeline, by the mid-1990s drug traffickers—not the state—ran the protection rackets at the plazas. They demanded fees to move product through, and it was their armed forces, not the PJF or the DFS, who took out the independent smugglers.

The importance of the shift cannot be underestimated. It capsized eight decades of state drug policy. It outsourced drug protection to the traffickers themselves. The taxed became the tax collectors.

Yet it also did much more. Controlling territory had a series of unintended side effects. They would become increasingly evident over the next two decades. To run citywide protection rackets, traffickers now needed more gunmen. They started to outsource violence to local cops, deserting soldiers, local mobs, and cross-border gangs. The Tijuana Cartel pioneered the move, welding together a strange mix of San Diego thugs and Tijuana posh kids into Arellano Félix's private army. Then Carrillo siphoned off a group of Ciudad Juárez cops to form his group. First, they were known as "the Little Trees"; then they became "the Line." The Gulf Cartel upped the ante once more. From 1997 on, they recruited members of the Mexican army special forces. This group became known as the Zetas.

These changes radically increased the violence connected with the drug trade. State agents had rarely held back when extorting payoffs (especially when the PJF took over in the 1970s). And conflicts between state institutions for control of the rackets were frequent. But there were limits. As the former racketeers were policemen, punishment for not paying bribes could mean prison time, not simply torture or death. And really bad cops could be sacked, arrested, or even killed. Even the president's friend, Arturo "El Negro" Durazo, had been arrested. There were clear rewards for showing just a little bit of restraint.

By the mid-1990s, these incentives were disappearing. And so was the restraint.

Big traffickers now used their own hitmen or local cops to round up small-time smugglers and make them pay a fee for moving product through their plaza. The reluctant were tortured. And those who refused were killed. The fee was called the *derecho de piso* (best translated as the "right to work"). The term had been used by the PJF to denote the bribe paid for any illegal activity. In Mexico, underworld slang came from inside the state.

In Baja California Norte, if you were caught bringing drugs into the ports of Ensenada or Rosarito or at the border crossings at Tijuana, Mexicali, or Tecate, you were kidnapped and shot in the back of the head. Local journalists estimated that the Arellano Félix gang killed between 100 and 200 a year. They were mostly small-scale weed smugglers from the south of Mexico. Many could not even be identified. In 2001 alone, doctors had to bury at least forty bodies in unmarked graves.

Occasionally, the press took note. In 1997, the *New York Times* reported that an El Paso NGO had recorded over fifty disappearances in the past three years. Two years later, FBI agents working with Mexican investigators started to uncover bodies on a nearby ranch. And in 2004 later, they uncovered another hidden graveyard with the remains of a dozen bodies. The municipal police admitted in private that "the desert surrounding Juárez is a vast cemetery, a huge mausoleum full of corpses."

Quantifying any of this, even vaguely, is borderline impossible. There were no drug murder counts at the time. Most bodies were hidden. And corrupt cops reclassified those that were found as the victims of manslaughter or crimes of passion. The sole aim of the chief of the Tijuana murder squad in the mid-1990s was to "distract attention from the Arellano Félix cartel." The chief even came up with a sharp saying that distilled his investigative approach. *"Si quieres llegar a ser agente viejo … hazte pendejo"* (If you want to get to be an old agent … act like a fucking idiot).

As a result, estimates of drug-connected deaths were sketchy at best. The best approximation suggests that from 1997 on, these trafficker-controlled protection rackets were killing around 350 small peddlers a year. It was an alarming upsurge. Yet it was soon forgotten. Within a decade, there were similar numbers of murders committed in a month just in a single Mexican city.

# Chapter 22

## Wars

GROUND ZERO WAS NUEVO LAREDO. THOUGH IT HAD BARELY 300,000 residents, the city was the principal transport route for over a third of the border's trade. Over 3,700 trucks crossed a day. In a year they carried $90 billion worth of goods over the Río Bravo, up Interstate 35 to Dallas and then beyond, throughout the Eastern Seaboard. Nuevo Laredo was also the entry point, DEA agents claimed, for over half the U.S.'s cocaine.

Hostilities took off at the end of 2004. Police discovered five bodies in a safe house in an upscale neighborhood of the city. The victims had been blindfolded, bound, tortured, and shot in the head. Beside them the killers laid two pieces of cardboard. They were a challenge. They read, "This message is for you, 'Chapo' Guzmán, and for you, Arturo Beltrán Leyva" and "Send more idiots for us to kill."

By the beginning of 2005, a new, more brutal drug war had arrived in Nuevo Laredo. Sinaloa gunmen under Guzmán and Beltrán Leyva confronted the Gulf Cartel's armed wing, the Zetas. Over the next year, the homicide rate tripled. Over the following six months, it doubled again. Bodies were strung from underpasses and dumped by the sides of the roads; messages were scrawled on cardboard notices and painted on sheets; victims were mutilated; journalists were murdered; and police chiefs were cut down in the street. Four were killed in just one year.

In March 2005 hundreds of federal police and soldiers arrived in the city. Killings continued nevertheless. Local cops met the feds with a barrage of bullets and the feds had to fight their way into the city. Later that year the entire local police force was sacked for being on the Gulf Cartel's payroll.

Yet the move seemed to do little. On July 28, 2005, gunmen from both cartels exchanged gunfire, grenades, and bazooka missiles in the city's biggest shopping complex. The confrontation lasted thirty minutes. Yet neither the federal nor the local forces intervened. By the time they reached the battlefield, both groups of gunmen had removed their dead and wounded.

New fronts in the new drug war opened up at speed. Murder rates suddenly leapt along the border in Tijuana and Ciudad Juárez. Tactics changed. In December 2005, a U.S. newspaper released a short homemade movie clip. In a dark room in the southern beach resort of Acapulco, members of the Sinaloa Cartel questioned four alleged Zetas. At the end of the clip, they shot them in the head. It was the first narco video. Compared to what was to come, it was distinctly PG.

New organizations now burst on the scene armed not just with high-caliber weapons but also with prepacked political creeds and religious messages. In September 2006, a Sinaloa-linked group tossed the heads of five Zetas into a Michoacán bar. The note declared that the group was the Familia Michoacana. "The family does not kill for money. It does not kill women or innocent people. Those who die are those who must die. Everyone should know that this is divine justice."

Over the next six years, the conflict in Nuevo Laredo was repeated throughout much of Mexico. Conflicts gained a depressing rhythm. Certain cartels would begin fighting in a particular state or city. The conflicts involved a combination of extended shootouts, increasingly horrific forms of mutilation and torture, the public display of bodies or their complete disappearance. Politicians—and particular policemen—were often the targets of the violence. And so were journalists and media workers. And what started off as localized clashes often spiraled into killings and political assassinations half a country away.

During the Nuevo Laredo clashes, President Vicente Fox (2000–2006) was a reluctant drug warrior. Mexico's first president from the conservative, probusiness PAN, he was also the country's first leader to come from outside the PRI for over fifty years. A good-time rather than a wartime leader, he didn't want conflict. So he was reluctant to send more than a few hundred police and soldiers to the border.

The next president, Felipe Calderón (2006–2012), had few such reservations. He was elected with only the slimmest of margins and limited legitimacy. Supporters of his rival were still camped out in Mexico City, claiming electoral fraud. Calderón had so little legitimacy he was forced to sneak into the Congress through the back door at his inauguration.

Calderón needed a mission. Something to unite the country behind his rule. He chose the war on drugs. On December 11, 2006, he sent 6,500 troops into his home state of Michoacán. Soon afterward he sent another 7,000 soldiers to Acapulco and over 3,000 to Tijuana. By the peak of the campaign around 50,000 troops and the entire federal police force was involved in combating traffickers.

The Americans backed Calderón. They lent over a billion dollars to equip the army and the federal police with the latest guns, the newest helicopters, and the most advanced technology. They also sent hundreds of DEA and ICE agents south to infiltrate Mexican cartels, turn informants, and share information with the Mexicans.

Calderón played the wartime president. He flew to a military base in Michoacán, donned army fatigues, and urged soldiers "to persevere until victory is achieved.... We will give no quarter to the enemies of Mexico." Despite the trappings of the role, Calderón was less than convincing; he was a diminutive, balding man and with none of the easygoing charm voters looked for in a political strongman.

Commentators still disagree whether Calderón's policy was the product of firm belief or rank opportunism or, as I suspect, a mixture of the two. (As a right-wing Catholic, zeal and pragmatism were never mutually exclusive.) But all agree it was an unmitigated disaster. The government crackdown intersected with trafficker conflicts and local struggles in strange and destructive ways. Cartels faced off against cartels; cartels faced off against soldiers and police; and some soldiers and police linked up with cartels to eliminate their rivals.

Drug-related murders rose rapidly. Between 2006 and 2012, experts estimated that there were as many as 65,000. Journalists observed that, in the same time period, civilian deaths in Mexico outpaced those in Afghanistan and Iraq. Soon the number surpassed that of U.S. casualties in the Vietnam War. (Though, it should be said, it was far fewer than the estimated 3 million Vietnamese killed.) It was the death rate of a low-intensity war or, perhaps better, a series of low-intensity wars.

The violence was unprecedented in both scale and volume. For over sixty years, since the land-reform and religious conflicts of the 1930s, Mexican murder rates had been in steady decline. At the turn of the century, they were around the same as the United States during the 1980s. Calderón's drug war upended such progress. The murder rate more than doubled in just five years.

And it overshadowed Mexico's other brief periods of drug war violence. During the 1970s, at the height of Operation Condor, deaths from drug violence never exceeded a thousand a year; they were probably nearer to a few hundred. From 2006 on, drug-related deaths often surpassed a thousand in just a month. During the 1990s, when cartels first started to war for control of trafficking plazas, murders were vicious and frequent. But they rarely outstripped an average of one a day. Now they averaged over one per hour.

For over a decade, politicians, academics, and journalists have sought to understand this violence. Political science has met true crime. Discussion of the murderous logic of kingpins now rubs shoulders with graphs of local-ized Mexican homicide rates, 3-D charts of cartel behavior, and complex regression analyses. They dot academic journals. They fill the schedules of new think tanks and scholarly centers. Drug prohibition, it seems, has gen-erated yet another industry.

Researchers point to several changes that help explain the scale of the new conflicts. Shifts in American drug tastes changed the geography of Mexico's drug trade once more. Cocaine was a boom-time narcotic. But with the 2008 financial crash, the boom time ended. Cocaine users nearly halved overnight. U.S. users now switched to marijuana, methampheta-mines, and increasingly, opiates. More and more Americans had been turning to heroin after the federal ban on prescribing opiate-based pain medications in 2003. In the next decade, heroin use tripled.

To meet the need for marijuana and opiates, traffickers returned to their old haunts in the mountains of the Sierra Madre Occidental, where they teamed up with local village leaders in states like Nayarit, Michoacán, Guerrero, and Oaxaca to produce acres of poppies and weed. Potent, artisan-made black tar heroin, produced in rural cook shops, returned to U.S. streets. By 2014, the DEA estimated, Mexico had over 26,000 hectares devoted to poppy production. It produced 50 tons of heroin per year. It was ten times what Mexicans had produced during the 1970s. And it was killing around ten times as many Americans.

Traffickers also moved to control access to west coast ports like Lázaro Cárdenas and Manzanillo. Here they imported pseudoephedrine from Asia to make into methamphetamine. Outside the ports in the villages of Michoacán and Colima, you could smell the acrid stink of meth wafting out of small hillside shacks.

The other big change that worsened the violence was the availability of guns. In 2004, President George W. Bush ended the Public Safety and Recreational Firearms Use Protection Act. The act had prevented the sale of semiautomatic assault weapons to civilians. Lifting the ban generated a global boom in gun manufacture and gun sales. Many were sold to U.S. citizens. But many were also smuggled south to arm Mexico's cartels.

Mexico, since the 1970s, had gun laws very different from those of the United States. They were some of the strictest in the world. The country had a single gun shop located on a military base. And to get a gun license, a Mexican citizen needed to pass a series of stringent background checks with the Ministry of Defense. To circumvent these laws, traffickers went shopping north of the border. There were over 6,000 gun stores in the American Southwest. They were all within less than an hour's drive of the border.

Quite how many guns these stores sold to the cartels, no one really knew. (Asking this kind of thing was deemed unconstitutional.) In 2013 the United Nations suggested that there were over 20,000 being smuggled into Mexico per year. The U.N. number was probably an underestimate. Between December 2006 and July 2010 the Mexican forces confiscated 85,511 weapons. Ninety percent came from the United States. And whatever the numbers, these new imports were certainly having an effect. Homicides caused by guns accounted for just 15 percent of Mexico's murders in 1997. Twenty years later, they made up two-thirds.

If smuggling drugs had gotten easier, so had smuggling guns. And if the drug trade was killing Americans, the gun trade was now killing Mexicans. It was the borderlands version of Newton's third law of motion.

Changes in American narcotics demands and the gun market were significant, but scholars also point to other changes that began in Mexico.

For the first time since the Mexican Revolution, drug traffickers started to sell drugs in bulk to the domestic drug market. The move probably started in Baja California, where smugglers connected to the Arellano Félix brothers began to establish small *tienditas*, or drug shops. They sold meth, marijuana, and cocaine. But local trade spread across the length of the border. By 2008, cocaine and its derivatives had replaced inhalants as Mexicans' drug of choice. Over 2 percent of Mexicans regularly took the product, a tenfold increase in just over twenty years.

Drug use was focused in tourist areas (like Cancún and Acapulco) and in the border cities of Tijuana, Ciudad Juárez, and Matamoros. In Ciudad Juárez, the shooting galleries pioneered by La Nacha had expanded from a few hundred to around 2,000. They fed an estimated 150,000 addicts, or a rather staggering 10 percent of the city's population. In poorer barrios, crack pipes, coke wraps, and syringes now littered the streets. But it wasn't just in the big cities. By the end of the decade, a person could go to the outskirts of any small town and pick up hard drugs for personal use with relative ease. Cartel gunmen from rural Michoacán frequently mentioned the welcome anesthetizing effects of meth, marijuana, or even heroin.

Small local drug gangs, often only nominally attached to the larger trafficking networks, started to fight over control of drug selling areas. Corner dealers, tit-for-tat murders, and drive-by shootings increased.

But perhaps the most devastating change to criminal practices had precious little to do with drugs at all.

During the Calderón presidency, the more entrepreneurial gangs moved beyond narcotics completely. Instead, they took the practice of running protection rackets, which they had taken over from the state during the 1990s, and started to apply it to all manner of illicit and licit businesses. Those that controlled the regional rackets, or "plazas," no longer exclusively charged the old drug smugglers. Now they imposed protection fees on any commercial venture from selling knockoff DVDs, to vending medicines, to farming avocados. And as these regional rackets no longer needed narcotics, they spread from the old smuggling and growing zones to cover most of country.

The Gulf Cartel's enforcers, the Zetas, led the way. The Zetas were what one security expert has called "a point of inflection" for Mexican organized crime. Traffickers had been employing bodyguards since at least the 1980s. But the Zetas were something different. They weren't local paramilitaries (like the Guadalajara crowd). And they weren't local police (like the Ciudad Juárez gang) or local posh kids (like the Tijuana mob).

They were violence professionals. And, more important, they weren't local; they had no ties or allegiances to the places they commanded. It was just territory to exploit. Most were former members of the Mexican special forces, or GAFE. They came from the army's traditional recruiting zones of southern and central Mexico. In 1997 they had been sent to work as federal cops on the northeastern border. But they had either resigned or deserted and instead joined the Gulf Cartel as bodyguards.

As the conflicts increased, the reputation of the Zetas grew to monstrous proportions. Stories abounded. Some were the products of the organization's secrecy; others, twisted propaganda; others, flat-out fabrications. At their core, there were thirty, or forty, or fifty original GAFE operatives. (One observer remarked that they increased "like Gremlins," multiplying not with water but rather by contact with government rhetoric.) They were recruiting Guatemalan military death squads. They were hiring Gurkhas. They were running training camps manned by Mossad agents. They were an intercontinental death cult, worshiping the skeletal figure of the Santa Muerte (Saint Death), feeding their victims to caged tigers, or to their leader, Heriberto Lazcano Lazcano. ("All that was missing was Darth Vader," the same observer remarked.)

Setting such myths aside, the Zetas did popularize a spectacularly violent new way of making money. At first, they stayed within the traditions of Mexican trafficking groups—at least those established during the 1990s. They simply started to extend the drug protection rackets into new areas. They began in the northeast, charging local smugglers fees for moving drugs through regions they controlled. Then they moved south, to the ports and cities along the Caribbean coast, where independent gangs brought in cocaine in high-powered boats. And they went west to the weed- and opium-growing areas of Guerrero and Michoacán. Locals were shocked.

They said that anyone who grew marijuana had to pay them. People in my part of the mountains are rough and a lot of them told these men to fuck themselves. And then bodies started appearing on the streets. And people started paying up.

But soon the Zetas moved away from narcotics. It made sense. They weren't traffickers. They had limited contacts with Colombian cocaine exporters, or Asian chemical magnates, or Chicago street gangs. And they had little of the patience, skill, or business sense that putting together a narcotics network demanded.

Instead, they specialized in what they were good at—protection rackets. And they started to enforce protection rackets on all sorts of businesses. They started with the illegal ones. Units of ten to fifteen Zetas descended on cities throughout Mexico. They met the local car thieves, the illegal loggers, the CD and DVD pirates, the housebreakers, the kidnappers, and the local policemen, who had previously taken a cut of such businesses. They now ordered these groups to pay the Zetas a monthly fee. Those that refused or were unable to pay were killed.

The scheme was quick, efficient, and brutal. In 2007, Zetas arrived in the commercial center of Torreón. They immediately kidnapped a local police chief and filmed him listing the city's illegal enterprises. The chief was never seen again. They then sent a letter—together with the film—to local business representatives. Anyone the police chief mentioned was now ordered to pay off the Zetas. Those that refused were threatened with "irreversible consequences."

22 DE MAYO DE 2007

ABOGADO ███████████ NOS DIRIJIMOS A TI PORQUE
TENEMOS INFORMACIÓN PREVIA DE QUE TIENES RELACIÓN
ESTRECHA CON ALTOS FUNCIONARIOS Y EMPRESARIOS DE LA
REGIÓN Y QUEREMOS QUE SEAS EL CONDUCTO PARA HACER DE
SU CONOCIMIENTO ,LLAMESE EN ESTE CASO SOCIOS DE
CANACINTRA ,GEL Y CLIP INFORMACIÓN CONTENIDA EN CD YA
QUE DICHA INFORMACION VA A INTERESAR TANTO A
EMPRESARIOS COMO A LA SOCIEDAD EN GENERAL.

CON ESTO ACLARAREMOS QUE NOSOTROS, NO VENIMOS A
ROBAR A NADIE SIMPLEMENTE VENIMOS A HACER NEGOCIO.

ACLARANDO QUE SERA MOLESTADA LA PERSONA QUE TENGA
NEGOCIOS ILICITOS FUERA DE NUESTRA ORGANIZACIÓN.

ESTA ES UNA PETICIÓN DE CARACTER URGENTE E IRREVOCABLE.

EXIGIENDOLE REALICE LAS GESTIONES NECESARIAS PARA
ENVIR DICHO CD A LAS PERSONAS ANTES MENCIONADAS,
TENIENDO COMO LIMITE DE PLAZO PARA LA CONCLUSIÓN, Y
EJECUCIÓN DE DICHA PETICIÓN, EL DIA MIERCOLES 23 DE MAYO
DEL 2007 A LAS 1200 HORAS.

ENTENDIENDOSE QUE POSTERIOR A LA EXHIBICIÓN DE DICHO CD
SE LLEVARA A CABO REUNION DE PERSONAL DE NUESTRA
COMPAÑIA Y PERSONAS DEL SISTEMA EMPRESARIAL PARA
LLEVAR ACUERDOS QUE PLANTEAREMOS EN SU MOMENTO
ASI COMO ACLARAR DUDAS E INQUIETUDES QUE TENGAN.

SIN MAS POR EL MOMENTO SE LE INFORMA QUE CUALQUIER
DESACATO ANTE DICHA PETICIÓN, TENDRA CONSECUENCIAS
IRREVERSIBLES PARA CON SU PERSONA Y SOCIOS DEL SISTEMA
EMPRESARIAL

ATENTAMENTE
CARTEL DEL GOLFO.
GRUPO Z

*During the 2000s, the Zetas started to extend protection rackets over both licit and illicit businesses. This letter was sent to a prominent Torreón lawyer. It demands that the businessmen of the region meet the Zetas demands or face the consequences.*

Next, the Zetas moved to the licit world. They tracked down shopkeepers, farmers, and small business owners and demanded that they also pay regular fees. These were often small—between 200 and 500 pesos. Yet they could build up, especially after the economic crash of 2008, and especially when nearly half of Mexicans earned less than 600 pesos a week. And again, the punishments for nonpayment were brutal. Burly men armed with semiautomatics now visited car mechanics in small-town Michoacán, taxi drivers in Veracruz, or cantina owners in Oaxaca City in the middle of the night and demanded a cut of the profits.

> If not, they said they would kill my wife and my children. Then they would kill me. I knew they weren't joking. They had already disappeared a lot of others.

The Zetas soon found that the most vulnerable were the easiest to squeeze. They were also the least risky; the chance of any comeback was essentially zero. In San Fernando, near the Mexico–Texas border they set up an extortion production line. They employed the local police to drag the Central American migrants off the buses that crossed the town. Or they scoured the streets of Matamoros and Nuevo Laredo looking for recent deportees. They brought these victims back to San Fernando, where they beat them, cut them, tied them to the back of trucks, and dragged them through the streets. They forced them to phone their relatives and demand money for their release. Those that couldn't pay were killed or sold as prostitutes or forced to become cartel lookouts.

Highway 101, which passed through San Fernando, became known as the "highway of death." In 2010 the authorities found seventy-two dead migrants on a farm in the area. They had all been shot in the head. Less than a year later, they uncovered another 193 bodies dumped into a dozen hastily dug graves.

The importance of this change in criminal practices cannot be underestimated. In less than a decade the Zetas extended the old drug protection rackets first to other criminals and then to everyday citizens. By the middle of Calderón's reign, they were alleged to extract fees in at least half of the country's states.

Other criminal groups soon adopted similar tactics. Even the Zetas' opponents took note. The Familia Michoacana had announced its arrival by hurling five Zetas' heads onto a barroom floor and declaring that it was firmly against such indiscriminate extortion. Yet within less than a year it was doing exactly the same. At one point, analysts estimated that criminals were charging protection from as many as 85 percent of Michoacán licit businesses from small stores and lime farms through to large multinational mining conglomerates. By 2012 that old plaza term—the *derecho de piso*, or fee—had become general Mexican slang. Everyone knew someone who was paying.

As the criminals diversified and the protection rackets spread, the violence increased. During the Calderón era, tens of thousands of murders were listed as "drug-related." Yet all this really meant was that the presumed perpetrators had at least a passing interest in the drug trade. The motive was increasingly unlikely to concern access to narcotics or trafficking corridors. Instead, it was frequently about the messy business of extracting protection money.

Yet, if the bloodshed of the past fifteen years has been shaped by recent changes to drug markets, firepower, and patterns of everyday crime, it also has longer-term roots. The two triggers for the sudden explosions of violence that wracked border cities like Nuevo Laredo, Tijuana, and Ciudad Juárez and caused the majority of drug-related homicides were the same triggers that had been causing drug violence for nearly a century. They were the struggle between powerful groups for the control of particular drug protection rackets and the pursuit of aggressive counternarcotics policing.

No doubt, as before, these had their own stand-alone consequences. But these factors now mixed and intertwined on a grander scale, in more damaging ways, and in a compound fashion. Struggles between rival groups sparked aggressive policing; and aggressive policing, in turn, generated increasing struggles between rival groups.

As violence increased, both Mexican and American police services put increasing pressure on drug traffickers to inform on other traffickers. Such a strategy had been part of drug policing for decades. But now the authorities repeatedly employed the tactic despite knowing that the consequences could be catastrophic.

The authorities called the strategy "divide and conquer." At best, police forces felt that they were taking advantage of existing divisions; they were arresting or assassinating traffickers who would soon be dead anyway. Those who got in the way—or were killed as suspected informants—were unfortunate collateral.

At worst, it was the Mexican and the U.S. authorities that were deliberately causing many of the divisions between trafficking groups. And once these fissures had been exposed, they effectively wedged them open. Divisions encouraged informants, which in turn generated high-level arrests. Divisions delivered up kingpins, they secured the funding for institutions, and they made careers. Those who got in the way—or were killed as suspected informants—were traffickers anyway. As long as they coughed up their networks before they died, who cared?

Perhaps the best way to illustrate how old and new forces interlinked in potent and destructive ways is to look closely at the conflict that devastated Ciudad Juárez in the last years of the decade.

In late 2007, gunmen from the Sinaloa Cartel started to arrive in Ciudad Juárez. Their mission—to take over the city's drug protection racket, or plaza. They numbered at least 500 and squatted in dozens of half-finished houses in the sprawling slums to the south and west. They called themselves the "the New Arrivals." And they started by killing the Juárez Cartel's enforcers. These were dubbed "the Line" and most—as they had been under Amado Carrillo Fuentes—were still local cops.

By the end of January 2008, the New Arrivals made their intentions clear. Sinaloa gunmen exited a dark sedan, walked up to the city's monument to dead police officers, and placed two white poster boards at the foot of the statue. On one they wrote, "For those who did not believe." Beneath were the names of five dead "the Line" policemen. On the other, they wrote, "For those who still do not believe." Beneath were the names of seventeen more Ciudad Juárez cops. This became known as "the black list," a register of intended victims.

Shootouts between the New Arrivals and the Line became frequent. On February 23, 2008, cameras beamed a firefight live on TV. It was in broad daylight on one of the city's main streets. Gunmen fired .50-caliber machine guns at each other as they crouched behind cars or ducked behind the doors of the family restaurants that lined the street. Off-camera, there were also kidnappings and murders. The federal police that raided drugs and arms stashes would often find corpses, partially dissolved in slaked lime, buried in hastily dug graves out back.

Both the Sinaloa and the Juárez Cartels increasingly swelled their ranks with young members of the city's smaller gangs. There were over 500 of these organizations, from relatively large cross-border groups like Los Aztecas to smaller cliques that barely covered a city block like "the Fucked Up." The cartels gave these new recruits high-powered guns, a measure of protection, and an enemy to attack. The intercartel conflict quickly meshed with and transformed into dozens of small-scale fights. The kind of every-day beefs over girls, over tagging walls, and over who sold weed where now became bloody conflicts.

To try to quell the violence, Calderón reacted according to script and sent in troops and federal police. They only made the situation worse.

Immediately, murders leapt up. Locals thought the soldiers as dangerous as the traffickers: they dubbed them "the military cartel." There were immediate accusations of torture, arbitrary detention, forced entry, property damage, and disappearances. And there were rumors of army-run death squads targeting the small local gangs and committing "social cleansing." Most commonly, soldiers dragged suspects from their houses, took them to the base, and proceeded to demand information by dunking their heads underwater, shocking them with Tasers, or covering their heads with plastic bags. In 2009 alone, there were 1,400 human rights complaints. One community spokesman declared, "Abu Ghraib would be a kindergarten compared to the military camp here in Ciudad Juárez."

The lucky ones were forced to confess and handed over to the police. But many didn't return at all. On December 29, 2009, troops dragged away José Ángel Alvarado Herrera and his cousin, Nitza Paola Alvarado, outside their house. Later, their relatives asked for their whereabouts at the local military base. But the soldiers refused to acknowledge taking them. On February 3, 2010, Nitza phoned her parents and got out the words, "Help me, get me out of here, I'm still alive" before being cut off. It was the last they heard of her.

The federal police were just as bad. Under security chief Genaro García Luna, the organization grew. In 2006 there were 6,500 federal cops; by 2012 there were 37,000. They were more educated than ever before (8,000 had university degrees!); they were better armed; and they were better organized. But their tactics were distinctly old-school. Human rights abuses climbed almost in lock step with increasingly numbers. They were the usual litany of torture, threats, attacks on family members, false imprisonment, attacks on property, and murder.

One Juárez woman, who had escaped to the United States, told me how police had stormed her house in March 2009. They were looking for her husband, a former cop and a suspected trafficker. They grabbed her two-year-old child off the bed, held him by the leg, and dangled him headfirst over the bath. They threatened to drown him if she didn't reveal her husband's whereabouts. When she went to complain to the local human rights office, the same cops tracked her down and arrested her. They picked up her brother at the same time. She never saw him again.

How many of the bodies slung onto Ciudad Juárez trash heaps or secreted in hidden graves in the desert were put there by the military or the police?

Aside from the trauma for the victims and their families, Calderón's strategy of aggressive policing also created and cemented divisions between trafficking groups. Threatened with capture, torture, or assassination, many Mexican traffickers now decided that the safest policy was to work—at least in part—with the authorities. It became less of a hasty survival mechanism and more of a studied combat strategy. They sent out emissaries to U.S. and Mexican agencies and employed informers to snitch on their enemies.

The group that was most successful at pursuing this strategy was the Sinaloa Cartel. So while Sinaloa gunmen were assassinating Ciudad Juárez's small-time dealers, cartel hitmen, and local cops, the Sinaloa chiefs—Joaquín "El Chapo" Guzmán and Ismael "El Mayo" Zambada—were also cooperating with the authorities.

In general, they used Guzmán's lawyer, Humberto Loya Castro, to leak the information to the U.S. and the Mexican agents. They began this strategy as early as the 1990s, selling out the rival Arellano Félix brothers in return for limited state interference. Zambada's son explained the system:

> [El Chapo said] that Loya was with the DEA with his permission and that all they were doing, all the detentions and all of that was on the information of him and my father, and that it was the DEA that acted together with the Mexican government.

As the pressure increased, the Sinaloa chiefs also used this system to fight the war in Ciudad Juárez. They employed a former city police captain to operate as an intermediary between their organization and U.S. agents. He gave the authorities the names of corrupt fellow cops and Juárez Cartel killers. The authorities then either arrested or killed them.

And when the pressure got too much, the Sinaloa chiefs used the strategy to turn on their own associates. Zambada's son even started to give intel to the DEA. The cooperation allowed the Calderón government to make dozens of high-level arrests. They included members of the Juárez Cartel, former Arellano Félix hitmen, independent Culiacán smugglers, and even—so the rumors went—Guzmán's own cousin, Alfredo Beltrán Leyva, who was arrested in January 2008.

Yet the strategy had devastating secondary effects. Selling out allies like Beltrán Leyva may have appeased the drug hawks, who captured another kingpin. And it may have kept Zambada and Guzmán out of jail. But it also started another round of bloody conflicts. Zambada and Guzmán now not only confronted the Juárez Cartel and the Zetas but also the Beltrán Leyva brothers. New struggles involved new fronts, and fighting broke out in Sinaloa and in the Beltrán Leyva stronghold of Acapulco.

The strategy also led to repeated accusations—first by rival cartels, then by journalists—of a tacit agreement between the Sinaloa Cartel and the authorities. According to these charges, the authorities were doing the Sinaloa Cartel's dirty work, and they were probably taking Sinaloa bribes in order to do so. Such accusations eventually culminated in the arrest of Calderón's chief security official, Genaro García Luna, by U.S. agents in 2019.

García Luna currently awaits trial. But whether the former security chief is personally guilty or not, there is no doubt that many officials did take Sinaloa money. Why not take a life-changing sum of cash to follow a tip-off and arrest a killer?

Yet, in reality, such collusion was not simply a matter of money or corruption. It was embedded in the process of drug war policing. To get arrests, you needed informants. To get informants you essentially had to back one group against another. And when rivalries didn't exist, you needed to create them.

Divide and conquer. What looked like intercartel struggles were often just extensions of drug policing. It was the drug war's dirty little secret. It was covered up by the traffickers, who didn't want to reveal themselves as snitches. And it was covered up by the authorities, who didn't want to unmask themselves as the authors of so much of the resulting bloodshed.

This combination of cartel conflicts over protection rackets, gang fights, and aggressive policing generated what the Ciudad Juárez mayor called "a perfect storm." The homicide rate skyrocketed. Murders increased from just over 200 in 2007 to 1,580 in 2008. By 2010 there were 3,798. It was a homicide rate of 272 per 100,000. Only two cities had ever outpaced the border city's murder rate—Medellín in the 1990s and Baghdad in 2006.

The subsequent conflict between the Sinaloa kingpins and the Beltrán Leyva brothers generated similar upsurges. In May 2008 the brothers' gunmen murdered Guzmán's son Édgar Guzmán López in a Culiacán parking lot. And over the next six months the official number of homicides in Sinaloa increased threefold. Hundreds more were kidnapped, killed, and buried in unmarked graves.

# Epilogue

## *Drugs and Violence*

ISELA REMEMBERS THE DAY THEY CAME. "IT WAS APRIL 3 [2014]. IT WAS MY daughter's birthday." They rode into the suburb on the edge of Acapulco in the back of Ford F-150s; they wore ski masks and carried automatic rifles slung over their shoulders. One had a pistol in his belt. Isela and her family were sitting around the table in the back of their small shop. It was early evening and they had just finished singing the Mexican version of "Happy Birthday": "Las Mañanitas." They were divvying up her daughter's favorite dessert, a tres leches cake.

They heard the sound of engines outside the shop. Isela thought it was probably one of the neighbors showing off a new car. But suddenly two men burst into the shop. The family dog barked a frightened warning. One man raised his pistol and shot the dog dead. "It was so loud, so unexpected, we all screamed." He looked around the shop, spied the fridge full of cold *caguamas* (liter beers) and proceeded to stuff them into a rucksack. The other man walked toward the family. "We are La Maña; we own this place now. You pay us, not the government, not the army, not that fat fuck Beto. You pay us. Now where's the fucking money." Isela father pointed to a metal box up on one of the shelves. The man emptied the contents into his pocket; then they left.

La Maña (the Knack or the Skill) was the local slang for what security analysts and drug agents precisely termed the Independent Cartel of Acapulco or CIDA. The group appeared in their formal charts and intricate color-coded maps. They claimed that it was an offshoot of the southern branch of the Beltrán Leyva Cartel, and it was now fighting for control of the drug trade with other groups, including "the Reds" and "the Squirrels."

But for Isela and her family, it was just La Maña. It was both less defined and more terrifying. It was manned by a group of street kids and drunks; it was run by "El Chino," a young, tattooed man rumored to be a former soldier; and it was involved in a turf war with a former policeman also known as "that fat fuck Beto." Isela was never privy to the inner logic of El Chino or La Maña, but the goal didn't seem to be some prized drug transshipment route or even control of the suburb's drug retail market. "I didn't know anyone who did drugs. Everyone in the Colonia Altamira, we were just young families."

For Isela the goal seemed to be extortion, or more precisely, the monopoly control of the suburb's extortion racket.

> From then on La Maña had the derecho de piso. They charged everyone, shop owners, businessmen, truck drivers, even the schools had to pay. And if you didn't pay, they gave you one chance and then they killed you … just like that.

At this point, Isela started to choke up. Her husband, Luis, who was also sitting in the Oakland lawyer's office, took up the story.

> They wanted so much. First it was 500 pesos [a week]. Then they found out that we also had a commercial oven, so they wanted 1000 pesos. Then they demanded 10,000 pesos. They said that they would leave us alone afterwards. But where were we going to get 10,000 pesos from?

On October 6, 2014, Luis, his uncle, and his brother left the shop to go into the center of Acapulco. They were going to pick up a part for the oven. Just before they got to the end of the road, a Ford F-150 pulled up beside them. One masked man stuck his head out of the window. "We're going to fuck you up for not paying." Then there was the noise; the deafening sound of automatic gunfire. Luis still has no memory of what happened next. When he woke up, he was in the hospital with a bullet in his chest and another in his arm. His uncle was also gravely wounded. His brother had been shot dead at the scene.

After 2012, the Mexican government employed the same militarized counternarcotics policies as President Calderón. And they had the same effects. Soldiers killed civilians; trafficking groups became increasingly divided. Divide and conquer. As Isela discovered, these smaller gangs were still termed cartels. But now they mostly engaged in other forms of crime. In fact, by the mid-2010s the everyday violence that most Mexicans experienced had little to do with the drug trade at all.

And despite government tactics, the flow of drugs northward continued unabated. Incentives remained high; the demand for opiates in particular boomed. And traffickers adapted to the shifting U.S. market, moving smoothly from marijuana to heroin to the synthetic opiate fentanyl. For American addicts, it is as if the drug war never happened. Now it is cheaper and easier to get high than ever before.

In 2012, voters kicked out the PAN and elected a president from the old PRI party. A slick, photogenic politician, married to a soap star, Enrique Peña Nieto also had a prestigious heritage. He was close to the former president Carlos Salinas and part of the Atlacomulco group, a famed inner circle of well-connected and politically able PRI apparatchiks. Many anticipated that such contacts would help the president negotiate a new status quo with the country's trafficking organizations.

At first, hopes were high. Peña Nieto promised to focus on the reduction of violence rather than the elimination of drug trafficking. He cut the overt links between his administration and the U.S. drug police. And he ended the shrill anticartel rhetoric that had marked Calderón's regime. He wore suits, not ill-fitting army fatigues. He concentrated on pushing ambitious new education and petroleum laws through Congress.

Initially, the approach seemed to work; homicides didn't halve as Peña Nieto promised. But they did decrease by 15 percent during his first year. (Though some cynics speculated that officials were massaging the figures and gunmen were simply burying the bodies deeper.) In public, newspapers lauded the new president's regime. In February 2014, *Time* magazine even published a front cover of a beaming Peña Nieto with the words "Saving Mexico" across his chest. Off the front pages, even security experts seemed impressed. They pointed knowingly to the Colombian officials who had "beaten" the Colombian cartels and now advised Peña Nieto.

Yet such hopes were short-lived. Whatever political skills Peña Nieto's allies brought, they relied on the same defunct institutions and the same tired, counterproductive strategies.

Mexico's security forces were particularly ill suited to any kind of peacekeeping role. Initial proposals to reform the police and create a new national gendarmerie failed almost immediately. Big plans to bring in 40,000 young recruits were shelved; and when the new institution eventually took to the streets in 2014, it consisted of little more than 5,000 former cops. Initiatives to bring together Mexico's 1,600 town police forces under single state commands also failed.

The army, which had often been Calderón's go-to security solution, was equally ineffective. Wages were still low; morale, rock-bottom; and corruption, endemic. Desertions were common. "I think of my battalion, around half of us left, I was one of the last to go," confessed one soldier who had fled his post for the United States in 2014. "All we did was guard the merchandise for the narcos. And we never saw any of it. It all went to the general." (It was a testament to the fear he still felt that he refused to name this general despite the threat of deportation.)

Furthermore, there were increasing reports of official atrocities that even Peña Nieto's upbeat press campaigns found difficult to hide. In June 2014, troops executed twenty-two civilians suspected of links to Michoacán traffickers in the village of Tlatlaya. In January 2015, federal police officers shot dead sixteen unarmed protesters outside Apatzingán's city hall. And

five months later, the federal police—backed by a helicopter gunship—
shot dead over forty suspected cartel members just outside the town of
Ecuandureo, also in Michoacán. Though the police claimed it was a firefight, none of their colleagues died, and three-quarters of the dead gunmen
had been shot in the head at point-blank range.

Most notoriously, on September 26, 2014, gunmen kidnapped and
killed forty-three students from the Ayotzinapa teaching training college in
Guerrero. Initially, the government claimed that organized criminals in
league with local officials had mistaken the students for cartel rivals and
killed them. But doubts immediately arose. Despite dozens of arrests, official investigators were unable to find any of the students' remains.
Subsequent investigators concluded that the federal police and the nearby
army battalion had also been involved in the massacre. They speculated
that the remains were most probably stashed in the army base.

Furthermore, though Peña Nieto was reluctant to play the strutting
strongman, his government continued to pursue the policy of arresting or
killing "high value" drug-trafficking targets. Such an approach had a name.
It was what the DEA dubbed the "kingpin" strategy and was designed to
break up leadership structures and trafficking networks. Quite why Peña
Nieto adopted such a strategy remains unclear. Was it the advice of his
Colombian advisors who thought the tactic had functioned with Pablo
Escobar in Medellín? Was it at the covert behest of the Americans? Or was
it a throwback to the old 1970s barbarians-of-the-north tactic of cowing
traffickers before forcing them into a deal on the PRI's terms.

Whatever the underlying reason, Peña Nieto's regime took down many
of what they claimed to be Mexico's most important traffickers. In 2013,
officials boasted that in just a year they had killed or captured 69 out of 122
cartel leaders, including the feared Zeta leader, Miguel Ángel Treviño
Morales, or Z-40. And in February 2014, Mexican marines, with DEA
help, caught the Sinaloa trafficker Joaquín "El Chapo" Guzmán in a
Mazatlán hotel.

The arrest, which seemed to cap off an impressive first fourteen
months, actually proved to be a disaster. A year after his arrest, Guzmán
fled from Mexico's leading high-security facility using a tunnel. It was clear
that he had high-level help. The escape was not only utterly humiliating for

the Peña Nieto regime, but also prevented his government from retreating from their kingpin policy even if it wanted to. Instead, intense U.S. pressure meant officials were forced to redouble their efforts.

In January 2016, Mexican police finally caught Guzmán, and a year later he was extradited to the United States. At the same time, now with the close cooperation of the United States, they continued to eliminate other "high value" targets. By the end of Peña Nieto's presidency, they had killed or captured 110 on the 122-man list.

Yet by 2018 it was clear that such an approach was completely ineffective. In fact, it was the very dilution of every bad drug war policy—big show; all blowback; no beneficial effects.

What it did do was what aggressive drug policing always did, but now on a countrywide scale. First, as U.S. and American agents put pressure on certain traffickers to sell out others, it split networks. Paranoia increased; bodyguards turned on capos and smugglers on wholesalers; informants or suspected informants were killed; and any residual trust disappeared. Even the bonds between the old Sinaloa families diminished, and Ismael "El Mayo" Zambada's family members turned on their old ally Guzmán.

Second, after leaders were captured, their lieutenants inevitably fought to control what remained. Front-page captures were almost inevitably followed by escalating murder rates. In the wake of Guzmán's 2016 arrest, Dámaso López Núñez, Guzmán's right-hand man, battled Guzmán's sons. In 2017, murders in Sinaloa increased by over a third.

Third, as established networks dissolved, organizations fractured. By the end of 2018, Mexicans confronted a bewildering landscape of cartel factions and criminal gangs. Quite how many, no one really knew. It depended on how you were counting. Incoming president Andrés Manuel López Obrador recognized the existence of thirty-seven cartels, a step up from the half-dozen around in 2006. Crisis Group Mexico listed 463 criminal gangs and speculated that this was probably an underestimate.

These new gangs were small and isolated. They often had little contact with Colombian cocaine magnates, Asian pharmaceutical wholesalers, or cross-border smugglers. So, as Isela discovered, they kept their U.S.-bought guns; they kept the same cartel identities (what better way to instill fear than tap into the country's most fearsome subculture); and they turned to other forms of crime. These included extortion but also kidnapping, robbery, forced sex work, human trafficking, illegal logging, illegal mining, and the theft of gasoline.

Few Mexicans denounced these crimes to the police. (In a country where less than 1 percent of crimes were ever solved, they saw little point.) So statistics were endlessly debated. But some stood out. Surveys estimated that around a third of Mexican citizens suffered a crime in any given year. And around 70 percent felt insecure in their town or city. During any year around a third of victims were robbed but nearly a fifth experienced the kind of extortion that Isela and her family suffered. Kidnapping, in particular, is almost impossible to quantify; it is almost never reported. But in one particularly alarming report, the Mexican statistics office speculated that there might be as many as 100,000 kidnappings every year. Or to put it another way, one Mexican got kidnapped every six minutes.

These depressingly everyday crimes were joined by a host of innovative practices. Stealing gasoline and tapping petrol lines became so popular that it even acquired shorthand slang. Criminals who engaged in the practice were dubbed *huachicoleros*, an old indigenous term for the runners of illegal alcohol stills, now repurposed for a new criminal age. There was even a patron saint of fuel thieves. El Santo Niño Huachicol, a Christ child holding a siphon and a jerry can, now shares Mexico's underworld pantheon with Jesús Malverde (the patron saint of drug traffickers), San Judas Tadeo (the patron saint of addicts), and the Santa Muerte.

Nowhere were such changes clearer than in the small, rather conservative state of Guanajuato just a couple of hundred miles northwest of Mexico City. Until recently, Guanajuato was known for its leather goods, its colonial architecture, and its petrol refineries. It has not been mentioned in this book before and with good reason. It has no real history of drug growing. (Though in the early twentieth century, weed aficionados did claim that the state produced Mexico's best marijuana.) It has no port to introduce precursors; it has no discernible chemicals industry; it has no entry point to the United States; and though it lies on a road from the drug-growing regions of Michoacán up to the Mexico–Texas border, there are plenty of other available routes to move heroin and meth.

Yet between 2013 and 2018, annual murders in Guanajuato increased by nearly 400 percent—from 700 to 3,412. It was the most of any Mexican state. Here at least half-a-dozen local gangs fought for control of a variety of criminal enterprises. In the big industrial city of León, conflicts centered on selling weed and crystal meth to the unemployed youths unable to find work in the declining leather goods factories. In mid-sized towns, like Guanajuato and Celaya, they focused on kidnapping and extortion. While around the big Salamanca oil refinery, groups struggled to monopolize the theft of petroleum.

Some of these gangs claimed broad national affiliation. The Cártel de Jalisco Nueva Generación—which both the Mexican and American authorities regularly described as Mexico's most powerful drug cartel—was involved. But so were much smaller local groups, including the Santa Rosa de Lima Cartel, a media-savvy group of bandits, kidnappers, and fuel thieves from around Celaya, or the Unión León, a gang of drug peddlers and petty criminals who worked the streets of León.

These new groups with their new crimes pushed rates of violence even higher. In 2010, at the height of the Ciudad Juárez conflict, Mexico had registered 24,374 murders. In 2019 the country suffered over 36,000.

Yet if Peña Nieto's kingpin strategy fragmented trafficking organizations, it did nothing to stop the flow of narcotics heading north. Divide, perhaps; conquer, less so. As usual, the trade had a completely independent rhythm, connected to the fluctuations in U.S. tastes. So though some gangs fought, the economic incentives remained so powerful that trafficking groups frequently came together to organize transnational trades. And peasants often decided that the punishments for growing opium were less than the risks of poverty, hunger, or traveling and working in the United States.

Since 2012, the demands on the Mexican drug trade have changed radically. Cocaine use failed to recover after its dramatic fall in 2008. And the weed market disappeared almost completely. U.S. legalization of recreational marijuana, first passed in Washington and Colorado, extended to many states. Now in 2020 over two-thirds of Americans can smoke pot legally. A third can do so without a medical certificate. And they no longer have to rely on variable south-of-the-border dope. Instead, they can choose from an array of homegrown strains. (The weed trade, it should be noted, was one of the first industries to embrace Trump's call for America First.)

U.S. opiate use, however, grew. Experts now talked of not one but three interlinking epidemics, one of black-market prescription opioids like OxyContin, another of black tar heroin, and another one of the superstrong synthetic opioid fentanyl. As dealers often mixed all three, controlling doses was tough. This had catastrophic consequences. In 2017 over 70,000 Americans died from opiate overdoses. This was nearly double the total number of car crash victims. In fact, the numbers were so great that they even managed to shave a few months off the country's average life expectancy.

Yet the trade showed little sign of slowing. Since the 1960s, Mexican traffickers have learned to be flexible regarding the fickle tastes of their northern neighbors. So, as cocaine use bottomed out and marijuana demand dropped, traffickers increasingly concentrated on producing opium poppies. Most were still grown in the Golden Triangle and Guerrero, where peasants had been growing them for decades. But the practice also spread throughout many of the poor mountain villages of southern Mexico.

It was there that I first came across their transformative power. I first visited the tiny village of San Pablo (not its real name) in 2007 while researching a book on indigenous religion. It stood on the border between the states of Oaxaca and Guerrero. The first time I was there, what struck me was the silence. There were no cars, no tractors, and no hum of market commerce. Many of the men, I was told, had left to work in the fields of the San Quintín Valley in Baja California. There was an internet café, which doubled as the town's Western Union office; there was a small, tired, adobe church which, if you looked carefully, revealed that it still had some blocks from the old pre-Hispanic temple. Noise, when there was any, came from the morning calls of dozens of caged fighting cocks the local landowner had decided to locate next to what the villagers rather generously termed "the hotel." (It was actually two concrete cells with a shared outdoor

bathroom.) Even religious festivities were quiet, somewhat sad affairs, populated by old couples, women, and bored-looking kids.

By contrast, when I returned in 2015, it was the noise that first hit me.
The town square was flanked by a mass of 4-by-4s and flatbed trucks. It
was evening and many flashed with neon underglow kits. Dozens of young
men stood around; some revved their engines; others blasted out cumbia,
narcocorrido, or reggaeton. The internet café was no more. But the whole
village was a mess of rapid construction. There was a row of clothes shops,
three new hotels, and what would have been called a "pop-up food market"
in London but was in fact six taco stands, two juice stalls, and a hotdog
seller. Even the church had a freshly painted front, gold leaf details, and a
pimped-out marble interior.

Shocked and somewhat concerned that I had arrived in the wrong village, I headed to see the priest. It was the same man I had met eight years
ago. I gave him a copy of my book. He was visibly underwhelmed. "I don't
know English and it's very long. Are there any pictures of the village?"—"Sorry, no." We made small talk and danced around what had tran-
spired. Finally, he relented. "You want to know what has happened?" "Yes,"
I replied. He pointed up the hill behind the church. It was the same answer
the British agronomist Paul Yates had received four decades earlier.
"Poppies."

He shrugged and seemed unconcerned. "At least they know to treat the
saint." He pointed to the flashy new church exterior. Visiting traffickers
now paid farmers around $1,000 for a kilo of opium. In a year—if they
could stretch to two harvests—they could earn enough to pay for a car, a
second storey for their house, or a lavish, weeklong fiesta.

And San Pablo was not alone. Between 2009 and 2017, the hectares
devoted to poppy growing more than doubled, increasing from 19,000 to
44,000 hectares. The Mexican military claimed that over 800—or a
third—of the country's municipalities grew the drug. The crop provided 90
percent of the U.S. heroin market and earned rural producers $1 billion a
year. In all, it was worth nearly double the earnings from the country's
wheat or cotton crops.

For Mexico's poorest, most remote villages, the U.S. opium crisis was a
comparative boom time. It floated rural communities that were struggling

because of the termination of farming subsidies enforced by NAFTA. And it meant that their men did not have to spend years north of the border away from their families. Poppy profits were remittances without the heartache.

Yet if Mexico's traffickers knew how to jump-start a rural drug boom, they also knew how to outlast one.

Around 2015 the demand for heroin started to decline. The United States had not suddenly decided to treat their addicts. The addicts had just got hooked on an alternative—fentanyl. Principally, it was a question of strength. Fentanyl is thirty to fifty times stronger than heroin. But it was also about supply. Chinese fentanyl manufacturers were starting to use the dark web to advertise the narcotic to American dealers. They would then ship the product across the United States cheaply and easily via the Postal Service, DHL, and Fedex. Drugs were meeting the digital economy. U.S. journalists had started to rename America's opium crisis the "fentanyl crisis."

Initially, this cut into Mexican profits. As Americans turned to fentanyl, the street price of heroin fell. It dropped 10 percent in the last quarter of 2016 alone. By the following year, Mexican farmers were suffering similar shortfalls. Visiting buyers now offered them just above $300 per kilo, a 70 percent drop from two years before.

But while village booms declined, Mexico's big traffickers just adapted. First, they started to import fentanyl directly from China, bringing in loads through the west coast ports of Manzanillo and Lázaro Cárdenas and then taking them over the border. But by 2017 they were also importing precursor chemicals, setting up labs, and producing their own versions of the drug. They also started to experiment. They mixed fentanyl with heroin and methamphetamine. They even started to manufacture carfentanil pills, which were 100 times more powerful than fentanyl and usually used on elephants.

Traffickers were not only sensitive to market demands; they were also wise to changes in antismuggling technology. When the U.S. authorities started to use massive X-ray imaging machines to monitor trucks as they crossed the border, the traffickers simply returned to the air and the sea. Some groups constructed massive catapults and flung packages of narcotics over the border to waiting gangs. Others purchased drones, attached small bags of fentanyl, and flew them north. Others started to invest in GPS-directed submersibles and move drugs through the Caribbean.

In fact, Mexican traffickers were so quick to recognize changing demands and shifting technologies that wholesale drug prices in the United States actually dropped over the past decade. This is despite the billions of dollars both governments have spent on police, border guards, guns, armored trucks, and other security paraphernalia. A kilo of heroin that was $73,000 in 2007 was worth just over $50,000 in 2015. A kilo of cocaine dropped around 10 percent in the same period.

If the war on drugs was ever really about pricing out addicts and reducing addiction, it was a dramatic and costly failure.

It is something that the new president has—it seems—recognized. Andrés Manuel López Obrador has also avoided any inflammatory martial rhetoric. (During his campaign, he paraded the slogan *"abrazos, no balazos,"* or "hugs, not bullets"). He has also avoided the counterproductive kingpin strategy. In October 2019, he did this quite explicitly, ordering military units to stand down rather than capture El Chapo Guzmán's son and risk another round of intracartel fighting. He has attempted to refocus concern on U.S. arms smuggling and push money toward social projects in some of Mexico's most deprived areas. And he has reduced the army's rural eradication campaigns.

Yet some problems have not gone away. In 2018, López Obrador ran on a promise to send the soldiers back to the barracks. He was going to end the militarization of the drug war. But the army remains a key public security force. And the new 90,000-strong National Guard—though nominally under civilian control—actually comprises an uneasy blend of former soldiers, former navy personnel, and former members of the notoriously corrupt federal police. Similar accusations of kidnapping, torture, and extrajudicial murder leveled at the security forces during Calderón's and Peña Nieto's regimes have dogged both institutions.

Furthermore, U.S. pressure on Mexican drug policy remains. When Trump was in power, López Obrador managed to evade disapproval by agreeing to American demands to round up and detain Central American migrants. Trump was happy; the drug hawks were quiet. And when the DEA pushed a more aggressive line, arresting the former head of the army General Salvador Cienfuegos in October 2020, the Mexican president pushed back. He threatened to kick the DEA out of Mexico. The Americans capitulated and released Cienfuegos.

But more intense U.S. pressure may return. Without the ability to use Central Americans as bargaining chips, will López Obrador be able to guide Biden the same way he has guided Trump? Will the DEA seek revenge for its humiliation over Cienfuegos?

Such matters of realpolitik may shape future U.S.–Mexican relations; they may even decide the fate of the next few kingpins the Americans choose to demonize and the Mexicans decide to give up. But they provide little comfort to Isela and others like her. The war on drugs has already turned her once-quite-suburban barrio of Acapulco into a no-go zone. El Chino and La Maña have taken over her shop. And if she returns, El Chino and La Maña have vowed to kill her and her surviving family. They remain in Oakland, awaiting the immigration court's decision.

Such realpolitik will also do nothing to the trade itself. As long as narcotics remain illegal, incentives to produce and smuggle them will outweigh any economic alternatives. A handful of authorities on both sides of the border will always take a bribe. And whether the Americans choose to focus on the air, the Eastern Seaboard, or the desert frontier, traffickers will always find a way through. A century and counting; the Mexican drug trade shows no sign of slowing.

# Acknowledgments

MOST HISTORY BOOKS ARE, IN THE END, COLLABORATIVE EFFORTS. THEY are the culmination of the research of hundreds of other scholars and researchers. Yet this book is even more collaborative than most. An extensive Arts and Humanities Research Council grant and a rather less extensive—but nonetheless useful—British Academy Newton grant provided the funds for myself and others to do much of the research that has gone into this book. In particular, I would like to thank my colleagues for these grants—Peter Watt, Wil Pansters, Nathaniel Morris, and Juan Antonio Fernández Velázquez. I would also like to thank my colleagues at the University of Warwick—Mark Philp, Sheilagh Holmes, Katie Klaassen, James Green, Colette Kelly, and David Duncan—whose help in applying for and administering these grants was invaluable.

Thanks must also go to my agent and editors—Will Francis, Tom Mayer, Andrew Goodfellow, Nneoma Amadi-obi, and Suzanne Connelly—who provided such important guidance and encouragement for the project. It may surprise those who have got this far in the book that it was—at one point—around 50 percent longer. You have Tom, in particular, to thank for making the book both shorter and better. You also have Tom to thank for the fact that it does not all read like a James Ellroy offcut. (And you have me to blame for all the bits that do.) Thanks also to Paul Gillingham, who set me off on this journey into the wilds of pop history in the first place.

Though it is based on a lot of research, *The Dope* is not an academic text. Instead, I have tried to reach out to as broad an audience as possible. I hope that my academic colleagues forgive the simplifications and the stylistic tics. In order to make it both readable and broadly correct, I have relied on a group of friends, colleagues, and family members, who read the (uncut) manuscript, pointed out a litany of errors and problems, improved the prose, and molded the final text. In particular, I must thank Sergio Aguayo and Pablo Piccato, whose own works on state repression, crime, violence, and the public sphere have shaped the work of a generation of scholars including my own; Carlos Pérez Ricart, whose sharp mind, filthy footballing, poor running skills, even poorer map-reading skills, pretentious taste in music, and work on Mexican and U.S. counternarcotics policies have proved so entertaining and influential over the past decade; Colby Ristow, an old friend who would love to be all "fine suits, firm handshakes, and veiled menace" but is actually relatively pleasant; Jonathan Marshall, whose knowledge of both the broad arc and finer details of the U.S.–Mexican drug trade is incredible; Regnar Kristensen, John Waller and Andrew Paxman, three friends whose enthusiasm and talent for readable history have been both liberating and influential; and finally Nigel Smith and Alex Buckley, whose own talents at writing clear, understandable, and entertaining English helped shape this book.

Beyond these readers of the text, I must also thank a mass of brilliant, kind, and influential scholars and friends whose work, support, tweets, and encouragement have all helped the production of this book in one way or another. They include Guy Thomson, Javier Garza, Salvador Maldonado, Rebecca Earle, Rosie Doyle, David Anderson, Roger Fagge, David Lambert, Dan Branch, Mark Knight, Joachim Haeberlen, Laura Schwartz, Peter Guardino, Duncan Wood, Michael Lettieri, Meleisa Ono-George, Romain Le Cour Grandmaison, Diana Ávila Hernández, Elizabeth O'Brien, Sarah Osten, Mike Bess, Jay Pan, Adela Cedillo, Alex Aviña, Isaac Campos, Elaine Carey, Nidia Olvera Hernández, Alan Knight, Thom Rath, Bill Booth, Julia McClure, Ben Fallaw, María De Vecchi, Ariel Rodríguez Kuri, Tanalís Padilla, Timo Schaefer, Carlos Flores Pérez, Christy Thornton, Alex Dawson, Natalia Mendoza, Jayson Porter, Louise Walker, Aaron Van Oosterhout, and John Milstead, Back to the Duke, Ed, Susanna, Tom,

Andy and JP, as well as members of the unfortunately named SHAME and the less unfortunately named NORIA. Thanks in particular to all of you who made the journey over to Warwick to discuss the regional history of the Mexican drug trade.

Special thanks must also go to all those journalists, professionals, scholars, and historians who were kind enough to share some of their own research, interviews, and documents with me. They include the Yates family, Alegría Magali Ocaña Salazar, Juan Carlos Ramírez-Pimienta, Amílcar E. Challú, Michael Kenney, Carlos Flores Pérez, Nidia Olvera Hernández, Adela Cedillo, Noah Hurowitz, Sara Daniela Hidalgo Garza, Nicholas Schou, Tony Ricevueto, Phil Jordan, and Paul Cuschieri. Really heartfelt thanks must go to Peter Maguire and Mike Ritter (whose book *Thai Stick* is outstanding and whose knowledge about and contacts with 1960s weed smugglers were invaluable), Douglas Valentine (whose generosity with so many classified documents went way beyond kind), and Craig Pyes (whose insights and early journalism on the 1970s drug war were invaluable). Many of the most interesting findings in this book are really based on their own hard work and discoveries. Finally, I should also thank a handful of journalists not only for their own pathbreaking work, but also for the support they have given me over the years. They include Ioan Grillo (whose *El Narco* is still the best English-language text on the current drug war), J. Jesús Esquivel (whose work on the Camarena killing was so influential), Falko Ernst, Duncan Tucker, and, of course, Anabel Hernández.

The staff at many libraries and archives have been particularly kind and helpful in helping me track down some of the more obscure sources consulted for this book. I feel bound to mention all the staff at the University of Warwick Library, especially those in the Interlibrary Loan office; Claudia Rivers at UTEP Special Collections; everyone in the Archivo General de la Nación's Galleries 1 and 3; the staff at the Archivo Histórico de la Tribunal Superior de Justicia, and the staff at the the Casas de la Cultura Júridica in San Luis Potosí, Ciudad Juárez, and Oaxaca who helped guide me and others through Mexico's labyrinthine judicial archives.

Researching the Mexican drug trade has been in turns fascinating, depressing, surprising, and at least once downright terrifying. But it has— once more—allowed me to spend time among friends and family in Mexico.

This is more than a simple added bonus. It is why I first studied the country and why I keep coming back again and again. In particular, I would like to thank Daniel Gerschenson and Eiji Fukushima, whose friendship has been invaluable and on one occasion, possibly lifesaving; Michael Swanton and Bas Van Doesburg, who always make Oaxaca so enjoyable and entertaining; and as usual my extended family that includes Don Eloy, Doña Catalina, Efrain, Elvia, Eloy, Edith, Michael, Abi, Ceilmor, Didier, Patricia, Jeff, Serafin, Troy, and Melissa.

Finally, I must thank as always my mother, my father, and my sister, Nick, Sue, Sue and Paul, my partner Noemi, and my children. Emilia and Eleanor you have brightened up every day, kept me sane, and still for some reason insist that—despite at least some evidence to the contrary—my principal job is "finding pubs and playing computer games."

# Notes on Sources

THE DOPE IS A WORK OF POPULAR HISTORY. IT IS AIMED AT THOSE WHOSE knowledge of the history of Mexico and narcotics is perhaps limited to *Narcos: Mexico*, Don Winslow's *Cartel* trilogy, or (less likely, I admit) *Viva Knievel!* As such, the text is unencumbered by the usual footnotes, endnotes, and the nods to academic allies. I hope that this makes what is a tough and complex topic more accessible and readable.

Yet *The Dope* is also based on mountains of research by myself, my fellow grant applicants, and two generations of Mexican drug trade scholars. Without this work, this text would be little more than a reiteration of the standard drug war myths. As a result, I have compiled a brief list of the major sources that were consulted for each chapter. This list is not complete. In particular, I have left out a lot of the texts that helped add background to particular regions, cities, political situations, or social milieus. They are not central to the narrative and, as my editors remind me, space is at a premium. The names, for example, of Tijuana's dive bars or Nogales's Canal Street brothels were not picked from thin air, but based on hours of skimming through contemporary tour guides, local newspapers, and eyewitness accounts. My account of corruption in 1940s and 1970s Mexico was based on dozens of secret service reports, newspaper exposés, and U.S. consular memoranda.

I have also left out a lot of my own triangulation, particularly of the drug war statistics. As Peter Andreas and Kelly Greenhall have argued in their wonderful *Sex, Drugs, and Body Counts*, drug statistics are basically like lines of cocaine. The more you know about how they were produced, the less attractive they seem. Many are flat-out false—fictional data based on spurious calculations and designed to defend a particular policy and fund a particular tier of the bureaucracy or the private security industry. Yet statistics are important; they are often the best way to explain the scale of the industry and its shifts over time. As a result, when choosing which statistics to quote, I have usually looked at dozens of sources and chosen those that tie in best with other statistics and more qualitative appreciations of the industry. They are also predominantly (and unless stated as so) low-ball estimates of the Mexican drug trade's size. Carlos Pérez Ricart—in particular—has attempted to keep me honest about this and has a particularly fine nose for bullshit, at least mine.

Though some of the DEA agents and traffickers I spoke to were happy to be quoted, others were more reticent. To protect these interviewees, they have been cited as anonymous sources. Furthermore, when the words of Mexican deportees are cited, their names are changed or they are also cited anonymously.

Individual texts and documents guide and shape each chapter. But some texts are so significant that they have influenced great swathes of this book. I would encourage anyone who wants to delve further into the world of Mexican narcotics to read them. All translations are my own unless otherwise stated.

The first group consists of the handful of histories of the Mexican narcotics trade.

L. Astorga, *El Siglo de Drogas: Del Porfiriato al Nuevo Milenio* (Mexico City: Penguin Random House, 2016).

L. Astorga, *Drogas sin Fronteras* (Mexico City: Grijalbo, 2003).

L. Astorga, *Mitologia del Narcotraficante en México* (Mexico City: Plaza y Valdés, 1995).

I. Campos and P. Gootenberg, "Toward a New Drug History of Latin America: A Research Frontier at the Center of Debates," *Hispanic American Historical Review* 95, no. 1 (2015), pp. 1–35.

C. A. Flores Pérez, *Historias de Polvo y Sangre: Génesis y Evolución del Tráfico de Drogas en el Estado de Tamaulipas* (Mexico City: CONACyT: CIESAS, 2013).

J. García Robles, *Antología del Vicio: Aventuras y Desventuras de la Mariguana en México* (Mexico City: Laberinto, 2016).

R. Pérez Montfort, *Tolerancia y Prohibición: Aproximaciones a la Historia Social y Cultural de las Drogas en México, 1840–1940* (Mexico City: Debate, 2016).

C. Pérez Ricart, "Las Agencias Antinarcóticas de los Estados Unidos y la Construcción Transnacional de la Guerra Contra las Drogas en México (1938–1978)" (Ph.D. diss, Freien Universität Berlin, 2016).

L. Rodríguez Manzanera, *Los Estupefacientes y el Estado Mexicano* (Mexico City: Botas, 1974).

M. C. Toro, *Mexico's "War" on Drugs: Causes and Consequences* (Boulder, CO: Lynne Rienner, 1995).

W. O. Walker, *Drug Control in the Americas* (Albuquerque: University of New Mexico Press, 1989).

The second group consists of the histories of narcotics and narcotics policing in the United States.

E. Betram et al., *Drug War Politics: The Price of Denial* (Berkeley: University of California Press, 1996).

D. T. Courtwright, *Dark Paradise: A History of Opiate Addiction in America* (Cambridge: Harvard University Press, 2001).

J. Jonnes, *Hep-Cats, Narcs, and Pipe Dreams: A History of America's Romance with Illegal Drugs* (Baltimore: Johns Hopkins University Press, 1996).

D. F. Musto, *The American Disease: Origins of Narcotic Control* (New York: Oxford University Press, 2010).

E. Schneider, *Smack: Heroin and the American City* (Philadelphia: University of Pennsylvania Press, 2011).

The third group consists of the recent works of political science, sociology, anthropology, and journalism that have sought to understand and explain the recent upsurge in drug-related violence.

M. Bergman, *More Money, More Crime: Prosperity and Rising Crime in Latin America* (Oxford: Oxford University Press, 2018).

A. Durán-Martínez, *The Politics of Drug Violence: Criminals, Cops, and Politicians in Colombia and Mexico* (New York: Oxford University Press, 2018).

F. Escalante Gonzalbo, "Homicidios 2008–2009: La Muerte Tiene Permiso," *Nexos*, January 1, 2011.

I. Grillo, *El Narco: The Bloody Rise of Mexican Drug Cartels* (London: Bloomsbury, 2017).

A. Hernández, *Los Señores del Narco* (Mexico City: Delbolsillo, 2014).

A. Hernández, *El Traidor: El Diario Secreto del Hijo del Narco* (Mexico City: Grijalbo, 2020).

B. Lessing, *Making Peace in Drug Wars: Crackdowns and Cartels in Latin America* (Cambridge: Cambridge University Press, 2018).

M. Serrano and P. Kenny, eds., *Mexico's Security Failure: Collapse into Criminal Violence* (New York: Routledge, 2012).

G. Trejo and S. Ley, "Federalism, Drugs, and Violence: Why Intergovernmental Partisan Conflict Stimulated Inter-Cartel Violence in Mexico," *Politica y Gobierno* 23 (2017), pp. 11–56.

E. Vulliamy, *Amexica: War Along the Borderline* (London: Vintage, 2011).

P. Watt and R. Zepeda, *Drug War Mexico: Politics, Neoliberalism, and Violence in the New Narcoeconomy* (London: Zed Books, 2012).

I have used the following abbreviations:

| | |
|---|---|
| AGN | Archivo General de la Nación |
| AHSS | Archivo Histórico de la Secretaría de Salud |
| AHTSJ | Archivo Histórico del Tribunal Superior de Justicia |
| DFS | Dirección Federal de Seguridad |
| DGIPS | Dirección General de Investigaciones Políticas y Sociales |
| NARA, RG | National Archives and Records Administration, Record Group |
| SHSM, AIRE | State Historical Society of Missouri, Arizona Investigative Reporters and Editors Papers |

## SOURCES CONSULTED

### PROLOGUE: THE LOOKOUT

P. Andreas, *Smuggler Nation: How Illicit Trade Made America* (New York: Oxford University Press, 2013), p. 256. On addiction rates of morphine in early twentieth century. It should be said that this was most probably an exaggeration.

I. Bleynat, A. E. Challú, and P. Segal, "Inequality, Living Standards, and Growth: Two Centuries of Economic Development in Mexico," *LSE International Inequalities Institute, Working Paper 46* (June 2020) and subsequent email correspondence. On average Mexican wages.

M. E. Castro and Marcelo Valencia, "Drug Consumption Among the Student Population of Mexico City and Its Metropolitan Area: Subgroups Affected and the Distribution of Users," *UN Drug Bulletin*, 1/1/1980. On Mexican marijuana use. [NB: Date style throughout the Notes is Day/Month/Year.]

*El Paso Times*, 4/2/1932, "… in Dope"; "… with the traffickers."

G. R. Ford Presidential Library, Richard D. Parsons Papers, Box 19, DEA Office of Intel, "Alternative Sources to Mexico for Heroin Supply for North America and Europe." On U.S. heroin use in the 1970s.

D. Gambetta, *The Sicilian Mafia: The Business of Private Protection* (Cambridge: Harvard University Press, 1996). On violence and protection rackets.

Interview with "Cruz," a Mexican lookout, November 2018. Cruz is not his real name. Furthermore, the name of his hometowns in the US and Mexico, the exact number of siblings involved in the trade and other key details have also been changed.

J. Kamstra, *Weed: Diary of a Dope Smuggler* (London: Harper & Row, 1974), p. 240; *New York Times*; National Narcotics Intelligence Consumers Committee (NNICC), *Narcotics Intelligence Estimate* (Washington, DC, 1984); D. Musto, "Illicit Price of Cocaine in Two Eras: 1908–14 and 1982–89," *Pharmacy in History* 54, no. 6 (1991), pp. 321–25; UNODC Data on Drug Prices, https://dataunodc.un.org/drugs/prices. Consulted September 2019. On U.S. wholesale prices.

A. Knight, "Corruption in Twentieth Century Mexico," in Walter Little and Eduardo Posada-Carbó, eds., *Political Corruption in Europe and Latin America* (New York: Palgrave Macmillan, 1996), pp. 219–36. On Mexican corruption.

S. Quinones, *Dreamland: The True Tale of America's Opiate Epidemic* (London: Bloomsbury, 2015). On small-scale Mexican heroin dealers.

G. Valdés Castellanos, *Historia del Narcotráfico en México* (Mexico City: Aguilar, 2013), p. 130, "... in the DNA of the trade."

## CHAPTER ONE: THE KING OF THE *GRIFOS*

AGN, DGIPS, Caja 11, Exp. 33. On 1920s marijuana seizures.

AGN, Tribunal Superior de Justicia del Distrito Federal, Caja 729, Exp. 128284; D. Pulido Esteva, "La Marihuana a Debate: Una Querella antes de su Prohibición (1908)," *Historías: Revista de la Dirección de Estudios Históricos* 93 (2016), pp. 105–20. Newspapers, *El Imparcial, El País, La Iberia, La Voz de México.* On the case of José del Moral.

A. Brenner, *Idols Behind Altars* (New York: Dover, 2002), pp. 180, 181, 184. On the "vacilada."

I. Campos, *Home Grown: Marijuana and the Origins of Mexico's War on Drugs* (Chapel Hill: University of North Carolina Press, 2014). On use of marijuana by soldiers and prisoners and medical use of marijuana; pp. 74–75 on theories for the name marijuana.

E. Gómez Maillefert, "La Marihuana en México," *Journal of American Folklore* 33, no. 127 (January–March 1920), pp. 28–33. On the 1920s marijuana subculture.

P. Hersch Martínez, *Plantas Medicinales: Relato de una Posibilidad Confiscada: Al Estatuto de la Flora en la Biomedicina Mexicana* (Mexico City: INAH, 2000), p. 110, "... extremely low."

*El Imparcial; El País;* Campos, *Home Grown,* p. 99. On newspaper panic over marijuana and violence.

NARA, RG59, Mexico, 1910–1929, 812.114, Mexicali consul to Secretary of State, 7/7/1923. On Tijuana drug arrests.

R. Pérez Montfort, "Las Drogas en el México Posrevolucionario, 1920–1930, El Escenario Popular y el Vacilón," in Pilar Gonzalbo Aizpuru, ed., *Espacios en la Historia: Invención y Transformación de los Espacios Sociales* (Mexico City: Colegio de México, 2014), pp. 405–26, p. 419. On Lupe Rivas Cacho.

F. L. Urquizo, *Tropa Vieja* (Havana: Editorial Arte y Literatura, 1979), p. 155, "... was calmed"; p. 83, "... absolutely free."

F. Vallejo, *El Mensajero: Una Biografía de Porfirio Barba Jacob* (Bogotá: Alfaguara, 2003), pp. 72, 188, 356–57, 469. On Barba Jacob and marijuana.

## CHAPTER TWO: WHITE LADY, BLACK MARKET

AGN, DGIPS, Caja 46, Exp. 5 and Caja 1969B, Exp. 44, Various letters. On investigations of José Mascorro.

AHSS, Fondo Salubridad Pública, Sección Servicio Jurídico, Caja 55, Exp. 29, "Algunos Aspectos de la Actual Lucha Contra La Toxicomania en México," "… on the trade"; "… newspaper vendors."

A. Knight, *The Mexican Revolution: Counter-Revolution and Reconstruction* (Lincoln: University of Nebraska Press, 1986), pp. 405–6. On the Grey Automobile Gang.

N. A. Olvera Hernández, "Policías, Toxicómanos y Traficantes: Control de Drogas en la Ciudad de México, 1920–1942" (M.A. thesis, Instituto Mora, 2016). On initial drug policing.

R. Pérez Montfort, "Las Drogas en el México Posrevolucionario, 1920–1930, El Escenario Popular y el Vacilón," in Pilar Gonzalbo Aizpuru, ed., *Espacios en la Historia: Invención y Transformación de los Espacios Sociales* (Mexico City: Colegio de México, 2014), pp. 405–26, p. 417, "… and heroin."

V. Quintana and I. Muñoz, *Memorias* (Mexico City: Populares, 1961); P. Piccato, *A History of Infamy: Crime, Truth, and Justice in Mexico* (Berkeley: University of California Press, 2017), pp. 112–14. On Valente Quintana.

M. Renero, "Ligeros Apuntes Sobre la Toxicomania de las Drogas Heroicas en la Capital de la República" (thesis, Universidad Nacional, 1925). On opiate addiction in Mexico City.

J. D. Schievenini Stefanoni, "La Prohibición de la Marihuana en México, 1920–1940" (M.A. thesis, Universidad de Queretaro, 2012). On Mexican drug laws.

## CHAPTER THREE: PIPES AND PREJUDICE

AHSS, Fondo Salubridad Pública, Sección Servicio Jurídico, Caja 28, Exp. 6, Report of Juan N. Requeña, 20/6/1931, and Memorandum Confidencial, 26/6/1932; *Albuquerque Journal*, 11/3/1927; *El Siglo de Torreón*, 11/4/1925. On Antonio Wong.

Archivo de la Casa de la Cultura Júridica, Mazatlán, 1927, Exp. 19, Manuel Long et al. On 1927 Mazatlán bust.

I. Campos, "Imperialism and Mexican Drug Policy, 1912–1916: A Reassessment" (manuscript), "... noxious results."

R. Chao Romero, *The Chinese in Mexico, 1882–1940* (Tucson: University of Arizona Press, 2011). On Chinese immigration in Mexico.

*El Democrata*, 25/7/1923. On Topolobampo bust.

*El Democrata*, 8/4/1925. On Culiacán bust.

F. Dikotter, Z. Xun, and L. Laamann, *Narcotic Culture: A History of Drugs in China* (London: Hurst & Co., 2016), p. 74, "... all we had."

*El Imparcial*, 15/7/1906. On Chen Ta Fan.

NARA, RG59, Mexico, 1910–1929, 812.114, Mexicali consul to Secretary of State, February 1927. On opium den in Mexicali, 1927.

J. Oliver Chang, *Chino: Anti-Chinese Racism in Mexico, 1880–1940* (Urbana: University of Illinois Press, 2017); J. J. Gómez Izquierdo, *El Movimiento Antichino en México (1871–1934): Problemas del Racismo y del Nacionalismo Durante la Revolución Mexicana* (Mexico City: INAH, 1991). On anti-Chinese racism.

*El Pueblo*, 15/6/1918. On Cabaret X.

*El Siglo de Torreón*, 30/12/1923, "... opium pipe."

*El Siglo de Torreón*, 13/6/1924, "... of intrigue."

*El Siglo de Torreón*, 8/9/1927, "... other distractions."

*El Siglo de Torreón*, 5/7/1936, "... Japanese silks."

*El Tiempo*, 25/4/1906, "... called opium."

## CHAPTER FOUR: VICE AND VIOLENCE

*El Paso Herald-Post*, 14/9/1931; *La Prensa*, 7/5/1931, 8/8/1931, 5/7/1931, 5/3/1932. On Enrique Fernández's support for schools. Thanks to J. C. Ramírez-Pimienta for these.

Fondo Fideicomiso Archivos Plutarco Elías Calles y Fernando Torreblanca, Fondo Torreblanca, Exp. 58, Inv. 3007; Fondo Alvaro Obregón, Disposiciones, Exp. 3, Inv. 58; Fondo Alvaro Obregón, Concessiones, Exp. 2, Inv. 57; M. González Félix, "El Opio, una Fuente de Acumulación de Capital en el Norte de Baja California, 1910–1920," *Calafia* 10, no. 5 (2000), pp. 4–13. On Cantú's opium taxing.

J. Jonnes, *Hep-Cats, Narcs, and Pipe Dreams: A History of America's Romance with Illegal Drugs* (Baltimore: Johns Hopkins University, 1996), p. 36. On U.S. opiate addiction.

*Kansas City Star*, 9/8/1920, "... of the district"; "... read and write."

C. A. Marcial Campos, *Territorio en Disputa, Distrito Norte de Baja California, Durante el Gobierno de Esteban Cantú, 1915–1920* (La Paz: Gobierno del Estado de Baja California, 2016); J. A. Sandos, "Northern Separatism During the Mexican Revolution: An Inquiry into the Role of Drug Trafficking, 1910–1920," *The Americas* 41, no. 2 (1984), pp. 191–214; A. Ponce Aguilar, *El Coronel Esteban Cantú en el Distrito Norte de Baja California, 1911–1920* (n.p., 2010). On Cantú, taxation, and social programs.

N. Mottier, "Drug Gangs and Politics in Ciudad Juárez: 1928–1936," *Mexican Studies/Estudios Mexicanos* 25, no. 1 (2009), pp. 19–46; AGN DGIPS, Caja 11, Exp. 19, June 1928, Trafico de Drogas; AGN, DGIPS, Caja 280, Exp. 12, various letters; AGN, Presidentes, Obregón-Calles, 812-A 13, various letters. On Enrique Fernández's drug and other enterprises.

NARA, RG59, Mexico, 1910–1929, 812.114, Evans to Collector of Customs, 12/10/1916. On Ensenada drug ring.

NARA, RG59, Mexico, 1910–1929, 812.114, Father Burelbach to U.S. Consul, 4/7/1913, "... to the past."

*New York Times*, 15/1/1922, "... in this country."

*La Prensa*, 4/9/1932, "... of the United States."

J. C. Ramírez-Pimienta, email correspondence, 3/2/2019, "... all the young people."

R. E. Ruiz, *On the Rim of Mexico: Encounters of the Rich and Poor* (Berkeley: University of California Press, 2010), p. 44, "... play golf"; p. 45, "... in my travels."

*Sacramento Union*, 30/5/1916, "... demoralizing drugs."

*San Diego Union*, 9/6/1916, "... or cocaine."

*San Diego Union*, 6/1/1917, "... in the other."

J. A. Sandos, "Prostitution and Drugs: The United States Army on the Mexican-American Border, 1916–1917," *Pacific Historical Review* 49 (1980), pp. 621–45. On U.S. soldiers' drug use at the border.

E. Schantz, "From the 'Mexicali Rose' to the Tijuana Brass: Vice Tours of the United States–Mexico Border, 1910–1965" (Ph.D. diss., University of California, Los Angeles, 2001). On the Baja California vice trade.

Special Collections of University of Texas, El Paso, Middaugh Collection, Box 12, Folder 147, Enrique Fernández; NARA RG59, Mexico, 1930–1939, 812.114, Anonymous informant to Josephus Daniels, 3/5/1934. On Enrique Fernández's escape and murder; on murder of Enrique Fernández's associates.

E. C. Thomas, *The Wanderer in Tijuana: Gambling, Liquor, Ponies, Girls, High Life 'n' Everything* (Tijuana: Wanderer Publishing Co., 1922), p. 3, "… useless places."

## CHAPTER FIVE: DRUGS IN DEPRESSION

*Calexico Chronicle*, 19/9/1936, "… outright killed."

E. Carey, *Women Drug Traffickers: Mules, Bosses, and Organized Crime* (Albuquerque: University of New Mexico Press, 2014), pp. 77–90; G. Rock, *The Coin of Contraband: The True Story of United States Customs Investigator Al Scharff* (New York: Doubleday, 1964); Archivo de la Ciudad de México, Departamento del Distrito Federal, Sección Jefatura de Policía, Serie Investigación y Seguridad, Servicio Secreto, Caja 2, Exp. 11. On the *To the Ends of the Earth* gang.

F. González, *Paisanos Chinos: Transpacific Politics Among Chinese Immigrants in Mexico* (Berkeley: University of California Press, 2017), pp. 31–41; M. Lazcano Ochoa, *Una Vida en la Vida Sinaloense* (Los Mochis: Universidad del Occidente, 1992). On Chinese expulsions from Sonora and Sinaloa.

NARA, RG59, Mexico, 1910–1929, 812.114, Smith to Nutt, 22/12/1924; NARA, RG59, Mexico, 1930–1939, Roll 33, Yepis to Secretary of State, 9/9/1936; NARA, RG170, Box 22, Folder 1, Lane to Nugent, 13/5/1936; Creighton to Anslinger, 22/3/1938. On Sonora trade.

NARA, RG59, Mexico, 1930–1939, 812.114, Smith to Anslinger, 19/4/1933, "… Chinese communities."

## CHAPTER SIX: THE REVOLUTIONARY

My thanks must go to Alegría Magali Ocaña Salazar for her advice and insights, which shaped this chapter.

M. Flores Guevara, "Alternativa Mexicana al Marco Internacional de Prohibición de Drogas Durante el Cardenismo" (B.A. thesis, Colegio de México, 2013), pp. 118–24. On Manuel Tello; p. 116, "... nigger."

NARA, RG170, Box 22, Dr. Salazar Viniegra folder, Creighton to Commissioner of Customs, 23/4/1940, "... used in Mexico."

Gregorio Oneto Barenque, *La Mariguana ante La Academia Nacional de Medicina* (Mexico City, n.p., 1938), "... no remorse"; "... euphoric and dizzy."

*La Prensa*, 20, 21, 22/3/1940, "... yellow skin"; "... very thankful"; "... diseases."

A. Ríos Molina, *Cómo Prevenir la Locura: Psiquiatria e Higiene Mental en México, 1934–1950* (Mexico City: Siglo XXI, 2016). On social medicine and mental hygiene.

J. Segura Millan, *Marihuana* (Mexico City: Costa-Amic, 1972).

B. T. Smith, "The Dialectics of Dope: Leopoldo Salazar Viniegra, the Myth of Marijuana and Mexico's State Drug Monopoly," in Susannah Wilson, ed., *Prohibitions and Psychoactive Substances in History, Culture, and Theory* (London: Routledge, 2019), pp. 111–32. On Salazar's ideas, background, and intellectual formation; "... on you"; "... a clothes shop"; "... dangerous."

*El Universal*, 20/4/1940, "... the merchandise."

University of Pennsylvania, Special Collections Library, Papers of H. J. Anslinger, Box 10, File 11, "... whole thing."

## CHAPTER SEVEN: THE GOLDEN TRIANGLE

AGN, DGIPS, Caja 128, Exp. 17, Roberto Atwood to Jefe de Salubridad, 25/11/1938. On Cuen opium ring.

AGN, DGIPS, Caja 794, Exp. 5, Memorandum of Inspector X, 25/8/1947. On Badiraguato parties in 1947.

AGN, Presidentes, Manuel Ávila Camacho, 422.2, Various letters. On early opium intermediaries in Badiraguato.

M. Aguilar Alvarado and W. Ibarra Escobar, *Desarrollo Empresarial y Liderazgo Político de Melesio Cuen Cázarez: Empresario y Líder de Badiraguato* (Culiacán: UAS, 2013); M. Lazcano y Ochoa, *Una Vida en la Vida Sinaloense* (Los Mochis: Universidad del Occidente, 1992), p. 203. On Cuen.

C. M. Aguirre, *Los Carabineros de Santiago* (n.p., 1992). On the Carabineros.

Archivo de la Casa de la Cultura Júridica, Mazatlán, 1920–1950, 1946, Exp. 29, Paulino Mendivil Salomón.

J. A. Fernández Velázquez, "Los Clanes de la Droga en los Altos de Sinaloa, 1940–1970," *Revista Conjecturas Sociológicas* 4, no. 10 (2016), pp. 23–54; Hector Olea, *Badiraguato: Visión Panorámica de su Historia* (Culiacán: Ayuntamiento de Badiraguato, 1988); F.J. Osuña Félix, "Crecimiento y Crisis de la Mineria en Sinaloa (1907–1950) (M.A. thesis, Universidad Autónoma de Sinaloa, 2014). On Badiraguato.

J. A. Fernández Velázquez, *El Narcotráfico en los Altos de Sinaloa* (Xalapa: Universidad Veracruzana, 2018). On everyday nature of opium production; "… pick tomatoes"; prices of opium.

Interview with anonymous informant, January 2019. On Eduardo "Lalo" Fernández Juárez.

NARA, RG170, Box 22, Folder 3 (1941–43), Folder 4 (1944), Folder 5 (1945–6), Folder 6 (1947), Folder 7 (1948), Folder 8 (1949). These folders contain much of the evidence pulled together for this chapter, including the story of Peña in Durango; "… definitely of Mexican origin"; the factual basis of the rumors about official U.S. involvement in the trade; and much of the evidence on Roberto Domínguez Macías and Alejo Castro.

R. Rodríguez Benítez and M. C. Islas Flores, *Veneranda Bátiz Paredes: Primera Farmacéutica Del Colegio Rosales* (Culiacán: Universidad Autónoma de Sinaloa, 2013). On Veneranda Bátiz.

E. Ruiz Alba, "Lai Chang Wong o José Amarillas, Enamoraba con Música, Curaba con Opio," *Presagio*, August 1979, "… until damnation."

## CHAPTER EIGHT: THE GOVERNORS AND THE GYPSY

AGN, DGIPS, Caja 794, Exp. 5, Memorandum of Inspector X, 25/8/1947, "… open hands."

AGN, Presidentes, Manuel Ávila Camacho, 422/2, Loaiza to President, 17/4/1941. On police collecting opium; "… gold teeth."

Anonymous, *La Vida Accidentada y Novelesca de Rodolfo Valdéz el Gitano* (Mazatlán: El Correo de la Tarde, 1949); O.L. López Alvarez, "Homicidio y Sociedad, Culiacán 1940–1960" (M.A. thesis, Universidad Autónoma de Sinaloa, 2010). On Loaiza's murder, the Gypsy, and Los del Monte; "... vast graveyard."

J. S. Avilés Ochoa, *Mocorito, Presidentes Municipales, 1931–1959* (Culiacán: COBAES, 2010). On Mocorito finances; "... unexpected costs."

*Excélsior*, 27/11/1947, "... Sell Opium."

M. Lazcano y Ochoa, *Una Vida en la Vida Sinaloense* (Los Mochis: Universidad del Occidente, 1992), p. 202, "... foreign currency."

M. Leyzaola, *En Nombre de Mi Padre* (Mexico City: Porrua, 2010); O. Lara Salazar, *La Carraca* (Culiacán: Instituto Sinaloense de Cultura, 2010). On the Wild Cat and his murder.

NARA, RG84, Mazatlán, Macmillan memorandum, 23/1/1945. On theories about Loaiza's murder.

NARA, RG170, Box 22, Folder 3 (1941–43), Creighton to Commissioner of Customs, 7/1/1943; Macmillan to Messersmith, 11/11/1943. On Loaiza's arrangement with the opium traffickers.

NARA, RG170, Box 22, Folder 6 (1947), Ochoa to PJF chief, 25/4/1947, "... more suspicious."

NARA, RG170, Box 22, Folder 6 (1947), Delagrave to Commissioner of Customs, 20/8/1947. On journalist's sting and subsequent cover-up.

NARA, RG170, Box 22, Folder 7 (1948), Agent DJCTE2646987 Memorandum, 26/1/1948, "... pure opium."

F. Ponce, *Lo que el Tiempo no se Llevó: Los Conflitos Agrarios en el Sur de Sinaloa Durante el Periodo Cardenista, 1935–1940* (Culiacán: Dirección de Investigación y Fomento de la Cultura Regional, 1993). On Loaiza's initial career.

## CHAPTER NINE: THE CADILLAC BUST

AGN, Presidentes, Miguel Alemán Valdés, 606.3/67. Anslinger's speech at the U.N.

AGN, Presidentes, Lázaro Cárdenas del Río, 543.1/28. Charges against Carlos Serrano in Veracruz.

AGN, Presidentes, Miguel Alemán Valdés, 422.1. On the Drew Pearson case; "… of the car"; "… misunderstanding."

S. Aguayo Quezada, *La Charola: Una Historia de los Servicios de Inteligencia en México* (Mexico City: Grijalbo, 2001). On the DFS.

Archivo Histórico Genaro Estrada, OMR, 136–6. On journalist García Travesi.

NARA, RG59, Mexico, 1945–49, 812.105, Report of Maurice Holden, 16/7/1947. On Serrano's use of blackmail; "… marijuana sales"; "… in this group"; "… illicit dope business"; and estimate of $60 million in drug earnings.

NARA, RG59, Mexico, 1945–59, 812.00, Raymond Geist to Secretary of State, 6/4/1947, "… sale of narcotics."

NARA, RG170, Box 22, Folder 6 (1947), Raymond Geist to Secretary of State, 18/5/1947, "… lowest ebb."

NARA, RG170, Box 22, Folder 6 (1947), Anslinger to WSW, 25/7/1947, "… hot one."

NARA, RG170, Box 160, Special folder: Carlos Serrano. On Nuevo Laredo bust and Serrano's attempts to get the Cadillac returned.

S. Niblo, *Mexico in the 1940s: Modernity, Politics, and Corruption* (Wilmington, DE: Scholarly Resources, 1999), p. 260, "… without a qualm" and "… under another name"; p. 216. María Félix story.

N. A. Olvera Hernández, "De la Protección a la Salud a la Criminalización de las Sustancias Psicoactivas: El Control de las Drogas en la Ciudad de México, 1946–1948 (Ph.D. diss., Instituto Mora, 2019). On changes to drug laws in 1947; changes in policing; and the "Great Campaign."

M. R. Pembleton, *Containing Addiction: The Federal Bureau of Narcotics and the Origins of America's Global War* (Amherst: University of Massachusetts Press, 2017). There are many works on Anslinger, but I found this recent work particularly useful and well written.

B. T. Smith, *The Mexican Press and Civil Society, 1940–1976: Stories from the Newsroom, Stories from the Street* (Chapel Hill: University of North Carolina Press, 2018), pp. 81–115. On Alemán, corruption, and financial situation of Mexico in 1947–48; "… without a budget."

University of Pennsylvania, Special Collections Library, Papers of H. J. Anslinger, Box 2, File 17, "… dates and places."

## CHAPTER TEN: THE NEW STATUS QUO

AGN, DGIPS, Caja 1451A, Anonymous Memorandum to Alejandro Ortega Romero, 8/8/1955. On Chavez León brothers.

AGN, Presidentes, Adolfo López Mateos, 422/1, J. Jesús Arias Sánchez to President, 3/7/1959.

AHTSJ, Amparos, José Méndez García, 1949, Exp. 3568; Archivo de la Casa de la Cultura Júridica, Tijuana, Caja 7, Exp. 143, José Méndez. On Méndez and his gang.

L. Astorga, *Mitologia del Narcotraficante en México* (Mexico City: Plaza y Valdés, 1995), pp. 64–68. On General Alvarez; "... all the fields."

Email correspondence with Sara Daniela Hidalgo Garza, March 2020. For Mexican incarceration rates.

Interview with anonymous informant, January 2019. On the story of "A. Nacaveva."

*Los Angeles Times*, 13/2/1953, "... poppy crop."

S. Maldonado Aranda, "Caciques, Traffickers, and Soldiers: Drug-Trafficking in the Cardenista Territory of Michoacán (1960–1970)" (manuscript), "... deserved rest."

S. Maldonado Aranda, *Los Márgenes del Estado Mexicano: Territorios Ilegales, Desarrollo y Violencia en Michoacán* (Zamora: Colegio de Michoacán, 2010). On the Michoacán trade.

A. Nacaveva, *Diario de un Narcotraficante* (Mexico City: Costa Amic, 1967).

NARA at California Riverside, RG36, San Diego Customs Office Reports, 1948–1952. On dropping Mexican drug supply; "... black armband"; "... no takers."

NARA, RG170, Box 161, Informe, 20/1/1954. On Prisciliano Cabrera.

P. Nicholas and A. Churchill, "The Federal Bureau of Narcotics, the States, and the Origins of Modern Drug Enforcement in the United States, 1950–1962," *Contemporary Drug Problems* 39 (2012), pp. 595–640. For U.S. incarceration rates.

W. Pansters and B. T. Smith, "U.S. Moral Panics, Mexican Politics, and the Borderlands Origins of the War on Drugs," *Journal of Contemporary*

*History* 55, no. 2 (2020), pp. 364–87. On Gene Fuson and California panics over narcotics.

J. Veledíaz, *El General Sin Memoria: Una Crónica de los Silencios del Ejército Mexicano* (Mexico City: Debate, 2010), pp. 165–66. Story of Don Romulo.

## CHAPTER ELEVEN: QUEEN PIN

AGN, DFS, Versión Pública, Oscar Soto Maynez. On his propensity for bribes.

Archivo de la Casa de la Cultura Júridica, Ciudad Juárez, 1920–1950, Delitos Contra la Salud. Those that mention La Nacha directly include 1929, Exp. 29; 1930, Exp. 99; 1930, Exp. 104; 1948, Exp. 77; 1948, Exp. 84; 1929, Exp. 7; 1931, Exp. 11. These were discovered and read by Nathaniel Morris, Wil Pansters, and myself in Ciudad Juárez. They were used here to describe La Nacha's working practices, prison racket, family relations, and use of *picaderos*.

E. Carey, *Women Drug Traffickers: Mules, Bosses, and Organized Crime* (Albuquerque: University of New Mexico Press, 2014), pp. 91–126, 115. On Lola la Chata; "... rock of Mexico"; pp. 126–58. On La Nacha and particularly her 1942–43 run-ins with the law.

*El Paso Evening Post*, 13/10/1930, "... killed you."

*El Paso Herald-Post*, 14/3/1944, "... bible prodigy."

*El Paso Herald-Post*, 21/1/1961, "... to Christ."

*La Prensa*, 19/2/1934, "... Nacha's gain."

J. C. Ramírez-Pimienta, "El Pablote": Una Nueva Mirada al Primer Corrido Dedicado a un Traficante de Drogas," *Revista de Pensamiento Critico y Estudias Literarias Latinamericanos* 14 (December 2016), pp. 41–56. On Pablote; "... on owls"; "... defend my own."

R. Salazar, *Border Correspondent: Selected Writings 1955–1970* (Berkeley: University of California Press, 1988), pp. 43–47. On Hypo and La Nacha.

*Sucesos*, 21/7/1937, "... goof balls."

University of Texas at El Paso, Institute of Oral History, Interview with Robert Hudgins, No. 425, "... the Mafia."

## CHAPTER TWELVE: THE MEXICAN STOPOVER

AGN, DFS, Versión Pública, Narcotráfico, 1 of 3, Interrogation of Alma Escobedo Martínez de Nanclares, 29/2/1972.

H. Aguilar Camín, "Narco Historias Extraordinarias," *Nexos*, 5/1/2017; *Novedades*, 6/3/1948; *Proceso*, 29/4/1985; *Alarma*, 9/3/1966; *El Informador*, 13/11/1964. On the Izquierdo Ebrard brothers.

AHTSJ, Amparos, Arturo Izquierdo Ebrard, 1967, Exp. 2967. On the scheme of Moreno and the Izquierdo Ebrard brothers.

AHTSJ, Amparos, Jorge Moreno Chauvet, 1955, Exp. 4458; Jorge Moreno Chauvet, 1961, Exp. 1030; Jorge Moreno Chauvet, 1966, Exp. 10457; Private Archive of Douglas Valentine, Project Pilot III. Internal DEA report on French Connection. On Jorge Moreno Chauvet; "... in chic restaurants."

The Association for Diplomatic Studies and Training, Foreign Affairs Oral History Project, Interview with William Harben, 1998, "... milpa somewhere."

J. González G., *Lo Negro del Negro Durazo* (London: Editorial Posada, 1983); Interview with Richard Dunagan, September 2018. On Durazo.

NARA, RG170, Box 161, Rebasa to Anslinger, 3/12/1959; Jean-Pierre Charbonneau, *The Canadian Connection* (Montreal: Optimum, 1976); Archivo Histórico Genaro Estrada, III, 591/5 (72.00) 8; Private Archive of Douglas Valentine, Project Pilot III. Internal DEA report on French Connection. On D'Agostino, Chez Hélène, and the early French Connection.

## CHAPTER THIRTEEN: ACAPULCO GOLD

AHTSJ, Amparos, Ruperto Beltrán Monzón, 1969, Exp. 5788; Miguel Barragán, 1968; P. Maguire and M. Ritter, *Thai Stick: Surfers, Scammers, and the Untold Story of the Marijuana Trade* (New York: Columbia University Press, 2014); N. Shou, *Orange Sunshine: The Brotherhood of Eternal Love and its Quest to Spread Peace, Love, and Acid to the World* (New York: Thomas Dunne, 2010); Private Archive of Peter Maguire, Various interviews; Interview with David Ortiz and Mike Ritter, March 2018; Interview with Travis Ashbrook, March 2018; Interview with Jerry Kamstra, March 2017. On sinsemilla and Papa Grande.

R. Bibbero, *90 degrees to Zamboanga: Memoirs of a 20-Year Marijuana Smuggling Adventure* (New York: Lucky Shirt Press 2015). On Rick Bibbero and Ciro Mancuso.

Big D. Unlimited, *A Guidebook to the Psilocybin Mushrooms of Mexico* (Tucson: Mother Duck Press, 1976).

DEA Library, Folder Mexico, "Drug Seizures Along the Mexican Border, 1960–1970." Thanks to Peter Watt for this data.

A. Del Valle, *Los Sembradores* (Los Angeles: Galeria de la Raza, 1970). On *curanderos*.

D. Farber, "Foreword: When Innocence Must Become Experience," in Peter Maguire and Mike Ritter, *Thai Stick: Surfers, Scammers, and the Untold Story of the Marijuana Trade* (New York: Columbia University Press, 2014), p. iix, "... deviant globalization." The term was first coined by Nils Gilman.

J. A. Fernández Velázquez, "El Narcotráfico en los Altos de Sinaloa" (Ph.D. thesis, Universidad Veracruzana, 2016), "... something similar to gold."

J. García Robles, *The Stray Bullet: William S. Burroughs in Mexico* (Minneapolis: University of Minnesota Press, 2013); J. García Robles, *At the End of the Road: Jack Kerouac in Mexico* (Minneapolis: University of Minnesota Press, 2014). On the Beats in Mexico.

Interview with Travis Ashbrook, March 2019. On walking over the border with marijuana.

J. Kamstra, *Weed: Diary of a Dope Smuggler* (London: Harper & Row, 1974), p. 240. On weed prices, "pop-proof cars," and the structure of the weed trade.

J. Kamstra, "Highway 15 Revisited," *High Times*, April 1977, "... from Guadalajara"; "... bleachers."

R. King, *Andiamo: A True Story of Marijuana Smuggling* (n.p., 2016). On Manuel Mendoza; "... smoked it."

SHSM, AIRE, Box 311. This is a collection of interviews with Customs officers and DEA officials conducted by Arizona journalists in the late 1970s; AGN, DFS, Versión Pública, Pedro Avilés Pérez; Interview with Phil Jordan, June 2016. AHTSJ, Amparos, Juan Esparragoza Moreno, 1988; Rafael Caro Quintero, 1973; AGN, DFS, Versión Pública, Narcotráfico, 1 of 3, Report of Javier García Paniagua, 7/7/1977. On Pedro Avilés Pérez.

*Texas Monthly*, July 1987, "... set a price."

University of Texas, Austin, Briscoe Center for American History, Jay McMullen Papers, 1942–2012, Box, 2010–017/4, Mexican Connection Transcripts, "... above the middle class"; "... to the intermediaries"


## CHAPTER FOURTEEN: MEXICAN BROWN

AHTSJ, Amparos, Jaime Buelna Aviles, 1980, Exp. 1242. On Favela Escobosa cocaine racket.

J. Carter Presidential Library, Special Assistant to the President-Bourne, Mexico 1/27/77–5/9/77, Box 40, DEA Statistical Summary 1977. On provenance of U.S. heroin; on estimated workers in heroin industry; on cocaine coming through Mexico.

*Christian Science Monitor*, 3/8/1976. On Salvador Díaz and peasant earnings from drug trade.

D. Courtwright, *Dark Paradise: A History of Opiate Addiction in America* (Cambridge: Harvard University Press, 2001), p. 168, "... firewalls."

*El Paso Times*, 1/2/1970, "... noisy cantinas."

J. A. Fernández Velázquez, *El Narcotráfico en los Altos de Sinaloa* (Xalapa: Universidad Veracruzana, 2018), "... pay for it."

*Florence Morning News*, 23/10/1977, "... to buy food"

G. R. Ford Presidential Library, Richard Parsons Files, Box 22, Parsons, Cannon to Parsons, 2/2/1976; U.S. embassy in Mexico to Parsons, January 1976 telegram. On Mexican heroin going to U.S. and pricing.

G. R. Ford Presidential Library, Richard Parsons Files, Box 22, "A Potential for a Forward Strategy Against Heroin in Mexico," 15/8/1975, "... detailed analysis."

Interview with David Wilson, September 2018, "... like a ghost."

J. Jonnes, *Hep-Cats, Narcs, and Pipe Dreams: A History of America's Romance with Illegal Drugs* (Baltimore: Johns Hopkins University Press, 1996), p. 250, "... into acid"; p. 284, "... along the way."

A. McCoy et al., *The Politics of Heroin in Southeast Asia* (New York: Harper & Row, 1973), p. 181, "... Saigon."

NARA at California Riverside, RG170, Fugitive File, 1972–4, Box 7. On Arthur Martinez.

National Security Archive, Washington, DC, Edward Heath, "Mexican Eradication Campaign" (M.A. thesis, California State University, 1981). On addicts dead; on poppy scorers; on wages of poppy scorers; on opium yields; on Lalo Fernández and cocaine.

Private Archive of Tony Ricevueto. Newspaper Clippings relating to Herreras; *Arizona Republic*, 5/4/1979; Peter A. Lupsha and Kip Schlegel, *The Political Economy of Drug Trafficking: The Herrera Organization (Mexico and the United States)* (Albuquerque: University of New Mexico, Latin American Institute, Working Paper, 1990); Nathaniel Morris, "Heroin, the Herreras, and the Chicago Connection: The Drug Trade in Durango, 1930–1990" (manuscript). On the Herreras.

D. Rosen, "The Mexican Connection," *Penthouse*, May 1977, "... deal in heroin."

E. Shannon, *Desperados: Latin Drug Lords, US Lawmen, and the War America Can't Win* (New York: Viking, 1988), p. 56, "... army coming."

SHSM, AIRE, Box 310, Various reports. On Nogales heroin industry; "... Customs headquarters"; "... surrounding it."

SHSM, AIRE, Box 336, Renner to Greene, 29/1/1977. On Favela and Bonnano.

University of Texas, Austin, Briscoe Center for American History, Jay McMullen Papers, 1942–2012, Box, 2010–017/4, Mexican Connection Transcripts. On heroin profits for traffickers.

N. Vidales Soto, *Leopoldo Sánchez Celis: El Hombre del Paliacate* (Mexico City: SEP, 2006), p. 124, "... up these situations."

P. L. Yates, Unpublished autobiography. This manuscript is kindly provided by the Yates family, who are currently preparing it for publication; "... on here?"; "... healthy for you." Thanks so much to Thom Rath for arranging this.

## CHAPTER FIFTEEN: THE RACKETS

AGN, DFS, Versión Pública, Leopoldo Sánchez Celis; N. Vidales Soto, *Leopoldo Sánchez Celis: El Hombre del Paliacate* (Mexico City: SEP, 2006). On Sánchez Celis.

AGN, DFS, Versión Pública, Narcotráfico, 1 of 3, Interview with Oscar Venegas Tarín, 12/11/1972.

AGN, DFS, Versión Pública, Oscar Flores Sánchez, "... drug trafficking."

*Arizona Daily Star*, 1/4/1977. On Goldwater.

H. Berrellez, *The Last Narc: A Memoir of the DEA's Most Notorious Agent*, (Los Angeles: Renaissance, 2021), pp. 69-70.

D. Bloch, *Flying Uncle's Junk: Hauling Drugs for Uncle Sam* (Clearwater, MN: North Star Press, 2016) (ebook), "... more honest."

N. Córdova, *La Narcocultura: Simbologia de la Transgresión, el Poder y la Muerte, Sinaloa y la Leyenda Negra* (Culiacán: Universidad Autónoma de Sinaloa, 2011), p. 283, "... disturb you."

DEA-6 Interview with CI, 25/2/1991, "... to buy," https://reneverdugo.org/docs.html. Consulted September 2019.

Digital National Security Archive, Mexico-United States Counternarcotics Policy, 1969–2013, Intel Assessment of Mexico, 13/10/1974, "... anti-narcotics effort."

*El Paso Times*, 30/10/1975; 16/11/1975; 20/6/1976; G. Courtwright, *Dirty Dealing: Drug Smuggling on the Mexican Border & the Assassination of a Federal Judge* (El Paso: Cinco Puntos, 1984), pp. 72–76. On George Hough.

*El Heraldo*, 20/1/1975, "... exploit them."

Interview with David Wilson, September 2018, "... authority here."

M. Lazcano Ochoa, *Una Vida en la Vida Sinaloense* (Los Mochis: Universidad del Occidente, 1992), p. 190, "... do you harm."

*The Mexican Connection* (CBS documentary, 1973), "... we wanted to"; "... by them."

NARA, RG170, Box 161, Reese to Hamilton, 7/7/1963, "... old man"; "... poppy agriculture."

Private Archive of Douglas Valentine, Interview with Richard Blum, "... U.S. Customs."

SHSM, AIRE, Box 309, Interview with JWS 3, 4/11/1976. On Borane; Interview with JWS-3, 1/11/1976. On Yuma sheriff; Interview with DW-15, n.d. On Montoya busts; "... to Nogales."

SHSM, AIRE, Box 310. On Lukeville.

B. T. Smith, "The Rise and Fall of Narcopopulism: Drugs, Politics, and Society in Sinaloa, 1930–1980," *Journal for the Study of Radicalism* 7, no. 2 (2013), pp. 125–65. On police corruption in Sinaloa.

J. Veledíaz, "La Vendetta que Marcó el Epoca," *La Prensa*, 27/8/2018; AGN, DFS, Versión Pública, Rodolfo Váldez; *El Informador*, 5/2/1970. On Virrueta killing.

M. F. Wendland, *The Arizona Project: How a Team of Investigative Reporters Got Revenge on Deadline* (Mesa, AZ: Blue Sky Press, 1988). On Don Bolles and Arizona Project.


## CHAPTER SIXTEEN: NARCS

AGN, DFS, Versión Pública, Policia Judicial Federal, Reports, 16/2/1974 and 18/2/1974. On Sinaloa and Manuel "Crazy Pig" Salcido Uzeta.

AGN, DGIPS, Box 1451A. Various clippings and reports. On Operation Intercept; "... and users"; "... deserted."

*Arizona Daily Star*, 26/12/1976, "... Untouchables."

J. Bario, *Fatal Dreams* (Garden City, NY: Dial Press, 1985); Private Archive of Douglas Valentine, DEA—Application for Sante Bario FOIA. On Sante Bario.

F. Browning, "An American Gestapo," *Playboy* 23, no. 2 (1976). On Mark's tribulations; "... bottles' worth."

T. G. Carpenter, *The U.S. Campaign Against International Narcotics Trafficking: A Cure Worse than the Disease* (Cato Institute Policy Analysis, 1985), pp. 8–9, "... our will."

*El Paso Herald*, 26/11/1973, 13/8/1975; AGN, DGIPS, Caja 1798A, Report 17/3/1975. On Ciudad Juárez; "... their homes."

*El Heraldo*, 6/12/1971; *El Universal*, 10/7/1971; *La Prensa*, 16/3/1972. On Mexican panic over narcotics.

Interview with Hector Berrellez, March 2019, "... buy dope."

B. Magaloni, A. L. Magaloni, and Z. Razu, "La Tortura como Método de Investigación Criminal: El Impacto de la Guerra Contra las Drogas en México," *Politica y Gobierno* 25, no. 2 (2018), 223–61. On torture and changes in laws.

J. Mills, *The Underground Empire: Where Crime and Governments Embrace* (New York: Doubleday, 1986), p. 535, "... people."

*New York Times*, 22/5/1977. On Rafael Díaz.

C. Pérez Ricart, "Las Agencias Antinarcóticas de los Estados Unidos y la Construcción Transnacional de la Guerra Contra las Drogas en México (1938–1978)" (Ph.D. diss., Freien Universität Berlin, 2016). On U.S. spending on Mexican drug war; changes to drug laws in Mexico; PJF changes; "... undertrained."

*¿Por Que?* 13/11/1969; *¿Por Que?* 9/11/1971. On Armando Martínez Salgado.

Private Archive of Craig Pyes, Craig Pyes, "US Torture in Mexico: They Have Ways of Making You Habla," "... even have."

Private Archive of Douglas Valentine, Grand Jury Transcript, El Paso, Jack Compton, Affidavit 1975. On Joe Arpaio; "... pure bull"; "... shot to pieces"; "... all the time"; "... the questions either."

Private Archive of Douglas Valentine, Interview with Richard Blum. On creation of special antinarcotics unit; on Sahagún Baca murder of marijuana smugglers.

*Proceso*, 3/1/2002. On Tarín Chávez.

R. Reaves, *Smuggler: A Memoir* (n.p., 2016) (ebook), "... and lungs."

L. Rodríguez Manzanera, *Los Estupefacientes y el Estado Mexicano* (Mexico City: Botas, 1974). On changing drug laws.

SHSM, AIRE, Box 311, Report of Alex Drehsler, 6/12/1976; *Proceso*, September 1984; Sergio René de Dios Corona, *La Historia que Pudieron Borrar: La Guerra Sucia en Jalisco, 1970–1985* (Guadalajara: Casa del Mago, 2004). On Sahagún Baca; "... very sinister."

SHSM, AIRE, Box 336, *Chicago Sun Times* series on drug trade, 1975, "... way of life."

*El Sol de México*, 10/10/1971. On end to amparos for drug offenses.

A. C. Strong, *Corrido de Cocaine: Inside Stories of Hard Drugs, Big Money, and Short Lives* (Tucson, AZ: Harbinger, 1990), p. 201, "... get information."

M. C. Toro, *Mexico's "War" on Drugs: Causes and Consequences* (Boulder, CO: Lynne Rienner, 1995), p. 59. On number of drug arrests.

D. Valentine, *The Strength of the Pack: The Personalities, Politics, and Espionage Intrigues That Shaped the DEA* (New York: Doppelgang Press, 2019), pp. 105, 106, 296, 344. On Joseph Baca.

M. Vigil, *DEAL* (Bloomington, IN: iUniverse, 2014), p. 83, "... ricochets"; p. 3, "... federale couture"; p. 47, "... is law"; p. 61, "... their actions."

*Washington Post*, 2/9/1974; NARA, RG59, Mexico, 1970–1973, Report 30/3/1973; "Corridos de Nuevo Laredo," http://www.laits.utexas.edu/jaime/jrn/cwp/nlg/coverpage.html (consulted September 2019); *El Norte*, 23/5/2003; *Sentido Comun*, 25/3/2015. On Nuevo Laredo.

## CHAPTER SEVENTEEN: THE ATROCITIES

AGN, DFS, Versión Pública, Colegio de Abogados, Eustaquio Buelna. On torture in PJF cells in Culiacán, "… Mexican government." Thanks to Adela Cedillo for finding this.

AGN, Secretaría de la Defensa Nacional, Sección Estado Mayor de la Defensa Nacional, Exp. 820. On February 1979 runway killings.

AGN, Secretaría de la Defensa Nacional, Sección Estado Mayor de la Defensa Nacional, Exp. 896. On Daniel Rivera de la Rocha case.

AGN, Secretaría de la Defensa Nacional, Sección Estado Mayor de la Defensa Nacional, Exp. 1298, Agustín Ramón Bejarano to SEDENA, 28/11/1978. On Pino Gordo.

AGN, Secretaría de la Defensa Nacional, Seccion Estado Mayor de la Defensa Nacional, Exp. 1299, Letter, 8/11/1982. On Baltasar Ayon Ayon.

A. Cedillo, "Intersections Between the Dirty War and the War on Drugs in Northwestern Mexico, 1969–1985" (Ph.D. diss., University of Wisconsin–Madison, 2019), pp. 203–14; Richard B Craig, "La Campaña Permanente: Mexico's Anti-Drug Campaign," *Journal of Interamerican Studies and World Affairs* 20, no. 2 (May 1978), pp. 107–31. On the mechanics of Operation Condor.

N. Córdova, *La Narcocultura: Simbologia de la Transgresión, el Poder y la Muerte, Sinaloa y la Leyenda Negra* (Culiacán: Universidad Autónoma de Sinaloa, 2006), p. 285, "… Dozens."

DEA-6 Interview with Lawrence Harrison, "… floating there," https://reneverdugo.org/docs.html. Consulted September 2019.

G. R. Ford Presidential Library, Richard Parsons Files, Box 22, "A Potential for a Forward Strategy Against Heroin in Mexico," 15/8/1975, "… induced"; "… drug efforts."

G. R. Ford Presidential Library, Richard D. Parsons Papers, Box 22, Rangel to President Ford, 29/10/1975.

Interview with anonymous DEA agent, September 2018, "... down the
mountain."

Interview with anonymous San Ignacio resident, March 2019, Culiacán.
On torture in San Ignacio.

Interview with Craig Pyes, March 2019, "... my skin."

J. Mills, *The Underground Empire: Where Crime and Governments Embrace*
(New York: Doubleday, 1986); *Los Angeles Times*, 2/10/1986. On Sicilia
Falcón case.

*New York Times*, 20/4/1975; *Excélsior*, 21/4/1975, "... police chiefs."

*New York Times*, 18/12/1977. On Ocotlán massacre.

*Proceso*, 16/4/1979, "... with me."

*Proceso*, 17/11/1979; AGN, Secretaría de la Defensa Nacional, Sección
Estado Mayor de la Defensa Nacional, Exp. 970, Vecinos of Comisario
de Colorados to SEDENA. On treatment of Rarámuri.

R. Stratton, *Smuggler: A Memoir* (New York: Allen & Unwin, 2017), p. 280,
"... nothing grew."

D. Valentine, *The Strength of the Pack: The Personalities, Politics, and
Espionage Intrigues That Shaped the DEA* (New York: Doppelgang Press,
2019), pp. 244–60. On problems in the DEA.

M. Vigil, *Deal* (Bloomington, IN: iUniverse, 2014), p. 81, "... on his back";
pp. 92–93, "... flinching."

D. Weimer, "The Politics of Contamination: Herbicides, Drug Control, and
Environmental Law," *Diplomatic History* 41, no. 5 (2017), pp. 847–73. On
contamination from drug spraying.

## CHAPTER EIGHTEEN: THE BARBARIANS OF THE NORTH

AGN, DFS, Versión Pública, Oscar Flores Sánchez, "... activities."

AGN, DFS, Versión Pública, Raúl Mendiolea, "... the republic."

AGN, DGIPS, Box 1711-C, Exp. 13. On Montenegro killing.

AGN, Versión Pública, Policia Estatal de Tamaulipas, Report, 31/7/1978.
On PJF vs DFS.

AHTSJ, Amparos, Pedro Díaz Parada, 1991, Exp. 83; *Proceso*, 10/12/1984.
On Oaxaca marijuana plantations; "... planes land."

J. González G., *Lo Negro del Negro Durazo* (London: Editorial Posada, 1983), p. 58, "… into a fight"; pp. 212–13. On Durazo and cocaine sales.

Interview with James Abdul Monroe, May 2019. On Thai Stick racket.

Interview with Olga Breeskin, *Ventaneando*, 19/5/2019.

Interview with three anonymous DEA agents in September 2016, October 2016, and March 2018. On Pedro Avilés Pérez assassination. For obvious reasons these agents did not want to be named. One confessed to putting the bounty on the trafficker's head. Another sent me the photograph but refused to talk about the murder. The other told me the story about the morgue.

NARA, RG59, Mexico, 1977 State Department Telegrams, 22/8/1978. On Rodolfo Herrera Nevárez case.

*New York Times*, 18/12/1977. On Oaxaca killings. The *New York Times* article confused the PJF official in charge. It was Martínez Salgado, according to local newspapers. *Carteles del Sur*, 21/7/1977, 31/7/1977, 6/8/1977, 10/8/1977; *El Imparcial*, 22/9/1977.

T. A. Poppa, *Drug Lord: The Life and Death of a Mexican Kingpin* (Seattle: Demand Publications, 1988), pp. 42–59, on the plaza system; pp. 65–66, on torture in Ojinaga.

*Proceso*, 14/7/1984. On Durazo drug smuggling.

C. Pyes, "Legal Murders," *Village Voice*, 4/6/1979, pp. 11–15, "… who doesn't." On Martínez Montenegro murder.

*San Diego Union*, 17/2/1980, "… against anyone."

Texas A&M University–Corpus Christi Special Collections, Johnson-Bezdek Collection on Opposition Politics in Twentieth-Century Mexico, Oscar Monroy, "Historia de la Derrota de Lic Jorge Omar Villalobos Moguel como AMP Federal contra la mafia del Noroeste"; J. Villalobos, *Perseguidor Perseguido: Testimonios de una Abogado Investigador* (Mexico City: Alta Pimeria Pro Arte y Cultura, 1985). On the Villalobos case.

Wikileaks, Telegram, 25/9/1976, "… narcotics-related fields," https://wikileaks.org/plusd/cables/1976MEXICO10915_b.html. Consulted September 2019.

## CHAPTER NINETEEN: THE "GUADALAJARA CARTEL"

The majority of this chapter came from the DEA files and court transcripts that can be found at René Verdugo's online archive, https://reneverdugo. org/docs.html.

AGN, DFS, Versión Pública, Javier Barba Hernández; S. R. de Dios Corona, *La Historia Que No Pudieron Borrar: La Guerra Sucia En Jalisco, 1970– 1985* (Guadalajara: La Casa del Mago, 2004). On Barba Hernández; "... here before."

DEA, Miscellaneous Reports, https://reneverdugo.org/pdf/Related%20 Matters/DEA%20Reports/DEA%20Reports%20(Miscellaneous%20 Pgs).pdf. Consulted September 2019. On DFS involvement in drug trade; on Félix Gallardo and cocaine trade; on Zacatecas marijuana fields.

DEA, Miscellaneous Reports, https://reneverdugo.org/pdf/Related%20 Matters/DEA%20Reports/DEA%20Reports%20(Miscellaneous%20Pgs). pdf. Consulted September 2019; T. A. Poppa, *Drug Lord, The Life and Death of a Mexican Kingpin* (Seattle: Demand Publications, 1988); *El Porvenir*, 3–10/9/1986. On some of the conflicts between institutions over drug protection rackets.

P. Gorman, "Big-Time Smuggler's Blues," *Cannabis Culture*, 16/6/2006. On Caborca marijuana fields.

R. Hernández López, *Zorrilla, El Imperio del Crimen* (Mexico City: Planeta, 1989), "... Zorrilla Pérez."

Interview with anonymous San Ignacio inhabitant, March 2019, Culiacán; AGN, DFS, Versión Pública, Rafael Caro Quintero; AHTSJ, Amparos, Rafael Caro Quintero, 1973. On Caro Quintero.

J. Kuykendall, *O Plata o Plomo? Silver or Lead?* (Bloomington, IN: Xlibris, 2005), p. 205, "... revolving door."

National Narcotics Intelligence Consumers Committee (NNICC), Narcotics Intelligence Estimate (Washington, DC, 1984); J. Jonnes, *Hep-Cats, Narcs, and Pipe Dreams: A History of America's Romance with Illegal Drugs* (Baltimore: Johns Hopkins University Press, 1996), pp. 366–88. On rising cocaine use.

D. Osorno, *El cartel de Sinaloa: Una Historia del Uso Político del Narco* (Mexico City: Grijalbo, 2010), pp. 207–57. On Félix Gallardo.

H. Padgett, "Cuando los Tigres del Narco se Soltaron," *Sin Embargo*, 9/4/2013. On Chao López.

Private Archive of Tony Ricevueto. Operation Columbus, DEA-6s, DEA factsheets on Miguel Félix Gallardo; J. Kuykendall, *O Plata o Plomo? Silver or Lead?* (Bloomington, IN: Xlibris: 2005), pp. 193–202. On money laundering.

*Proceso*, 19/11/1984; *Washington Post*, 12/5/1985; *Los Angeles Times*, 15/11/1985; Interview with Hector Berrellez, March 2019. On Búfalo Ranch.

*Proceso*, 15/4/1989, "… move upwards."

*Proceso*, 27/6/2013. On Guadalajara de Día.

*San Diego Union*, 6/8/1955; AHTSJ, Amparos, Fidel Carrillo Elenes, 1956; On Fonseca.

E. Shannon, *Desperados: Latin Drug Lords, U.S. Lawmen, and the War America Can't Win* (New York: Viking, 1988), p. 194, "… enforcement agency."

*United States v. Juan Ramón Matta-Ballesteros et al.*, Testimony of Lawrence Harrison, 6/6/1990, "… close to them." Thanks to Noah Hurowitz for this.

E. Valle, "Ciudad Asediada," *El Universal*, 20/10/1987. On Guadalajara violence.

*Washington Post*, 12/5/1985. On wages among marijuana pickers.

## CHAPTER TWENTY: THE MARTYR AND THE SPOOK

Again the majority of this chapter came from the DEA files, court transcripts, and tape transcripts of the Camarena interrogation that can be found at René Verdugo's online archive, https://reneverdugo.org/docs.html.

S. I. Guerra, "Entre los Mafiosos y la Chota: Ethnography, Drug Trafficking, and Policing in the South Texas–Mexico Borderlands," in A. Ochoa O'Leary, C. M. Deeds, and S. Whiteford, eds., *Uncharted Terrains: New*

*Directions in Border Research: Methodology, Ethics, Practice* (Tucson: University of Arizona Press, 2013), pp. 121–39, p. 132. On Red Ribbon Week.

https://reneverdugo.org/docs.html; J. J. Esquivel, *La CIA, Camarena y Caro Quintero: La Historia Secreta* (Mexico City: Grijalbo, 2014); J. Kuykendall, *O Plata o Plomo? Silver or Lead?* (Bloomington, IN: Xlibris, 2005); E. Shannon, *Desperados: Latin Drug Lords, U.S. Lawmen, and the War America Can't Win* (New York: Viking, 1988); Interview with E. Heath, February 2019; AGN, DFS, Versiones Públicas, Rafael Caro Quintero, Ernesto Fonseca Carrillo, Miguel Ángel Félix Gallardo; DEA Library, Folder Mexico, Literature and clippings relating to killing of Enrique "Kiki" Camarena. On the Camarena murder and the subsequent investigation.

Interview with anonymous DEA agent, various dates, 2019. This DEA agent told me the story of the murder of Félix Gallardo's uncle and the killing of Salcido Uzeta.

Interview with Hector Berrellez, March 2019, "... zoologist."

Interview with Juan A. Valencia, May 2020; Interview with J. Jesús Esquivel, April 2018; J. J. Esquivel, *La CIA, Camarena y Caro Quintero: La Historia Secreta* (Mexico City: Grijalbo, 2014); Interview with Hector Berrellez, March 2019; R. Bartley and S. Erickson Bartley, *Eclipse of the Assassins: The CIA, Imperial Politics, and the Slaying of Mexican Journalist Manuel Buendia* (Madison: University of Wisconsin Press, 2015); C. Bowden, *Blood on the Corn,* https://medium.com/@readmatter/blood-on-the-corn-the-complete-story-488f55d4f9ea. Consulted September 2019; *The Last Narc* (Amazon Prime documentary, 2020). On Lawrence Victor Harrison and the parsing of the Camarena murder. See R. Bartley and S. Erickson Bartley in particular for an exhaustive discussion of literature on drugs-for-arms scandal.

*Proceso,* 21/4/1986. On upswing in Sinaloa violence.

*Proceso,* 27/10/2013, "... gave the orders."

D. Valentine, *The Strength of the Pack: The Personalities, Politics, and Espionage Intrigues That Shaped the DEA* (New York: Doppelgang Press, 2019), pp. 366–72; M. Levine, *Deep Cover* (Bloomington, IN: iUniverse, 2000). On the decline of DEA in early 1980s.

## CHAPTER TWENTY-ONE: THE TAKEOVER

P. Andreas, *Border Games: Policing the U.S.-Mexico Divide* (Ithaca: Cornell University Press, 2009), pp. 74–82, p. 75, "... than others?" On the effects of NAFTA.

J. Bailey, *The Politics of Crime in Mexico: Democratic Governance in a Security Trap* (Boulder, CO: Lynne Rienner, 2014); P. Reuter and D. Ronfeldt, *Quest for Integrity, Mexican-U.S. Drug Issue in the 1980s* (Santa Monica: RAND Corp., 1992). On the size of the Mexican drug trade.

J. Blancornelas, *El Cártel: Los Arellano Félix, la Mafia Más Poderosa en la Historia de América Latina* (Mexico City: Random House, 2009), "... hazte pendejo." On supposed divvying up of plazas in 1989; on first conflicts between "cartels" in 1993; on Arellano Félix cartel and gunmen; on trafficker control of protection racket in Baja California.

C. Bowden, *Down by the River: Drugs, Money, Murder, and Family* (New York: Simon & Schuster, 2004). On Amado Carrillo Fuentes; on $30 billion Mexican drug trade; on Raúl Salinas corruption scandal.

A. Durán-Martínez, *The Politics of Drug Violence: Criminals, Cops, and Politicians in Colombia and Mexico* (New York: Oxford University Press, 2018), p. 202, "... of corpses."

I. Grillo, *El Narco: The Bloody Rise of Mexican Drug Cartels* (London: Bloomsbury, 2017), p. 83, "... U.S. Customs."

A. Hernández, *El Traidor: El Diario Secreto del Hijo del Narco* (Mexico City: Grijalbo, 2020) (ebook). On El Mayo and Tirso Martínez Sánchez network; "... take money."

M. Kenney, "Summary of Guillermo Pallomari's Testimony in the 1997 Operation Cornerstone Trial of Michael Abbell and William Moran," *Transnational Organized Crime* 5, no. 1 (1999), pp. 120–38. On "one for one" deal.

M. Molloy and C. Bowden, *El Sicario: The Autobiography of a Mexican Assassin* (Lebanon, IN: Bold Type Books, 2011), pp. 75–77. On Ciudad Juárez police force.

T. A. Poppa, *Drug Lord: The Life and Death of a Mexican Kingpin* (Seattle: Demand Publications, 1988). On profits in Ojinaga.

J. Preston and S. Dillon, *Opening Mexico: The Making of a Democracy* (New York: Farrar, Straus & Giroux, 2004). On democratization and rapid decline of PRI authority in the 1990s.

Private Archive of Phil Jordan, DEA fact sheet, Carrillo Fuentes Organization, "... or cartel"; "... family syndicates"; "... from the PJF."

J. C. Reyna, *Confesión de un Sicario: El Testimonio de Drago, Lugarteniente de un Cartel Mexicano* (Mexico City: Grijalbo, 2011), pp. 57–60. Story of Drago and the Whale.

M. Serrano and P. Kenny, eds., *Mexico's Security Failure: Collapse into Criminal Violence* (New York: Routledge, 2012), pp. 54–87. On bribery and corruption of security forces.

G. Trejo and S. Ley, "Why Did Drug Cartels Go to War in Mexico? Subnational Party Alternation, the Breakdown of Criminal Protection, and the Onset of Large-Scale Violence," *Comparative Political Studies* 51, no. 7 (2017), pp. 900–37. On 350 drug-related murders per year in the late 1990s.

E. Valle Espinosa, *El Segundo Disparo: La Narcodemocracia Mexicana* (Mexico City: Océano, 1995), p. 68, "... narco-ecologists"; "... drug traffickers."

## CHAPTER TWENTY-TWO: WARS

R. C. Ainslie, *The Fight to Save Juárez: Life in the Heart of Mexico's Drug War* (Austin: University of Texas Press, 2013), pp. 149–53. On expansion of drug addiction in Ciudad Juárez; on the conflicts in Ciudad Juárez more generally.

L. Astorga, *Seguridad, Traficantes y Militares* (Mexico City: Tusquets, 2007), "... Darth Vader."

G. Correa-Cabrera, *Zetas Inc.: Criminal Corporations, Energy, and Civil War in Mexico* (Austin: University of Texas Press, 2017). On the Zetas.

I. Grillo, *El Narco: The Bloody Rise of Mexican Drug Cartels* (New York: Bloomsbury, 2012). On Nuevo Laredo, pp. 94–104; p. 113, "... enemies of Mexico"; p. 105, "... paying up."

Interview with anonymous Mexican asylum seeker, January 2016. On federal police raid on house in 2009.

Interview with anonymous Mexican asylum seeker, January 2018, "... a lot of others."

M. Meyer, "Abuso y Miedo en Ciudad Juárez, un Análisis de Violaciones a los derechos Humanos Cometidas por Militares en México," WOLA Paper, September 2010, https://www.wola.org/sites/default/files/downloadable/Mexico/2010/WOLA_RPT-SPANISH_Juarez_FNL-color.pdf. Consulted September 2019. On Nitza Paola Alvarado. The case of Nitza Paola Alvarado was presented to the Inter-American Court of Human Rights in 2018.

D. Pérez Esparza, S. D. Johnson, and P. Gill, "Why Did Mexico Become a Violent Country? Assessing the Role of Firearms Trafficked from the U.S.," *Security Journal* (2019), pp. 1–31; E. Weigland Vargas and D. Pérez Esparza, "Should Mexico Introduce Permissive Gun Policies from the United States?" *Mexican Law Review* XI, no. 2 (2019). On the rise in gun trafficking from the United States.

G. Valdés Castellanos, *Historia del Narcotráfico en México* (Mexico City: Aguilar, 2013), p. 164, "... inflection."

## EPILOGUE: DRUGS AND VIOLENCE

P. Andreas, *Killer High: A History of War in Six Drugs* (New York: Oxford University Press, 2020), pp. 251–68. On recent technological developments of Mexican drug trade.

M. Bergman, *More Money, More Crime: Prosperity and Rising Crime in Latin America* (Oxford: Oxford University Press, 2018). On Mexico's rising crime rate.

G. Calderon, G. Robles, A. Díaz Cayeros, and B. Magaloni, "The Beheading of Criminal Organizations and the Dynamics of Violence in Mexico," *Journal of Conflict Resolution* 5, no. 8 (2015), pp. 1455–85; J. M. Lindo and M. Padilla Romo, "Kingpin Approaches to Fighting Crime and Community Violence: Evidence from Mexico's Drug War," *Journal of Health Economics* 58 (March 2018), pp. 253–68. On the failure of the kingpin strategy.

J. Esberg, "More than Cartels: Counting Mexico's Crime Rings," *Crisis Group Mexico*, 8/5/2020, https://www.crisisgroup.org/latin-america-caribbean/mexico/more-cartels-counting-mexicos-crime-rings. Consulted September 2019. On number of Mexican cartels and gangs.

V. Felbab-Brown, *Changing the Game or Dropping the Ball? Mexico's Security and Anti-Crime Strategy Under President Enrique Peña Nieto* (Washington, DC: Brookings Institution, 2014); M. Serrano, "Del 'Momento Mexicano' a la Realidad de la Violencia Político-Criminal," *Foro Internacional* LX (2020). On Peña Nieto's security strategy.

Interview with "Isela" and "Luis" from Colonia Altamira, Acapulco, December 2016. These are not their real names. Furthermore the name of their neighborhood, the resident criminals, Beto and Chino, and other key details have also been changed.

Interview with "José," former soldier from Michoacán, September 2017. This is not his real name.

N. P. Jones and J. P. Sullivan, "Huachicoleros: Criminal Cartels, Fuel Theft, and Violence in Mexico," *Journal of Strategic Security* 12, no. 4 (2019), pp. 1–24.

R. Le Cour Grandmaison, N. Morris, and B. T. Smith, "The Last Harvest? From the US Fentanyl Boom to the Mexican Opium Crisis," *Journal of Illicit Economies and Development* (2019). On opium boom and subsequent slump.

P. McDonnell, "A Cartel War Has Transformed Once-Tranquil Guanajuato into One of Mexico's Deadliest States," *Los Angeles Times*, 2/8/2020, https://www.latimes.com/world-nation/story/2020–08–02/el-marro-vs-el-mencho-cartel-turf-war-roils-mexicos-guanajuato. Consulted September 2020. E. Reina, "Guanajuato, el Polvorín de la Nueva Lógica de los Carteles en México," *El País*, 24/6/2020. On Guanajuato crime wave.

# List of Illustrations

Maps on pages 2, 90, 168 and 236 by Noemi Morales Sánchez

Page 6: *El Imparcial*, 23 February 1903

Page 54: Courtesy Arreola Postcard Collection.

Page 68: AGN, DFS, Caja 368 bis Exp. 2–17–1944.

Page 78: From Jorge Segura Millán, *Marihuana* (Mexico City: Costa-Amic, 1972). Courtesy Costa-Amic Editores.

Pages 83 and 84: *La Prensa*, 3 May 1940. Material kindly given by the Fototeca, Hemeroteca y Biblioteca Mario Vásquez Raña/Organización Editorial Mexicana S.A de C.V.

Page 93: National Archives and Records Administration, RG170, Box 23.

Page 101: AGN, DFS, Caja 368 bis Exp. 17–2-1944.

Page 118: La Vida Accidentada y Novelesca de Rodolfo Valdez el Gitano. From Anonymous, *La Vida Accidentada y Novelesca de Rodolfo Valdez el Gitano* (El Correo de la Tarde, 1949).

Page 150: From *Diario de un Narcotraficante* (Mexico City: Costa-Amic, 1967). Courtesy Costa-Amic Editores.

Page 156: National Archives and Records Administration, RG170, Box 23.

Pages 174 and 179: Jean-Pierre Charbonneau, *The Canadian Connection*, (Montreal: Optimum, 1976). Courtesy Optimum Publishers.

Page 201: AGN, Presidentes, Miguel de la Madrid Hurtado, SDN, SDN, 07.01.04 Caja 2 Exp. 8.

Page 212: From an anonymous source.

Page 214: *Drug Enforcement*, February 1977.

Page 262: From *Hearing Before the Permanent Subcommittee on Investigations of the Committee on Government Operations*, United States Senate, Ninety-Fifth Congress, January 12, 1977.

Page 264: *Drug Enforcement*, February 1977.

Page 267: *Drug Enforcement*, Winter 1975–1976.

Page 284: From DEA agent, who wishes to remain anonymous.

Page 288: AGN, Presidentes, Miguel de la Madrid Hurtado, SDN, 07.01.04, Caja 2 Exp. 10.

Page 289: AGN, Presidentes, Miguel de la Madrid Hurtado, SDN, 07.01.04.00, Caja 3 Exp. 9.

Page 290: From an anonymous source.

Pages 294 and 295: AGN, Presidentes, Miguel de la Madrid Hurtado, SDN, 07.01.00.00, Caja 1 Exp. 17, Secretaría de Defensa Nacional, Memorias.

Page 298: Proceso Photographic Archive.

Page 299: Photograph of a DEA operations map taken by Nathaniel Morris.

Page 306: AGN, Presidentes, Miguel de la Madrid Hurtado, SDN, 07.01.04.00, Caja 1 Exp. 4.

Page 352: From Sergio Aguayo's personal collection.

# Index

Page references in *italics* indicate images.